# BIOGRAPHIES OF BOOKS

# BIOGRAPHIES OF
# BOOKS

§ § §

## The Compositional Histories of
## Notable American Writings

*Edited by*

James Barbour and Tom Quirk

University of Missouri Press
Columbia and London

Library of Congress Cataloging-in-Publication Data

Biographies of books : the compositional histories of notable American Writings / edited by
James Barbour and Tom Quirk.
    p.  cm.
   ISBN 0-8262-1044-9 (cloth : alk. paper)
   1. American literature—Criticism, Textual. 2. Literary form. I. Barbour, James,
1933–  .  II. Quirk, Tom, 1946–  .
PS25.B58  1996
810.9—dc20                                  95-40987
                                                                     CIP

Designer: Kristie Lee
Typesetter: BOOKCOMP
Printer and binder: Thomson-Shore, Inc.
Typeface: Minion

For Barbara,
*who was so much of our lives*

# Contents

# BIOGRAPHIES OF BOOKS

# Introduction

To a degree, this book is a sequel. A few years ago we published *Writing the American Classics* (1990), a collection of ten essays on important, or at least interesting, American literary texts, among them Franklin's *Autobiography, Moby-Dick, Walden, The Sound and the Fury,* and *Native Son.* This gathering of essays likewise explores the origins and shifting paths that the authors followed to the completion of several works that may or may not be considered "classics" but that nevertheless have exerted their imaginative appeal over professional and nonprofessional readers alike. The present collection comprises genetic studies of Emerson's *Nature,* Twain's *A Connecticut Yankee in King Arthur's Court,* Howells's *A Hazard of New Fortunes,* James's *The Ambassadors,* Dreiser's *Sister Carrie,* Wharton's *The House of Mirth,* Steinbeck's *The Grapes of Wrath,* Welty's *Delta Wedding,* Heller's *Catch-22,* and Kesey's *One Flew over the Cuckoo's Nest.*

The editorial principle that gives coherence to both collections is essentially a methodological one. For more than forty years, the critical and historical emphasis placed upon an interpretive understanding and aesthetic appreciation of "texts" as self-sponsored aesthetic wholes or linguistic artifacts has tended to eclipse or obscure an interest in literature as the product of the human imagination. In that emphasis, New Critics, structuralists, poststructuralists, and new historicists are not so very different after all. For whether one considers a literary work as a self-sufficient "verbal icon" or as a "site" wherein social and political meanings are produced and disseminated, there is the tendency, not to say convenience, of shunting the creative intelligence aside. By contrast, the contributors to this volume, as with the first one, seek to explore how certain works came to be, how they took shape under the ministry of their creators' art, but also how they were responsive or resistant to the several influences (social and political as well as private and incidental) upon them.

Whether or not it corroborates one's political or critical prepossessions, the story of the creation of a text may be as interesting, albeit in a very different way, as the text itself. *Writing the American Classics* sought to provide the biographies of books that many readers have found of some lasting interest. This second collection of essays offers more of the same, in the sense that the essayists represented here also explore the genesis and composition of certain well-known American works. But in another sense, this collection differs as much from the first volume as the essays do from one another. For if there is a single subject that binds these essays together, that subject is the imagination itself, and the imagination is as notoriously variable and unpredictable as the products of its efforts. Wallace Stevens considered the imagination to be a value, not merely some esemplastic force. It is "the power of the mind over the possibilities of things," he said, "but if this constitutes a certain single characteristic, it is the source not of a certain single value but of as many values as reside in the possibilities of things." If indeed the imagination is a value, like other values, it may be lost by gross neglect or simple inattention. At any rate, the essays gathered together here, in their focus upon the creative process, shed interesting and perhaps unexpected cross-lights on familiar American texts.

When we published *Writing the American Classics*, we meant to provide a collection of essays dealing with the compositional histories of certain familiar American literary texts and offered that collection of essays with a certain nervous confidence. We were nervous, in part, because we recognized that this sort of anthology stood in marked opposition to prevailing theoretical opinion. On the other hand, we were confident that these "stories of stories," as we described them, were in themselves worth telling and would appeal to those who find this sort of thing appealing.

Both our nervousness and our confidence, it appears, were unfounded. On balance, the collection was well received by those who read it; and to our knowledge, literary theorists have not read our collection, much less cared to dispute the underlying principles of genetic inquiry, though we had paved the way for just such an exchange by way of a cordial but firm and quasitheoretical defense of our project in the Afterword. On the other hand, the attention we paid to our potential adversaries inadvertently led us to neglect our natural allies, who not only read the essays but sometimes registered criticisms of their own. In retrospect, that was a mistake. Even in so short an interval as that between the publication of the first collection and this one, it appears that we have entered the age of "post-theory"; and while yesteryear's theorists assess the consequences, conventional scholars keep plodding along.[1] Perhaps it is too late, but we mean now to introduce this second group of essays by addressing the hesitations or complaints of our friends instead of attempting to appease those who by inclination and commitment could only regard scholarly effort of this kind as quaint or banal or repressive.

The most efficient and straightforward way to summarize those complaints is to recur to Linck C. Johnson's thoughtful and, we believe, largely sympathetic review essay of *Writing the American Classics* published in *Resources for American Literary Study*.[2] While he is, on balance, admiring of the essays in the volume, he registers several criticisms of the collection itself and the methodology it discloses both by way of example and self-conscious announcement. The questions he puts to the earlier volume, and by implication to this one, are well worth a considered response, and, more to the point, may help to frame the essays collected here.

In the opening paragraphs of his review, Johnson makes separate but related criticisms of the earlier collection: He believes that the title is misleading in the sense that nonclassics are included and suggests that if we had simply abandoned the word *classics* altogether, we might have achieved a greater coherence for the collection. He also observes that black writers and women writers are underrepresented in the collection of ten essays—apart from an essay on Wright's *Native Son* and another on Cather's *The Professor's House,* the essays deal with the work of dead, white males. (I might insert here that we have made up for another deficiency in the first volume, not commented upon by reviewers or critics: in this collection no fewer than three of the authors—Welty, Heller, and Kesey—are alive.)

There is no easy answer to Johnson's criticisms, but there is a simple response: the working title for the collection and the preferred title of the editors from the beginning was "The Path of the Creator," a phrase borrowed from Emerson's remark in "The Poet" that "art is the path of the creator to his work." One can easily see why readers, publishers, and librarians would

1. See Karen J. Winkler, "Scholars Mark the Beginning of the Age of Post-Theory," *Chronicle of Higher Education,* October 13, 1993, A9.

2. Linck C. Johnson, "Compositional History and the Composition of the Canon," *Resources for American Literary Study* 19:2 (1993): 301–8.

not appreciate such an orphic title. The choice of *Writing the American Classics*, not being ours, prompted us to attempt to get out from under the onus of that title. With an assist from Gertrude Stein, we tried to deconstruct the term *classic* (probably the only example of deconstruction in the entire book) by noting that the principal interest of compositional histories of literary texts has to do with matters that predate the identification of this or that work as a "classic" and the subsequent enshrining of it in the "canon."

Our requirements for that collection, as with this one, were simple and practical. We wanted essays that told engaging and, as far as possible, complete stories about the genesis of certain works of the imagination. Johnson laments the fact that women and minority writers are underrepresented in the first collection, and no doubt he might say the same about the present collection. One sort of answer to this complaint, one that may not be satisfactory simply by virtue of being true, is that we solicited essays on any number of texts, not merely those by women and black writers, but for various reasons they never materialized. Among other works, we wanted and tried to secure essays on *Their Eyes Were Watching God, Up from Slavery, The Narrative of the Life of Frederick Douglass, The Country of the Pointed Firs, Invisible Man,* and *The Awakening,* along with essays on "Song of Myself" and *The Waste Land.* The "classic" status of these works is not in question, but the resources for rehearsing their genesis and composition often are limited or nonexistent.

There were also deliberate exclusions, however. The stories of the composition of other classic texts, such as *The Great Gatsby,* have been told before and sufficiently well not to require repeating. Of course, even with such familiar works as Franklin's *Autobiography,* in the first collection, or Emerson's *Nature,* in this one, there may be some surprises. Leo Lemay and Albert von Frank went over pretty thoroughly plowed ground and yet were able to disclose new dimensions to the genetic history of these works. Still other works—*The Scarlet Letter* is a good example—were excluded because the record of their composition is neither extant in the form of manuscript or other materials nor, for the most part, even inferable from circumstantial evidence. Until some future day when the evidence of its composition may become available, the compositional history of Ellison's *Invisible Man,* like Hawthorne's masterpiece, will remain a mystery.

The point to be made here is that the inclusions or exclusions of texts in this or the earlier anthology have less to do with questions of "canonicity" than they do with such practical questions as "Is the evidence sufficient to describe the contours of composition of a given text?" "Is there someone willing and competent to write such a piece?" and "Will the contributors be able to complete the essay in good time?" These are the tedious and uninteresting facts that most editors of collections face, and, in the long run, they may have more to do with representations of the canon than most scholars and critics are willing to admit. But there are other determining factors as well.

The sad truth of the matter is that archival material relating to the work of women and minority writers is scantier and usually more poorly organized than has customarily been the case for white male authors. The collection and interpretation of information relating to authorial intention necessary for preparing authoritative editions has barely begun for many important American writers; obviously, it is more immediately important in canon reformation to make editions of previously neglected works generally available than it is to establish definitive editions of these texts, which of course involves, among other things, discerning the compositional history of the texts. Correspondence, notebooks, manuscripts, even reliable working bibliographies are in many instances yet to be published or even collected. Only in recent years has the invaluable Schomburg collection been systematically organized; the *Bibliographical Guide to the Study of the Literature of the U.S.A.* lists eighteen bibliographies of African American literature, only three of which were published before 1970. Prior to the publication of *Ebony* in the 1960s, no black periodicals were even indexed in the *Reader's Guide to Periodical Literature,* and for many important African American periodicals, *Opportunity,* for example, there remain no index sources. It was not until 1972, when the Modern Language Association established its "Commission on Minority Groups and the Study of Language and Literature," that the MLA could be said to have become hospitable to minority literature. In the case of African Americanists, the College Language Association was the preferred organization, and for some it still is. These instances are suggestive of the problem.

The massive scholarly work yet to be performed for most minority and many women writers is more urgent and probably more important than a narrowly focused essay on the composition of a single, though perhaps remarkable, text. While a host of dedicated scholars may be energized by new discoveries and new opportunities, they may feel, as well, the pressure of having to make up for lost time. Not so very many years ago, women and minority scholars were not admitted into the stacks of important research libraries. Authorized or even variorum editions of many important American works are still few. Definitive, or in some instances even preliminary, biographies of many major women and minority writers often do not exist. However, at long last we have, in Faith Berry, Arnold Rampersad, and David Levering Lewis, African American biographers rendering the lives of African American writers. The cultural consequences of this fairly new phenomenon have yet to be fathomed. As Arnold Rampersad has observed, the very ideas of preserving primary materials and of biography as an important genre are fundamentally affected and largely determined by African American cultural practices, and these are not always congenial to scholarly prerogatives. Similarly, for some Native American cultures, the very notions of authorship, canon, and text may be alien concepts.[3] In short, it may be some time before there exist the scholarly resources or the intellectual leisure to write the compositional histories of many significant American literary works.

A different sort of objection Johnson makes has to do with the "values" a collection of genetic essays implies. Our fear with the first volume was that postmodernists would cry "Positivism!"—a charge that theorists typically regard as damning and incontrovertible. But Johnson, who has himself written a fine genetic study of *A Week on the Concord and Merrimack Rivers,* by Thoreau, makes an antithetical objection when he observes that the contributors exhibit, explicitly or implicitly, a "romantic ideology." Since, as we announced in the first collection, genetic inquiry is largely empirical in its methods and inductive in its reasoning, and since, yes, most practitioners of this method do believe that the author had some shaping influence, however limited, over his or her work, it is perhaps best to accept the criticisms from both camps. "Romantic positivists": that description will do, we suppose; but we rather suspect that the combined epithets really amount to calling us pragmatists, a term that more accurately reflects the method and, to the extent that it has one, the ideology of genetic criticism.

3. Arnold Rampersad, "Biography, Autobiography and Afro-American Culture," *The Yale Review* 73:1 (Autumn 1987): 1–16. For an interesting example of this difficulty as it relates to Navajo culture, see James C. Faris, "Context and Text: Navajo Nightway Textual History in the Hands of the West," *Resources for American Literary Study* 20:2 (1994): 180–95.

The so-called new pragmatists may not recognize a common genealogy between genetic inquiry and their broader cultural critique, but it is there nonetheless. Likewise, new historicists and revisionist biographers may disprize the work of old historicism and traditional biography, more intent as they are on articulating differences than recognizing affinities. Still, there is an interesting implication imbedded in this apparent conflict, one that may bear, once again, on questions of the classic and the canon. For one of the terms conspicuously absent from the otherwise abundant vocabulary of current critical discourse, and indeed absent from much more conventional scholarship as well, is the word *imagination*. We offer no theory of the imagination here or elsewhere because, at least in terms of genetic inquiry, the imagination is known, if at all, primarily by its effects, not its causes. But, however much the creative imagination has made its several compromises with prevailing ideology alongside the pertinacious complaints of friends, relatives, and editors, that does not mean that its presence is not felt on the page and more precisely discerned in the compositional history of a given text.

The efforts of the imagination may be, in fact are likely to be, exposed to all manner of ideological pressures. Candace Waid and Albert Devlin observe how both Edith Wharton and Eudora Welty conceived of themselves as principally short-story writers and struggled with the whole concept of the extended narrative, the novel, which they conceived to be an essentially masculine genre. Their mastery of the form in, respectively, *The House of Mirth* and *Delta Wedding* may or may not determine their texts to be "classics" and thereby authorize their right to be included in the canon on aesthetic grounds. The genetic critic has little or nothing to do with that sort of determination. But the stories of their stories may shed valuable light on the actual, as opposed to the theoretical, relations between gender and genre as they are encountered in the recalcitrance of their material, the intractability of the marketplace, and the hesitations and blockages of the imagination itself.

Related to the supposed romantic ideology of geneticism is Johnson's observation that the authors tend to "perpetuate the notion that a 'classic' is a work undervalued or misunderstood in its own time. Images of the alienated artist crop up in various guises in these essays, possibly because so many American authors have themselves been ambivalent about commercial success, evidently fearing that efforts to appeal to a mass audience might compromise their aspirations to join an elite group of 'classic' writers." Apart from the fact that, in America, the image of the alienated artist itself has commercial possibilities (one of the canniest of American authors, Edgar Allan Poe, fostered such an image, as did, in very different ways but to the same effect, Ernest Hemingway and T. S. Eliot), the criticism certainly does not apply to *The House of Mirth* or *Catch-22*, discussed in this collection, or *Native Son,* discussed in the earlier volume, all best-sellers. Besides, if artists, or anyone else, were not in some measure "alienated" from someone or something, why, one wonders, would they write at all? And what would they have to say?

In any event, the status of the "classic" in American literature may, in fact, depend in some measure on its capacity to make a counterstatement to the prevailing culture, whether or not the public buys it by the hundreds of thousands or neglects it altogether. Surely this antinomian quality has something to do with how, in the twentieth century, the American "canon" has been understood and determined. Giles Gunn, in *Thinking across the American Grain: Ideology, Intellect, and the New Pragmatism,* has recently noted how, in their ability to resist, if only in the imagination, the edicts of the dominant culture, certain native writers have continually refused an official American culture by exposing its pompous and often sentimental self-satisfaction. More often than not, the effect of these counterstatements has typically been not to dismantle the republic but to regenerate a more productive and responsible American tradition. Melville's *White-Jacket,* Sinclair's *The Jungle,* and Steinbeck's *The Grapes of Wrath* actually had political and legislative consequences, but who can estimate the effect the phrase *Catch-22* has had on how we understand our national life and the means whereby we may call its public policies into question?

The image of the alienated artist may be a romantic, even a sentimental, one, but it is appropriate to the degree that such artists, by whatever means, enable us to cast a skeptical glance o'er main traveled roads. The symbolic gestures of this resistance may be as decorous as Lambert Strether's advice to "live all you can: it's a mistake not to!"; as rambunctious as Ken Kesey and his Merry Pranksters setting out to look for America; or as fantastic as Yossarian (a latter-day Huck Finn?) vowing to row to Sweden in an inflatable raft. Not as critics, but as readers do we respond, much, or little, or not at all, to such rebellions; and it may be that we do so because, though they are fantastic, these imaginative refusals are nevertheless more coherent than the compromises of everyday life. At all events, the acts of the imagination are as mysterious as their effects upon us. Some things are rather more certain, however. Responding to such anthropological explanations of artistic expression as were current in her own day, Willa Cather observed that the arts "did not come into being as a means of increasing the game supply or promoting tribal security. They sprang from an unaccountable predilection of the one unaccountable thing in man."[4]

The moment we begin to account for the unaccountable, we are perforce dealing with a diminished thing. Perhaps this was what Gertrude Stein was driving at when she remarked that "the creator of the new composition in the arts is an outlaw until he is a classic, there is hardly a moment in between."[5] Essays such as those included here, if they do nothing more, might serve to remind us of, and thus prolong, that moment "in between." At any rate, it is perhaps worth remembering that the "canonical" status of Thoreau, Melville, and Twain was conferred in the twentieth not the nineteenth century, and that the reputations of, for example, Wallace Stevens, Willa Cather, and William Dean Howells suffered from a perceived political incorrectness in the 1930s.

From quite a different perspective (one unlikely to have any use for genetic criticism), Hayden White has reaffirmed essentially the same point that Stein made so many years before: "The classic text seems to command our attention because it not only contains ideas and insights about 'the human condition' in general but provides an interpretative model by which to carry further our investigations in our own time or, indeed, any time." The classic text, he continues, "reveals, indeed draws attention to, its own processes of meaning production and makes these processes its own subject matter, its own content." So considered, a "classic" is the more valuable to us to the extent that "we de-sublimate it and return it to its status as an immanent product of the culture in which it arose." Though the means whereby White

4. Willa Cather, *Willa Cather on Writing: Critical Studies on Writing as an Art* (Lincoln: University of Nebraska Press, 1988), 19. W. B. Carnochan has recently reminded us that anthropological constructions of "culture" and the periodic "culture wars" that have ensued are more than a hundred years old. See *The Battleground of the Curriculum: Liberal and American Experience* (Palo Alto: Stanford University Press, 1993), 100–111.

5. Gertrude Stein, "Composition as Explanation," in *Selected Writings of Gertrude Stein*, ed. Carl Van Vechten (New York: Random House, 1946), 514.

might recuperate the immanence of the already existing text is quite different from that of the genetic critic, the end is the same. Or, as Stein would have it, readers "really would enjoy the created so much better just after it has been made than when it is already a classic."[6]

For our part, it hardly matters whether the image of the alienated artist is rendered as one who seeks to escape or break through the discourses imposed upon him or her and thereby discloses meaning-making models of some use to subsequent generations, or as one who out of inner compulsion or simple orneriness tries to do something a bit different. What does matter is that the study of the genesis of certain works of the imagination restores a certain imaginative, not to say meaning-making, vitality to a text. Twain's original intentions for *A Connecticut Yankee in King Arthur's Court*, for example, are straightforward enough, and, had he abided by them absolutely, his novel would have served as an unproblematic celebration of nineteenth-century progress and capitalistic culture. If this had happened, Twain's novel would have been of greater interest as a historical "document," to use White's term, than as a classic text worthy of attention on altogether different grounds, and Howard Baetzhold follows with meticulous detail the shifting intentions of Twain's novel.

The same might be said for the subjects of other essays in this volume. *The Grapes of Wrath, Nature, The House of Mirth, A Hazard of New Fortunes,* and *Sister Carrie* all are in one way or another, and sometimes in spite of themselves, imaginative refusals of their own time and place. But their interest for us does not lie solely in whatever meaning-making paradigms critics may discern in them, nor in their function as historical artifacts. We cannot finally possess our literature until we have in some fashion humanized it. And that will not happen until we recognize that the "canon," whether of the right or of the left, is not the work of saints but the product of uneven and imperfectly human performances that do not, in fact cannot, answer to interpretive prescription or political prepossessions.

6. Hayden White, *The Content of Form: Narrative Discourse and Historical Representation* (Baltimore: Johns Hopkins University Press, 1987), 211, 213; Stein, "Composition as Explanation," 514.

# The Composition of *Nature*

## Writing and the Self in the Launching of a Career

ALBERT VON FRANK

❦    ❦    ❦

> I like my book about nature & wish I knew where & how I ought to live.
>
> —Emerson, journal entry, September 6, 1833[1]

IN OCTOBER 1833, when Emerson returned to America from his first trip to Europe, he brought back an idea for a "book about nature," an idea that he strongly associated with the conviction that he was entering on a new life. Indeed, he seems to have felt that the issue of where and how he ought to live was immediately implicated not only in the new literary career that he was contemplating, but also in the particular book that would launch it. As recently as 1829 he had begun a very different sort of life, with his marriage to Ellen Tucker and his nearly simultaneous acceptance of a call to minister at Boston's Second Church. But that design crumbled in 1831 with the death of his wife, and crumbled again in 1832, when, literally sick and tired, and finding himself at odds with his congregation over the significance of the Lord's Supper, he relinquished his pastorate and set sail for Europe.

Following his return, he lived outwardly very much as he had before his marriage, residing with his mother, who, having no home of her own, depended on relatives for room and board. Still an accredited minister,

---

1. *The Journals and Miscellaneous Notebooks of Ralph Waldo Emerson*, ed. William H. Gilman et al., 16 vols. (Cambridge: Harvard University Press, 1960–1982), 4:237. Hereafter cited parenthetically in the text as *JMN*.

Emerson continued to preach at various Boston-area churches and did not yet rule out the possibility of a regular ministerial career. But his "book about nature" led him into new worlds of speculation, even as it put him, for the first time, before a lyceum audience. In the career of the scholar as he was beginning to conceive it, the book and the new life would evoke each other. *Nature* would be very much the product of its own command to "Build, therefore, your own world."[2]

In broad outline, the genetic history of *Nature* is simple enough and well known. When Emerson left the Second Church, he was already planning a career as a writer and had a number of literary projects in mind.[3] The trip to Europe happily included the famous revelation at the Jardin des Plantes, in which the phenomenal world seemed to Emerson suddenly unlocked, yielding, and intelligible; this experience brought his attention to focus on a "book about nature," though what he envisioned in September 1833 could hardly have resembled the slim volume called *Nature* that he published three years later. Immediately following his return to Boston he began to try out his ideas in a series of lectures on natural history, but he soon discovered that the form of the scientific lyceum lecture was not advancing him in the direction he wished to go. Over the next two years, as Emerson explored the "first philosophy," his inhibiting attachment to an avowedly scientific approach to his subject, although never entirely abandoned, waned to such a point that in the spring of 1836 he suddenly saw his way clear, and *Nature* was written within a few months, in two stages.

The significance of the "two stages" has not been sufficiently appreciated, and it is therefore a main purpose of the present essay to offer an interpretation of Emerson's divided conception of his subject. Very late in the process of composition, he had it in mind to publish his brief treatise in two parts, a first installment entitled *Nature* and a sequel entitled *Spirit*. This division

2. In *The Collected Works of Ralph Waldo Emerson*, ed. Joseph Slater et al., 5 vols. to date (Cambridge: Harvard University Press, 1971–   ), 1:45. Hereafter cited parenthetically as *CW*.

3. On January 6, 1832, Emerson sketched out topics for a book in nine chapters indicative of his speculative concerns toward the end of his ministerial career (*JMN*, 3:315–16). On November 19 of the same year he wrote to his brother William of "the projects that sprout & bloom in my head, of action, literature, [and] philosophy," including the conduct of a journal: see *Letters of Ralph Waldo Emerson*, ed. Ralph L. Rusk and Eleanor M. Tilton, 9 vols. to date (New York: Columbia University Press, 1939–   ), 1:358; hereafter cited parenthetically as *L*.

relates to two successive purposes; an early conception, much influenced by Thomas Carlyle, concerned to show the symbolic interrelation of science and ethics; and a later, more lyrical and ecstatic vision quickened by the influence of Bronson Alcott.

## I

In mid-October 1832, while Emerson was embroiled in the controversy with his congregation over the Lord's Supper, a Unitarian minister newly arrived from England came to dine at Emerson's rented quarters on Chardon Street. The guest spoke entertainingly of his acquaintance with Wordsworth and Coleridge, but his most valuable information was the identification of Carlyle, the anonymous translator of Goethe's *Wilhelm Meister*, as the author of a number of recent unsigned articles in the British quarterlies, principally but not exclusively on the subject of German literature. Emerson, who had already met with some of these and had read *Wilhelm Meister* in August, spent much of the last two months of his Boston pastorate ferreting out and avidly reading Carlyle's essays.[4]

Perhaps the most important and influential of these essays was "Characteristics," published in the *Edinburgh Review* in 1831. In it Carlyle bewails the hyperconscious and introspective cast of the present age as a morbid response—though an inevitable one—to the destructive work of the eighteenth-century rationalist fathers, who seemed to have made faith untenable. He asserts that "Belief, Faith, has wellnigh disappeared from the world. The youth on awakening in this wondrous Universe, no longer finds a competent theory of its wonders." To Emerson, already restive about the formalism of his Unitarian sect and conscious of the baleful legacy of his father's generation, this call to restore to the Universe its lost integrity through a renewal of faith came as a stirring challenge. Moreover, it fell in

4. See Charles Chauncy Emerson to Mary Moody Emerson, October 24, 1832 (Houghton Library, Harvard University, MS Am 1280.226 [70]), owned by the Ralph Waldo Emerson Memorial Association and quoted by permission, and Kenneth Walter Cameron, *Ralph Waldo Emerson's Reading* (1941; rev. ed., 1962; reprint, New York: Haskell House, 1966), 19. Emerson wrote to Mary Moody Emerson on August 19, "The Germans regard [Goethe] as the restorer of Faith & Love after the desolations of Hume & the French. In Wilhelm Meister he leads a child of Nature up from the period of 'Apprenticeship' to that of 'Self production' and leaves him, Schiller says, assured on the way to infinite perfection" (*L*, 1:354).

nicely with that aspect of Unitarian thought that most appealed to Emerson: the doctrine of self-culture, or the progressive empowerment of the self through a continual spiritual education. For Carlyle, the worst effect of the present loss of faith was not that it prompted men to write books of metaphysics (a symptom bad enough in itself), but that it disempowered and paralyzed the individual, rendering heroism—and action itself, almost— groundless and nugatory. "Faith gave [man] an inward Willingness; a world of Strength wherewith to front a world of Difficulty." Now, conscious of the diseased state of society, man anatomizes and analyzes, hoping to cure the ailment of which the very substitution of analysis for action is a primary symptom. As Emerson was to do in *Nature,* Carlyle posits a golden age of unselfconscious moral grandeur prior to what has variously been called the dissociation of sensibility or the emergence of dichotomous public and private spheres, an anterior existence seen as a paradise of "wholeness" from which Man has fallen. "Characteristics," like Carlyle's other great diagnostic essay, "Signs of the Times," is an impassioned lament over the birth pangs of a bourgeois modernist sensibility, a eulogy for the passing of the heroic age, and, finally, a suggestion that the cure for the derangements of modernity is, in a word, transcendentalism.[5]

## II

When Emerson finally severed his connection with the Second Church and left for Europe in December 1832, his mind was saturated with Carlyle and with Carlyle's authors, Goethe and Schiller. It is tempting to speculate that an intention to meet Carlyle may have been responsible for Emerson's last-minute decision not to go to Puerto Rico, as he had first planned, and where he might have joined his tubercular brother Edward, but to travel instead to Europe.[6] Emerson left Boston shortly before Christmas and spent the remainder of the winter sightseeing in Sicily and Italy. As the weather

5. Carlyle, "Characteristics," in *Critical and Miscellaneous Essays* (Philadelphia: A. Hart, 1850), 305. For the definitive treatment of the doctrine of self-culture, see David Robinson, *Apostle of Culture: Emerson as Preacher and Lecturer* (Philadelphia: University of Pennsylvania Press, 1982). Carlyle felt that Unitarians in general were ineffectual and in "Characteristics" (298) spoke slightingly of "Socinian Preachers."

6. Emerson checked out half a dozen books on the West Indies from the Boston Athenaeum between December 3 and 12 (Cameron, *Emerson's Reading,* 20). "I suppose if I had sifted the

improved, he worked his way north, and summer found him in Paris. It is a noteworthy fact that Emerson's "conversion" to the study of nature occurred here rather than in America—not while "crossing the bare common," but while touring in the heart of an ancient city. In mid-July, at the Jardin des Plantes in Paris, Emerson was struck with the "inexhaustible riches of nature":

> The Universe is a more amazing puzzle than ever as you glance along this bewildering series of animated forms,—the hazy butterflies, the carved shells, the birds, beasts, fishes, insects, snakes,—& the upheaving principle of life everywhere incipient in the very rock aping organized forms. Not a form so grotesque, so savage, nor so beautiful but is an expression of some property inherent in man the observer,—an occult relation between the very scorpions and man. I feel the centipede in me—cayman, carp, eagle, & fox. I am moved by strange sympathies, I say continually "I will be a naturalist." (*JMN*, 4:199–200)

The Jardin des Plantes was not nature, of course, but already a quotation from nature. It was a book about "life" rendered immediately in arrangements of symbolic natural facts without the problematic mediation of human language; it was to the instructed human eye rather what the aeolian harp was to the ear.

Although this well-known journal passage has the look of an epiphany, Emerson had in fact said much the same thing to his Boston congregation in 1830 and 1831, in Sermon LXVII:

> Such is [the] dominion of the spirit that the outward world seems only a mirror to reflect the thoughts of the soul. Every animal in nature is to our eye a symbol of some moral quality in ourselves; the fox is cunning, the ape is folly, the viper is ingratitude, the ant is industry, the light is our emblem of knowledge, and darkness of ignorance; warmth is our emblem of charity and cold for selfishness, and so the mind goes up and down the world writing its own name on every phenomenon.[7]

---

reasons that led me to Europe, when I was ill and was advised to travel, it was mainly the attraction of these persons [Coleridge, Wordsworth, Landor, De Quincey, and Carlyle]" (*CW*, 5:4).

7. *The Complete Sermons of Ralph Waldo Emerson*, ed. Albert J. von Frank, Andrew Delbanco, Teresa Toulouse, Ronald A. Bosco, and Wesley T. Mott, 4 vols. (Columbia: University of Missouri Press, 1989–1992), 2:146.

To see the world as named and authorized rather than accidental—or as an inwardly necessitated array of surfaces to be penetrated by the mind in search of meaning—can be construed as a religious or as a scientific project. It was Emerson's impulse at this time to keep any such distinction in abeyance. His response to the Jardin des Plantes, and generally to the symbolic aspect of nature, was colored by a mode of thought and feeling that was possible perhaps only for a brief moment in human history, abetted by a disappearing religious conviction that the world was nothing in itself—nothing but the means to a higher end elsewhere—and by a dramatically rising valuation of the individual human consciousness. The special historical circumstances that shaped this response in Emerson seem also to distance Emerson from us. A modern sensibility, particularly one imbued with an environmentalist tendency to see nature as under the shadow of swords, will likely be appalled at the suggestion of a mean egotism in Emerson's observation, subordinating as it does the world to the self, or "life" to the "principle of life," and valuing the Not-Me as an index to the observer's own interiority. Yet Emerson's intoxication at seeing his mind—as he would have it—so richly expressed in natural objects is directly an effect of a new theory of consciousness, gathered by Samuel Taylor Coleridge and Thomas Carlyle out of German sources. Coleridge had expressed it by saying, "What we have within, that only can we see without."[8] Carlyle likewise proposed that "Matter has an existence . . . only as a Phenomenon; were we not there, neither would it be there."[9] Such romantic idealism inevitably privileged self and consciousness over external nature, but it also provided a fresh and compelling motive for paying attention to nature at all.

There had in fact been little in Emerson's upbringing to make him espe-cially attentive to nature. Born in the city of Boston, Emerson was educated to eighteenth-century values, centering much less on nature than on the moral sublime as exemplified in the actions of ancient heroes. Like other American

8. Coleridge, *The Friend,* in *The Works of Samuel Taylor Coleridge,* ed. William G. T. Shedd (New York: Harper & Brothers, 1853), 2:377–78. Kenneth Walter Cameron makes much of this point in *Emerson the Essayist,* 2 vols. (1945; reprint, Hartford: Transcendental Books, 1972); see the index under "Like can only know like" and "Quantum sumus scimus." See also *JMN,* 3:213 n, and *Nature,* where the observation takes the form "What we are, that only can we see" (*CW,* 1:45).

9. Carlyle, "Novalis," *Critical and Miscellaneous Essays,* 175. Carlyle is explaining the thought of Johann Gottlieb Fichte.

children of that era, he was taught to regard nature as the providentially supplied fuel of human progress, a realm over which man was meant to exercise an ever more complete dominion. Nature was an arena of work for adults and of play for children, as Emerson knew well enough from childhood summers spent with his brothers at Concord.[10] His early puzzlement over Wordsworth's reputation suggests how his mental culture had made any but a utilitarian concern with the natural world seem childish and unserious. It was not until he was out of college that his Aunt Mary Moody Emerson, "an idolater of Nature," as he said, set her reluctant nephew to reading Nature and Wordsworth both (*L*, 1:133–34). Even in the fullness of his developed transcendental thought he was often inclined to regard nature as a toy[11] and was at times skeptical and condescending about Thoreau's excessive attachment to it; he once addressed his younger colleague in a letter that read in its entirety: "My dear Henry, A frog was made to live in a swamp, but a man was not made to live in a swamp. Yours ever. R" (*L*, 8:562; compare *JMN*, 14:203).

Trained to subordinate nature to a higher concern with moral issues, Emerson was quick to appreciate how the new idealism, like other recent intellectual developments, "transferred nature into the mind, and left matter like an outcast corpse" (*CW*, 1:34). He could, in *Nature*, genuinely value the Not-Me for its formative and tutelary effects (most especially as to beauty, language, and discipline) on the human subject (often represented as a child),[12] but always in the context of a progressive need to possess and

10. This association is perhaps best recorded in Emerson's poem "Dirge" (*The Complete Works of Ralph Waldo Emerson*, ed. Edward Waldo Emerson, 12 vols. [Boston: Houghton Mifflin, 1903–1904], 9:145–47 [hereafter cited parenthetically as *W*]), written in 1838. One of the purposes of Thoreau's *Walden* would seem to be the deconstruction of this work/play binary.

11. See Emerson's comments to Carlyle on his purchase of a Walden woodlot in 1845: "I too have a new plaything, the best I ever had—a woodlot" (*The Correspondence of Emerson and Carlyle*, ed. Joseph Slater [New York: Columbia University Press, 1964], 399; hereafter cited parenthetically as *CEC*). Compare *Nature*, 9: "Nature never became a toy to a wise spirit." For Emerson's early attitude toward Wordsworth and the literary uses of nature, see *JMN*, 1:162, and Joel Porte, *Emerson and Thoreau: Transcendentalists in Conflict* (Middletown, Conn.: Wesleyan University Press, 1966), 62.

12. The child in *Nature*—as often in Wordsworth—is regarded as a figure of faith and innocence, and, somewhat paradoxically, as the subject of education (compare Emerson's reading of *Wilhelm Meister*, cited in note 4 above); the image was aggrandized under Bronson

transcend it. The objective in *Nature,* then, is not primarily to foster a love of natural forms or to provide a basis for rejecting or superseding them, as has sometimes been argued; the avowed purpose of the essay is to indicate how one might assert a power over the world as circumstance, a position still redolent of Emerson's eighteenth-century moral training.

In the early 1830s, while still ministering at the Second Church, Emerson was swept up in the resurgence of popular interest in natural history, which was grounded in a similar agenda of human empowerment.[13] His own interest in the subject seems to have deepened suddenly in December 1831 with his reading of J. F. W. Herschel's *Preliminary Discourse on the Study of Natural Philosophy,* "a noble work enough," he said, "to tempt a man to leave all duties to find out natural science" (*L,* 1:342–43). Herschel's conception of science was Baconian (the frontispiece of the book is a portrait of Bacon): the study of science was construed as the investigation of the laws impressed by God on matter at the moment of creation, and the purpose of studying these laws was to facilitate human power. In September 1833, when Emerson wrote in his journal that he liked his book about nature, he was reading another work by Herschel, the *Treatise on Astronomy* (*JMN,* 4:238). What

---

Alcott's influence and eventually came to serve Emerson as the image of the leader or messiah of a spiritual revolution. See, for example, "The Song of Nature" (*W,* 9:245) and Emerson's letter to Caroline S. Tappan, October 13, 1857 (*L,* 5:86). In the early 1830s Emerson was fond of quoting lines 18–20 of Coleridge's "The Destiny of Nations: A Vision": "For all that meets the bodily sense I deem / Symbolical, one mighty alphabet / For infant minds." See *The Early Lectures of Ralph Waldo Emerson,* ed. Stephen E. Whicher, Robert E. Spiller, and Wallace E. Williams, 3 vols. (Cambridge: Harvard University Press, 1959–1972), 1:25 (hereafter cited parenthetically as *EL*), and *JMN,* 6:173–74, 218–19.

13. This popular interest in natural history was directly responsible for the organization of the lyceum system in New England by Josiah Holbrook in 1826. This system was by design a vehicle for disseminating scientific information. Holbrook had combined the scientific interests of his teacher Benjamin Silliman with the educational interests of his friend Bronson Alcott. See Carl Bode, *The American Lyceum: Town Meeting of the Mind* (New York: Oxford University Press, 1956), 8–26. In 1830, Emerson's kinsman and parishioner George B. Emerson, an accomplished botanist, participated in founding the Boston Society of Natural History and the American Institute of Instruction; it was he who arranged Emerson's first lectures, given in 1833 and 1834 on scientific topics (see *EL,* 1:xx–xxii, 1–4). Emerson thought these institutions useful principally as a check on the tendency of science toward abstraction and objectivity: "It will be the effect of the popularization of science to keep the eye of scientific men on that human side of nature wherein lie grandest truths. The poet, the priest must not only receive an inspiration, but they must bring the oracle low down to men in the market-place" (*EL,* 2:38).

excited Emerson at this time was, again, not nature itself, but science, which, following Bacon, he would define in 1836 as "the reconstruction of nature in the mind" (*EL*, 2:27); what in turn particularly excited him about science was the progressively clearer perception it offered of the absolute governance of the universe by law.[14]

Just how and when the excitement of these ideas would result in a book had much to do with Emerson's generalized ambitions as a writer. These ambitions, piqued by his scientific investigations in Paris (which also included lectures at the Sorbonne), were brought to a focus immediately thereafter by his literary investigations in England—that is to say, by meetings with Wordsworth, Coleridge, and Carlyle—which on the one hand significantly demystified the figure of the writer, and on the other encouraged Emerson in the belief that he had something to say—that he had a finer "insight into religious truth" (*JMN*, 4:79) than any of them. It was Carlyle, though, who reacted most strongly on Emerson, and who seems to have given a specific impetus to his literary plans.

Emerson's meeting with Carlyle at Craigenputtock in August 1833, just days before his departure for America, had been exceptionally congenial. Yet nine months elapsed before Emerson wrote to him, initiating what was to become one of the finest, longest sustained, and most celebrated of literary correspondences. In that first letter Emerson offered much fulsome praise for the ideas and some tentative criticism of the prose style of *Sartor Resartus*, then issuing serially in *Fraser's Magazine*. He was acutely aware that his comments on Carlyle's antic style bordered on presumption, coming as they did from one who had not as yet written for publication: "And though with all my heart I would stand well with my Poet," Emerson wrote, "yet if I offend, I shall quietly retreat into my Universal relations wherefrom I affectionately espy you as a man, myself as another" (*CEC*, 100). Emerson must have seen that this universal democratic masculine relation was no

14. See the conclusion of Emerson's lecture "The Humanity of Science," *EL*, 2:39–40. In the important late lecture "Historic Notes of Life and Letters in New England," Emerson characterized the intellectual revolution of his younger days as "a return to law" (*W*, 10:338). See also Harry Hayden Clark, "Emerson and Science," *Philological Quarterly* 10 (July 1931): 225–60, and Gay Wilson Allen, "A New Look at Emerson and Science," in Robert Falk, ed., *Literature and Ideas in America: Essays in Memory of Harry Hayden Clark* (Athens: Ohio University Press, 1975), 58–78.

adequate basis for the continued contact he emphatically desired. The only way to put their relationship on an assured footing and to satisfy his yearning for equality with Carlyle would be for Emerson to become a "Poet" himself. If *Nature* was not written expressly *for* Thomas Carlyle, he was without doubt *the* reader whose approval Emerson most coveted.[15]

Then, too, *Sartor Resartus* was itself an important instigation to Emerson's writing. In that first letter, Emerson showed that he valued the book principally for "the brave stand you have made for Spiritualism" (*CEC*, 98). Soon, therefore, he would exercise a similar bravery in the cause that Carlyle had defined, and which Carlyle had shown could be treated in a secular and literary manner at an appreciable distance from the snares of traditional religious discourse. In this regard the term *spiritualism* may itself be a significant clue to the genesis of *Nature*. The earliest citation for it in the *Oxford English Dictionary* is to Carlyle's *Sartor;* Emerson himself had never used it before. The word thus given was immediately and happily received by a number of American transcendentalists whose views were not adequately represented by the term *idealism*.[16] It was not Plato or Bishop Berkeley whom they proposed to advance as their counter to the deadening materialism of the times, but something not as yet well named, something obscurely allied to what the Calvinists had called the religious affections. Indeed one of the important turns that Emerson's argument takes in the course of *Nature* occurs when, in the sixth and seventh chapters, he rejects classical idealism in favor of a more specific and human vision of a life of the spirit. "Spiritualism," this suggestive gift from Carlyle, embodied no

15. The only recent studies of the Emerson-Carlyle relationship are Joseph Slater's introduction to *CEC*, and Kenneth Marc Harris, *Carlyle and Emerson: Their Long Debate* (Cambridge: Harvard University Press, 1978).

16. Writing before his first visit to Emerson in 1835, Bronson Alcott referred to him as "one of the purest spiritualists of the day": see *The Journals of Bronson Alcott*, ed. Odell Shepard (Boston: Little, Brown, 1938), 68. Emerson's general avoidance of diction that carried much theological freight (the tendency is present even in his sermons) is obviously paralleled in Carlyle, and relates, especially in Emerson, to the project of freeing ethical discourse from the burden of history. The usefulness of the term *spiritualism* was eventually lost to the mesmerists and spirit-rappers. Harris (*Carlyle and Emerson,* 16) notes that Carlyle avoids the term *idealism* altogether in *Sartor Resartus.* In a sketchy description of his first meeting with Carlyle, included in *English Traits,* Emerson mentions that Carlyle did not read Plato, and that he "disparaged Socrates" (*CW,* 5:16).

radically new perception, but seems to have had for Emerson and his friends
an orienting rightness of perspective in its implied mediation between the
old religious issues and the newer, nonprescriptive and ahistorical ways in
which they were—in some measure enabled by this term—to talk about and
to revalue the inner life of man.[17]

### III

Emerson gave the first of four lectures on scientific subjects before the
Boston Society of Natural History on November 4, 1833, within a month
of his return from Europe. These lectures, considered as a vocational experiment, were related both to the question of where and how their author
would live and to the substance of his "book about nature." The first lecture,
"The Uses of Natural History," though it makes numerous concessions to its
immediate audience, has much in common with portions of the 1836 *Nature,*
including an early version of Emerson's theory of language. As he was to
do in *Nature,* Emerson organized his lecture discussion in ascending order
through the physical to the spiritual uses of nature. Retaining the utilitarian
implication of the term *uses,* Emerson, still professionally a minister, would
no doubt have been attentive also to its sermonic associations, seeing a
relation between religious and secular modes of meaning and straddling
them in a kind of mild irony. He was in any event moving the already
established genre of the scientific lyceum lecture away from its focus on
practical or applied science, showing that a knowledge of nature could
contribute to more than the health of the body or the wealth of the nation.
Still, Emerson did not despise these aspects of the question, but implicated
them directly in the unifying theme of nature's assistance to man.

The argument of these early lectures relies much on a providential and
teleological view of the universe. In "The Relation of Man to the Globe," the
second lecture in the series, Emerson argues on the basis of new geological

17. Without acknowledging Emerson's debt to Carlyle, Merton M. Sealts Jr. discusses the
importance of "Spiritualism" to the concluding scheme of *Nature,* observing that its deployment
got Emerson past the "useful introductory hypothesis" of idealism; see *Emerson on the Scholar*
(Columbia: University of Missouri Press, 1992), 79–80. It would be difficult to determine
whether Emerson's "introductory hypothesis" is merely a heuristic device or reflects an earlier
stage in his own thinking.

evidence that "Man . . . has been prophesied in nature for a thousand thousand ages before he appeared," and that the planet's geological career was a process of fitting itself out to be, in time, the home of man (*EL,* 1:29–30). Thus God made worms to keep the surface of the soil open for agriculture, and the upward thrust of the geologic strata purposefully brings coal and minerals within man's reach. Similarly, "modern chemistry has discovered some facts of striking fitness between the atmosphere and the creature who breathes it" (*EL,* 1:32).[18] The point to which Emerson ultimately brings the argument in "The Uses of Natural History" is that the world exists to serve its highest product, human consciousness; it follows, therefore, that "it is . . . the greatest office of natural science . . . to explain man to himself" (*EL,* 1:23). While these observations seem consistent with the older conventional "argument from design," Emerson does not deploy them, as Bishop Paley had done, to confirm the existence of God, the producer of these effects, but instead to draw attention to the effect itself, showing how nature is to be understood as a medium for self-regarding human consciousness. The study of nature will not, in its finest development, serve the "uses" so far expected by lyceum lecturers and lyceum audiences, but will search the "Mind of Man" as the essential middle term between the visible and invisible worlds:

> The strongest distinction of which we have an idea is that between thought and matter. The very existence of thought and speech supposes and is a new nature totally distinct from the material world; yet we find it impossible to speak of it and its laws in any other language than that borrowed from our experience in the material world. We not only speak in continual metaphors of the morn, the noon and the evening of life, of dark and bright thoughts, of sweet and bitter moments, of the healthy mind and the fading memory; but all our most literal and direct modes of speech—as right and wrong, form and substance, honest and dishonest etc., are, when

18. Modern readers, steeped in the evolutionary thought of Charles Darwin and his successors, will find these "scientific" observations painfully naive and wrongheaded, but it can be said in their favor that they are less divergent from the science of Emerson's day than they are from ours, and that they observe a venerable principle of science, that the purpose of explanation is to "save the appearances." (Emerson's defense of idealism against materialism in *Nature* appeals directly to this principle.) Science would be a very different affair today had it followed Emerson's (and Goethe's) penchant for referring phenomena to the human situation—but it would still be science.

hunted up to their original signification, found to be metaphors also. And this because the whole of Nature is a metaphor or image of the human Mind. The laws of moral nature answer to those of matter as face to face in a glass. "The visible world," it has been well said, "and the relations of its parts is the dial plate of the invisible one." (*EL*, 1:24–25)

In outlining what was to become the important "Language" chapter of *Nature*, Emerson is announcing a romantic, human-centered vision of science. His view rejects the empiricism of Baconian science while accepting Bacon's belief that science was to be *the* road to human empowerment. In short, the intrinsic idealism of Emerson's religious training had given him a definition of empowerment as essentially spiritual and inward, which caused him in turn to value science as an eligible vehicle for investigating the moral law. "To the powers of science," he said, "no limit can be assigned" (*EL*, 1:13), suggesting that the practical materialism of his day was an unnecessary and shortsighted acceptance of limits, a failure of imagination, or a resting in the Understanding where the highest success was reserved to the Reason.[19]

While many of his conservative contemporaries were driven to defend biblical models against the challenges of the new scientific revelations, Emerson met them in ways that strengthened rather than diminished his faith, finding that scientific truth supported what was "spiritual" and degraded only what was historical or superstitious. As he later recalled the impact of the new science, he found that "the religious nature in man was not affected by these errors in his understanding. The religious sentiment made nothing of bulk or size, or far or near; triumphed over time as well as space; and every lesson of humility, or justice, or charity, which the old ignorant saints had taught him, was still forever true" (*W*, 10:336–37). Like Christ, "a minister of the pure Reason" (*JMN*, 5:273), Emerson would come, as he hoped science would, not to destroy the law but to fulfill it, to redeem spiritualism from

19. It is interesting to see how Bronson Alcott's thought paralleled Emerson's in the years just prior to their first meeting. From a reading of Herschel in 1831, Alcott progressed to a repudiation of Bacon in the spring of 1834. For Alcott, the problem with Bacon was that he "narrowed the range of the human faculties, retarded the progress of discovery by insisting on the supremacy of the senses, and shut the soul up in the cave of the Understanding" (*Journals*, 27, 39). Compare *Nature:* "And there are patient naturalists, but they freeze their subject under the wintry light of the understanding" (*CW*, 1:44).

the Egyptian bondage of the conventional and sensual tropes in which it had
been fixed or enslaved for ages.[20]

The emphasis on spirit in Emerson's thought will suggest to a modern
mind that he altogether lacked a scientific sensibility, and yet in 1830 even
Herschel would acknowledge the moral side of science, and could wax
eloquent about the ennobling love of general truths and the enlargement
of the human character provoked by such study:

> There is something in the contemplation of general laws which power-
> fully persuades us to merge individual feeling, and to commit ourselves
> unreservedly to their disposal. . . . And this it does not by debasing our
> nature into weak compliances and abject submission to circumstances, but
> by filling us, as from an inward spring, with a sense of nobleness and power
> which enables us to rise superior to them; by showing us our strength and
> innate dignity, and by calling upon us for the exercise of those powers and
> faculties by which we are susceptible of the comprehension of so much
> greatness.[21]

It is safe to say that Emerson was very much more interested in such
possibilities than was Herschel, for whom they seem a lucky side effect. The
corresponding claims that Emerson makes in "The Uses of Natural History"
and later in *Nature* are pointedly much grander, amounting almost to belief
that by nature we are saved:

> Whosoever would gain anything of [science,] must submit to the essential
> condition of all learning, must go in the spirit of a little child. . . . I
> apprehend that every man who goes by himself into the woods, not at

---

20. It is in this regard that one sees most clearly the influence of radical protestantism on
Emerson. Just as his arguments against respecting the ritual *form* of the Lord's Supper were all
drawn from Quaker sources, so the Quakers' emphasis on inwardness and their independence
from formalism—as exemplified in the life of George Fox—became a primary model for "an
original relation to the universe." See Mary C. Turpie, "A Quaker Source for Emerson's Sermon
on the Lord's Supper," *New England Quarterly* 17 (March 1944): 95–101, Emerson's 1835 lecture
on Fox (*EL*, 1:165–82), and F. B. Tolles, "Emerson and Quakerism," *American Literature* 10 (May
1938): 142–65. Before the transcendentalists took to themselves the title of "spiritualists" (an
older word than *spiritualism*), the term had been most often and regularly applied to Quakers.

21. J. F. W. Herschel, *A Preliminary Discourse on the Study of Natural Philosophy* (London:
Longman, Rees, Orme, Brown & Green, 1830), 16.

the time occupied by any anxiety of mind, but free to surrender himself to
the genius of the place, feels as a boy again without loss of wisdom. In the
presence of nature he is a child. (*EL*, 1:21; compare *Nature, CW,* 1:9–10)

This benign, redemptive vision of juvenility, a complex and emotionally
charged motif in *Nature,* is one strong mythical alternative to the fallen,
adult hyperconsciousness that Carlyle had lamented in "Characteristics"; as
a motif it exerted a particularly strong pull on Emerson, who was, as we
shall see, at this time struggling to establish, belatedly, his own productive
adulthood in becoming a writer and a father. He is deeply ambivalent
about taking on such a generative self, which he sees, from one angle,
as further removed from the richly aggrandized figure of the child and
a closer approach to that oppressive and sepulchral, yet envied, figure of
the fathers on which the opening paragraph of *Nature* dramatically turns.
These important generational anxieties color Emerson's evolving theory of
the self, which had its roots in the religious ideal of the submission of
the self (as a dependent child) to a paternal God. It was a model that
of course discountenanced the rebellious, imperial, productive adult will
in favor of "yielding to the perfect whole," as Emerson said in his 1834
poem "Each and All," or, as Christ had said, "not my will, but thine,
be done" (Luke 22:42).[22] In the passage just quoted from "The Uses of
Natural History," Emerson echoes Christ's proposition that "Whosoever
shall not receive the kingdom of God as a little child shall in no wise
enter therein" (Luke 18:17), an illustration that the virtues of humility,
submission, and self-forgetfulness (kenosis) are substantially greater than
any self-regarding piety. If, as Emerson would shortly propose, "Nature is
the symbol of spirit" (or, in the alternative, "the kingdom of God"), then
one truly enters Nature in this humble, self-effacing manner or not at all.

22. Emerson again refers to this episode in Luke when, on March 21, 1834, he commends
the belief of his Quaker friend, Mary Rotch, that the progress of religion is toward an ever
more "inward & spiritual dispensation," a position he had himself consistently argued from the
Second Church pulpit, and which was the basis for his opposition to the vestigial historicism
and superstition he found in contemporary religion. "These dispensations she compared to
the progressive stages of the human heart in the work of religion, from loving our neighbor as
ourselves to loving our enemies & lastly arriving at that state of humility when self would be
totally abandoned & we could only say Lord be merciful to me a sinner" (*JMN*, 4:268; compare
Luke 18:13).

He is arguing, in these early lectures, for a science that is capable of making use of this insight.

But this lesson in humility comprises at most only half the message in the scientific lectures: in "The Naturalist," delivered in May 1834, Emerson argues a position that seems at first quite incompatible with the discipline or submergence of the self:

> But it is said that Man is the only object of interest to Man. I fully believe it. I believe that the constitution of man is the center from which all our speculations depart. But it is the wonderful charm of external nature that man stands in a central connexion with it all; not at the head, but in the midst: and not an individual in the kingdom of organized life but sends out a ray of relation to him. (*EL*, 1:71)

This was the revelation of the Jardin des Plantes—that the immense variety of nature was miraculously unified in the consciousness of the observer, that it was all, in its organic perfection, somehow "connate" and "familiar." All made sense and was to be accounted for not in the relations of part to part, but in the relation of all to that interpreting consciousness for which it was made. Clearly this view makes the self the organizing center of the universe, and indeed, this principle lies at the heart of Emerson's project, as it certainly did not lie at the heart of emergent Victorian science. On April 10, 1834, when Emerson moved with his mother to the exceptionally quiet and secluded town of Newton, Massachusetts, he asked himself whether it were "possible that in the solitude I seek I shall have the resolution . . . to work as I . . . project in highest most farsighted hours? Well, & what do you project? Nothing less than to look at every object in its relation to Myself" (*JMN*, 4:272).

Emerson's theory of the self has been a stumbling block to innumerable readers who are not without cause confused about the distinction between the mean egotism of the Understanding in its imperious dealings with time and space, and the divinely sanctioned egotism of the Reason, which relates man to the absolute, and about the consequent need to discipline and subdue the former and prevent it from usurping the place and privileges of the latter. The perception that Emerson had moved beyond recognizably Christian attitudes by the middle 1830s disguises the fact that these crucial distinctions rather closely mirror conventionally religious exhortations to be suspicious of the self and to rely on God instead. The paradox of the valuable, reliable self and the unworthy, distorting self seems to have become suddenly clearer to Emerson at just this time—the spring of 1834—when his attention came to rest on Coleridge's distinction between the Reason and the Understanding.[23] Emerson believed in divine immanence, believed that the core of the human self was "the God within": this was the Reason, the "door of access" to God and the realm of the absolute. To the Reason, or the "renewed understanding," as Emerson called it, the phenomenal world is perceived as referring to the noumenal, and it educates us constantly by that reference. But in our fallen condition, the Reason is obscured, eclipsed by the lower faculty of the Understanding, and man, corrupt and shortsighted, lives at odds with his own spiritual origins, thinks of himself as one circumstance among many, and comes to rely on his Understanding to deal with the phenomena as though they were real and ultimate. "Man," according to Emerson, "is conscious of a two-fold nature which manifests itself in perpetual contradiction" (*JMN*, 5:271). Emerson had arrived at this point in his thinking while still a minister delivering sermons, but in 1834 and 1835 he worked it out again in the philosophical context supplied by Coleridge, where its anti-Lockean implications were still more evident.[24] As he did so, he moved quickly from his earliest conception of *Nature* to the form it would take in 1836.

## IV

When Emerson said at the Jardin des Plantes "I will be a naturalist," he was making a statement about how (if not where) he would live. *Science* had become for him simply another name for education, conceived essentially as

23. Emerson explained these concepts at length to his brother Edward in a letter of May 31, 1834 (*L*, 1:412–13), as though they were new to himself. He had certainly read, years earlier, the several works by Coleridge that define them, but the terms become functional and instrumental for Emerson only at this point.

24. Most specifically he worked it out in Journal RO in June 1835, which is his summary explanation to himself of the "First Philosophy," a term borrowed from Bacon (*JMN*, 5:269–76). It is worth mentioning that Emerson is never very directly or explicitly concerned with John Locke or his arguments against intuition, though the issue was certainly "in the air": the first meeting of the Transcendental Club, according to the later recollections of Frederic Henry Hedge, centered on Locke's baleful influence on contemporary Unitarianism.

the mind's use of the world. "Nature," he had said in his first lecture, "is a language and every new fact we learn is a new word; but it is not a language taken to pieces and dead in the dictionary, but the language put together into a most significant and universal sense. I wish to learn this language—not that I may know a new grammar but that I may read the great book which is written in that tongue" (*EL*, 1:26). Thus the famous distinction in *Nature* between the Me and the Not-Me, which follows immediately from this perception, amounts, as a matter of science, to a distinction between the reader and the "great book." The distinction turns out to have played a significant role in Emerson's thinking about "how to live"—as we may infer from the earliest reference to the terminology, in a letter of October 8, 1835, from Emerson's brother Charles to his friend Joseph Lyman. The terms are already so familiar that they are humorously rendered in French: "To find the fit sphere of our activity; & then to mix, in just proportions, study & action: & still farther, rightly to divide study between the 'Moi' & the 'Non Moi,' between listening to the voice within, & acquiring the languages that are from without, here observing the phenomena, & there recognising the law of association—to do this is to know how to live; is to live."[25]

It seems clear that if Emerson's lecture series on Science did not advance him immediately to the book he wished to write, it was because he had involved himself in the naturalist's tendency to privilege what Charles was calling the "Non Moi." Emerson wrongly supposed that science, which seemed to be pointing "more and more steadily at Method, at a Theory" (*EL*, 1:82), would soon arrive at its apotheosis by a conscious methodological commitment to joining the Me and the Not-Me. He would himself help this process along in a book that would propose in its introduction "to find a theory of nature" that would "explain all phenomena" (*CW*, 1:8). This project, which is not quite what *Nature* accomplishes, belongs to the first half of Emerson's divided purpose—to "Nature," as opposed to its sequel, "Spirit"—and reflects the moral/ethical vision of the recently liberated min-

---

25. Charles Emerson, letter to Joseph Lyman, Houghton MS Am 1280.220 (53), folder 13, owned by the Ralph Waldo Emerson Memorial Association and quoted by permission. Emerson's own first recorded use of the terms (March 17, 1836) recounts Charles's observation that the Greek chorus represented the Not-Me (*JMN*, 5:141). Ultimately, of course, they derive from Fichte's *Ich* and *Nicht-Ich*, as Emerson might have learned from Carlyle ("Novalis," *Critical and Miscellaneous Essays*, 175).

ister of 1833, the Emerson who "loves" Carlyle and is "enamoured of moral perfection" (*JMN*, 4:79, 87). In the spring of 1834, Emerson took leave of the subject of science with these words: "No truth can be more self-evident than that the highest state of man, physical, intellectual, and moral, can only coexist with a perfect Theory of Animated Nature" (*EL*, 1:83).

During the winter of 1834–1835, he pursued another, in some respects more manageable, interest. The new lectures on Biography were a welcome relief from the relative sterility of the Science series: "Natural history by itself," he said, "has no value; it is like a single sex; but marry it to human history, and it is poetry."[26] The impulse to the Biography series was essentially similar, however, to the foregoing lectures: in "The Uses of Natural History," he had asked, in reference to the variety of animal life, "Where is it these fair creatures . . . find their link, their cement, their keystone, but in the Mind of Man?" (*EL*, 1:24). Just so do great men assume their place, and Emerson's experience in the church of Santa Croce in Florence while examining the bust above the tomb of Michelangelo is strictly analogous to his experience at the Jardin des Plantes: "As I beheld that head I felt that I was not a stranger in the foreign church for this man's great name sounded hospitably in my ear. He was not a citizen of any country; he belonged to the human race; he was a brother and a friend to all who acknowledge the beauty that beams in universal nature and who seek by labor and denial to approach its source in Perfect Goodness" (*EL*, 1:117). He might easily have said at that point "I will be a biographer"—had he not already said it a year earlier (*JMN*, 4:35; compare *JMN*, 4:256). Of the six lectures in the Biography series, delivered between January 29 and March 5, 1835, much the most important was the one devoted to Michelangelo, for it was an occasion to expound a theory of beauty that eventually became the core of the third chapter of *Nature*.

The Biography series allowed Emerson to see his evolving project more in terms of its essential subject/object configuration; that is to say, it focused his attention more sharply on the "Mind of Man" and relaxed its hold on Nature

26. The evolution of this proposition is typical of many in *Nature:* it first occurs in a journal entry for August 15, 1834 (*JMN*, 4:311); then it, or versions of it, turns up in a lecture at Concord (presumably a revision of "The Uses of Natural History") on January 1, 1835, in the introductory lecture to the English Literature series the following November (*EL*, 1:221), and in a revised version of the first lecture on Shakespeare (*EL*, 1:289) before making its appearance in *Nature* (*CW*, 1:19).

as the significant object. A large part of the old "book about nature" could
now be spun off as a subordinate project, reconceived in terms strikingly
more Thoreauvian than Emersonian: "If life were long enough," he wrote in
his journal on March 28, "among the thousand & one works should be a
book of Nature whereof '[William] Howitt's [Book of the] Seasons' should
be not so much the model as the parody. It should contain the Natural
history of the woods around my shifting camp for every month in the year.
It should tie their astronomy, botany, physiology, meteorology, picturesque,
& poetry together. No bird, no bug, no bud should be forgotten on his
day & hour" (*JMN*, 5:25). The reconceptualizing—and demotion—of some
large part of Emerson's original project immediately opened up space for the
writing of a more daring and ambitious book, which was still, however, not
the book of 1836. On June 25, 1835, he informed Frederic Henry Hedge that
his literary plans for the upcoming winter included "8 or 10 lectures before
the Diffusion Society" and "by & by a book of Essays chiefly upon Natural
Ethics with the aim of bringing a pebble or two to the edification of the new
temple whilst so many wise hands are demolishing the old" (*L*, 1:447).[27]
The relative dissatisfaction with a "scientific" subject is compensated for by
a rising interest in the spiritual subject. If *Nature* in its first version was to
redefine science, this version of 1835 would redefine religion, presumably
along the lines finally laid out in the Divinity School Address of 1838. These
were the poles between which Emerson's thinking about his book vibrated
as he approached the writing of it.

## V

The reference to the "shifting camp" that centers the projected "Seasons"
book provides a clue to the important local conditions of Emerson's thought
at this time. What in fact most occupied Emerson's attention in 1835 was,
quite simply, the wholesale reorganization of his private life. In January he
was engaged to Lydia Jackson of Plymouth, a woman he seems not to have
known especially well; by the time they were married in September, he had
bought a house in Concord large enough to accommodate also his mother

27. Emerson delivered eleven lectures on English literature before the Society for the Diffusion
of Useful Knowledge between November 5, 1835, and January 14, 1836. The series as a whole
contributed little to *Nature*, though the first of two lectures on Shakespeare contains a lengthy
passage, revised from "The Uses of Natural History," used in the "Language" chapter of *Nature*.

and his brother Charles, who was himself on the verge of marriage, and whose bride, Elizabeth Hoar, would then join this extended family. What made all of this possible was the inheritance that had come from Emerson's deceased first wife, Ellen Tucker, literally the angel in the house.[28] One can see these events, and several other related ones, as Emerson's deliberate assumption of his majority, a firm decision, finally, about where and how he ought to live. By becoming the central, settled male figure in an extended household (moving out of his step-grandfather's Old Manse), he is, at age thirty-two, at last empowered to move forward in a literary career he felt was sputtering or stalled.[29] Within a year he was significantly more connected to the world, having come into a considerable amount of money, acquired a home and a home town, and (perhaps the overriding goal) secured the continued presence of the most important intellectual influence on him, his brother Charles.[30] Moreover, the period during which *Nature* was actually composed—April through July, 1836—fell entirely within the span of his wife Lidian's first pregnancy, and for a while it may have seemed doubtful whether Waldo or *Nature* would be delivered first. Eighteen thirty-six was the year that Emerson became a father.

On March 27, about the same time that Emerson wrote a brief preface for the first American edition of *Sartor Resartus,* he wrote in a journal entry a

28. Emerson received half the legacy in 1834 and would receive the other half in 1836; it came to about $22,000 in all, more than twelve times his highest annual salary at the Second Church.

29. "When will you mend Montaigne? When will you take the hint of nature? Where are your Essays? Can you not express your one conviction that the moral laws hold?" (*JMN*, 5:40). This journal entry for May 14, 1835, goes on to list and review virtually all of the important themes of Emerson's private speculations, couched in terms of his present exasperating inability to write them out. The single most astonishing fact about *Nature* is how little it overtly deals with these themes: the "doctrines" of self-reliance and compensation, for example, had been extensively worked out in the sermons, and yet his formal presentation of them had to wait until the publication of *Essays* in 1841. Just as the events of 1835 put a social and domestic foundation under Emerson's literary career, *Nature* provides a general intellectual basis for the exposition—and reception—of important specific issues. *Nature* is thus intrinsically a prospective work, an "entering wedge," as he described it to Carlyle (*CEC*, 149).

30. Charles had earlier located in Concord, where he had taken over the law practice of his fiancée's father, Samuel Hoar. The deliberateness of Emerson's shaping of the "private sphere" at this time also shows in his eagerness to deliver the Concord bicentennial address on September 12, 1835, just two days before his marriage. Even more than his purchase of the Coolidge house, the address (which also became his first significant publication) cemented his relations with the town at the very outset of his forty-seven-year residence there. However, in agreeing to deliver the address, he seems to have deprived Charles of that honor.

sketchy outline of the four central chapters of *Nature:* Commodity, Beauty, Language, and Discipline, the four "uses" that nature serves in its ministry to man (*JMN,* 5:146–47). Of these, the two central ones had already been largely worked out in the lectures: "Beauty" in "Michel Angelo Buonaroti" and "Language" first in Sermon LXVII, then in "The Uses of Natural History," and then again in the first of the two lectures on Shakespeare. The "lower" use of "Commodity" and the "higher" use of "Discipline" were as yet undeveloped.

Soon after he sketched the outline, on Saturday, April 2, perhaps thinking of the sermons he would deliver the next day at East Lexington, Emerson reminded himself, in an oddly deferred afterthought, that Nature is ultimately to be referred to the Deity, and considered adding a chapter on Worship (*JMN,* 5:149). In early April, while the snow melted and the grass in the Concord meadows turned green, Emerson was deeply engaged in his writing. He may have devoted some of this time to revising lectures for delivery later that month in Salem, but generally when Emerson stops writing in his journal and curtails his correspondence (as was the case through the first half of April), it means that he has cleared the decks for original composition.

What could Emerson have written between March 27, when the organization of the work became clear to him, and April 18, when he began delivering his Salem lectures? As we shall see, he did not in fact begin the chapter on "Beauty" before the very end of May, so it would seem likely that he was engaged on "Commodity" and, probably, some sort of introduction.

Any introduction that Emerson might have written in early April would necessarily have been an introduction to a book consisting only of the four chapters outlined on May 27. The final chapters, "Idealism," "Spirit," and "Prospects," belong to a subsequently expanded conception of the work. Perhaps in part an elaboration of his idea that Nature was to be referred, at last, to the Deity, these chapters were not combined with the original four until very late in the process of composition. On July 20, Emerson supposed (and had been supposing for at least a month) that he could issue *Nature* as a work of fewer than fifty pages, to be followed shortly thereafter by a sequel entitled "Spirit."[31] This fact presents a number of

---

31. Emerson thus described his plan to Hedge; see *L,* 2:30. On June 28, he told his brother William that the contents of *Nature* would "not exceed in bulk S[ampson] Reed's Growth of

difficulties for anyone trying to understand how *Nature* was put together, but it may, on the other hand, help to explain why the book has, in effect, two introductions—one so called, and another, following it, entitled "Chapter I. Nature." These two introductions are in fact rather different: the first is a relatively straightforward laying out of premises, concerned with definitions and the niceties of logical argument; the second is distinctly more poetic and transcendental. The first, which allies itself to the "one aim" that science has of finding a "theory of nature," points at once to the four central chapters and to the earliest conception of the book; the second seems more attached to the concluding discussion of Spirit and to the final sense of what *Nature* was to accomplish.

The two introductions differ in another important respect: in the Introduction so called, only four sentences and two phrases can be traced to Emerson's prior writings; Chapter I, however, is a veritable patchwork of self-quotation. Apart from the final paragraph, which clearly alludes to the death of Charles Emerson on May 9, virtually every sentence adapts or repeats some text in the journals. That these two expository units were composed according to such radically different methods does not in itself establish the priority of the Introduction, but it does perhaps imply that they were not written consecutively, or in near succession, or for very similar purposes. What seems a great deal more likely is that the Introduction and the Commodity chapter were written consecutively,[32] and that Chapter I was composed as part of a belated effort to accommodate the concluding portion of the work, whether before or immediately after Emerson's decision in August to issue *Nature* and *Spirit* together.[33]

One is also led to suppose that the early and shorter version of *Nature* must at one time have had some sort of conclusion, that it did not simply

------

the Mind" (*L*, 2:26). Reed's work was forty-four pages long; *Nature*, as finally issued, spanned ninety-five pages.

32. A somewhat crude statistical analysis further supports this conclusion: 17.2 percent of the text of the "Introduction" and 18.2 percent of the text of "Commodity" can be traced to sources in Emerson's prior writings. The remaining chapters range between 24 percent ("Chapter VII. Spirit") and 68.9 percent ("Chapter I. Nature") and average 46.3 percent.

33. Bronson Alcott wrote in his journal on August 2 that Emerson "is now writing a work, of a high intellectual character, which he calls 'Nature and Spirit.' In beauty and finish of style, he is unrivalled among American writers. There is also more philosophical depth than in any other writer" (*Journals*, 65).

break off at the end of the "Discipline" chapter. Evidence for the existence of such a conclusion may be found in a brief outline written in Journal B on June 4:

> Man puts things in a row
> Things belong in a row
>> The showing of the true row is Science
>> History teaches
>>> 1. The presence of Spirit
>>> 2. The antecedence of Spirit
>>> 3. The humanity of Spirit
>> Corollary
>> Science must be studied humanly. (*JMN*, 5:168–69)

By this hypothesis, then, the abandoned conclusion of *Nature* became the core of Emerson's "Humanity of Science" lecture, delivered in December as a rather unassimilated part of the Philosophy of History series.[34]

The "Humanity of Science" lecture has an ambitious argument, but that argument is still the logical and relatively prosaic extension of the science lectures of 1833–1834: "When science shall be studied with piety; when in a soul alive with moral sentiments, the antecedence of spirit is presupposed; then humanity advances, step by step with the opening of the intellect and its command over nature" (*EL*, 2:36). Emerson is still true to his earliest insight into the "radical analogies" (*EL*, 2:26), and is still fascinated by the prospect of deploying science in the Carlylian project of moral and social reformation: "The highest moral of science," Emerson contends, "is the transference of that trust which is felt in nature's admired arrangements, light, heat, gravity,—to the social and moral order" (*EL*, 2:39).

The main point of the book that might have ended this way would be to advise scientists on how they ought to conceive of their field, and to involve natural history in a moral and spiritual intervention in the condition of

---

34. Merton M. Sealts Jr. shrewdly notes (*JMN*, 5:169 n) that the outline relates both to the "Humanity of Science" lecture and to the opening passages of the "Prospects" chapter of *Nature*: "Nor has science sufficient humanity" (*CW*, 1:40). But that the outline has its most immediate reference to *Nature* is irresistibly implied by the date of its inscription: Emerson did not begin to plan his winter lectures until the middle of October (see *JMN*, 5:221–22).

the public sphere. Such a book clearly envisions and advocates immediate alterations in the way the public understands nature, and, in a voice that presumes to know what is best for the community, adopts a position with respect to its audience that is distinctly more ministerial (and Carlylian) than orphic or bardic. There is no basis for supposing that at some specific time Emerson became aware that this approach was not the strongest he could take. For some time, as we have seen, the science-centered approach to the book was losing the strength of its initial appeal; simultaneously, other motives, both complementary and competing, arose in its place. The presence of Bronson Alcott, whom Emerson first met in October 1835, is in many ways paradigmatic of these "other motives," for while Alcott may have contributed few essential ideas to the composition of *Nature*, it is likely not only that he prompted Emerson to confront "the Ideal Theory" head on, but also that he gave Emerson a sharply new conception of what his audience might be and of what capacities of reception he might count on.

## VI

The influence of Bronson Alcott helps to explain why *Nature* as finally issued was more a prose poem than a scientific treatise. It was not just that Alcott was in all likelihood the inspiration for the orphic poet who presides over the final chapter; a more fundamental contribution was, in 1835, to have challenged or complicated the influence of Carlyle, and to have done so by representing a necessary connection between idealism and poetics. Emerson's lecture on Bacon, written shortly before its first delivery on Christmas Eve, 1835, signals a turn in Emerson's interests towards "a poetry . . . of insight" (*CW* 1:3), which Alcott seems to have abetted and encouraged. Bacon had taught Emerson to think of "the perfect man" as "the Interpreter of Nature and the priest of the world"; in the lecture he praises Bacon for that "Universal Curiosity" that would make the mind of man "a second Nature, a second Universe" (*EL*, 1:326–28). Perhaps Emerson had, early on, some vague hope that by bringing science to acknowledge the symbolic character of nature, he could accomplish in his own book what he felt Bacon had earlier done: "he would put his Atlantean hands to heave the whole globe of the Sciences from their rest, expose all the gulfs and continents of error, and with creative hand remodel and reform the whole" (*EL*, 1:328). But Bacon's reformation—or the quality of his example—was problematical: as a human being he was seriously flawed, a sycophant who allowed himself to grovel before authority, a man who did not, in the end, know "where and how he ought to live." His work, therefore, suffered a similar disintegration: "He did not arrange," Emerson declares, "but unceasingly collect[ed] facts. . . . Each of Shakspeare's dramas is perfect, hath an immortal integrity. To make Bacon's works complete, he must live to the end of the world" (*EL*, 1:335). The allusion to Shakespeare is not accidental: Emerson was coming to see that the kind of general or "abstract" speculation that science ought to arrogate to itself, as he had argued, was perhaps more naturally the province of the poet. He had recently felt the strong rising of a poetic gift within himself, and had addressed an emphatic premarital argument to Lidian in favor of living in Concord on the basis of his needs as a poet.[35]

Emerson's turn toward poetry and the language of the Reason would place some increased distance between himself and Carlyle, just as it would simultaneously promote a relationship between Emerson and Bronson Alcott. It was not just that Carlyle could "not approve of rhyme at all," as he would later confess (*CEC*, 410), but that he consistently deplored Emerson's "abstractness," his unwillingness to address directly the real conditions of contemporary social life, as he had himself done in his preeminently prosy jeremiads in the quarterlies. Alcott, on the other hand, performed an important service in confirming Emerson's belief that it was an error "to fight for Reason with the Weapons of the Understanding."[36] Typologically, Carlyle *was* Jeremiah, with perhaps a bit of the Baptist thrown in; but Alcott, wholly

35. See Carl F. Strauch, "The Year of Emerson's Poetic Maturity: 1834," *Philological Quarterly* 34 (October 1955): 343–77. It is a fact supportive of Strauch's hypothesis that Emerson began his first major poetry notebook ("P") in 1834. For Emerson's assertion that his "nature & vocation" is to be a poet, "in the sense of a perceiver & dear lover of the harmonies that are in the soul & in matter, & specially of the correspondences between these & those," see his letter to Lydia Jackson, February 1, 1835 (*L*, 1:434–35). Emerson's explicit preference for poetry over the "half-sight of science" is expressed in the "Prospects" chapter of *Nature* (*CW*, 1:41).

36. This was Emerson's response to reading John Norris's *Essay towards the Theory of the Ideal or Intelligible World* (1701–1704) in July 1835. In calling this "the common error of the first philosophers," Emerson implicitly extends the judgment to Bacon as well (*JMN*, 5:57). It is perhaps worth mentioning in this connection that when Carlyle met Alcott in 1842, they found they were wholly opposite types and could barely communicate with each other; Carlyle wrote that Alcott wanted to "*be* something," whereas it was Carlyle's goal to "*do* something" (*CEC*, 326).

in the optative mood, and suffering the little children to come unto him, was the very embodiment of new faith.

The first extended conversation between Emerson and Alcott, on October 18, 1835, turned chiefly on the life of Christ.[37] "Mr. E's fine literary taste is sometimes in the way of the clear and hearty acceptance of the spiritual. Carlyle is his ideal," Alcott wrote (*Journals*, 68–69). The implication would seem to be that Carlyle's influence was relatively a clog to Emerson's acceptation of a more spiritual, less grounded way of talking, and in fact Emerson seems to have looked upon Alcott's influence as liberating in precisely this way: after their first meeting, Emerson's brother Charles remarked on "the nimbleness & buoyancy which the conversation of a spiritualist awakens; the world begins to dislimn" (*JMN*, 5:99). In February 1836, Emerson's immediate reaction to reading Alcott's unpublished "Psyche" was to write in his journal: "The book is always dear which has made us for moments idealists. That which can dissipate this block of earth into shining ether is genius" (*JMN*, 5:123).

Alcott's spiritual and idealizing influence arrived at a crucial time. Between Emerson's reading of "Psyche" in February and his reading of Alcott's private journal for 1835 in late May and early June, his brother Charles succumbed to tuberculosis, dying in New York on May 9. A letter of June 7 from Elizabeth Hoar, Charles's fiancée, to Mary Moody Emerson testifies to the depth of Emerson's grief and depression at this time,[38] though he managed to work through it on various parts of *Nature*, outlining the "Beauty" chapter, for example, on May 31 (*JMN*, 5:166).

Alcott paid three or four brief visits to Emerson during June, the earliest period to which any of the concluding parts of *Nature* can be dated. Emerson wrote a draft of "Prospects" on June 22 or 23, interrupting his reading of a

---

37. Before this, Emerson had heard Alcott described by their mutual friend George P. Bradford as "a consistent spiritualist" (*JMN*, 5:57) and had read *Record of a School; Exemplifying the General Principles of Spiritual Culture*, a description of Alcott's methods at his Temple School, written by his assistant, Elizabeth Palmer Peabody. In his journal, Emerson particularly commended Alcott's instruction through emblems, concluding, "Good writing & brilliant conversation are perpetual allegories"—a sentence he later used in the "Language" chapter of *Nature* (*JMN*, 5:63).

38. Elizabeth Maxfield-Miller, "Elizabeth of Concord: Selected Letters of Elizabeth Sherman Hoar (1814–1878) to the Emersons, Family, and the Emerson Circle (Part Two)," *Studies in the American Renaissance: 1985* (Charlottesville: University Press of Virginia, 1985), 141–43.

manuscript version of Alcott's *Record of Conversations on the Gospels*.[39] This shows that Emerson was working on *Spirit* before he completed *Nature*, or at least before he was ready to present the first of his two essays to his publisher, James Munroe. On a visit to Boston on July 6 Emerson consulted with Munroe, who quoted an estimate of $100 to produce the volume (*L*, 2:28); this figure appears low, and would seem more consistent with the costs of a pamphlet than a book. As late as July 20, as we have seen, Emerson maintained his intention to issue *Nature* first and its sequel some time later. Evidently, as Emerson wrote out the chapters on "Idealism," "Spirit," and "Prospects" in June and July, it became clearer to him that he would be able to join them with the earlier chapters, which were still not quite ready for the printer. The two segments actually came together during the memorable first visit of Margaret Fuller to Concord. She arrived on July 21 or 22, stayed for three weeks, and left on August 11, and although virtually nothing is known of this visit except that it happened, it would seem at least plausible that Emerson would have read portions of the work to her, and that they would have discussed it. On August 8, before Fuller left, Emerson wrote to his brother William, mentioning a recent visit from Alcott, and saying, "The book of Nature still lies on the table. There is, as always, one crack in it not easy to be soldered or welded, but if this week I should be left alone after the probate affair [settling the estate of Charles Emerson] I may finish it" (*L*, 2:32).[40] The "crack" could be nothing other, of course, than the joint between "Discipline" (from which, perhaps, a conclusion somewhat

39. See *JMN*, 5:181–82, which shows that he was particularly pleased with a section entitled "Annunciation of Spirit to Paternity. Paternal Sentiment." Emerson was reading the manuscript in several distinct capacities: as one interested in learning about Alcott, as a parent-to-be, and as a surrogate parent. Emerson had the care of Hillman B. Sampson, the child of his late friend George Adams Sampson, and would within a month enroll Hillman in Alcott's school.

40. The will of Charles Emerson was probated on August 9; after the payment of debts, he had an estate of $236.83. It is difficult to assess the effect of the loss of Charles on the concurrent writing of *Nature*, despite Emerson's two distinct references to it (*CW*, 1:10–11 and 28–29), the latter the powerful conclusion of the "Discipline" chapter. Charles died before his planned marriage to Elizabeth Hoar, a marriage that had been put off until Charles could establish himself professionally. This linking of the public and private spheres is observable in the lives of the older brothers, William and Ralph Waldo, as well, and seems to mark a very distinct coming-of-age, which Charles failed to reach. Ralph Waldo had arrived at that point in 1829, but had to repeat the process in 1835–1836.

like "The Humanity of Science" had already been detached) and the chapter
on "Idealism." That he felt the need of an uninterrupted week to make repairs
suggests that he meant to do more than revise a few paragraphs. Emerson's
biographer, James Elliot Cabot, supposed that this joinery work involved
the interpolation of "Idealism" (hence the last-written chapter) between
"Discipline" and "Spirit."[41] Yet the "Spirit" chapter, which formally qualifies
the position of the idealist, seems logically dependent on the foregoing
explanation.

Another theory suggests itself: that Emerson was conscious of a tonal
dissonance as well as of an abrupt topical transition in the argument in the
movement from "Discipline" to "Idealism," and that he repaired the "crack"
by composing and inserting a second chapter of introduction, the better to
prepare his readers to accept so lyrical a conclusion. This would account for
the qualitative differences discussed earlier between the two introductions,
and leads to a consideration of further evidence, including the fact that the
latest of all the borrowings from the journals occurs in the introductory
chapter entitled "Chapter I. Nature." On August 12, the day after Margaret
Fuller left, Emerson went for a walk to Walden Pond and recorded in his
journal that "a little before sunset . . . I behold somewhat as beautiful as my
own nature" (*JMN*, 5:189). In the completed chapter, this becomes: "In the
tranquil landscape, and especially in the distant line of the horizon, man
beholds somewhat as beautiful as his own nature" (*CW*, 1:10). There can
be no certainty, of course, that this was not added at the last moment to
a chapter otherwise completed much earlier, but the fact that it dates from
the very week that Emerson had set apart to mend the crack in his book
and the fact that this chapter manifestly does function to hold the two parts
of the work together argue against the supposition that the presence *here* of
the latest journal borrowing is mere chance or coincidence.

Another link between this new introduction and the concluding chapters
further supports the theory: only in these chapters does Emerson make
important use of the first person singular. The autobiographical element—
from the famous eyeball passage in Chapter I to the admission in "Idealism"
that "I have no hostility to nature, but a child's love to it," and so on

---

41. James Elliot Cabot, *A Memoir of Ralph Waldo Emerson,* 2 vols. (Boston and New York:
Houghton, Mifflin, 1887), 1:259.

through "Spirit" and "Prospects"—is almost completely suppressed in the "original" chapters, the Introduction, "Commodity," "Beauty," "Language," and "Discipline," where he generally employs "we" or "Man."[42] It was Alcott who, from his very first meeting with Emerson, encouraged him in the direction of autobiography (*JMN*, 5:99). The foregrounding of the Emersonian "I" in what we can perhaps now call the "poetic" chapters is invariably characterized by an open, receptive, passive stance, sometimes avowedly related to a childlike persona. This effect is certainly connected with the influence of Alcott, one who had "retained the spirit of infancy even into the era of manhood," as Emerson described the ideal "lover of nature" (*CW*, 1:9). Contrasted with Carlyle, whom Emerson described in *English Traits* as "a man from his youth" (*W*, 5:15), Alcott represented spiritualism in its relation to faith, innocence, and the sources of poetry. Even as Emerson now launched himself on the adult world of professional authorship, fatherhood, and engagement with the larger world; even as he established himself as a kind of father to other transcendentalists—largely on the strength of his connection to Carlyle—he had, in the writing of *Nature*, placed his career-making debt to Carlyle in manageable perspective—had in fact nearly outrun it by the time *Nature* was finished and published on September 9, 1836.

42. Emerson uses a rhetorical, non-autobiographical "I" from time to time as the conductor of an argument, as in "I shall use the word in both senses." Otherwise, I believe there is only a single exception to this suppression of the "I" in the earlier chapters, a passage in "Beauty" (13) that is closely based on a journal passage of January 1835 (*JMN*, 5:13).

# "Well, My Book Is Written—Let It Go. . . ."

## The Making of *A Connecticut Yankee* in *King Arthur's Court*

H O W A R D   G.   B A E T Z H O L D

❦   ❦   ❦

GESTATION PERIODS for literary works often far exceed those of other species. *A Connecticut Yankee,* conceived in December 1884, developed slowly. A full five years would pass before its birth on December 10, 1889.[1] Still, it was not really unusual for Mark Twain's works to be so long in progress. *Tom Sawyer* (1875) took *almost* five years; *Huckleberry Finn* (1884) was six years in the making. These were not, of course, continuous periods of composition. Much of the author's writing was restricted to the summer vacations which he, his wife, Olivia, and their children spent at Quarry Farm near Elmira, New York, the home of Olivia's foster sister, Susan Crane, and her husband, Theodore. At home in Hartford, literary activities were often interrupted for long periods, or even halted entirely, by multifarious business and social distractions, all of which engendered voluminous correspondence. Samuel Clemens's many interests and enthusiasms often make him appear,

---

1. The chief studies of the composition of *A Connecticut Yankee,* listed chronologically, include John B. Hoben, "Mark Twain's *A Connecticut Yankee:* A Genetic Study," *American Literature* 18 (November 1946): 197–218; Howard G. Baetzhold, " 'The Autobiography of Sir Robert Smith of Camelot,' Mark Twain's Original Plan for *A Connecticut Yankee,*" *American Literature* 32 (January 1961): 456–61, and "The Course of Composition of *A Connecticut Yankee:* A Reinterpretation," *American Literature* 33 (May 1961): 195–214; James D. Williams, "The Genesis, Composition, Publication and Reception of Mark Twain's *A Connecticut Yankee*" (Ph.D. diss., New York University, 1961); James Russell, "The Genesis, Sources, and Reputation of Mark

as Tom Quirk has so aptly put it, like "an acrobat who spins a dozen plates atop as many sticks—rushing back and forth between and among the plates to keep them spinning while starting yet another that will further scatter his attention."[2]

In 1884 business prospects were bright. Though he had been disappointed with the sales of *The Prince and the Pauper* (1882) and *Life on the Mississippi* (1883), Mark Twain was confident that his recently completed *Huckleberry Finn* would be hugely successful. In May, to insure that success, and because he was convinced that his earlier publishers had always cheated him in one way or another, he established his own publishing firm, Charles L. Webster & Co., naming it for his nephew, who would serve as manager. During the remainder of 1884, besides seeing *Huckleberry Finn* through the press, seeking a producer for *Colonel Sellers as a Scientist* (a play he had written with William Dean Howells), and helping to market a pair of grape shears invented by Howells's father, he deserted the Republican party to proclaim himself a "Mugwump" and became deeply involved in the Cleveland campaign for president in 1884. Meanwhile, with expenses of the fledgling publishing company added to those of the lavish scale of living in Hartford, he badly needed a new source of income. In November, therefore, he once more took to the lecture platform, which in the 1870s had won him both wide reputation and financial reward. This time he was joined on tour by George Washington Cable, whose stories and novels of Creole Louisiana had also won considerable fame.

---

Twain's *A Connecticut Yankee in King Arthur's Court*" (Ph.D. diss., University of Chicago, 1966); Baetzhold, chapters 6 and 7 of *Mark Twain and John Bull: The British Connection* (Bloomington and London: Indiana University Press, 1970), 102–61; and Henry Nash Smith, introduction to *A Connecticut Yankee in King Arthur's Court,* Iowa-California Edition, ed. Bernard Stein (Berkeley and Los Angeles: University of California Press, 1979) (this edition is hereafter cited as *CY*). While not strictly a study of the composition of the novel, Everett Carter's "The Meaning of *A Connecticut Yankee,*" *American Literature* 50 (1978): 418–40, is an especially important study of the author's intention and other matters affecting the novel's progress. The completed holograph manuscript is in the Henry W. and Albert A. Berg Collection, New York Public Library, Astor, Lenox, and Tilden Foundations. Two multipage deletions are in the Mark Twain Papers, Bancroft Library, University of California, Berkeley. All of Mark Twain's deletions and other revisions are recorded in "Alterations in the Manuscript," Iowa-California Edition, 706–825. For more information on sources, see *Mark Twain and John Bull,* Notes, 339–51.

2. Tom Quirk, "Nobility Out of Tatters: The Writing of *Huckleberry Finn,*" in *Writing the American Classics,* ed. James Barbour and Tom Quirk (Chapel Hill: University of North Carolina Press, 1990), 83.

The grueling tour—104 performances in 16 states, the District of Columbia, and eastern Canada from early November 1884 to the end of February 1885—proved doubly rewarding. Not only did it provide a much-needed $16,000,[3] but a chance occurrence on the tour ultimately resulted in the writing of *A Connecticut Yankee.*

Clemens and Cable were taking advantage of a rare free Saturday for a sightseeing stroll in Rochester, New York, when a sudden rain shower forced them to duck into a nearby bookstore. There, in searching for something to read during the potentially dull Sunday to come—Cable insisted on strict observance of the Sabbath—Clemens came upon a green-cloth-bound Globe edition of Sir Thomas Malory's *Le Morte Darthur.* As Cable later remembered it, he encouraged his friend to buy the book, assuring him that he would find it fascinating.[4]

Cable was right. Though Clemens liked some of Malory's tales that he had read in Sidney Lanier's abridged and slightly bowdlerized edition of *The Boy's King Arthur* (1880), the original charmed him even more. Almost ebullient, he wrote to his daughter Susy, urging her to read this "quaintest and sweetest of all books," which he told her was "full of the absolute English of 400 years ago." Sir Ector's lament for his dead brother Launcelot Clemens found no less than "perfect," and he later would praise Malory's description of the death of King Arthur as "one of the most beautiful things ever written in English, and written when we had no vocabulary."[5]

An additional result of the Rochester bookstore incident, however, was an inclination to play with Malory's style. Soon Clemens, Cable, and their friends took to badgering each other in Malory's "quaint language." They dubbed Ozias Pond, brother of tour manager James B. Pond, "Sir Sagramore le Desirous," and when Ozias fell ill, "Sir Mark Twain" and "Sir George W.

3. *Mark Twain's Notebooks & Journals*, vol. 3, ed. Robert Pack Browning, Michael B. Frank, and Lin Salamo (Berkeley and Los Angeles: University of California Press, 1979), 63. Hereafter cited parenthetically as *N&J3*.

4. Arlin Turner, *Mark Twain and George W. Cable: The Record of a Literary Friendship* (East Lansing: Michigan State University Press, 1960), 135–36.

5. For a full account of Clemens's prior knowledge of Malory, see Alan Gribben, " 'The Master Hand of Old Malory': Mark Twain's Acquaintance with *Le Morte D'Arthur*," *English Language Notes* 16:1 (September 1978): 32–40; Olivia Susan Clemens, *Papa: An Intimate Biography of Mark Twain by Susy Clemens, His Daughter, Thirteen, with a Foreword and Copious Comments by Her Father*, ed. Charles Neider (Garden City: Doubleday, 1985), 168; Twain, *N&J3*, 159; Albert Bigelow Paine, *Mark Twain: A Biography*, 3 vols. (New York: Harper, 1912), 3:1320.

Cable" wired him: "Now wit you well, Sir Sagramore, thou good knight and gentle, that there be two that right wonderly do love thee, grieving passing sore and making great dole at thy heavy travail. And we will well that thou prosper at the hand of the leech, and come lightly forth of thy hurts, and be as thou were tofore."[6]

From that same mood of banter and burlesque came Mark Twain's first notebook "germ" for the book:

> Dream of being a knight errant in armor in the Middle Ages. Have the notions and habits of thought of the present day mixed with the necessities of that. No pockets in the armor. No way to manage certain requirements of nature. Can't scratch. Cold in the head—can't blow—can't get at handkerchief, can't use iron sleeve. Iron gets red hot in the sun—leaks in the rain, gets white with frost & freezes me solid in winter. Suffer from lice & fleas. Make disagreeable clatter when I enter church. Can't dress or undress myself. Always getting struck by lightning. Fall down and can't get up. See Morte DArthur. (N&J3, 78)

One must note here that Mark Twain's idea of taking a modern man to Arthurian England probably did not result entirely from the Rochester incident. In 1881 Charles Heber Clark, a humorist who wrote as "Max Adeler," published a collection containing a story called "Professor Baffin's Adventures" (issued the following year as "The Fortunate Island"). In that tale, Professor Baffin's dream encounter with Arthurian inhabitants of a floating island which had broken off from the mainland centuries before featured a number of situations similar to those experienced by Twain's hero. In November 1889, in fact, the publication in a Philadelphia paper of excerpts from the *Yankee* that were to appear in that month's *Century* magazine brought a telegram to the *New York World* charging Mark Twain with plagiarizing from "The Fortunate Island." Though he later took pains in an interview for the *World* (January 12, 1890) to dispel those charges by misdirecting readers' attention to "The Old Fogy," another of Adeler's stories involving a dream visit to the past, Clemens at the same time implied the possibility of "unconscious" borrowing. As David Ketterer and Horst Kruse

---

6. Clemens quoted the telegram in a letter to his wife, February 4, 1885, Mark Twain Papers (quoted in Smith, introduction to *CY*, 2).

have shown, however, the likelihood that the borrowing was *conscious* is very strong.[7] Nevertheless, *A Connecticut Yankee* soon went far beyond "The Fortunate Island" in numerous directions.

In a note written across the original "dream inspiration" passage, Clemens later said that he immediately began to make mental notes for the book. But the story did not get under way until almost a year later. When the tour ended in February 1885, Clemens busied himself overseeing the activities of the fledgling Webster Company, especially the publication of General Ulysses Grant's *Memoirs,* negotiations for which had just concluded. As the year wore on, he also became deeply involved with the promotion of James W. Paige's typesetter, a project which would continue to enchant him with promises of untold riches—and would drain his financial resources—for almost a decade to come. So concerned was he with these matters that except for an account of his brief Civil War experience, "Private History of a Campaign That Failed," and an unimportant article on child-rearing titled "What Ought He to Have Done?" he all but abandoned his writing for most of 1885.

Early in December, however, perhaps because the publication of the first volume of Grant's *Memoirs* had relieved some of the pressures, Twain took up the Yankee's story in earnest, listing further ideas for the novel. The first entry carried on the burlesque spirit of the "dream" idea, with the brash, self-assured Yankee announcing: "Wouldn't fight the knight with a lance, 'but I will just try him a whirl with a hay-fork—& I bet I'll show him that I warn't brought up on a Conneticut farm for nothing'" (*N&J3,* 216). But then, after Twain's further suggestion that the story be brought out "as a holiday book" titled "The Lost Land," a romantic strain emerges, which, along with the realism of the first entry, reflects the warring strains of realism and romance that would dominate the story and contribute to the author's eventual ambivalent attitude toward his protagonist.

Twain's notes indicate that the Yankee's tale was to be preserved on an "ancient yellow parchment (palimpsest)" with "remnants of monkish legends" showing through. The last chapter, however, would be on new paper with a watermark depicting the British coat of arms and the date

---

7. David Ketterer, "'Professor Baffin's Adventures' by Max Adeler: The Inspiration for *A Connecticut Yankee* . . . ," *Mark Twain Journal* 24:1 (Spring 1986): 24–34; Horst H. Kruse, "Mark Twain's *A Connecticut Yankee:* Reconsiderations and Revisions," *American Literature* 62:3 (September 1990): 464–83.

"1885" (the then present year). The Yankee, now back in modern England, would find all changed: "He mourns his lost land," which now has become "old, so old!—& it was so fresh & new, so virgin before." Hence, he "has lost all interest in life" and "is found dead next morning—suicide" (*N&J3*, 216).

Besides this forecast of something very like the eventual ending of the novel, Mark Twain also proposed to add a love interest, with the Yankee "grieving to see his sweetheart, so suddenly lost to him," and he considered several possibilities from Malory. Additional short notes proposed that the Yankee would start a printing office and that at some time the country was to be placed under the Church's Interdict (*N&J3*, 216–17).

Within a week after these entries he was well into further planning stages, if not the actual writing. "I am plotting out a new book, & am full of it," he told his nephew Webster on December 16. Business matters, however, continually threatened to tear him away, so much so that Susy and Olivia worried that his current deep involvement with Grant's *Memoirs* might make him forget his own literary work entirely.[8]

He was obviously working on the *Yankee*, however, for on February 13, the day after Susy's notation, he was begging Webster to spare him from business matters since he had gotten "into the swing" of work on the novel. And on the 22nd Susy reported the family's enjoyment the night before when "papa read to us the beginning of his new book . . . founded on a New Englanders [*sic*] visit to England in the time of King Arthur and his round table."[9] By the time business again called a halt late in February or early in March, Mark Twain had managed to finish the introductory "A Word of Explanation" and three more chapters; after that, business forced the time-traveler from Hartford to remain shut up in Arthur's castle for almost a year and a half.

Mark Twain did release his hero briefly on November 11 for an appearance at the Military Service Institution on Governor's Island in New York Harbor. There, for the large and colorful audience of military officers and their guests, he read the completed chapters and sketched the Yankee's subsequent career in what he billed as an "outline," with "extracts" from the journal of his hero—then called Sir Robert Smith.

8. Clemens to Webster, December 16, 1885, *Mark Twain, Business Man*, ed. Samuel L. Webster (Boston: Little, Brown, 1946), 343; Olivia Susan Clemens, *Papa*, 187.
9. *Mark Twain, Business Man*, 355; *Papa*, 191–92.

Detailed accounts in the New York papers—particularly in the *Herald* and the *Sun*—verify how much of the book Mark Twain had actually completed by that time. Though he said he would read one chapter, the extensive quotations—many almost exactly as they would appear in the final work—and the other summaries show that he read all or part of the introduction and the first three chapters. The *Sun's* reporter summarized the initial encounter of the narrator and the stranger at Warwick Castle, who introduced himself as the superintendent of the Colt Arms Factory, "a Yankee of the Yankees, a practical man, nearly barren of sentiment— or poetry," but a man who could make or invent "anything that anybody wanted"; the Yankee's transmigration; his capture; the journey to Camelot "amid scenes of human life" that afforded the author "many opportunities for quaint philosophic contrasts and dry humor"; and the meeting with the page whom the Yankee names Clarence, who would become his chief aide. The *Herald* provided additional details of the castle's furnishings, the feasting at the great oaken table "big as a circus ring"; the lies of boastful knights; and, finally, Merlin's putting the company to sleep by "telling an old story for the thousandth time," the tale that ends chapter 3.[10]

In the meeting with the "practical" Yankee, who first tells the narrator of his brush with a crowbar and awakening in ancient Britain, and then leaves him the parchment manuscript, Mark Twain made use of the "frame" structure originally learned from other nineteenth-century humorists. And the first three chapters embody many instances of the broad burlesque and implicit ridicule suggested by the initial "dream" idea and common to nineteenth-century humor in general.[11] And here Twain also revealed both sides of his own initial reaction to Malory, first in the narrator's early enjoyment of the "rich feast of prodigies and adventures" in "old Sir Thomas Malory's enchanting book," and then in the comic picture at the end of

10. For the full newspaper reports of the Governor's Island reading, which are the sources for this account, see *CY*, Appendix A. The *Sun's* reference to Sir Kay's "embroidering" the story of his capture of Smith may possibly suggest, as James Russell has claimed (16–17), that Mark Twain had also written chapter 4 (or perhaps part of it) by this time. But if he had, a change of ink and handwriting in the manuscript at the beginning of chapter 4 shows that he later rewrote the passage. Moreover, contrary to Russell's assertion, there is no break in the manuscript after chapter 4.

11. See David E. E. Sloane, *Mark Twain as a Literary Comedian* (Baton Rouge: University of Louisiana Press, 1979), 146–67, for the fullest and best discussion of these elements.

chapter 3, when Merlin's story, quoted directly from *Le Morte Darthur,* serves as a general anesthetic.

For the rest of the story as outlined in his Governor's Island appearance, the "extracts" from Sir Robert's journal reveal Mark Twain's current plans for his hero's subsequent adventures. As the newspaper accounts of the speech show, he briefly developed some of the difficulties with armor envisioned in the original "dream" plan—the inability to scratch, problems with weather (especially rain), and Robert's fears that his "boiler-iron strait jacket" made him "a perambulating lightning-rod." Included also was a hint about the Yankee's later fight with the knights—in Sir Bob's comment that a "hardware suit" is merely a hindrance and that without it he could "dodge around and tucker out any duffer in armor, lasso him, and yank him in."

Among his other exploits the Yankee was to be commissioned by King Arthur to take a castle, kill its ogre, and rescue the sixty princesses held captive there. The wily Sir Bob would finally decide not to bother with such a dangerous scheme, but in true tall-tale fashion would tell "a majestic lie about it like the rest of the Knights," whereupon his superiority "in the lofty realms of that art" would soon make him the king's favorite.

Deciding that the "education of the nineteenth century" was "plenty good enough capital to go into business in the sixth century with," this brash entrepreneur figured that before long he would be running the entire kingdom—"on a moderate royalty of forty per cent." At the same time, in a partial preview of the Yankee's final battle, Sir Robert contracted with Arthur "to kill off, at one of the great tournaments, fifteen kings and many acres of hostile armored knights" and from behind "a barbed wire fence charged with electricity mowed them down with Gatling guns that he had made for the occasion." Within three and a half years he would have "cleared out the fuss and flummery of romance" and put the kingdom on a "strictly business basis," with Launcelot running a kind of Louisiana lottery, the search for the Holy Grail given up for a hunt for the Northwest Passage, and the 140 illustrious knights of Arthur's court forming a stock board, with a seat at the Round Table selling for $30,000.

Press reports of the reading brought an immediate cry of consternation from Clemens's Cleveland friend, Mary Mason Fairbanks, who had been something of a watchdog over his literary propriety ever since they met on board the *Quaker City* during the trip to the Holy Land that resulted in his first widely successful book, *The Innocents Abroad* (1869). Fairbanks evidently expressed her fear that he planned to ridicule Malory's characters. Hastening to calm her fears that he was overstepping the bounds, Clemens wrote just five days after the reading to assure her that the book would not offend. "The story isn't a satire peculiarly," he explained, "but more especially a *contrast*" between Arthurian times and the present. He was only "after the *life* of that day that is all: to picture it; to try to get into it; to see how it feels & seems." He certainly had no plans to demean Galahad, Launcelot, and Arthur—"the great & beautiful *characters* drawn by the master hand of old Malory."[12]

The first chapters and the "outline" did indeed emphasize the mostly comic contrasts between the Yankee's bumptious and somewhat vulgar modernity and the romantic world of chivalry as conceived by Malory (and Scott in *Ivanhoe* and Tennyson in *Idylls of the King*). Much like Twain's Sir Wissenschaft in "Legend of the 'Spectacular Ruin'" (*A Tramp Abroad*, chapter 17), who slew a dragon with a fire extinguisher invented for the purpose, demanded a monopoly on the sale of spectacles for his reward, and grew rich on the proceeds, Sir Bob, as "operator," would turn his wits and inventive skill chiefly to his own profit. The few signs of medieval cruelty that are included seem to be there primarily for local color. The Yankee's battered fellow prisoners are not downtrodden peasants, but knights wounded in chivalric combat. And the town itself, "with its naked brats, and joyous dogs, and shabby huts," and the hog wallowing in the street, resembles the Bricksville of *Huckleberry Finn*, whose wretched inhabitants received little of the author's pity. In these chapters particularly, Launcelot and Arthur are treated with considerable respect.

The novel did not have very high priority at this time, for Mark Twain also told Mrs. Fairbanks that he intended to write three chapters every summer for the next thirty years as "holiday amusement." But when he took it up again at Quarry Farm the next summer, he wrote more than sixteen chapters (not including chapter 10, "Beginnings of Civilization," which he would insert later). Most of these would develop elements of the earlier notes and the Governor's Island outline, like the Yankee's manipulation of the eclipse to gain his freedom, and his rise to Bossdom (with his "royalties" now reduced

12. *Mark Twain to Mrs. Fairbanks,* ed. Dixon Wecter (San Marino: Huntington Library, 1949), 257–58.

from 40 percent to 1 percent). The introduction of the Demoiselle Alisande la Carteloise—Sandy—as a non-stereotypical "maiden-in-distress" provided the vehicle for expanding the quest for the captive princesses (now only forty-five of them, rather than sixty) and the Yankee's difficulties with armor, and for adapting additional episodes from Malory into Sandy's garrulous tales. At first merely an annoyance, Sandy would later prove to be also the "lost love" mentioned in the early note. Other episodes not suggested in the Governor's Island reading would bring the wanderers through the encounter with the group of "freemen" and the horrors of Morgan le Fay's castle to the borders of the Valley of Holiness.

Sometime between the Governor's Island reading and resumption of work on the story, Mark Twain's concept of the Yankee's role and of his character changed significantly. The burlesque would continue throughout the novel—often effectively, but sometimes to the detriment of mood and atmosphere. But instead of merely profit for himself and for the king's treasury, the Yankee's goal would be no less than total reform of political and social evils in Arthur's kingdom. Instead of dodging the quest for the captive princesses and lying about it, he would carry it through to reveal that the princesses (and by implication all royalty and nobility) were actually hogs. And instead of using his Gatling gun and electrified fence to defeat Arthur's enemies, he would turn them against the whole chivalry of England and the values for which they stood. The Yankee himself would later be called Hank Morgan, and though maintaining many elements of his original characterization—especially his inventiveness—would become more and more the spokesman for Clemens's current opinions, revealing a knowledge of history, economics, and politics far beyond what the entirely "practical" arms factory superintendent would be likely to possess. And in episode after episode, directly or indirectly, comically or seriously, he would castigate the attitudes fostered by the feudal ideal.

Admittedly, Mark Twain never entirely succeeded in reconciling the Yankee's initial role as bumptious "operator" with that of the relatively intellectual would-be political savior. He himself recognized at least part of that "split," for he later declared in a letter to his daughter Clara that an inept dramatization of the story by Howard Taylor had bored and enraged him because Taylor had captured only the "rude animal side," the "circus side" of the Yankee's character, leaving the "good heart & the high intent" of this "natural gentleman" unrevealed.[13] Revisions in the manuscript also show that he was attempting to indicate a *gradual* development from operator to humanitarian.

One should perhaps note here that space does not permit discussion of *all* the elements that went into the making of this novel. And though the discussion will concentrate on the social and political attitudes that contributed to the serious themes, it should be remembered that the book was conceived as, and was meant to be, a humorous adventure story, with the Yankee as a hero who faces almost overwhelming odds and (almost) succeeds in overcoming them.

Why the change of purpose? The reasons are complicated. There was the purely practical consideration of what might appeal to the preferences of the American public. Selling books was always a major concern for Clemens. He was also afraid that the extensive quotations in the press might have prejudiced his copyright. But there obviously were other considerations. His involvement in the Cleveland campaign for president in 1884 had brought an admiration for Cleveland's policies, among them the advocacy of free trade, which would find its way into the Yankee's comment on the disadvantages of "protection," that is, protective tariffs, in chapter 33. More important, Clemens had developed a new sympathy for egalitarian democracy far from his "elitist" stance of the 1870s, when he thought that unrestricted suffrage, which put too much power in the hands of the ignorant and incompetent, was largely responsible for governmental corruption. In the mid-1880s he also developed a new enthusiasm for the union movement represented by the Knights of Labor. But whatever these or other elements contributed, a major impetus for the serious concerns that came to underlie the humor of the novel was a growing antagonism toward certain aspects of the England he had loved so well in the 1870s.[14]

13. Clemens to Clara, July 20, 1890, *Love Letters of Mark Twain*, ed. Dixon Wecter (New York: Harper, 1949), 257.

14. For a fuller treatment of his 1870s attitudes, see Baetzhold, "Mark Twain: England's Advocate," *American Literature* 28 (November 1956): 328–46, and *Mark Twain and John Bull*, chapter 2. For his 1880s interest in unions, see Paul J. Carter's "Mark Twain and the American Labor Movement," *New England Quarterly* 30 (September 1957): 382–88.

His antipathy was by no means directed at all things British, but only toward those elements which seemed obstacles to progress and to the preservation of human dignity. In becoming a "Mugwump" in his support of Cleveland, he actually had moved fairly close to the position of the British Liberal Party, the Mugwumps being "well-defined politically as the American branch of middle-class Liberalism."[15] Many of the "improvements" that the Yankee was to propose were, in fact, those currently advocated by the British Liberal Party, especially by its Radical wing. Hence it was primarily a new sense that ancient evils fostered by monarchy and the Established Church were still evident that led to a number of the more serious elements not envisioned in the Governor's Island "outline."

During this period he seems to have kept in fairly close touch with developments in Britain. Reacting in November 1886 to news of Welsh protests against the tithes imposed by the Church of England, he launched a notebook blast at this "frightful tax" and described the reaction of a Welsh farmer's wife with eleven children, who, faced with confiscation of a tenth of her livestock, asked the parson–tithe collector: "You take the tenth pig; will you have the tenth child?" (N&J3, 265–66). This incident he would later adapt for his novel. Very likely he also read about the demonstrations of Scottish crofters against their landlords' setting aside grazing lands as private deer-parks and the harsh penalties against tenant farmers for killing rabbits or other "vermin" even on their own plots of ground, for echoes appear in the novel.

Clemens's growing animosity was doubtless spurred when Matthew Arnold's review of Grant's *Memoirs* appeared in the January and February issues of *Murray's* magazine. Surprisingly, he had reacted only briefly in 1882 to Arnold's "A Word about America," in which the critic, referring to a ludicrous minor character in *David Copperfield*, had specifically cited Mark Twain's "Quinionian" humor to illustrate the sad condition of American literature. But the present criticism of Grant, a man whom Clemens all but idolized, was another question.

Though Arnold's review was generally favorable, what must have rankled were the critic's references to the American propensity for boasting, now

---

15. Louis J. Budd, *Mark Twain, Social Philosopher* (Bloomington: Indiana University Press, 1962), 110.

implicitly aimed at Grant, as well as the several criticisms of Grant's style. That April Clemens took advantage of a speech at the Army and Navy Club of Connecticut to defend his hero. Citing H. H. Breen's *Modern English Literature: Its Blemishes and Defects* in order to "prove" that Grant's grammatical flaws were no more numerous nor serious than those of many universally acknowledged literary masters, he took Arnold to task for certain egregious stylistic faults in the review itself. In concluding, he flung Arnold's charges of American chauvinism back in his face, with an eloquent tribute to the grandeur of Grant's *Memoirs* and their soldier-author, "who, all untaught of the silken phrase-makers, linked words together with an art surpassing the art of the schools."[16]

Of all the elements that contributed to the new direction, however, none was more important than a book—*The People's History of the English Aristocracy*—sent to him in May 1887 by its author, George Standring, an English printer and publisher whom Clemens had known and corresponded with for more than a year. A fervid advocate of abolishing the British monarchy and the privileges of aristocracy, Standring charged particularly that the vast wealth of the English nobles gave them control not only of the House of Lords, but of the military, the professions, business, and even "that one bulwark which the nation is supposed to possess against tyranny—the House of Commons." Feudal principles of primogeniture and entail helped maintain this control, but almost more important was the British devotion to what Standring called the "fetish" of nobility, an irrational reverence that kept the commoner in a state of slavery more hopeless than if his chains were real ones.[17]

What Clemens no doubt found most striking were the case histories, up to the present day, of most of England's noble families, many of whose titles had resulted from the liaisons of kings and courtesans, and the amazing catalogue of "crimes," both serious and petty, that Standring marshaled to show how totally undeserved was the respect, let alone the loyalty and devotion, traditionally lavished upon the nobility. Almost invariably, he climaxed his accounts with sarcastic gibes, like that which followed his recital

16. *Mark Twain Speaking*, ed. Paul Fatout (Iowa City: University of Iowa Press, 1976), 227.

17. George Standring, *The People's History of the English Aristocracy*, 2d ed. (London, 1891), Introduction (unnumbered) and 1, 2, 6, 161–65.

of the misdeeds of Thomas Howard, Third Duke of Norfolk: "Yet this is the stock to which our nobility point with pride when they prate over their long descent."[18]

Clemens probably had already encountered a good bit of Standring's "evidence" in his own extensive reading in history, but nowhere had he found in such detail the intimate stories of so many of England's noble houses. He was so enthusiastic about *The People's History,* in fact, that shortly after its arrival he proposed to publish it, along with three of his very favorite volumes—St. Simon's *Memoires,* Taine's *Ancient Regime,* and Carlyle's *French Revolution*—in a high-priced, elaborately illustrated edition to be called "Royalty and Nobility Exposed" (*N&J3,* 295). Though this scheme failed to materialize, here was firsthand evidence from a native Englishman that British slavery to a totally corrupt ideal was far from dead.

Once he resumed work on his manuscript at Quarry Farm that July, the sharper tone—minor at the outset, perhaps, but still significant—soon emerged. In the earlier chapters, the Yankee had found the speech of the knights and ladies "gracious and courtly" and had seen "something attractive and lovable" in the ignorant and simple knights, whose countenances reflected "a fine manliness" and even "a certain loftiness and sweetness." But here his observations become much more critical, for the aristocrats now conversed in "language that would make a Comanche blush." And the Yankee adds that books like *Tom Jones, Roderick Random,* and others of that kind had convinced him that such talk and "the morals and conduct which such talk implies" were common among English ladies and gentlemen "clear into our own nineteenth century" (*CY,* 66, 69, 78).

Though Twain had expressed objections to the coarseness of *Tom Jones* and *Roderick Random* as early as 1879, it seems evident that the recent reading of *The People's History* played its part here, for, probably close to the time he wrote this passage, he included "Standring's book" in a list of some fourteen sources for an appendix that would document the assertion that laxity in language and morals had lingered far beyond medieval times.[19] In reading Standring he could hardly have missed the aristocratic elegance and delicacy of the Duchess of Marlborough, whose "volley of oaths and streams of foul

18. Standring, *People's History,* 15.
19. See *CY,* 515.

language would have done credit to a Billingsgate fish fag," and a law-clerk's subsequent comment that though he did not know her, he "was sure she was a lady of quality, *as she swore so dreadfully*." It is tempting also to imagine Mark Twain remembering other instances from *The People's History* when the Yankee comments that the "squaws" of these Arthurian "Comanches" were always ready "to desert to the buck with the biggest string of scalps at his belt." He could, of course, also have been recalling episodes from Malory in which damsels became the property of victorious knights, but most of those ladies were simply passive spoils of combat. Standring, besides observing that the "flood of filth and garbage" flowing from English divorce courts was typical of "the daily life of the Modern English Aristocracy," later described how Lady Shrewsbury disguised herself as a page in order to attend the duel between her husband and George Villiers, the second Duke of Buckingham, and how "*when her husband lay cold and dead on the ground she rode off with his murderer.*"[20]

In the following episodes Mark Twain remained pretty much detached from his protagonist up through the destruction of Merlin's ancient stone tower in chapter 7. But in chapter 8, the mask slips considerably when the Yankee, by then firmly established as King Arthur's second-in-command and affectionately named "The Boss," launches into his first direct diatribe against English reverence for rank and pedigree. With much the same scorn that Standring so often heaped upon the British bondage to the "fetish of nobility," Twain established major themes that would continue throughout the book—the power of "training," and the "slavery" it engendered. These "inherited ideas," the Yankee says, made ostensibly free Englishmen into slaves, proud to grovel before king, Church, and noble. Calling "*any* kind" of royalty or aristocracy an "insult," Mark Twain even more specifically related the criticism to the present with the Yankee's ironic observation that in Arthur's England, "just as in the remote England of my birth-time, the sheep-witted earl who could claim long descent from a king's leman . . . was a better man than I was" (*CY*, 113).

In further developing the Boss's tirade, Mark Twain stressed the "awful power" of the Church as it perpetuated those "inherited indignities," and

---

20. Standring, *People's History*, 61, Introduction, and 42; his emphasis. The possibility of a play on the first syllable of *Buck*ingham's name in the matter of the "squaws'" readiness to desert is also intriguing.

also laid a basis for the Yankee's eventual downfall: the Yankee says that though he is now equal in power to the king, the Church is "stronger than both of us put together" (*CY*, 109–13).

For his description of the Church's role, Twain turned to a longtime favorite, W. E. H. Lecky's *History of European Morals from Augustus to Charlemagne*, and especially to Lecky's discussion of how the Church, by creating the theory of "divine right," had maintained its influence when secular monarchs seemed to be trying to break away. And here the Yankee adds another contemporary jab by declaring that the "poison" fostered by the Church still remained strong in the nineteenth century, when even "the best of English commoners" was not only contented but proud "to see his inferiors impudently continuing to hold a number of positions, such as lordships and the throne, to which the grotesque laws of his country did not allow him to aspire" (*CY*, 113).

Obviously it was not only the Roman Catholic Church that was under fire. The Yankee's conviction that "any Established Church is an established crime, an established slave-pen" pointed a direct finger at the Anglican Church. And again Twain injected a reference to his own day when he had the Yankee ironically observe that there were still Englishmen "who imagined that they had been born in a free country, a 'free' country with the Corporation Act and the Test still in force in it—timbers propped against men's liberties and dishonored consciences to shore up an Established Anachronism with" (*CY*, 185–86). Then, too, the "slave-pen" image specifically linked the Church with physical as well as mental slavery, a connection that the author would develop further.[21]

The charge that the presence of an Established Church was purely political in its nature and the Yankee's plan to create numerous sects which could

---

21. The passages involving the Church and its evils were doubtless also enhanced by Lecky's *History of the Rise and Influence of Rationalism in Europe* (1865), which Clemens had read and annotated at Quarry Farm in 1885 and probably again the following summer. For instance, on p. 127, inspired by Lecky's description of the Scottish Church, he noted in the margin: "There are people, even in this day, who long for a 'united church.' There never was a united church which did not usurp the privileges of <hell> tyranny." Quoted by Mary Boewe, who discovered this volume in the present Quarry Farm Library, in "Twain on Lecky: Some Marginalia at Quarry Farm," *Mark Twain Society Bulletin* 8:1 (January 1985): 4 (angle brackets indicate Mark Twain's deletion).

compete with each other and so undermine the power of a united Church reflected current agitations for Disestablishment in England and Wales. That connection Mark Twain would later underline in his adaptation of the Welsh widow's experience with the tithe-gatherer who demanded the tenth pig (chapter 20). At that point the Yankee notes the "curious" fact that the same thing had happened in his own day "under this same old Established Church, which was supposed by many to have changed its nature when it changed its disguise" (*CY*, 231).

Work went fairly well that July of 1887. Up to chapter 13 Mark Twain again worked chiefly in the spirit of the original burlesque contrast. In the account of the tournament in chapter 9, for instance, he introduced a humorous gibe at courtly morality when the fair ladies, instead of being appalled at the hacking and maiming, crowded in for a closer view, except "sometimes one would dive into her handkerchief, and look ostensibly broken-hearted," a sure sign that "there was a scandal there somewhere and she was afraid the public hadn't found it out." In that chapter, too, Twain prepared for the Yankee's eventual fight with the knights (chapter 39) by having Sir Sagramour[22] challenge him to combat, the encounter to take place three or four years hence, when Sagramour would return from a quest for the Holy Grail.

As the Yankee's own quest proceeded, the encounter in chapter 13 with the band of ragged "freemen" laboring on their lord's road again introduced a more serious note. In terms of plot, here is the awakening of the Yankee's desire to reform Arthur's kingdom, for even in the chapter 8 diatribe, the Boss's anger (as opposed to that of Mark Twain) was directed almost as much at the Arthurians' failure to appreciate his personal merit and his position as the king's second-in-command as at the system itself.

Twain drew upon Carlyle's *French Revolution* and other works on that period and its backgrounds—principally Taine's *Ancient Regime*—to describe the plight of commoners in Arthur's realm. After detailing a number of horrors to which these "freemen" were subjected, including the enforced road work, he explicitly acknowledged his sources with the Yankee's comment: "Why, it was like reading about France and the French, before the ever

---

22. For Sir Sagramour, and in the case of Guenever later, I use the spelling adopted by the Iowa-California Edition.

memorable and blessed Revolution, which swept a thousand years of such villainy away in one swift tidal wave of blood" (*CY*, 157). In addition, he again implicitly underlined the close connection of the Church with the secular oppression by noting that the lord on whose road these peasants were working was a bishop.

By early August Mark Twain had brought his travelers as far as Morgan le Fay's castle, with its additional evidences of aristocratic and ecclesiastical oppression—especially the pitiful prisoners whom the Yankee releases from the queen's dungeons: "Skeletons, scarecrows, goblins, pathetic frights every one: legitimatest possible children of Monarchy by the Grace of God and the Established Church" (*CY*, 216). Something of his mood in dealing with these materials is suggested by his complaint to Webster on August 3 that a cloud of "funereal seriousness" had settled over the novel. But by August 15, having reread the 350 pages completed by that time, which took the story through the chapter 20 meeting of Sandy and the Yankee with Sir Madok de la Montaine, purveyor of Peterson's Prophylactic Tooth-Brushes, he could tell Webster and his assistant Fred J. Hall that he found he was producing an "uncommonly bully book" and hoped to finish by the end of the year.[23]

A short time later, in a letter to Howells, Twain revealed some of the emotions that underlay the writing during these months. Speaking of Carlyle's *French Revolution,* which he had first encountered in 1871, he said he was amazed at how radically his attitudes had changed. He had initially sided, like Carlyle, with the Girondins, the moderates who advocated establishment of a constitutional monarchy. But, he said, "Every time I have read it since, I have read it differently—being influenced & changed, little by little, by life & environment (& Taine, & St. Simon): & now I lay the book down once more, & recognize that I am a Sansculotte!—and not a pale, characterless Sansculotte, but a Marat."[24] That change was indeed drastic. In *A Tramp Abroad* (1880), for instance, he had strongly deplored the excesses of the French Revolution. Now his sympathies lay with the most radical of the revolutionaries.

Following the meeting with Sir Madok, Twain further demonstrated his current state of mind regarding the serious elements of his story when he had the Boss and Sandy encounter one of the elderly prisoners freed from

23. *Mark Twain's Letters to His Publishers,* ed. Hamlin Hill (Berkeley and Los Angeles: University of California Press, 1967), 222, 224.

24. *Mark Twain–Howells Letters,* ed. Henry Nash Smith and William M. Gibson, with assist. of Frederick Anderson (Cambridge: Harvard University Press, 1960), 2:595.

Morgan le Fay's dungeons and returned to his home. Here the fact that the sad old man's sufferings had brought no outburst of rage from his friends and loved ones made the Yankee realize the depth of slavery into which these citizens had sunk, their entire being "reduced to a monotonous dead level of patience, resignation, dumb, uncomplaining acceptance of whatever might befal them in this life." And then, in the manuscript, with smaller and heavier writing, as if he were bearing down hard on the pen, Twain described the Yankee's concern about his prospects of accomplishing a peaceful revolution. The townspeople's reaction discouraged him, the Yankee said, because it raised the "ungetaroundable fact that, all gentle cant and philosophising to the contrary notwithstanding, no people in this world ever did achieve their freedom by goody-goody talk and moral suasion: it being immutable law that all revolutions that will succeed must begin in blood, whatever may answer afterward. . . . What this folk needed, then, was a Reign of Terror and a guillotine." But then Twain had the Yankee add, for the sake of plot: "and I was the wrong man for them" (*CY*, 228–29).

As it turned out, Mark Twain's earlier hopes for finishing by the end of the year proved far too optimistic. After bringing his traveling pair to "The Ogre's Castle" (chapter 20) and seeing through their rescue of the "enchanted" hog-princesses in chapter 21, the author's "tank" began to run dry. At this point he tried to adapt a satire of contemporary business practices written earlier that year. But the material did not fit the story well, and the following summer he would delete it.[25]

Once the family was back in Hartford in mid-September, the myriad business and social activities totally eliminated any hope of finishing that may have lingered. "This kind of rush is why parties write no books," Clemens grumbled to Mrs. Fairbanks late in November.[26] And the Yankee again had to wait until the family's next visit to Quarry Farm.

The new directions taken in 1887 actually made *A Connecticut Yankee* a more logical next step after *A Tramp Abroad* (1880), *The Prince and the Pauper* (1882), *Life on the Mississippi* (1883), and *Huckleberry Finn* (1884) than the original burlesque would have been. In *A Tramp Abroad*, besides blasting the revolutionary excesses, Mark Twain had blamed the French

25. See *CY*, 753–61, for the deleted text. The satire, as originally directed at Olivia's cousin Andrew Langdon, was published after Clemens's death as "Letter from the Recording Angel." The specific reasons for Clemens's antipathy to Langdon are unknown.

26. November 25, 1887, *Mark Twain to Mrs. Fairbanks*, 262.

problems primarily on the ineptness of Louis XVI and the meddling of Marie Antoinette. In *The Prince and the Pauper* he was still governed by his convictions of the 1870s that monarchy itself was not necessarily evil but that a cure for political and social ills could be achieved through the paternalistic rule of those best qualified. The "Sansculottism" of *A Connecticut Yankee,* then, embodied a significant step in the author's political outlook.

The novel also revealed a new development in Clemens's own basic philosophy. Here again Lecky's *History of European Morals* was a primary stimulus. From the time he had first dipped into the book in 1874, he had been intrigued by Lecky's discussion of the two major strains of moral philosophy that had influenced thought through the ages: the argument of those (sometimes called "intuitionists") who held that individuals possess an innate moral perception which governs moral choices; and the view of those ultimately called "utilitarians" who denied that man possesses any such innate perception of virtue, holding instead that standards of right and wrong, and all choices, moral or otherwise, are determined solely by the degree of pleasure or pain that might result, that is, by outside forces rather than by any intuitive perception of good and evil. Over the years Clemens had become increasingly attracted to the utilitarians' deterministic philosophy, which Lecky had sought to refute.

By the time he wrote *Huckleberry Finn,* he had come close to accepting the utilitarian view. But not quite, for the final victory of Huck's "sound heart" over his society-trained conscience when he decides not to write Miss Watson of Jim's whereabouts dramatizes the fact that Clemens had not entirely lost faith in innate moral perceptions.

In *A Connecticut Yankee* the importance of "training" by outside forces— especially the kind of training which ultimately defeats the Yankee—looms even more important than in *Huckleberry Finn.* And in dramatizing Hank Morgan's reactions to an incident at Morgan le Fay's castle in chapter 18, Mark Twain moved a step closer to total acceptance of the utilitarian position. When the queen breezily rationalizes her callous stabbing of a page who had accidentally brushed against her, the Yankee is at first astonished. But then— and obviously speaking in his creator's voice—he reasons that he should not have been surprised, considering her background and the life she had been bred to. "Training—training is everything," he says; "training is all there is *to* a person." As for ideas, "We have no thoughts of our own, no opinions of our own: they are transmitted to us, trained into us."

So far he agrees completely with the utilitarian view, but then Hank hedges slightly. He says, "All that is original in us . . . can be covered up and hidden by the point of a cambric needle," and he goes on to vow that he will devote all his efforts to saving that "one microscopic atom in me that is truly *me*" (208). Thus, though he still clings to some small sense of innate originality, the reduction of Huck Finn's "sound heart" to the "one microscopic atom in me" shows Twain a step closer to the total determinism that he would adopt in his later "gospel," *What Is Man?* (1906).

When Mark Twain returned to his manuscript in the summer of 1888, he did so under a full head of steam, his anti-British emotions freshly fueled that spring by yet another of Matthew Arnold's essays—"Civilisation in the United States," which had appeared in the *London Nineteenth Century* for April (and was reprinted in the *New York Evening Post* on April 9). When an invitation came from Lorettus Metcalf, editor of *Forum* magazine, to answer Arnold's charges, he eagerly accepted, and signaled the onset of his attack with a terse notebook entry: "Matthew Arnold's civilization is *superficial polish*" (*N&J3,* 383).

The *Forum* article never appeared, however. On April 13 Clemens wrote Metcalf that his wife's sudden illness would probably prevent him from completing the piece in time for the next issue (*N&J3,* 383 n. 280), and the publisher may well have decided that the delay would seriously decrease the timeliness of the piece. Or perhaps he decided that the sudden death of Arnold on April 15 made a subsequent attack seem inappropriate. Even so, Clemens would continue to pile up ammunition for a barrage that ultimately filled many notebook pages and drafts of a half-dozen essays, all blasting Arnold's ideas.

One of his special targets was the critic's contention that the United States sadly lacked the quintessential quality of any truly civilized society, "a spirit of reverence," and that the American press and the American "funny-man" were responsible for perpetrating much of that irreverence. Somewhat erroneously, and perhaps intentionally, interpreting Arnold's "spirit of reverence" as total acceptance of monarchy, aristocracy, and the British caste system, he voluminously attacked the fallaciousness of that position.

His only public expression at the time came in late June, when he permitted the *Hartford Courant* to print his letter accepting an honorary master of arts degree from Yale. That award, he wrote, represented a tribute to all humorists, and had been rendered "all the more forcible and timely" by "the late Matthew Arnold's sharp rebuke to the guild of American 'funny men' in his latest literary delicacy." All but stating the theme that had come to dominate *A Connecticut Yankee,* he declared that the honor would also remind the world of the humorist's real purpose—"the deriding of shams, the exposure of pretentious falsities, the laughing of stupid superstitions out of existence"—and that in pursuing that aim, the humorist was inevitably "the natural enemy of royalties, nobilities, privileges, and all kindred swindles, and the natural friend of human rights and human liberties."[27]

Obviously this was not a new anger, but Arnold's essay surely strengthened Mark Twain's resolve to try to laugh away those "stupid superstitions" through the Yankee's adventures. And sometime in July he took up a new batch of manuscript paper and began his tale again, at the point (in what ultimately became chapter 21) where Sandy assembles the hog-princesses and Hank Morgan comments, in almost the exact words of some of the notebook attacks on Arnold, that her solicitous attentions to the hogs manifest "in every way the deep reverence which the natives of her island, ancient and modern, have always felt for rank, let its outward casket and the mental and moral contents be what they may" (*CY,* 237).

Mark Twain's continued concern for developments in Britain was evident again the same month when he commented on a newspaper dispatch to the *New York Tribune* concerning a Liberal measure hotly contested in both Parliament and press for several years. After copying into his notebook a sentence from the article declaring that the Liberals welcomed "the passage of the Local Government bill through committee as almost a revolution which transfers the control of county affairs from the privileged few to the people," he almost cheered: "There—the handwriting on the wall! There's a day coming!" (*N&J3,* 409).

In the novel, once Hank and Sandy had dispensed with the "princesses," Mark Twain again dramatized the pervasive presence of religious and secular superstition and slavery when he had his pair encounter first a band of religious pilgrims bound for the Valley of Holiness, there "to be blest of the godly hermits and drink of the miraculous waters and be cleansed from sin" (*CY,* 241), and almost immediately thereafter a band of literal slaves, limping along in chains, encouraged by the overseer's lash. During one

27. *Hartford Courant,* June 22, 1888, 5, col. 1.

especially severe whipping of a young mother, the reactions of the basically kindhearted and sincerely religious pilgrims provided vivid evidence for the Yankee of what slavery and the institutions which fostered it could do in "ossifying what one may call the superior lobe of human feeling." All of these basically good and kindhearted pilgrims watch the cruel punishment and comment "—on the expert way in which the whip was handled" (*CY*, 246, 245).

For his portrait of the pilgrims and the slaves, Mark Twain turned to two other important sources, one of them immediately contemporary. Most of the details of the slave-band, both here and later, he drew from Charles Ball's *Slavery in the United States*, a slave narrative first published in 1837. But his description of the chains worn by the Arthurian slaves shows that he was also remembering portraits of gangs of prisoners in the graphic illustrations of George Kennan's articles on Russia and the Siberian exile system, which were then running in *Century* magazine. Moreover, Kennan also provided evidence of the still-powerful influence of the Church and of "medieval" attitudes. In the July 1888 *Century*, for instance, he featured a "strange and medieval" procession of priests and peasants bearing a famous icon from village to village so that the inhabitants could have an opportunity to pray to "the miracle-working image." And the destination and mission of Twain's Chaucerian group seem to reflect those of the Russian pilgrims in the first of Kennan's articles (June 1887), who were bound for "the Canterbury of Russia," the Troitskaya monastery, and were willing to suffer any hardship in order to "drink out of the holy well of St. Sergius."[28]

In the Valley episodes, after further drawing on Lecky's *History of European Morals* for details concerning the failure of the Holy Fountain and the portraits of the disgusting hermits, Mark Twain presented two more instances of the Yankee's defeat of the forces of superstition—his besting of Merlin's necromancy with the spectacular restoration of the fountain (after simply plugging a leak) and his discrediting the alleged clairvoyance of the "Rival Magician" with his own foreknowledge based on a telephone connection with Camelot.

28. *Century*, 14:355, 12:253–54. Kennan's eyewitness accounts of Russian atrocities and religious fervor appeared in June and November 1887, and then monthly, with few exceptions, through November 1889, and then occasionally through 1891. For additional documentation see Baetzhold, "The Course of Composition," 207–10.

It should perhaps be noted here that although Merlin is presented primarily as another representative of the superstition that dominated the Arthurians' minds and is not closely identified with either the monarchy or the Church, Mark Twain was surely relying on his readers' familiarity with Merlin's role as Arthur's counselor, especially in Tennyson's *Idylls of the King.* Sir Edward Strachey, in his introduction to the Globe edition of Malory, had also introduced a religious note in describing Merlin as "half-Christian, half-magician, but always with dog-like devotion to the house of Uther Pendragon."[29] And the fact that the monks look first to the magician as the one who will restore their fountain suggests a strong bond between him and the Church.

Though notebook entries during August show that Mark Twain planned episodes which would ultimately take him to the Church's invoking of the Interdict and the final downfall of the Yankee's new civilization, his story had probably not progressed beyond chapter 24. Sometime shortly thereafter, doubtless realizing that he had not adequately prepared for the telephone's presence in the Valley, nor for the subsequent appearance of the West Pointer at "The Competitive Examination" (chapter 25) and of "The First Newspaper" (chapter 26), he provided additional background and inserted the new material as chapter 10, "Beginnings of Civilization." There he established a four-year period between the tournament of chapter 9 and the beginning of the quest with Sandy. During that time—all in secret for fear of the Church's power—the Yankee created schools, a West Point and a naval academy, industries, a telephone and telegraph system, a weekly newspaper with Clarence as editor, and "a complete variety of Protestant congregations" (*CY,* 127) which would keep the power away from any one sect and eventually undermine that of the Established Church.

. Work on the book was going well enough that just a week before the return to Hartford in mid-September he wrote his English publisher, Andrew Chatto, that though he had not progressed as far as he had wished, if he found he had finished two-thirds of his story by the time they left Elmira, he would try to persuade himself "to do that other third before spring."[30] And once back in Hartford he kept at the task, even amid the noise of

---

29. *Morte Darthur,* Globe edition, ed. Edward Strachey (London: Macmillan, 1866–1870), xiii.
30. Clemens to Chatto, September 17, 1888, quoted in *N&J3,* 394.

carpenters' hammers at his minister friend Joseph Twichell's house, where he fled for several days in early October to escape distractions at home. At the same time a letter to his brother-in-law Theodore Crane announced that he wanted to finish his book on the same day as the Paige typesetting machine was completed, and named October 22 as the factory's best calculation. But he added a caveat, noting, "experience teaches me that their calculations will miss fire, as usual."[31] His fears proved all too correct, and though he probably had not finished two-thirds of the book before leaving Elmira, his earlier prediction, to Chatto, ultimately was the more accurate.

His mention of the typesetter here—the invention which had enchanted him since 1881—points to another element that periodically had interfered with work on the book. As suggested earlier, Clemens was often beset with business worries, primarily the financial problems of the publishing company. Though he blamed its current difficulties on mismanagement by Charles Webster, he himself had been draining its resources in order to support the tremendous costs—some $3,000 per month during the latter part of 1888—of perfecting a demonstration model of the typesetter now under construction in the Hartford plant of Pratt and Whitney. Hence, though the machine promised great rewards, it was also a source of great worry.

James M. Cox has argued that Mark Twain felt an almost mystical connection between the typesetter and himself, that his letter to Crane was saying, in effect, that he saw himself as a machine-driven writer, and that his novel, too, had reached some strange sort of identification with the machine. There also was an element of doubt, at least at the time, about the machine's eventual completion and, by implication, that of the book. But Cox further notes that Twain's ability finally to finish his novel and thus "break the vicious identification between it and the machine signified a victory for the writer." What effect these anxieties and frustrations had on the later chapters of *A Connecticut Yankee*, however, is probably impossible to determine. As Henry Nash Smith has said in discussing the matter of the typesetter, one should not place too much weight on the writer's personal problems, for Mark Twain almost always had trouble finishing his books.[32]

31. Clemens to Crane, October 5, 1888, quoted in *CY*, 11.
32. James M. Cox, "*A Connecticut Yankee in King Arthur's Court:* The Machinery of Self-Preservation," *Yale Review* 50 (Autumn 1960): 89–102, reprinted in *A Connecticut Yankee in*

Whatever the doubts and difficulties, among the portions of the book completed at Twichell's house, "The Competitive Examination" (chapter 25) showed an especially skillful blending of current concerns and older sources. During these years, Standring and others, besides deploring reverence for hereditary rank, were attacking abuses in the military system and aristocratic opposition to technical education. Sometime in August 1887, Clemens had copied a set of statistics from Standring's *People's History* concerning the vast oversupply of high-ranking officers in the army and navy, and he later echoed Standring when he commented, "Rank in the army is still restricted to the nobility—by a thing that is stronger than law—the power of ancient habit and superstition. Let a commoner become an officer—he will be snubbed by all his brethren, ostracized, driven out" (*N&J3*, 306, 399).

This opinion is amply illustrated as the Yankee's West Pointer, eminently qualified in military matters and in general knowledge as well, vies with two young nobles for a lieutenancy in the newly established army. The alliance of Church and State in matters of aristocratic prerogative appears once more, both in the Yankee's comment that of course the examiners were all priests and, more vividly, in his questioning the requirement (borrowed from Carlyle's *French Revolution* and Taine's *Ancient Regime*) that the candidates must prove their descent from at least four generations of nobility. Such a question, the examiner haughtily exclaims, "doth go far to impugn the wisdom of our Holy Mother Church itself," since the same rule applies to the canonizing of a saint.[33]

That condition, of course, immediately eliminates the Yankee's candidate, whose father was a weaver. And though the others both have the requisite four generations of noble background, the board's final choice is not difficult. Sir Pertipole's great-grandfather had been elevated to the rank of first Baron

---

*King Arthur's Court*, Norton Critical Edition, ed. Alison Ensor (New York: Norton, 1982), 390–401 (quotation on 398); Henry Nash Smith, *Mark Twain's Fable of Progress: Political and Economic Ideas in "A Connecticut Yankee"* (New Brunswick: Rutgers University Press, 1964), 60.

33. Mark Twain identified Carlyle and Taine as his sources for the "four-generation" rule and "Cyclo. Am" for the requirement for sainthood in notebook plans for an appendix to document these and other assertions (*N&J3*, 506). Though no four-generation requirement actually exists for sainthood, he probably devised that rule from the statement in the article on "Canonization" in Appleton's *American Cyclopedia* (1883, 3:716) that "before a beatified person can be canonized in the Roman Church four consistories must be held."

of Barley Mash for building a brewery (a not-so-subtle gibe at the "beer peerages" that had been awarded in the 1880s to such notables as Guinness and Bass, the latter as recently as 1886). The wife of the founder of his noble line, a lady from "the highest landed gentry," had led a blameless life, marked with graciousness and charity. But his rival had an advantage. *His* great-great-grandmother had been "a king's leman," who "did climb to that splendid eminence by her own unholpen merit from the sewer where she was born." This, said the examiners, awarding the lieutenancy, "indeed is true nobility, this is the right and perfect intermixture" (*CY,* 294). The satire of the passage is also analogous to Standring's indignation over practices in the British military establishment, exemplified by the anomaly of one of Nell Gwyn's sons being commissioned colonel of a cavalry regiment at age fifteen, even though "like many royal and aristocratic officers of today, he did nothing besides drawing his pay."[34]

Following the introduction of the first newspaper (chapter 26), Mark Twain sent Hank Morgan and King Arthur on an "educational" tour of the kingdom, much as Prince Edward had toured with Miles Hendon in *The Prince and the Pauper* (1882). During the journey both the basic "manhood" of King Arthur and the strength of his "training" are revealed as he braves the danger of "The Small-Pox Hut" and grieves for the widow and her daughter, but can see no justification for the widow's sons' rebellion against the lord of the manor, nor any reason not to hang them for their presumption.

The subsequent episodes involving Marco and Dowley (chapters 31 to 33) permitted Twain to introduce matters of economics and comments concerning the benefits of unions and free trade. Moreover, the Yankee's humiliation of the pair also provided for a plot reversal when Marco's revenge led to the king and the Yankee's being captured and sold into the same slave band they had encountered near the Valley of Holiness, an experience that greatly enhanced King Arthur's understanding of the plight of his subjects.

The nick-of-time rescue of Hank and the king by the arrival of the "cavalry"—Launcelot and his 500 knights, on high-wheeled bicycles—provided an additional contemporary jab at the English, very likely based on newspaper reports in 1888 of the attempts to introduce the bicycle into the military maneuvers of certain British volunteer companies. As one historian

34. Standring, *People's History,* 29.

has said, in an impressive understatement, "The high bicycle did not lend itself well to such uses."[35]

Bringing Hank and the king back to Camelot, Mark Twain developed his Governor's Island mention of a lasso and the Yankee's superior agility into "The Yankee's Fight with the Knights" (chapter 39). The battle, which arises from the necessity of answering Sir Sagramour's challenge of years before, becomes a crucial struggle between "the two master-enchanters of the age," the Yankee and Merlin (who had allegedly imbued Sir Sagramour's armor with supernatural powers). And Hank Morgan, "champion of hard unsentimental common-sense and reason," with rope and cow-pony and six-shooter once more defeats the forces of superstition by dispatching Sir Sagramour and all the other knights who dare to come against him.

That victory allows him to reveal his mines, factories, and schools, and for three years all is serene, with progress on every front. Here Twain introduced—somewhat suddenly—a picture of marital bliss into which he injected much of his own deep love of family. Entered into at first merely for the sake of propriety (since Sandy insisted on staying with Hank), the marriage had evolved into an almost ideal relationship, especially after the birth of a beloved daughter.

To finish his book, Mark Twain devised an ending that would combine the final breakup of the Round Table, the suppression of the Yankee's civilization by the Church and its forces, and a final spectacle, when Hank and his small group would make their last stand against the whole chivalry of England at the Battle of the Sand Belt. From Malory he borrowed the story of the Arthurian wars which followed Arthur's learning of the love affair between Launcelot and Guenever. That account he presented primarily in the form of a vernacular but accurate report by Clarence to the Yankee, who had

35. R. H. Gretton, *Modern History of the British People, 1880–1910,* 2 vols. (Boston, 1913), 1:239. Gretton cites files of the *London Times* as his chief source of "dates and facts" and *Punch* as his authority for some of "the popular interests of the moment." Clemens often read *Punch,* and if he did not see the *Times* itself, excerpts often appeared in American newspapers. He doubtless would have been interested later to see an item in *Frank Leslie's Illustrated Newspaper* (June 1, 1889, 287) noting the *Pall Mall Budget*'s description of military maneuvers on bicycles, the prediction of "a distinguished army officer" that the cyclist will be "the cavalry of the future," and seriously suggesting adoption of the bicycle by the United States Cavalry. My thanks to Horst Kruse for calling this item to my attention.

just returned to England from France, where he and Sandy had gone for their daughter's health on advice of their doctors, who were under secret orders from the Church. In relating the events, Clarence also quoted (as a newspaper report) Malory's much-admired description of Arthur's death. The only major factual change Twain made in Malory's tale was to develop Sir Robert Smith's early reference to the formation of a stock board into an incident that actually caused the war. In this version one of Launcelot's "manipulations" as head of that stock board resulted in severe losses for Mordred and Agravaine. It was their anger, then, that led the pair to tell Arthur of his queen's affair.

With the Church's imposition of the Interdict, ostensibly to halt the war but actually to destroy the Yankee's new civilization and reestablish its own power, Mark Twain developed another of the earliest notes, which was perhaps originally suggested by the Pope's *threat* in Malory to invoke the Interdict during the Arthurian wars (book 20, chapter 12). Here the Church's action, officially directed against Mordred's attack on the Tower of London in his attempt to force Guenever to marry him, effectively snuffs out the Yankee's "improvements" by shutting down the whole country. And the culmination of Hank's long-held dread of the Church's power comes with the realization that, except for Clarence and the fifty-two youths who had been trained by the Yankee since childhood, the rest of the fearful populace had deserted him.

For the group's final stand Twain transformed the Governor's Island idea that the Yankee would use his modern weapons to defeat Arthur's enemies in a tournament into a total and horrific destruction by dynamite, Gatling guns, and electrified fence of the whole body of England's knighthood, twenty-five or thirty thousand strong. Many modern critics, especially since the revelation of the mass killings of the Nazi Holocaust and the atom bomb, have deplored the violence of this episode and the insensitivity to human life that could envision such annihilation. The episode is indeed horrible, but it seems obvious that Twain, and probably the early critics such as Howells, regarded it primarily as a spectacular variant of the traditional adventure-story ending in which the hero uses exceptional means to overcome the "bad guys." Twain no doubt expected his readers to react in much the same way as modern viewers react to the violence in animated cartoons and other movies. The cataclysmic finales of most James Bond films provide an exceptionally close present-day analogy.

The Yankee's own manuscript record, after an exultation over his and his small band's now being "masters of England," ends with a note that within an hour a misfortune happened—his own fault—which he did not have the heart to relate. To describe what happened, and to provide for the Yankee's return to the present, Twain wrote a "Post-Script by Clarence" that revealed a final triumph of the forces of superstition and unreason. Hank, stabbed by a dying knight he had tried to help, is cared for by Merlin, who had come to the cave disguised as a peasant woman a few days after the battle, offering to cook for the group. The magician enjoys his brief moment of victory—before accidentally brushing against the electrified fence—as he places a spell upon Hank which will cause him to sleep for thirteen hundred years. Hemmed in by the corpses of the slaughtered knights, the young boys in his band are destined to sicken and die. Clarence's note closes by describing the means taken to hide the sleeping Yankee and his manuscript before the fatal illness overtook the whole group. By sometime in March 1889, then, Mark Twain made good his vow to finish "before spring," completing the frame structure which began the novel by bringing the Yankee back to modern England to die, not by suicide as forecast in the initial note, but still in a way longing for his "lost land," and especially for the wife and child he had left behind.

One should note that Mark Twain obviously did not intend *A Connecticut Yankee* to serve solely as an attack upon England and certainly not just as an inverted satire on the nineteenth century. The sources he used for the sections written in 1887 and 1888, which encompass most of the ages of Western history from Roman times until the present, show that he intended a much wider scope.[36] As the novel itself illustrates over and over again, what Twain sought from most of the sources were examples of the people's "slavery" to the combined religious and secular "superstitions," not only as they existed in medieval times, but as they had persisted through the centuries into his own age. That the idea of contemporary subjection to social and religious forces was on his mind while he was writing the novel is clearly revealed by one of the fragmentary responses to Arnold, in which he defined a slave as "anyone owned by another person," anyone, that is, who is subject by law, custom, or tradition to any requirement "not required of

---

36. For a fuller discussion of Mark Twain's use of his sources, see Baetzhold, *Mark Twain and John Bull,* chapters 6 and 7, and James D. Williams, "The Use of History in Mark Twain's *A Connecticut Yankee,*" *PMLA* 80 (1965): 102–10.

all men in his country" or anyone who is denied "anything that is privileged to another."[37]

By the middle of April 1889 a letter from Webster & Co. announced that two typed copies of the manuscript were ready for his attention. After further revisions in May and June, Clemens sent a copy to Edmund C. Stedman for comment and then busied himself with production matters. He saw to the hiring of Dan Beard, whose illustrations pleased him immensely in their further enhancement of the novel's contemporary implications, arranged for the book's publication in England, and involved himself in planning the typesetting, printing, and marketing of the story. In July, elated by Stedman's hearty approval of the work as a whole, he rewrote all of the eight or nine scattered passages that the critic had objected to as crude or overexaggerated, such as the reference to an anchorite "who never washed any part of herself but her fingers" and the pseudoscientific computations of poundage of slaughtered knights in the Battle of the Sand Belt (see *CY*, Appendix D).

That August, as was often his custom, he enlisted Howells's aid in proof-reading, which resulted in a few additional changes. In the ensuing months, he continued to involve himself closely in the book's production and pro-motion. Among other matters, he battled with company proofreaders who insisted on regularizing his punctuation and made an absolutely impossible last-minute demand that his new manager, Fred Hall, who had succeeded Webster, have Standring's *People's History* set up in type so that it could be distributed along with the *Yankee*. About mid-November the final forms went to press, and finally, on December 10, 1889, almost exactly five years since the notebook "dream" had envisioned a modern man in medieval armor, *A Connecticut Yankee* reached full term, and Hank Morgan sallied forth, full-grown, from the portals of Charles L. Webster & Co. His mission—or at least part of it—was to strive by satire and ridicule to laugh away the past and present "superstitions" represented by monarchy, aristocracy, and the Established Church.

In September of that year, Clemens had underscored that mission in a letter to Howells thanking him for helping with the proof. All but repeating his emotions of 1887, he rejoiced that Howells had approved of the book's

---

37. Paine 102b, Mark Twain Papers, quoted in Baetzhold, *Mark Twain and John Bull,* 159.

comments on the French Revolution, and continued: "Few people will. It is odd that even to this day Americans still observe that immortal benefaction through English & other monarchical eyes, & have no shred of an opinion about it that they didn't get at second hand." Next to July 4th and its aftermath, this was the "noblest & holiest" of events, he said, "and its gracious work is not done yet—nor anywhere in the remote neighborhood of it." With some regret he concluded: "Well, my book is written—let it go," adding that if it could be done over, he would not have left out so many things: "They burn in me; & they keep multiplying & multiplying; but now they can't ever be said. And besides, they would require a library—& a pen warmed up in hell."[38]

Events of 1889, especially the establishment of a republic in Brazil, the official announcement of which closely resembled the Yankee's "Proclamation" in chapter 42, undoubtedly solidified Clemens's perception of his novel's relevance to the present. And the possibilities that such relevance offered for sales promotions must have been all but irresistible. Moreover, he was always concerned with the critical reception of his book, and he no doubt thought its "timeliness" would be appreciated. But there is little question of the sincerity of emotion in the letter to his friend Howells, or in another two months later which extolled news of these "Immense days! Republics & rumors of republics from everywhere in the earth."[39]

Nor was he entirely insincere when, after having arranged with Sylvester Baxter of the *Boston Herald* to review the *Yankee,* he cautioned Baxter not to let on that "there are any slurs at the Church or Protection" since he wanted "to catch the reader unwarned & modify his views if I can."[40] He was doubtless concerned about the potential loss of sales to those who might

38. *Twain–Howells Letters,* 2:613.
39. Ibid., 621. Horst Kruse has recently argued brilliantly (in "Mark Twain's *A Connecticut Yankee:* Reconsiderations and Revisions," 471–75) that events in 1889 after the book was completed caused Clemens to "realize the true significance of what he had achieved in writing the novel" and that Clemens also realized he could, by directing the ensuing publicity to the politically significant aspect of the novel, further distance himself from the charge of plagiarizing from Max Adeler's "The Fortunate Island." Though Clemens's perception of the *Yankee*'s democratic message was surely enhanced by these developments, to say it suddenly changed seems an overstatement.
40. Clemens to Baxter, November 20, 1889, quoted in *CY,* 23.

be offended, but there is little question of how strongly he felt about the Church's evil influence and of his desire to influence public opinion.

There are confusions and ambiguities in *A Connecticut Yankee,* to be sure, doubtless reflecting confusions in the author himself, and they are abundantly noted in numerous and conflicting scholarly and critical interpretations. Mark Twain's own statements were somewhat contradictory. In 1906 he said, "I think I was purposing to contrast . . . the English life of the whole of the Middle Ages with the life of modern Christendom and modern civilization—to the advantage of the latter, of course . . . if we leave out Russia and the royal palace of Belgium."[41] But the contemporary allusions in the novel make it obvious that he was not just comparing the backwardness of past centuries with the progress of his own. Much more to the point, in fact, was his tribute to Dan Beard in December 1905, when he praised the artist's drawings for supplementing his own ideas in their "vast sardonic laugh at the trivialities, the servilities of our poor human race, and also at the professions and the insolence of priestcraft and kingcraft—those creatures that make slaves of themselves and have not the manliness to shake it off."[42]

In the novel itself, despite the implicit hope that the nineteenth century might finally achieve the Yankee's dreams, there lies the strong suggestion that the "trivialities and servilities" are too deeply ingrained to be educated out of the human race. One striking example of juxtaposed hope and gloom occurs at the end of chapter 30 and beginning of chapter 31. There the willingness of the citizens of Abblasoure to support the lord of the manor in hanging their fellows (supposedly responsible for burning the manor house) reminds Hank of the actions of the "poor whites" in the American South who, though oppressed themselves, supported the slaveholders in all political moves to perpetuate slavery. But the admission of Marco, the charcoal burner, that he and the others had pursued their fellow-citizens simply because their own lives were at stake, that he hated the lord and now would be willing to support Hank's cause leads to the Yankee's eloquent statement: "A man *is* a man, at bottom. Whole ages of abuse and oppression cannot crush the manhood clear out of him." And in the final paragraph of chapter 30, he concludes that he need not give up his dream for a while, since "there

41. *Mark Twain in Eruption,* ed. Bernard DeVoto (New York: Harper, 1940), 211.
42. *Mark Twain Speaking,* 473.

is plenty good enough material for a republic even in the most degraded people that ever existed—even the Russians . . . even in the Germans, if one could but force it out of its timid and suspicious privacy" (*CY,* 346).

Yet in the next chapter, in the very first paragraph, Mark Twain implicitly illustrated the immensity of that "if" and fragility of that dream as Marco's greetings to passersby underscore "the nice and exact subdivisions of caste." His respectful bows to those of higher rank and his scorn for those lower than himself provoke Hank to comment about this charcoal-burner whose "manhood" he had so recently praised, "Well, there are times when one would like to hang the whole human race and finish the farce." And in the next paragraph the author clinched his point concerning the strength of traditional training by having the group rescue a boy who is accidentally strangling after being hanged by his playmates as part of their game. "It was some more human nature," the Yankee says, "the admiring little folk imitating their elders; they were playing mob" (*CY,* 349).

Such comments are remarkably close to the spirit of a notebook entry from July 1888. Among a group of planning notes, many of which concerned influences of the Church and false loyalty to institutions and traditions, and immediately following a reminder to have the Yankee "run across the slaves again," Mark Twain wrote: "There are in Conn., at this moment, & in all countries, children & disagreeable relatives chained in cellars, all sores, welts, worms & vermin—cases come to light every little while—2 recent cases our state." This suggests, he said, "that the thing in man which makes him cruel to a slave is in him permanently & will not be rooted out for a million years" (*N&J3,* 414).

The ending of a novel often makes clear the author's intention. In this case, however, the conclusion itself embodies the same sort of ambiguity and ambivalence as does the experience with Marco. Though history itself dictated the Yankee's failure, the fact that Merlin's spell would be lifted in thirteen hundred years *could* be read as a sign that in the nineteenth century people would eventually triumph over the forces of superstition and unreason and possibly achieve the real civilization the Yankee had failed to establish in Arthur's sixth-century England. If so, Hank's final delirium and death might be considered simply a partial working out of the original idea of having him commit suicide in modern England, yearning for his "lost land" and medieval sweetheart, a convenient way to end the novel with a pathetic scene designed to draw sympathetic tears from sentimental readers.

On the other hand, Hank's conviction that his nineteenth-century life, as well as his attempts to superimpose the ideals of nineteenth-century American civilization on sixth-century England, had all been an illusion could also imply that any hope for progress against superstition and ignorance was also an impractical dream. Hank's last ramblings, though they again reveal Clemens's own conviction of the importance of love and family, actually come ironically close to a view expressed by the author he had so often attacked. For as Hank deliriously begs Sandy to stay by him every moment so that he will not have to endure again "those hideous dreams" of progress and defeat, and as he declares death preferable to separation from loved ones, he is a close relative of the disillusioned speaker in Matthew Arnold's "Dover Beach," who pleads:

> Ah, love, let us be true
> To one another! for the world, which seems
> To lie before us like a land of dreams,
> So various, so beautiful, so new,
> Hath really neither joy, nor love, nor light,
> Nor certitude, nor peace, nor help for pain;
> And we are here as on a darkling plain
> Swept with confused alarms of struggle and flight,
> Where ignorant armies clash by night.

In 1889 and 1890, with the Paige typesetter still promising riches almost beyond his dreams, he had certainly not consciously lost faith in technological progress, believing like Lecky that such progress combined with education *could* help eradicate the old limiting ideas.[43] And he would continue to champion various reforms for the rest of his life. At this time he surely hoped that his book, through its broad farce, burlesque, serious satire, and direct diatribe, would help laugh away the nineteenth-century remnants of the "superstitions" that defeated Hank Morgan. But he was also aware of just how strong ingrained ideas could be. As one of the epigrams in *Pudd'nhead Wilson's New Calendar* later put it: "Let me make the superstitions of a nation and I care not who makes its laws or its songs either."[44] Hence, it was not so

---

43. See Lecky's *History of European Morals* and *England in the Eighteenth Century.*
44. Epigraph for chapter 51, *Following the Equator* (1897).

much that he had unconsciously lost faith in technological progress, as some have argued, but that he had now become at least partly convinced, perhaps subconsciously, that "the thing in man which makes him cruel to a slave"— superstition, ignorance, subservience to custom and social position—could not be rooted out permanently by technology or by any other means.

Mark Twain's own final judgment of the novel came in a letter to his daughter Clara on March 12, 1910, just six weeks before his death on April 21. He had reread the *Yankee* the day before for the first time in many years, he said, and was "prodigiously pleased with it—a most gratifying surprise."[45] Most critics of recent years have concluded, however, that artistically, *A Connecticut Yankee* is a failure. Some have argued that it is great despite its faults, but more have pronounced its excellences significantly inferior to its flaws. Inconsistencies of characterization form the most obvious flaw. As suggested earlier, the Yankee, first presented as a brash entrepreneur learned in little but technological skills, soon exhibits knowledge far beyond what might logically be expected. Sandy, the humorously garrulous nuisance of the early journey-quest, suddenly emerges toward the end as devoted wife and mother. Too often, dramatization yields to direct diatribe, with Twain's own voice supplanting that of his narrator. In certain instances the seeming inability to resist striving for a laugh destroys a carefully crafted and essentially serious mood. Though he stresses the importance of the individual, Hank Morgan becomes a dictator, forcing his reforms upon the nation. More broadly, the novel merely mentions the Yankee's reforms, rather than providing significant evidence of the benefits of the new civilization. These flaws, and the presence of elements so various as to defy any real amalgamation—comedy, burlesque, satire, diatribe, melodrama, sentimentality, parody, pathos, and social commentary—cause serious problems, to be sure. But many of them are also intriguing. If the book is indeed a failure, it is the failure of a great writer.

Despite its faults and confusions, *A Connecticut Yankee* remains a classic, and continues to delight, if not to instruct. Its adaptation (though considerably revised and weakened) for a silent movie in 1921, "talkies" with Will

45. Clara Clemens, *My Father, Mark Twain* (New York: Harper, 1931), 289. This source dates this letter March 10; *Union Catalogue of Clemens Letters*, ed. Paul Machlis (Berkeley and Los Angeles: University of California Press, 1986) dates it March 12.

Rogers in 1931 and Bing Crosby in 1949, and two musical stage versions by Rodgers and Hart (1927 and 1943), not to mention a Bugs Bunny cartoon and an issue of *Classic Comics,* helps to substantiate its continuing popular appeal. And even as this is being written, production is planned for yet another film version.[46]

Moreover, the very variety of scholarly criticism suggests a richness and a fascination with the work: *A Connecticut Yankee* has been studied from biographical, historical, political, sociological, psychological, theological, economic, mythic, and linguistic perspectives. The humor—even some of the broad burlesque—is often of a high order. Hank Morgan's voice does sometimes lapse into Mark Twain's own, but at its best it reveals the same mastery that animates *Huckleberry Finn.* And though the book has defied attempts to fit it exactly into established genres, its place in American literature remains secure.

46. Indianapolis *Star,* August 23, 1992, Section G, 3.

# The Unsmiling Aspects of Life

## A Hazard of New Fortunes

JOHN W. CROWLEY

ᔓ   ᔓ   ᔓ

Overfamiliar metaphor: The novelist destroys the house of his life and uses
its stones to build the house of his novel. A novelist's biographers thus
undo what a novelist has done, and redo what he undid. All their labor
cannot illuminate either the value or the meaning of a novel, can scarcely
even identify a few of the bricks.

—Milan Kundera, *The Art of the Novel*

IN SEPTEMBER 1886, soon after occupying the "Editor's Study" in
*Harper's Monthly,* W. D. Howells "rather absently dynamited his own
reputation for the next century."[1] Writing of *Crime and Punishment,* which
he had recently read in a French translation, Howells related the "hardly less
tragical story" of Dostoevsky's life: how he had once been marched before a
firing squad and then reprieved at the last instant—only to be sentenced to
six years at hard labor in Siberia. "Whatever their deserts," Howells added
sardonically, "very few American novelists have been led out to be shot,
or finally exiled to the rigors of a winter at Duluth; one might make Herr
Most the hero of a labor-question romance with perfect impunity; and in
a land where journeymen carpenters and plumbers strike for four dollars
a day the sum of hunger and cold is certainly very small, and the wrong
from class to class is almost inappreciable. We invite our novelists, therefore,

1. Gore Vidal, "William Dean Howells," in *At Home: Essays, 1982–1988,* 164.

to concern themselves with the more smiling aspects of life, which are the more American, and to seek the universal in the individual rather than the social interests."

Howells was undoubtedly correct in asserting that life in the United States was less arduous, *on average,* than life in Russia. Appropriately, then, an American realist committed to the representation of ordinary experience—an indigenous reality of the commonplace defined in part by contrast to such reality elsewhere—should concern himself, as a Dostoevsky could not, with the relatively "more smiling aspects" of life. Precisely because "there were so few shadows and inequalities in our broad level of prosperity," the native realist could not honestly write an American *Crime and Punishment:* "whoever struck a note so profoundly tragic in American fiction would do a false and mistaken thing."[2]

Although the logic here is impeccable *if* one accepts both Howells's theory of realism and his undergirding premise about American prosperity, some of his readers over the last century have gagged on the "smiling aspects of life" and pilloried Howells for his supposed complacency about "social interests"—seen as an unforgivable blindness to the less smiling aspects of the Gilded Age. Even his advocates have deplored the "single phrase [that] has succeeded in damning him in the eyes of subsequent critics."[3]

By 1889, in the midst of writing *A Hazard of New Fortunes,* Howells himself seemed to know better. As he confessed to Edmund Gosse, a friend privy to his inmost thoughts, his mood had darkened considerably: "No, black care has not left so much laugh in me as there used to be." And when he later incorporated the notorious "Editor's Study" into *Criticism and Fiction* (1891), Howells subtly revised it: " . . . and the wrong from class to class *has been* almost inappreciable, *though all this is changing for the worse*" (my emphasis).[4] He also deleted the clause about Herr Most and the labor-question romance.

2. James W. Simpson, ed., *Editor's Study by William Dean Howells* (Troy, N.Y.: Whitston, 1983), 40–41.

3. Everett Carter, *Howells and the Age of Realism* (Philadelphia: Lippincott, 1954), 185.

4. Howells, letter to Edmund Gosse, George Arms et al., eds., *Selected Letters of W. D. Howells,* 6 vols. (Boston: Twayne, 1976–1983), 3:245 (hereafter cited parenthetically as *SL*). W. D. Howells, *Criticism and Fiction* (New York: Harper, 1891), 128; the sentence following was also revised to be less *prescriptive* and more *descriptive*: "Our novelists, therefore, concern themselves with

I

Johann Most set forth from London in 1882 to carry the gospel of European anarchism to the new world. Preaching violent resistance to the capitalist order, Most published a handbook on revolution in which he proffered the recipes for dynamite and other explosives.

Few Americans perceived any difference among the various "foreign" doctrines—anarchism, socialism, communism—that were suspected of breeding discontent throughout the 1880s, a tumultuous decade of unprecedented strife between Labor and Capital. Whatever the political principles espoused by workers, however modest or reasonable their goals, all "agitation" was "connected in the public mind with attacks upon the dearest beliefs of Americans: religion, freedom, and prosperity."[5]

Early in 1886, in one of many such conflicts across the United States, workers subjected to a general lockout picketed the McCormick Reaper Works in Chicago. On May 3, about a month before Howells endorsed the "smiling aspects,"[6] a clash between strikers and their scab replacements triggered police intervention; several workers were beaten and shot, at least two of them fatally. The following evening a protest in Haymarket Square was attended by the mayor of Chicago as well as by labor organizers and political radicals. The rally was rhetorically supercharged but uneventful until the end—after the mayor had departed—when the police unnecessarily moved to disperse the already diminishing crowd and a bomb exploded, killing one policeman, mortally wounding six others (all of whom died within a few weeks), and injuring dozens more. As the enraged police fired at fleeing workers, many of them were also wounded.

The bombthrower's identity was never determined, but the police nevertheless rounded up eight prominent anarchists—George Engel, Samuel Fielden, Adolph Fischer, Louis Lingg, Oscar Neebe, Albert Parsons, Michael Schwab, and August Spies—and charged them with the murder of officer Mathias J. Degan. In effect, the accused were indicted for their incendiary political beliefs. Whether they had been present at the Haymarket rally or not—

---

the more smiling aspects of life, which are the more American, and seek the universal in the individual rather than the social interests."

5. Carter, *Howells and the Age of Realism*, 180.

6. The lag between composition and publication of the "Editor's Study" was normally three months; the September column was probably written in late June 1886.

most of them had, in fact, been elsewhere when the bomb exploded—the anarchists were held strictly accountable for inciting the violence. Promptly brought to trial, all were convicted on August 20, 1886. In October, the presiding judge denied a defense motion for a new trial and condemned seven of them to hang. The executions were stayed, however, while the lawyers appealed to higher courts. Meanwhile, a vindictive national mood, fomented by the press, magnified the anarchists' case into a symbol—not of "wrong from class to class," but rather of the peril to basic American values.

A year later, just before the prisoners' appeal was denied by the Illinois Supreme Court, Howells explained that his "original feeling that the trial of the anarchists was hysterical and unjust" had been strengthened by reading an account one of their partisans had sent him anonymously.[7] "I feel that these men are doomed to suffer for their opinions' sake," he told George W. Curtis, editor of *Harper's Weekly;* "the trial was for socialism and not for murder." The case had taken "deep hold" of the novelist: "I feel strongly the calamity which error in it must embody. Civilization cannot afford to give martyrs to a bad cause; and if the cause of these men is good, what an awful mistake to put them to death!" (*SL,* 3:193).

Although Howells was well aware that *Harper's Weekly* had allied itself editorially with the vast majority demanding retribution, he hoped that Curtis, whose record of social activism Howells had long admired, might still be persuaded to speak out. There was time, perhaps, to temper public fury before the United States Supreme Court rendered its final judgment. But Curtis, an erstwhile abolitionist, retreated from his earlier, privately confessed doubts of the anarchists' guilt, pleading that he was too ignorant of the trial to take a position on its fairness. He urged Howells to pursue the matter himself: "Now your name would give great weight to any statement or plea proceeding evidently not from emotion, but from conviction." Yes, *Harper's Weekly* might print such a plea, but it "would have to be very conclusive, undoubtedly, to strike our friends in Franklin Square favorably."[8]

---

7. Howells had received *August Spies' Autobiography: His Speech in Court, and General Notes,* as compiled by Niña Van Zandt, the woman who was married to Spies by proxy while he was in prison. He later read Dyer D. Lum's *Concise History of the Great Trial of the Chicago Anarchists in 1886, Condensed from the Official Record.* A superb modern study is Paul Avrich, *The Haymarket Tragedy* (Princeton, N.J.: Princeton University Press, 1984).

8. Quoted in Clara M. Kirk and Rudolf Kirk, "William Dean Howells, George William Curtis, and the 'Haymarket Affair,'" *American Literature* 40 (January 1969): 490. After reading the

Howells's friends in Franklin Square were the publishers who had recently signed him to an exclusive contract. Following the failure of James R. Osgood and Company in Boston, Howells, who had been a freelance since resigning his editorship of the *Atlantic Monthly* in 1881, came to lucrative terms with Harper & Brothers in October 1885. For a salary of $10,000, he agreed to produce one novel a year for serial and book publication as well as other material for *Harper's Monthly* and *Harper's Weekly*—for all of which work he would also receive generous royalties and piecework payments. For an additional $3,000, he would write the "Editor's Study," beginning in January 1886. Other than Howells's letters, in fact, the Harpers owned the rights to everything he wrote.[9]

Thus when it became clear that Curtis would not budge, Howells decided to make his views public through a letter to the *New York Tribune*. The passionate tone of this letter contrasted sharply with the gently ironic voice of Howells's fictional narrators. The question of justice or injustice, he sternly prophesied, "must remain for history, which judges the judgment of courts . . . and I, for one, cannot doubt what the decision of history will be" (*SL*, 3:199).

Howells's appeal appeared just five days before Engel, Fischer, Parsons, and Spies went to the gallows on November 11, 1887. Lingg had committed suicide on the eve of his execution; the other two had been spared the death penalty.

Among prominent literary figures, Howells was not merely "for one" in decrying the hangings; he was alone. He had implored John Greenleaf Whittier, for instance, to appeal for clemency from the governor of Illinois: "A letter from you would have great weight with him. I beseech you to write it, and do what one great and blameless man may to avert the

---

material sent by Howells (Lum's *Concise History*)—and sharing it, as Howells had requested, with Charles Eliot Norton—Curtis concluded that "the men are morally responsible for the crime. . . . They are not condemned for their opinions, but for deliberately inciting, without any pretence [*sic*] of reason, to a horrible crime which was committed with disastrous results" (494–95).

9. Howells's awareness of this constraint was explicit in his letter of December 1, 1887, to William M. Salter, one of the anarchists' chief supporters. Howells regretted that although he wished "not to leave his [Spies's] memory and that of the others to infamy," he could not edit a proposed memorial volume "because my Harper engagement covers all my work. . . . I will contribute a letter—the only form not cut off by my contract" (*SL*, 3:209).

cruellest wrong that ever threatened our fame as a nation" (*SL*, 3:198). But a man who, like Curtis, had once defied authority in the cause of abolition proved to be timorous now, washing his hands of the anarchists on the punctilious grounds that he had "never interfered with the law as it affects individual cases" (*SL*, 3:199 n).[10] Isolated in an extremely unpopular stand, Howells became a lightning rod for the shafts of those who cheered what he denounced, on November 11, as "the thing forever damnable before God and abominable to civilized men" (*SL*, 3:200).

A day later, in a second letter to the *Tribune*, Howells apologized with fierce sarcasm for intruding "a note of regret" upon the "hymn of thanksgiving for blood going up from thousands of newspapers all over the land this morning." He insisted that the hangings had been nothing less than a "political execution": *They died, in the prime of the freest Republic the world has ever known, for their opinions' sake.* At great length he excoriated those responsible, in their "paroxysmal righteousness," for "a trial by passion, by terror, by prejudice, by hate, by newspaper." Intending, perhaps, to shame Curtis and Whittier, Howells invoked the spirits of Emerson, Garrison, Parker, Phillips, Thoreau, and others who had dared to fight against slavery— all of whom, by the contorted logic of the anarchists' trial, should also have merited death for inciting the violence of John Brown. "I dread the Anarchy of the Courts," he defiantly concluded, "but I have never been afraid of the prevalence of the dead Anarchists' doctrine, because that must always remain to plain common sense, unthinkable; and I am not afraid of any acts of revenge from their fellow conspirators because I believe they never were part of any conspiracy" (*SL*, 3:201–4).

This letter, titled "A Word for the Dead," was evidently never sent. A draft addressed to Whitelaw Reid, editor of the *Tribune*, was found among Howells's papers by Edwin H. Cady and first published by him in 1958. It

10. Whittier later told an interviewer that Howells had privately begged him to join in "'protesting' against the execution of the Anarchists at Chicago." Howells, upon reading this report, angrily set the record straight: "What I asked you to do was to join me in petitioning the governor to commute the mens' [*sic*] sentence, and in urging you to do this I gave as my reason that I did not think they had been fairly tried" (*SL*, 3:240). In appealing to Whittier, Howells had been strategically careful to delimit his commitment to the anarchists' cause: "The fact is, these men were sentenced for murder when they ought to have been indicted for conspiracy" (*SL*, 3:198).

seems more likely that Howells never mailed the letter than that Reid received but refused to publish it. Cady believes that once Howells had vented his wrath in the writing of "A Word for the Dead," he thought better of exposing himself to "unfair but even more withering attack from a press and public opinion already passionately decided. It had destroyed the Anarchists and it might destroy him."[11]

The same day, November 12, 1887, that Howells banked the fire of his indignation, Johann Most was arrested for delivering an inflammatory speech in protest of the executions. Most's subsequent incarceration struck Howells as yet another injustice: "This can't last. Sometime the conscience of the people will be stirred" (SL, 3:210).

Howells's own conscience had already been stirred, more deeply than he would have thought possible a few years earlier. But his reaction to the Haymarket affair was far more circumspect than Johann Most's. In demanding justice for the anarchists, Howells never committed himself to their cause. Although he believed that August Spies was "a noble, unselfish and heroic soul," he also had his "reservations in regard to him" (SL, 3:209), and he distanced himself from those who perceived Spies as a revolutionary martyr. "How hard it is," he reflected, "when a great wrong has been done, not to say and then to think that its victims were wholly right! That is the devil of it; the train of evil seems to warp and twist all things awry as it goes on, when once its infernal impetus is given" (SL, 3:212). In shying from more confrontational tactics, Howells was not simply protecting himself or defending bourgeois interests in which he had a stake. He was evincing his aversion to extremes, political and otherwise.


## II


"It's no use," Howells told his sister Annie a week after the hangings. "I can't write about it. Some day I hope to do justice to these irreparably

---

11. Edwin H. Cady, *The Realist at War: The Mature Years 1885–1920 of William Dean Howells* (Syracuse, N.Y.: Syracuse University Press, 1958), 77–78. Gore Vidal puts it less charitably: "I suspect that the cautious lifetime careerist advised the Tolstoyan socialist to cool it. Howells was in enough trouble already." But Vidal's praise of "A Word" is justly generous: "As polemic, Howells's letter is more devastating and eloquent than Emile Zola's *J'accuse;* as a defense of the right to express unpopular opinions, it is the equal of what we mistakenly take to be the thrust of Milton's *Areopagitica*" (*At Home,* 166–67).

wronged men" (*SL,* 3:208). His sense of injustice came to bear almost immediately, however, on his fiction, where the force of the anarchists' ideas was tested against his distrust of radical solutions. Although anarchist doctrine might be "unthinkable" to "plain common sense," he was, in fact, thinking it through in *Annie Kilburn* (1889), *A Hazard of New Fortunes* (1890), *The Quality of Mercy* (1892), and *The World of Chance* (1893).

What was also at issue in these novels was the radical challenge of Leo Tolstoy. In justifying his own refusal to plead for the anarchists, Whittier suggested that Howells's admiration of Tolstoy had induced him—as if against his better judgment—"to take an interest in those creatures" (*SL,* 3:240). There was certainly a connection. In the same letter to Annie, Howells confided that he and his wife, Elinor, "both no longer care for the world's life, and would like to be settled somewhere very humbly and simply, where we could be socially identified with the principles of progress and sympathy for the struggling mass" (*SL,* 3:207). That he was expressing these sentiments while living in a swank hotel in Buffalo made Howells acutely aware of the gap between the asceticism he avowed and the material ease of his own circumstances. This was the same contradiction that Tolstoy had hoped to escape by renouncing aristocratic privilege and attempting to live as if he were one of the peasants on his estate.

Howells initially discovered Tolstoy in 1885. By the following summer, with mounting excitement, he had devoured *The Cossacks, Anna Karenina, My Religion,* and *War and Peace,* and proceeded to Tolstoy's stories, autobiographies, and social writings. "I know very well that I do not speak of these books in measured terms; I cannot," he professed in an introduction to *Sebastopol,* which he edited in 1887. "As yet my sense of obligation to them is so great that I neither can make nor wish to make a close accounting with their author." Whereas "all other fiction at times *seems* fiction," Tolstoy's books "alone seem the very truth always." It does not matter where one starts with him; "you feel instantly that the man is mighty, and mighty through his conscience; that he is not trying to surprise or dazzle you with his art, but that he is trying to make you think clearly and feel rightly about vital things with which 'art' has often dealt with diabolical indifference or diabolical malevolence."[12]

12. W. D. Howells, "Leo Tolstoï," *Sebastopol* (New York: Harper, 1887), 11, 6, 8. Originally published in *Harper's Weekly* (April 23, 1887), this essay was Howells's first extended discussion of Tolstoy, to whom he returned again and again in his "Editor's Study" columns.

The influence of Tolstoy was apparent in Howells's letters. In February 1887, for example, the sight of the gigantic textile mills at Lowell, Massachusetts, gave him pause. Although he judged them to be "as humanely managed as such things can be," they made him think nonetheless that civilization was "all wrong in regard to the labor that suffers in them. I felt so helpless about it, too, realizing the misery it must cost to undo such a mistake. But it is slavery" (*SL*, 3:182). A week later, writing to Curtis, Howells defended "commonplace people" from the aspersions of those American fiction writers in whom "the very, very little culture and elegance with which our refined people have overlaid themselves seems to have hardened their hearts against the common people: they seem to despise and hate them." In disgust, Howells found himself turning "to the barbarous nations with a respect I never expected to feel for them" (*SL*, 3:183).

In April 1887, while Howells was reading *Que Faire?*, he admitted how "very unhappy" Tolstoy made him feel about the "terrible question" of prosperity's responsibility for poverty. He could not, however, emulate Tolstoy's renunciation of luxury and superfluity. "I don't exactly see how this helps," he told his father, "except that it makes all poor alike, and saves one's self from remorse" (*SL*, 3:186).[13] To Edward Everett Hale, a fellow Tolstoy enthusiast, Howells owned that the ethical writings had "shown me the utter selfishness and insufficiency of my past life, without convincing me that Tolstoi offers quite the true solution. To work for others, yes; but to work with my hands, I'm not sure, seeing that I'm now fifty, awkward and fat." But Tolstoy had nonetheless freed Howells by "flooring" him: "Never again can I be a snob; my soul is at least my own henceforth" (*SL*, 3:189).

As Howells asserted in a letter to Henry James, he was "not in a very good humor with 'America,'" which now seemed "the most grotesquely illogical thing under the sun." Whatever James might think of his old friend, Howells seemed to be shocking himself by his declaration that "after fifty years of

13. Howells publicly acknowledged his doubts in his "Editor's Study" of July 1887. Calling Tolstoy "the greatest living writer, and incomparably the greatest writer of fiction who has ever lived," Howells pondered his call to humble toil: "It is a hard saying; but what if it should happen to be the truth? In that case, how many of us who have great possessions must go away exceeding sorrowful!" After reading *Que Faire?*, he concluded, "you cannot be quite the same person you were before; you will be better by taking its truth to heart, or worse by hardening your heart against it" (Simpson, *Editor's Study*, 87).

optimistic content with 'civilization' and its ability to come out all right in the end, I now abhor it, and feel that it is coming out all wrong in the end, unless it bases itself anew on a real equality." Then, in an oscillation from the "audacity" of such "social ideas," Howells added ironically: "Meantime, I wear a fur-lined overcoat, and live in all the luxury my money can buy" (*SL*, 3:231).

Such self-deprecation was entirely characteristic of Howells; it reflected his skepticism of extremes as well as his cognizance of personal imperfections. Howells later joked to his father that he and Samuel Clemens, along with their wives, were "all of accord in our way of thinking: that is, we are theoretical socialists, and practical aristocrats. But it is a comfort to be right theoretically, and to be ashamed of one's self practically" (*SL*, 3:271). Writing to Hale, he linked his pessimism about social conditions to awareness of his own "prejudices, passions, follies," which he believed could be surmounted only by "unselfishness" and an "immediate altruism dealing with what now is." The maddening dilemma was how to translate these ideals into action: "Words, words, words! How to make them things, deeds,—you have the secret of that; with me they only breed more words" (*SL*, 3:233).

Howells immersed himself in radical literature and, to a degree, in socialist politics. Had there been a labor party "embodying any practical ideas" (*SL*, 3:223), he would have voted with it. He told Hamlin Garland, in January 1888, that although he had not joined Henry George's Single Tax crusade, he had been "reading and thinking about questions that carry me beyond myself and my miserable literary idolatries of the past" (*SL*, 3:215). He was especially attracted to Laurence Gronlund's blend of Marxian social analysis and utopian socialism—Gronlund preferred the term *collectivism*—in *Co-operative Commonwealth* (1884). Howells, who had heard Gronlund lecture in Buffalo, praised the book's "reconciliation of interests which now antagonize one another, the substitution of the ideal of duties for the ideal of rights, of equality for liberty."[14]

Like Gronlund, Howells felt uneasy about labeling his political identity, given the stigma attached to "socialism" by the American public. Former

14. Ibid., 129. In the same April 1888 "Editor's Study," Howells also mentioned Richard T. Ely's *Land, Labor and Taxation*. Two months later, he admired Edward Bellamy's *Looking Backward* for its "force of appeal": "whether Mr. Bellamy is amusing himself or not with his conceit of the socialistic state as an accomplished fact, there can be no doubt that he is keenly alive to the defects of our present civilization" (141).

president Rutherford B. Hayes (Howells's cousin by marriage), after reading *Annie Kilburn,* reflected in his diary: "I do not find a ready word for the doctrine of true equality of rights (expressed in the novel). Its foes call it nihilism, communism, socialism, and the like. Howells would perhaps call it justice. It is the doctrine of the Declaration of Independence, and of the Sermon on the Mount. But what is a proper and *favorable* word or phrase to designate it?"[15]

As Hayes shrewdly sensed, Howells preferred to detach his own beliefs from dubious European origins by conceiving of "socialism" as no more "foreign" than the American Revolution and the New Testament—indeed, as nothing really unfamiliar. "Socialism, as I understand it, is not a positive but a comparative thing," he explained in another of his unmailed letters to the editor, this time to the *New York Sun;* "it is a question of more or less in what we have already, and not a question of absolute difference" (*SL,* 3:237).

Howells took such care in this statement to palliate his "socialism" because he had come once more under suspicion for his "radical" commitments. On November 11, 1888, at an anniversary service in Boston for the Haymarket anarchists, a letter from Howells was read in which he allegedly "reiterated his well-known views that the execution of Spies and his companions was an outrage."[16] Henry Mills Alden, editor of *Harper's Monthly,* was alarmed at this report. With permission from Howells, he hastened to publish a correction, to the effect that Howells's position had been grossly misrepresented: he had merely sent a polite note declining an invitation to address the anarchists' meeting; rather than renewing his condemnation of the executions, this note had referred to Howells's 1887 *Tribune* letter as his last word on the matter.

The anniversary of the hangings occasioned a rehearsal of all the old arguments; and by tying himself, however tenuously, to the Boston anar-

---

15. Quoted in Clara M. Kirk and Rudolf Kirk, *William Dean Howells* (New York: Twayne, 1962), 110.

16. From a report of the anarchists' meeting, titled "A Letter from W. D. Howells," in the *Chicago Tribune,* November 12, 1888. Quoted in Clara Marburg Kirk, *W. D. Howells: Traveler from Altruria, 1889–1894* (New Brunswick, N.J.: Rutgers University Press, 1962), 22. It is likely that the *New York Sun* carried the same story, for Howells's unsent letter of November 23, 1888, was prompted by "the two articles you have printed this week on my 'socialism,' supposed or actual." Neither article has so far been located, but Howells's response suggests that the second was an editorial on the first.

chists, Howells became vulnerable once again to the abuse he had endured in 1887 from papers like the *Sun*. He was understandably wary of exploitation by those eager to appropriate the worth of his good name to their own radical ends. Not only his reputation but also his livelihood seemed in danger.

In fact, as protective as they were of Howells's public image on this occasion, his "friends in Franklin Square" had exhibited surprising tolerance during his earlier campaign against the Haymarket executions. In recalling his long association with his publishers, Howells supposed that although his *Tribune* letter had not appeared in a Harper publication, it must have been "as distasteful to the House as it was to the immeasurable majority of the American people. It raised a storm above my head, but no echo of the tempest ever reached me from Franklin Square any more than if the House there had quite agreed with me."[17] It had not, of course. But the House did recognize some advantages in Howells's social activism.

During negotiations in 1885, Joseph W. Harper had proposed that Howells write "a *feuilleton* for 'Harper's Weekly,' embracing current social, literary & artistic topics, with story & incident" (*SL*, 3:128 n). In September 1888, just before the anniversary incident, Alden was prompted by Harper to remind Howells of this idea. Quoting the publisher directly, Alden outlined an ambitious series of articles for the *Weekly*: " 'a powerful presentation of the life of our great metropolis, social, educational, economical, political—as shown in our schools, colleges, charitable organizations, reformatory institutions, prisons, courts of law, occupations & amusements—our streets & parks & factories & clubs—the rich & the poor, the idler & the worker, the silly men & bad men & frivolous women—the elevated railroads, the monopolies, the nuisances—& Hunter's Point.' " Neither Alden nor Harper doubted that Howells would infuse this material with his " 'sympathy, his altruism—in other words, his warm democratic heart.' " Ideally, the feuilletons would have a (covertly) didactic effect: " 'Possibly lessons might be drawn from these observations, showing the real assimilation of interests in these diverse classes & occupations of the community, with suggestions for the improvement of society.' " The series, moreover, " 'would command the interest of all

17. Quoted in J. Henry Harper, *The House of Harper: A Century of Publishing in Franklin Square* (New York: Harper, 1912), 322.

classes, afford food for reflection & conversation in society, & would be largely quoted.' "[18]

Viewed in this light, Howells's "socialism" became a relatively innocuous "altruism": not political but educational, not divisive but synthetic, demonstrating not the radical polarization of class interests but rather "the real assimilation of interests in these diverse classes." Such "altruism" was topical and therefore a means to good publicity and social influence. Ironically, if Howells's "socialism" was subject to appropriation by the anarchists, it was also open to commodification by the Harpers. While they protected their investment in Howells, his publishers meant to capitalize on the market value of his "radical" reputation.


### III

As Harper's proposal suggests, Howells was expected to relocate himself imaginatively, if not actually, in New York. For most of his career, he had been closely identified with Boston, in the environs of which he and his family had lived since 1866, when Howells first assumed his duties as assistant editor of the *Atlantic Monthly*. By 1887, however, he had come to feel "that there is little or nothing left for me in Boston, and in New York there may be a good-deal" (*SL*, 3:195).

Howells and his family had always been peripatetic, moving from house to house, leaving the city for summer vacations, and occasionally traveling through Europe. This pattern became all the more pronounced during the 1880s, as Winifred Howells, his elder daughter, suffered her slow decline.

Born in Venice in 1863, Winny (as her father called her) was a precocious child with literary ambitions. A published poet at thirteen—in *St. Nicholas,* a children's magazine—Winifred seemed favored to reach the goal she once set for herself in her diary: "to be a great writer." Three years later, however, she began to experience vertigo and other mysterious symptoms that were ultimately to render her an invalid. Treated by "rest cure" during 1880–1881, Winifred made a temporary recovery—just as Howells himself collapsed during the composition of *A Modern Instance* (1882).[19]

18. Quoted in Kirk, *Traveler from Altruria,* 19.

19. Winifred Howells, quoted in W. D. Howells, *Winifred Howells* (privately printed, 1891), 20. On Howells's 1881 breakdown, see John W. Crowley, *The Black Heart's Truth: The Early Career of W. D. Howells* (Chapel Hill: University of North Carolina Press, 1985), 110–46.

The burden of family illness—Elinor too was becoming a confirmed invalid—forced the Howellses to abandon the commodious home they had just recently designed and built for themselves in the Belmont hills and to return to Boston. The house there, at 302 Beacon Street, was no more permanent. When Winifred, at age twenty-one, suffered a relapse of "nervous prostration" during the fall of 1885, her parents began their "wandering about in the health-search" (*SL*, 3:228): first to suburban Auburndale and then to Lake George, New York, for the summer of 1887. That fall Winifred was confined for several months to an expensive sanitorium in Dansville, New York. It was during this period, while Howells and his wife lived nearby in a Buffalo hotel, that he became preoccupied with the anarchists' case. Indeed, the growth of his political consciousness and the erosion of his confidence in America were concurrent with his deepening concern about Winifred's health—as if the problems of his own family sharpened his sensitivity to the unsmiling aspects of the world at large.

This awareness was also expanded by Howells's impressions of New York, where he and Elinor moved from Buffalo in February 1888. The city was "immensely interesting" but nearly overwhelming for the self-consciously middle-aged novelist. Compared to the "abounding Americanism" of New York, Boston now seemed "of another planet" (*SL*, 3:223). From temporary quarters on West Ninth Street, the Howellses moved in April to the Chelsea on West Twenty-third Street: "one of the vast caravanseries [*sic*] which are becoming so common in New York,—ten stories high, and housing six hundred people" (*SL*, 3:225). In the fall they undertook an exhausting hunt for a permanent residence, inspecting over a hundred flats before settling on an old-fashioned apartment house at 330 East Seventeenth Street, overlooking Stuyvesant Square. In the same letter to James in which he railed against American "civilization," Howells confided that "at the bottom of our wicked hearts we all like New York" (*SL*, 3:232). The novelist was soon at home in various clubs and social circles, and he enjoyed informal dinners at Moretti's (renamed Maroni's in *Hazard*), where the literati gathered.

The family now included Winifred again. She had rejoined her parents and her younger siblings (John and Mildred) after her release from Dansville in the spring of 1888. The sanitorium had proven to be worse than ineffectual; it had reinforced, her father thought, "every bad habit of invalidism" (*SL*, 3:226). Home care in New York and then near the sea at Little Nahant, Massachusetts, worked no better. It is impossible at a century's remove to be certain about any diagnosis, but Winifred's case seems to fit the picture of "anorexia nervosa" that was then first being drawn by European physicians.[20]

As Winifred would reach plateaus of stable weakness and then sink again into vales of depression, her parents alternated between hope and dejection. For all of his devotion to his daughter, Howells sometimes betrayed frustration with her helplessness. "She has fairly baffled us, and has almost worn her mother out," Howells complained to his father in November 1888. "There are some proofs that she suffers little or no pain, but she manages to work upon our sympathy so that we are powerless to carry out our plans for her good." The latest such plan, which the Howellses did carry out, was to enlist the services of Dr. S. Weir Mitchell, the inventor of the "rest cure" and the most distinguished psychiatrist in America. Winifred would be sent to Mitchell's clinic in Philadelphia. "It will be a fearfully costly experiment,—perhaps $2000 in all—but we *must* make it, or else let her slide into dementia and death. Of course we are glad that Mitchell will even try to do anything for her, but we are not very hopeful" (*SL*, 3:235).

Elinor Howells, it seems, reluctantly yielded to her husband "in all the details of this last attempt to restore Winny to health" (*SL*, 3:249 n); and when Howells personally delivered his daughter to Mitchell, he was anxious to put the best face on a desperate situation. "If you could once see Dr. Mitchell," he wrote to his father, offering the same reassurances he had probably given Elinor, "you would see how he differed from all other specialists, and would not have a doubt but she was in the best and wisest and kindest hands in the world. He did not conceal from me that he thought it a very difficult case; her hypochondriacal illusions and obstinacy in her physiological theories complicate it badly; but everything that can be done will be done, 'As if she were my own daughter,' he said" (*SL*, 3:235 n).

Convinced that Winifred's illness was hysterical, Mitchell tried to undermine her own stubborn belief in a somatic etiology of her health problems through a combination, standard to the "rest cure," of forced feeding and psychological persuasion. Early in 1889, the doctor reported that Winifred

---

20. See Joan Jacobs Brumberg, *Fasting Girls: The Emergence of Anorexia Nervosa as a Modern Disease* (Cambridge: Harvard University Press, 1988). Anorexia nervosa, or "hysterical anorexia," was first identified clinically during the 1870s—independently by William Gull in England and Charles Lasègue in France. It is unlikely that Winifred's American physicians were aware of the European medical literature; they consistently diagnosed her illness as hysteria.

was "in a very good way physically," but that "she still continues rebellious, and wont admit that she's at all better, though she has gained fifteen pounds, and is able to do anything she likes."[21] During a visit the next month, Howells too was encouraged by Winifred's appearance, but disturbed by the persistence of her "hypochondria."

Once she had gained twenty pounds, Winifred was transferred to Merchantville, Pennsylvania, where Mitchell maintained a rural retreat for patients on the mend. There, in her twenty-sixth year, she died on March 2, 1889, the day after her father's fifty-second birthday.[22]

"The blow came with terrible suddenness, when we were hoping so much and fearing nothing less than what happened," Howells reflected (*SL*, 3:249). In the stupor of grief, he struggled to comprehend the death of Winifred—with "her gentleness, her divine intelligence, the loveliness of her most angelic character, and the beauty of her patient wisdom"—as anything other than the senseless slaughter of innocence. "As I can conceive of no hate that could have framed a law so dreadful as the law of death," he told an old friend, "I must believe that Love did it" (*SL*, 3:250).

Blaming himself for Winifred's tragedy, her father was haunted by grotesque dreams. In one of them, he shared the fate of the Chicago anarchists: "Last night I was to be hanged for something, and I had a chance to escape; but I reflected, 'No, I am tired of living; and it's only a moment's wrench, and then I shall be with *her*'" (*SL*, 3:270). The dreadful "law of death" was even more harrowing than the "awful mistake" of the Haymarket hangings. The execution of innocent men had shaken Howells's faith in human justice, but Winifred's death compelled him to question Divine Providence. To John Hay, he quoted a sentence from Henry James's letter of condolence: "'To be young and gentle, and do no harm, and to pay for it as if it were a crime.' That is the whole history of our dear girl's life. What *does* it mean?"[23]

---

21. Howells to William Cooper Howells, January 27, 1889. Quoted in John W. Crowley, *The Mask of Fiction: Essays on W. D. Howells* (Amherst: University of Massachusetts Press, 1989), 98.

22. The immediate cause of death was a "heart clot." The relationship, if any, between Winifred's chronic illness and her fatal heart attack cannot be established definitively, but sudden heart failure is sometimes a consequence of anorexia nervosa. For a full discussion of the physical and psychological dimensions of Winifred's case, see Crowley, *The Mask of Fiction*, 83–114.

23. George Monteiro and Brenda Murphy, eds., *John Hay–Howells Letters: The Correspondence of John Milton Hay and William Dean Howells, 1861–1905* (Boston: Twayne, 1980), 96.

## IV

Howells was then in the midst of writing *A Hazard of New Fortunes,* the novel he had started the previous October with a rush of enthusiasm. But by February 1889, with Winifred "a wreck of health and youth," he was feeling alienated from the mindless and carefree vitality of New York. "I suppose if I were not old and sore and sad I should like life here," he told Gosse. "It's very simple and irresponsible, and hell seems farther than at Boston, because people agree not to think about it" (*SL,* 3:245).

Howells had no choice but to think about it; after Winifred's death, he was living in hell. Seeking distraction from grief, he labored in vain at his desk. "I thought I was never going to be able to get anything done," he later told an interviewer. "For weeks I made start after start, and tore up everything I wrote. I was in perfect despair about it."[24] In the draft of his retrospective preface to the novel, Howells recalled how sorrow had "so palsied the hand and brain that it seemed as if the work added to the anguish." Through "leaden hours and days," he had hewed to his task, but the stress "had its effect in the formlessness of the passages following the opening, or rather their dispropotionate [*sic*] length."[25]

Many critics have agreed about the "disproportionate length" of the early chapters in which the Marches search for an apartment, and they have accepted the explanation Howells gave more than once. As he wrote on January 30, 1891, in reaction to Thomas Wentworth Higginson's criticism of the opening: "But you are quite right . . . long stretches of carpentery [*sic*], where I arrived at little or nothing of the real edifice. I may tell you that they were done when we were losing, when we lost, our Winny, and that I was writing in that stress because I *must.* Afterwards I could not change them" (*SL,* 3:304).[26] Twenty years later, he told Brander Matthews that he still liked

24. Quoted in Cady, *The Realist at War,* 99.

25. W. D. Howells, "Autobiographical," *A Hazard of New Fortunes,* ed. Everett Carter (Bloomington: Indiana University Press, 1976), 509–10. All quotations from the novel are taken from this standard edition and are hereafter cited parenthetically as *HNF.* The draft of Howells's preface, written in June 1909, is far more detailed and revealing than the version first published in the Library Edition of *Hazard* (New York: Harper, 1911).

26. Howells was given to heightened and somewhat disingenuous deference in dealing with Higginson, one of Boston's most distinguished and also most pompous literary personages. It is possible, then, that Howells exaggerated his own dissatisfaction out of courteous agreement

the novel, "all but the beginning, where I was staggering about, blind and breathless from the blow of my daughter's death, and trying to feel my way to the story" (*SL*, 5:361).

These letters contradict, however, the published preface to the Library Edition, in which Howells recalled his *pleasure* in writing these chapters: "There is nothing in the book with which I amused myself more than the house-hunting of the Marches" (*HNF*, 5). Furthermore, his letters from 1888–1889 suggest that this first section of the novel was completed well *before* Winifred's death.

In the absence of the manuscript of *Hazard*, it is difficult to say exactly how far Howells had progressed by March 1889. However, he could not have written chapter 10 before November 23, 1888, because he used there an incident mentioned in his unsent letter to the *New York Sun*: "Yesterday afternoon, I went out to walk on the Avenue—not Fifth, but Third,—and I saw a decently dressed man stoop and pick up from the pavement a dirty bit of cake or biscuit, which he crammed into his mouth and greedily devoured. Then I saw this man go along the curbstone, and search the garbage of the gutters like a famished dog for something more to eat" (*SL*, 3:238). By Christmas 1888, he had finished 500 pages, with 300 more to go before typesetting could begin for the serial in *Harper's Weekly* (*SL*, 3:241). In mid-February, he was still "working very hard on my story" (*SL*, 3:244).

Howells was referring to 500 manuscript pages. It is, of course, impossible to know precisely how many printed pages would have been equivalent, but a rough estimate may be ventured on the basis of the partial manuscript of *A Modern Instance*, the only manuscript of a Howells novel from the 1880s that has survived. For that book, the conversion factor was about $3\frac{1}{2}$ manuscript pages for 1 printed page. Using the same proportion, we can speculate that 500 manuscript pages of *Hazard* would have corresponded to 143 printed pages.[27] It so happens that "Part Second," set *after* the

with Higginson's. In any case, the same objection had already been voiced in some of the reviews. George W. Curtis, for instance, observed: "It might be alleged that the tale lags a little in getting under way, but the shrewd humor of the dalliance is full compensation" ("Editor's Easy Chair," *Harper's Monthly* 80 [January 1890]: 314).

27. This is a conservative estimate. A comparison of the first editions shows that whereas *A Modern Instance* was set at 37 lines per page, the type body of each page measuring $3\frac{1}{2}$ by $5\frac{3}{8}$ inches, *Hazard* was set, in a slightly smaller font, at 31 lines per page, with a type body of 3

Marches have finally signed their lease, begins on page 133 in the first hardcover edition.

It is probable, then, that "Part First" and even more of the novel was drafted before the end of 1888 and thus before Winifred's death induced the block. No doubt, Howells wrote the house-hunting chapters under emotional pressure, but his attributing the stress to losing her was hindsight possible only after she had indeed been lost. His later sense of the composition of *Hazard* was, therefore, somewhat distorted.[28] That Howells did not revise the opening may also have resulted from his writing "with the printer at my heels" (*HNF*, 3), for serialization began long before the novel was finished, and he likely had no more time than inclination to make changes.

Despite the urgency of deadlines, Howells was unable to move ahead until he fled New York in May 1889 and retreated to a rented house near Belmont. Then the novel flowed "so easily from the pen that I had the misgiving which I always have of things which do not cost me great trouble." As *Hazard* advanced, "it compelled into its course incidents, interests, individualities, which I had not known lay near, and it specialized and amplified at points which I had not always meant to touch, though I should not like to intimate anything mystical in the fact." The action developed "as nearly without my conscious agency as I ever allow myself to think such things happen" (*HNF*, 4–5).

This imaginative surge makes psychological, if not "mystical," sense. In effect, Howells came full circle to Belmont, the place where Winny's troubles had all begun. She lay now a few miles away, in the Cambridge cemetery, and one spring day her father prostrated himself beside her grave and

---

by 4⅞ inches. That is, *A Modern Instance* contains about 25 percent more copy on each page than *Hazard* does. If Howells followed his usual practice of writing on half sheets, then 500 manuscript pages of *Hazard* was really equivalent to *more* than 143 printed pages.

28. Clearly, Howells was not sure in 1909 about the sequence of events twenty years earlier. In his "Autobiographical" preface, he wrote and then deleted this internally revised sentence: "But after the first chapters were written, something befell me were already in the hands of the printers, such sorrow as comes to all of us if we live and outlive, came to me suddenly, swiftly, in the dawn of new hopes, where there had never yet been despair" (*HNF*, 509). The editors of *Selected Letters* note that Howells's 1911 letter to Brander Matthews is "almost certainly incorrect" in its timing of the novel's composition (*SL*, 5:361 n).

"experienced what anguish a man can live through."[29] He was, in fact, living through his anguish by writing through it, by releasing strong emotions into a novel that seemed wondrously to be writing itself.

Howells later thought that *Hazard* became "the most vital" of his fictions "through my quickened interest in the life about me, at a moment of great psychological import." It reflected, he believed, his concern during the later 1880s with the "humaner economics," the visionary dreams of Henry George and Edward Bellamy, and the "bombs and scaffolds of Chicago" (*HNF*, 4). Although he traced its origins to such social interests, he also knew it was rooted in private agony. *Hazard* became an act of psychic recovery; Howells's profound sense of loss lay inevitably at its core. This loss was multifarious: of his daughter and hope for her afterlife, of his former identity as a Bostonian writer, of whatever Christian beliefs he held before Tolstoy's unsettling challenge, of his faith in American society and its institutions.

## V

The keynote to *A Hazard of New Fortunes* is struck by its Shakespearean title. Chatillion, the French ambassador to the English court in *King John*, warns his own monarch of an invasion by those who, divided among themselves in Britain, have united in their predatory design upon disputed French territories. With a mixture of apprehension and contempt, Chatillion describes the band of adventurers who have swarmed across the channel:

> And all th' unsettled humours of the land,
> Rash, inconsiderate, fiery voluntaries,
> With ladies' faces and fierce dragons' spleens,
> Have sold their fortunes at their native homes,
> Bearing their birthrights proudly on their backs,
> To make a hazard of new fortunes here.[30]

29. Henry Nash Smith and William M. Gibson, eds., *Mark Twain–Howells Letters: The Correspondence of Samuel L. Clemens and William D. Howells, 1872–1910* (Cambridge: Harvard University Press, 1960), 603.

30. William Shakespeare, *The Life and Death of King John*, ed. Stanley T. Williams (New Haven: Yale University Press, 1927), 13–14. The best study of the novel in light of its Shakespearean

In the context of Howells's novel, the passage applies most pointedly to the Dryfoos family, displaced by new fortunes from their farm in Moffitt, Indiana, and cast adrift in the chaotic modern city, where they are condemned never to feel at home. As Mela and Christine proudly await the social triumph that is not, as they imagine, their birthright in New York, Jacob Dryfoos brings his rash and fiery temperament to bear on Wall Street, where he is determined to attain a position of commanding wealth. Meanwhile, his wife pines for their abandoned western homestead, and his son, Conrad, renounces all earthly ambition.

The fate of such a family had been the seed of the novel. Howells's curiosity was aroused in 1886 about some "Cincinnati men who had come to New York to become part of Eastern society." A year later, during a visit to the Natural Gas Jubilee in Findlay, Ohio, he was amazed by the booming new industry that had transmogrified farmers into entrepreneurs. "The wildest dreams of Col. Sellers are here commonplaces of everyday experience," he gushed to Samuel Clemens, adding that he wished he could "blow off a gas-well in this note" to give some sense of what he had witnessed.[31] "It was a wonderful spectacle gaseously, materially and morally," as he told John W. De Forest. "I believe I shall try to write a story about it" (*SL*, 3:188).

Howells did use "A Hazard of New Fortunes" as the title for a sketch he never finished "about Pennsylvania emigrants to Ohio" (*HNF*, 523 n). But he soon shifted to a much larger scale, more on the order of Tolstoy than of Ivan Turgenev, whose compressed novels, centered on a few characters, had earlier been his fictional paragon. Before *Hazard*, no American writer had managed to capture what Howells described to James as the "vast, gay, shapeless life" of New York (*SL*, 3:232). In taking up what he soon realized would be his "longest story" (*SL*, 3:241), Howells explicitly rejected his publisher's "plan of short stories" (*SL*, 3:230). This project was reassigned to Basil March,

---

title is Fred G. See, "Howells and the Nature of Fathers," *American Literary Realism* 20 (Spring 1988): 38–54.

31. Everett Carter, introduction to *Hazard*, xix; Smith and Gibson, *Mark Twain–Howells Letters*, 593–94. In his "Autobiographical" preface, Howells connected the idea of the Dryfoos family to his experience in Findlay. He also noted that the family "name itself is a misnomer, being a Jewish name, and not that of such people of Pennsylvania Dutch origin as I was imagining" (*HNF*, 506).

who spends most of *Hazard* gathering material for New York feuilletons that remain unwritten at the end.

First employed in *Their Wedding Journey* (1872), Basil and Isabel March were quasi-autobiographical, but decidedly fictional, surrogates for Will and Elinor Howells. The Marches, whom Howells seemed to revive whenever he was exploring personally difficult material, served as the "mask of fiction" that was, paradoxically, the enabling condition of self-revelation. In *Hazard*, the Marches' move from Boston to New York, their quest for an apartment, and their reactions to the city all resemble the Howellses' own experience.[32]

Consider, for example, Howells's use in the novel of his encounter with a man scavenging for food in the gutters of Third Avenue. Howells had been moved to speak to the man (in rudimentary French) and to give him a little money: "he caught my hand between his work-hardened palms, and clung to it, and broke down, and cried there on the street in the most indecent manner. For me, I went away sorrowful, not because there were not places enough for that hapless wretch to go to, for charity if he could find them, but because the conditions in which he came to such a strait seemed to me Christless, after eighteen hundred years of Christ" (*SL*, 3:238). Similarly, Basil March "pulled himself away, shocked and ashamed, as one is by such a chance . . . and the man lapsed back into the mystery of misery out of which he had emerged." Although Basil and his wife Isabel see the social significance of this encounter in the same terms Howells had used, they are incapable, at this early point in the novel, of sustaining his moral seriousness. To Isabel's plea "Then we must change the conditions," Basil replies facetiously, "Oh no; we must go to the theatre and forget them" (*HNF*, 70–71); and they end in irresolution about what, if anything, can be done.

Throughout the novel, Howells maintained an ironic narrative distance from the Marches even as he used them as a point of reference, a relatively

---

32. In a famous passage in *Years of My Youth* (New York: Harper, 1916), Howells wrote: "No man, unless he puts on the mask of fiction, can show his real face or the will behind it" (127). In retrospect, Basil seemed much more like Howells than he had realized when he imagined him: "I too was of the Middle Western birth and growth, and of Bostonian adoption; I had been a journalist as those things went in the simple days of my youth; I had thought myself a poet, and my life was in my literary hopes. I had been all that March was; except an insurance man, and perhaps he never was really an insurance man" (*HNF*, 507).

stable center around which the plot and the other characters revolve. The force of the novel is powerfully centrifugal, however.[33] Not only does everything seem to be flying off, but the center itself does not finally hold. In a crucial passage, Basil has the vertiginous realization that "accident and then exigency" are the only forces at work amid the "frantic panorama" of the city: "The whole at moments seemed to him lawless, Godless; the absence of intelligent, comprehensive purpose in the huge disorder, and the violent struggle to subordinate the result to the greater good, penetrated with its dumb appeal the consciousness of a man who had always been too self-enwrapt to perceive the chaos to which the individual selfishness must always lead" (HNF, 184).

Implicit here is a saving hope that individual *unselfishness* might work to undo the Godless chaos by leading to restored harmony within, and then among, individuals and thus to the reconciliation of human society with a divine order. The moral logic of Basil's thinking, like all of the Marches' efforts to make sense of the bewildering New York environment, is inflected by their fundamentally bourgeois values—values that Howells himself shared but that he felt were disintegrating under the weight of social disorder.

The narrative coherence of the novel depends on the loosely organizing device of *Every Other Week,* a literary magazine for which Jacob Dryfoos is the financial angel and to which all the other characters are more or less connected. March is enticed to join the staff by Fulkerson, an old Midwestern friend. As it happens, March has little choice in the matter: his prospects in Boston are as dim as were Howells's after the ruin of James R. Osgood. Although March's arrangement recalls Howells's contract with Franklin Square, Fulkerson's character was not based on either Alden or Harper, but rather on Ralph Keeler, a flamboyant and amusing California writer whom Howells knew well during the 1870s.[34]

---

33. Amy Kaplan, *The Social Construction of American Realism* (Chicago: University of Chicago Press, 1988), 61.

34. Ulrich Halfmann, ed., *Interviews with William Dean Howells* (Arlington, Tex.: American Literary Realism, 1973), 41. Halfmann asserts that Fulkerson "is generally thought to be modeled more after S. S. McClure [the hyperkinetic publishing magnate] than after Keeler" (124 n). But Howells's "Autobiographical" preface confirms what he told Robert Louis Stevenson in 1893: he had taken Fulkerson's name from a boyhood friend and his nature from Keeler (HNF, 504–5; SL, 4:49).

Fulkerson also recruits Angus Beaton, Alma Leighton, and Colonel Wood-burn, to whose daughter Madison he becomes engaged. The Woodburns, whom Howells regarded as "truthful types" of Southern aristocracy, were drawn from his memory of "a visit, already remote in time, which I had paid an Old Virginia capital" (*HNF*, 508). Alma Leighton, a type of the New Woman, owed something as well to the New York art school experiences of Howells's younger daughter, Mildred, and the frustrated literary aspira-tions of his favorite sister, Victoria, whose early death in 1886 had deeply affected him.[35]

Dryfoos's motive in backing *Every Other Week* is to dissuade the unworldly Conrad from entering the ministry by making him a publisher instead. The idea for a plutocrat's son turned socialist may have come to Howells after he attended a fashionable tea party one afternoon and met a "very rich young fellow" whose family owned a house at Newport, but who was also a member of the socialist cell whose meeting Howells had visited the same day (*SL*, 3:243). Conrad, with his piety and meekness, was meant to represent the nonviolent, Christian socialism that Howells connected with Tolstoy, in which religious vocation obviated political activism.

Berthold Lindau, on the other hand, reflected the fervid radicalism of the Haymarket anarchists. Inspired by an exiled revolutionist named Limbeck who had taught Howells German in his youth, Lindau engaged the novelist's sympathy. Howells later said that he felt "a tenderness for this character which I feel for no other in the book, and a reverence for an inherent nobleness in it" (*HNF*, 505)—a statement that suggests August Spies was another model for Lindau.

Lindau's radicalism is represented as a diabolical force in the novel. Not only does it breed discord among the staff of *Every Other Week*, causing a rift even between March and Fulkerson; it also leads to the death of an innocent man. The imaginative energy of *Hazard* is generated by the conflict between its ordering and disruptive elements—the struggle of the reasonable characters, especially the Marches, to contain the social and moral chaos that Lindau unleashes. As the problems of the surrounding city overrun the

35. On Alma Leighton and Victoria Howells, see Eric Cheyfitz, "*A Hazard of New Fortunes*: The Romance of Self-Realization," *American Realism: New Essays*, ed. Eric J. Sundquist (Baltimore: Johns Hopkins University Press, 1982), 62.

secure enclave of *Every Other Week,* it becomes clear that no sanctuary exists. The novel's "failures" of formal coherence—the "disproportionate length" of its opening and the meandering inconclusiveness of its final chapters— may be seen to mark its imaginative engagement with social realities too intractable for realistic treatment.[36] The narrative fabric of the novel itself unravels in the streetcar strike.

This episode was based on events that unfolded even as Howells was writing. Between January 29 and February 6, 1889, New York was convulsed by turmoil between striking traction workers and city authorities. The police were called in, ostensibly to protect nonunion replacements, and violence erupted. According to the *Times,* a medical student was bludgeoned by police as he tried to restrain an officer from attacking a crowd of strikers; it was later reported (erroneously) that a bystander in another such incident had been killed by police blows. The only confirmed death was that of a stableman, shot through the head. "The strike, the arrogance of the utility companies, the weakness of the state and its failure to intervene, the reported deaths, one by clubbing, the other by shooting, the victimization of bystanders as well as strikers—from this reality Howells built the climax of his novel."[37]

Into the shooting of Conrad Dryfoos and the grief of his father, Howells poured his anguish about Winifred. Like Winny, Conrad dies to no apparent purpose other than to satisfy the dreadful "law of death." Like Howells, Jacob Dryfoos is consumed by guilt, desperate to find some answer to the riddle of the painful earth. It is significant that Dryfoos seeks compassion from Beaton, who is too self-absorbed to comprehend the old man's need. If Dryfoos the stricken father echoed Howells's remorse about his beloved child, then Beaton the egoistic artist reflected Howells's ambivalence about his own literary career. In his youth, he had been instilled with his father's Swedenborgian belief that selfishness is the greatest of sins, and he never escaped the fear that his own success was founded on selfishness.[38] Had

36. As Kaplan remarks, "*Hazard* both fulfills and exhausts the project of realism to embrace social diversity within the outlines of a broader community, and to assimilate a plethora of facts and details into a unified narrative form." The disordered ending of *Hazard* "exposes the drive toward moral unity in realism as a dream of mastery to compensate for the lack of control" (*Social Construction,* 62–63).

37. Carter, introduction to *Hazard,* xxi–xxii.

38. On Howells's childhood religious training, see Rodney D. Olsen, *Dancing in Chains: The Youth of William Dean Howells* (New York: New York University Press, 1991).

fame and fortune made him incapable of "the immediate altruism dealing with what now is," which, as he told Hale (*SL*, 3:233), was prerequisite to social reform? Beaton is marked as the secret sharer of Howells's darkest self-doubt by his fur-lined overcoat—a sign, as Howells had admitted to James, of his own mental and moral insulation from the suffering of others (*SL*, 3:231).

Although *Hazard* is mainly concerned with the modern city as a site of social strife, the novel also explores the inner conflict of the writer torn between the aesthetic imperatives of his art and the political demands of his social conscience. One major theme is the chastening of Basil March as he moves from regarding New York, at an aesthetic distance, as "picturesque" material for a feuilleton to recognizing his moral implication in the life around him. What remains unanswered, however, is Tolstoy's question, "What to do?" Uncertain about the efficacy of fiction finally to do anything, Howells wished that his words could somehow become deeds as well. The most he could achieve in *Hazard*, as William Alexander remarks, was painfully to acknowledge his compromises and limitations and to hope that "by mirroring for Americans their own complacency and revealing the nature of the society for which they were ultimately responsible, he could still fulfill a mission to men's souls, and thus a mission to civilization."[39]

Howells's imaginative impetus during the 1880s—toward addressing public issues through insistently social realism—lost velocity in the course of *Hazard*, which ends with the brooding introspection of the Marches. Howells turned inward and backward in the next two books he would write in rapid succession during 1889–1890: *The Shadow of a Dream*, a Hawthornean tale in which the Marches confront not the perplexities of the city but the involutions of the human heart; *A Boy's Town*, a veiled autobiography in which Howells examined his own boyhood place in the vanished world of antebellum Ohio.

## VI

*A Hazard of New Fortunes* ran as an illustrated serial from March 23 to November 16, 1889. Placement in *Harper's Weekly* rather than *Harper's*

---

39. William Alexander, *William Dean Howells: The Realist as Humanist* (New York: Burt Franklin, 1981), 129.

*Monthly* (the usual venue for Howells's fiction) was a consequence of its extraordinary length, which only weekly installments could accommodate within one year. More important, the publishers regarded the *Weekly* as the more "political" of their magazines and thus more appropriate for a work with strong social content. Although Howells had substituted *Hazard* for the series of sketches urged on him by Harper and Alden, he still met the spirit of their expectations.[40]

Because they hoped that *Hazard* would attract a wider readership than Howells ordinarily enjoyed, the Harpers decided to issue it first in cheap paperback format. This edition, which was reset from the serial text in small type and double columns, was published on November 27, 1889 (although the title page was dated 1890); five thousand copies were printed. Meanwhile Howells attended to the trade editions. *Hazard* was issued first, for copyright purposes, by David Douglas of Edinburgh, his regular British publisher, and then in two volumes by Harper & Brothers on January 27, 1890.

Given his emotional investment in *Hazard,* Howells was unusually anxious about its reception. To his father, he expressed gloomy expectations: "Sometimes I think the public is thoroughly tired of me; heaven knows I'm tired of the public" (*SL,* 3:263). But *Hazard* proved to be a huge success: over 20,000 copies were sold in the first year. Howells boasted in 1898 that despite the "quiet indifference" of the public to the serial and his fears that the book "would fall stillborn," it had become "quite popular, and twice as many copies of it have been sold as of any one of my other novels."[41]

Contemporary reviews of *Hazard* were almost uniformly positive. Newspapers and magazines from all regions admired the ambitious scope of the novel, judging it an advance over Howells's Bostonian fiction. George W. Curtis was partisan but also representative in his opinion, delivered from the "Easy Chair" in *Harper's Monthly,* that *Hazard* "is what has long been desired and often attempted, but never before achieved, a novel of New York life in the larger sense." William Sharp in the *Academy,* reflecting the cooler British reception, doubted that Howells would endure but asserted that he was "the genuine connecting link between crude realists in method like Tolstoi, and

40. During the 1890s, Howells did finally write a few New York sketches. The best of them—including "An East-Side Ramble," "Tribulations of a Cheerful Giver," "New York Streets"—were collected in *Impressions and Experiences* (New York: Harper, 1896).
41. Halfmann, *Interviews with William Dean Howells,* 58.

the crude realists in thought like Zola."[42] Although reviewers acknowledged the novel's seriousness, noting the importance of Howells's "socialism," they also appreciated its humor—more fully, perhaps, than twentieth-century critics—and agreed that Fulkerson was the most vital character.

Privately, Howells's friends also heaped praise upon what Edward Everett Hale pronounced a "masterly" work: "It is good. It is good in all ways—chiefly because it will make people better. It will make them think and it will make them think right" (*SL*, 3:281 n). James Russell Lowell, Howells's revered Bostonian mentor, also valued the "deep moral" of the novel, which he liked "all the more, since it isn't rammed down my throat." These were the sentiments exactly of Samuel Clemens (seldom of one mind with the likes of Lowell), who admired the "high art" by which *Hazard* "is made to preach its great sermon without seeming to take sides or preach at all." The James brothers too were united in acclaim. "Never a weak note," wrote William James, "the number of characters, each intensely individual, the observation of detail, the everlasting wit and humor, and beneath all the bass accompaniment of the human problem, the entire Americanness of it, all make it a very great book." "The *Hazard* is simply prodigious," declared Henry James. "The life, the truth, the light, the heat, the breadth and depth and thickness . . . are absolutely admirable."[43]

Henry James's letter about *Hazard*—so prolix that he feared Howells might think him "demented with chatter"—was, in effect, both a private review of the novel and a declaration of artistic differences that sprang from amiable rivalry. Admixed with lavish praise were James's reservations about Howellsian realism, especially its formal looseness: "there's a whole quarter

---

42. Curtis, "Editor's Easy Chair," 313; Sharp, quoted in Clayton L. Eichelberger, *Published Comment on William Dean Howells through 1920: A Research Bibliography* (Boston: G. K. Hall, 1976), 105. British antagonism to Howells had been aroused by his 1886 essay on Henry James, in which he championed American realism at the expense of Dickens and Thackeray, and by his critical polemics in "The Editor's Study" throughout the later 1880s. Indignant about an upstart American's denigration of their native idols, British reviewers often avenged themselves on Howells's novels; and although the original intensity of the feud was waning by 1890, the reaction to *Hazard* was colored by transatlantic literary politics.

43. M. A. DeWolfe Howe, ed., *New Letters of James Russell Lowell* (New York: Harper, 1932), 335; Smith and Gibson, *Mark Twain–Howells Letters,* 630; Henry James, ed., *Letters of William James* (Boston: Houghton Mifflin, 1920), 1:298–99; Leon Edel, ed., *Henry James Letters; Volume III, 1883–1895* (Cambridge: Harvard University Press, 1980), 281.

of heaven upon which, in the matter of composition, you seem consciously—
*is* it consciously?—to have turned your back." More bluntly, James had
written to his brother William: "I have just been reading with wonder
and admiration, Howells's last big novel, which I think is so prodigiously
good and able and so beyond what he at one time seemed in danger of
reducing himself to, that I mean to write him a gushing letter about it. . . .
His abundance and facility are my constant wonder and envy—or rather not
perhaps, envy, inasmuch as he has purchased them by throwing the whole
question of form, style and composition overboard into the deep sea—from
which, on my side, I am perpetually trying to fish them up."[44]

More gratifying to Howells, perhaps, than the praise of friends and critics
was the knowledge that in reaching a broader audience *Hazard* might
influence ordinary readers. With quiet pride, he told his father about one of
them in describing a visit to Henry George's homely New York apartment:
"His family is fond of my books and they are reading the 'Hazard' aloud
to one daughter, who is sick" (*SL*, 4:102 n). *A Hazard of New Fortunes*
remained popular throughout Howells's lifetime; it went through numerous
reprintings, including a 1917 edition in Boni & Liveright's "Modern Library
of the World's Best Books."

By then, as he had confided to Henry James two years earlier, Howells
appraised himself as "comparatively a dead cult with my statues cast down
and the grass growing over them in the pale moonlight" (*SL*, 6:80). This
vision of pacific neglect did not foresee the vehemence of the assault launched
after his death in 1920 by H. L. Mencken, Sinclair Lewis, and other agents of
the ascendant moderns. Not content to let grass gently blanket the toppled
statues of The Dean's literary reputation, they were keen to drag these icons
into broad daylight and smash them to smithereens. As a result, all of
Howells's novels—*Hazard* no more or less than the others—suffered a steep
devaluation during the 1920s.

Since then, the fortunes of *Hazard* have followed the general trends in
Howells criticism, in which a rise in social consciousness has correlated with
renewed attention to Howells's "critical realism," especially his "socialist"
novels of the 1880s and 1890s. During the 1930s, when many critics were

44. Edel, *Henry James Letters,* 282; Albert Mordell, ed. *Discovery of a Genius: William Dean
Howells and Henry James* (New York: Twayne, 1961), 137.

mobilized by Marxism, *Hazard* was read as evidence of Howells's "bourgeois" and/or "reactionary" tendencies, his failure to be radical enough. Granville Hicks, the most influential and perceptive of American Marxist critics, treated Howells respectfully, but he ruefully noted that Howells was a victim of his middle-class loyalties. "No other American novel of the nineteenth century, except possibly *The Gilded Age,* can be compared in its scope with *A Hazard of New Fortunes,*" Hicks allowed. But "the reader, feeling that something important is being neglected, becomes impatient with the amount of attention devoted to the progress of the magazine, the home life of the Woodburns, and the various love stories."[45]

However scorned in some quarters, Howells was still a public figure in the 1930s. By the 1940s, like most writers of the nineteenth century, he was becoming a ward of the academic establishment, whose role was increasingly curatorial in regard to American literary history. That is, Howells's readership shrank almost exclusively to professors and their students; and, as Kenneth Eble bleakly predicted, he is not again "likely to become a common cultural possession."[46] With few exceptions, then, commentary on *Hazard* over the last fifty years has been confined to the intramural world of the university.

Whenever the mainstream of academic culture has drifted leftward, readings of *Hazard* tend to recapitulate Hicks's caveats. Thus Kenneth Lynn, writing early in the 1970s (before his own neoconservative turn), asserted that *Hazard* "fails to come to grips with the meaning of the life it spreads before us." Although Howells "endeavored to write a serious, indeed a tragic, study of human suffering and class antagonism," he defensively fell back on "all the devices of intellectual irony, anesthetizing wit, and comic perspective by which he had avoided the unpleasant implications of his urban material in *Silas Lapham.*" Likewise in the 1980s, in a study influential with proponents of political "intervention" by academic means, Alan Trachtenberg dismissed Howellsian realism, in *Hazard* and elsewhere, for its obliviousness to social realities: "Realism, then, brings Howells to the point where, in spite of himself, his fictions of the real disclose the unresolved gaps and rifts within the traditional world view he wishes to maintain, to correct and discipline. . . .

45. Granville Hicks, *The Great Tradition: An Interpretation of American Literature since the Civil War,* rev. ed. (New York: Macmillan, 1935), 87–88.
46. Kenneth E. Eble, *William Dean Howells* (Boston: Twayne, 1982), 190.

Resorting to romance, Howells conceded, without acknowledgment, the fundament of illusion on which his realism rested: the illusion and romance of 'America' itself."[47]

Howells's position has improved, however, whenever criticism has taken an aesthetic, rather than political, turn. A modern Howells revival began during the 1940s among those sympathetic to the emergent New Criticism and to the liberal anticommunist ethos of the Cold War academy. In an introduction to the 1952 reprint of *Hazard* in Dutton's "Everyman's Library"—the first reprint in many years—George Arms stressed the novel's comic and artistic elements, arguing that Howells was best understood as a satiric novelist of manners in the tradition of Jane Austen. In their major studies of Howells, such revivalists as George N. Bennett, Edwin H. Cady, Everett Carter, and Clara M. Kirk celebrated both the formal qualities of *Hazard* and its balanced vision of life. Richard Foster summed up this line of criticism in his 1959 essay on *Hazard* in which, following Lionel Trilling, he reclaimed Howells as a prophet of the liberal imagination. Howells's "freely skeptical but liberally humane intelligence . . . understood with such moral clarity the predicaments of our time": specifically, "the severance of the commercially structured present from the ways of life of the traditional past," and the consequent "displacement of the intellectual as the traditional spokesman for intelligence and responsibility in the arena of public action."[48]

During the 1960s, such critics as George C. Carrington and Kermit Vanderbilt explored a psychological and existential version of Howells that was extrapolated from Foster's alienated intellectual. Carrington, for instance, read *Hazard* as a bitterly satiric "anatomy-fiction" (a term borrowed from Northrop Frye) in which Howells "quashes one expectation and standard after another until we can be sure of little more than that the sun will

---

47. Kenneth S. Lynn, *William Dean Howells: An American Life* (New York: Harcourt Brace Jovanovich, 1971), 298–99; Alan Trachtenberg, *The Incorporation of America: Culture and Society in the Gilded Age* (New York: Hill & Wang, 1982), 192.

48. Richard Foster, "The Contemporaneity of Howells," *New England Quarterly* 32 (March 1959): 54–55, 78. In Trilling's landmark essay, "Howells and the Roots of Modern Taste," dis-ease with Howells's balanced and comic vision was linked to a modernist fascination with evil and apocalyptic tragedy: "It is possible that our easily expressed contempt for the smiling aspects and our covert impulse to yield to the historical process are a way of acquiring charisma. It is that peculiar charisma which has always been inherent in death" (*The Opposing Self: Nine Essays in Criticism* [New York: Viking, 1955], 102).

continue to rise." The reliability of the Marches is undercut at every turn; the plot is twisted into a parody of realism; any possibility of making sense of urban chaos is denied. "Having destroyed the possibility of solutions and the authority of solvers, Howells leaves us alone with the problem of the world itself. In no other Howells book is this problem thrust so rudely in the reader's face."[49]

*Hazard* largely disappeared from critical view during the 1970s and early 1980s as Howells was refashioned from an existential nihilist into a Freudian case, a man racked by neurotic vastations and sexual repression. Even George N. Bennett, who had emphasized Howells's social consciousness in an earlier study, now reread his "critical realism," including *Hazard*, as a deviation from the main line of his psychological realism.[50]

With the predominance of literary theory during the 1980s, *Hazard* regained a privileged place in the Howells canon. For those concerned with the articulation of gender, race, and class, his novels offered a multitude of interpretive possibilities; and along with *A Modern Instance* and *The Rise of Silas Lapham*, *Hazard* has elicited some of the best recent commentary. Just over a century since its publication, having withstood the vicissitudes of Howells's literary reputation as well as many changes in taste and critical ideology, *A Hazard of New Fortunes* remains a "classic" of American realism.

49. George C. Carrington Jr., *The Immense Complex Drama: The World and Art of the Howells Novel* (Columbus: Ohio State University Press, 1966), 82, 99.

50. George N. Bennett, *The Realism of William Dean Howells, 1889–1920* (Nashville: Vanderbilt University Press, 1973).

# "Quite the Best, 'All Round,' of All My Productions"

## The Multiple Versions of the Jamesian Germ for *The Ambassadors*

RICHARD A. HOCKS

§ § §

O NE OF THE better-known cases in American literature of a single generative incident which gave rise to a masterpiece by a major novelist is the famous "germ" of Henry James's *The Ambassadors:* when William Dean Howells purportedly stood in a Parisian garden owned by James McNeill Whistler sometime in 1894 and declared to his thirty-year-old confrere, Jonathan Sturges, "Live. Live all you can: it's a mistake not to." Rarely has a single genetic source so successfully initiated and eventually pervaded a great and hefty novel, playing itself out in multiple directions and culminating in what James later called "frankly, quite the best, 'all round,' of all my productions."[1]

It is fascinating to consider that, whereas *The Ambassadors*—presumably just because of this happy germ—was among the easiest of James's long novels to compose, it became one of the most difficult for him to publish.

---

1. Henry James, *Literary Criticism: French Writers, Other European Writers, the Prefaces to the New York Edition,* ed. Leon Edel and Mark Wilson (New York: Library of America, 1984), 1306; hereafter cited parenthetically in the text as *LC.* This, of course, is from James's preface to the New York Edition. For a possible "subconscious" connection between Strether's "live" speech and James's early character Louis Leverett in "A Bundle of Letters" (1879), see Oscar Cargill, *The Novels of Henry James* (New York: Macmillan, 1961), 304.

He had problems galore before it eventually ran in *The North American Review* in 1903 (not in *Harper's Monthly* as he expected) and was then published in England by Methuen and in America by Harper & Brothers with texts substantially different from the serial publication. And these texts, given James the incessant reviser, in turn differed significantly from one another. Add to all that the fact that the English and American editions had chapters 28 and 29 in reverse order and that both were different from the serial text—which had omitted chapter 28 altogether!—and you catch just a glimpse of the complications attending the publication and text of *The Ambassadors*.[2] Such combination of amazing ease in composition, answered in turn by maddening difficulty in publication, suggests that all of us in American literature might consider more sympathetically the validity of Emerson's doctrine of compensation. Interestingly, several years later, in his New York Edition preface, while commenting on *The Wings of the Dove*, a book that did get published pretty much on time even while *The Ambassadors* still endured its delays, James went out of his way to emphasize the severe composition problems of *The Wings* by contrast with *The Ambassadors* (*LC*, 1306).[3]

Perhaps by 1909 James had traveled sufficient distance from the publication problems of *The Ambassadors* that he did not say what he might well have: that *The Ambassadors* wrote easily but published hard, whereas *The Wings of the Dove* wrote hard but published rather easily. What he did say that bears directly on these questions, however, was that *The Wings of the Dove* had finally freed him from the restrictions of serial publication: indeed, neither *The Wings* nor its successor, *The Golden Bowl*, was published serially before their first English and American editions.[4] Besides its being James's last novel published serially, *The Ambassadors* is also the only James novel with a surviving, very Jamesian, prose Scenario, sent to Harper's in 1900 and entitled "Project of Novel," a document the novelist himself in a letter to H. G.

2. For an excellent concise summary of these publishing difficulties see Henry James, *The Ambassadors: A Norton Critical Edition*, ed. S. P. Rosenbaum (New York: W. W. Norton, 1994), 354–70. Further references are to this edition unless stated otherwise; hereafter cited as *A*.

3. Compare *A*, 3; also Henry James, *The Wings of the Dove: A Norton Critical Edition*, ed. J. Donald Crowley and Richard A. Hocks (New York: W. W. Norton, 1978), 459.

4. For James's comments on this issue, see his letter to H. G. Wells in Crowley and Hocks, *Wings of the Dove*, 455, and *A*, 407.

Wells two years later wrongly stated was destroyed.[5] I shall return to that Scenario document presently. What I propose is to concentrate not on James's publishing woes but on the multiple reiterations of the generative germ that seem to have made his composition so easy; this germ has set the initial parameters and guidelines for our criticism and interpretation ever since.

It may surprise even readers familiar with this book and some of the vast scholarship it generated to realize that there are probably more than half a dozen extant versions of the germ, some before the novel, one within it, and some after it. Of course the actual number of versions depends, as such things generally do, on how you count. The very first instance of the germ speech is not preserved because it was only related orally to James by Sturges. But whatever Howells actually said in McNeill Whistler's garden was less than what James said in his first entry in his *Notebooks* eighteen months later, October 31, 1895—the second version, if you will, of the incident and speech: "Oh, you are young, you are young—be glad of it and *live*. Live all you can: it's a mistake not to. It doesn't so much matter what you do—but live. This place makes it all come over me. I see it now. I haven't done so— and now I'm old. It's too late. It has gone past me—I've lost it. You have time. You are young. Live!"[6] James immediately adds, "I amplify and improve a little—but that was the tone. It touches me—I can see him—I can hear him."

Henry James, I hope we can agree, not only "hears" Howells, he rather begins to reinvent Howells's outburst on the spot; he responds with more than Wordsworthian "wise passiveness" to the impulse transmitted by Sturges's account the previous evening. Just how drastically nonpassive James can be in this regard is flagged by his own words *amplify* and *improve;* such nonpassivity is really borne out by the full notebook passage itself, which turns out to be a model of germ-plus-reflection through productive self-talk. By the end of it, James has come an astonishingly long way into his "Howellsian" character and situation, all in the space of roughly 1,400 words; the man is a widower, coming out to retrieve the son of a widow to whom he is engaged to be married; he is fifty-five; he undergoes a total volte-face of his mission; he feels the dumb passion of desire even though "it's too late now,

5. Letter to Wells, in Crowley and Hocks, *Wings of the Dove,* 454–55, and *A,* 406–7.

6. Henry James, *The Complete Notebooks of Henry James,* ed. Leon Edel and Lyall H. Powers (New York: Oxford University Press, 1987), 141 (hereafter cited parenthetically as *CN* ); compare *A,* 374.

for HIM to live"; he is "literary almost . . . The Editor of a Magazine . . . not at all of a newspaper" (*CN*, 141). James even thinks in terms of the tale's burgeoning genre, of his "deepen[ing] the irony, the tragedy" (*A*, 375–76). In short, James's 1895 notebook entry is an ideal exemplum of the operation of the generic germ or "suggestive virus" he later explained at once so ponderously and so poetically in his New York Edition preface to *The Spoils of Poynton.* We could say that a figure originating in Howells might well be "literary almost," might surely be an "Editor of a Magazine"; yet the notebook entry is impressive precisely by the extent that Howells seems to disappear into the enveloping field of the burgeoning figure whose character, as with the earlier Isabel Archer, for example, is in process of determining his incidents, of turning the Aristotelian relationship inside out.

Another feature of this first entry, or second version of the germ, is that James conceives the fundamental ambience of character and situation to be one of sorrow, of tragedy and irony. Later he will add more consciously the element of comedy to the novel. To this day, however, all readers and critics alike of *The Ambassadors* have to deal with its beautifully mixed tonal mode. Like *Don Quixote*, which elicits its "hard" and "soft" readings, each of which may go in and out of fashion, *The Ambassadors* can modulate from a sort of Freudian "Mourning and Melancholia" text to a sharp comedy of manners tethered to curiosity, bewilderment, miscalculation, and misinterpretation—somewhat like Molière. James preserves this mixed mode right to the very last lines of the novel itself, when we read that Maria Gostrey "sighed it at last, all comically, all tragically, away" (*A*, 347). Her "sigh," we might well say, started all the way back with his, the man in the garden's, in the earliest versions of the germ. Et in Arcadia Ego.

The third version of the germ comes from James's remarkable "Project of Novel," the 20,000-word Scenario sent in the autumn of 1900 to Harper & Brothers after his agent, James B. Pinker, had first seen it. We know from James's 1902 letter to Wells not only that he thought it had been destroyed, as earlier mentioned, but also that this scenario was twice the length of the one he wrote for *The Wings of the Dove,* the latter read at one stage by Joseph Conrad and afterward lost.[7] Perhaps simply because of its length and amplitude, one guesses that, by comparison with other scenarios

7. See the letter to Wells in Crowley and Hocks, *Wings of the Dove*, 454–55, and in *A*, 406–7.

that may not have survived, James's "Project of Novel" is an extraordinary
piece of writing, at times resembling one of his own nouvelles, at other
times reminding the reader, almost with a jolt, that this "text" is actually
an extended statement to his publisher, and yet one that also resembles
the procreative self-talk found in the *Notebooks*—with which, by the way,
James's successive sets of editors, Matthiessen and Murdock, and now Leon
Edel and Lyall Powers, have consistently published it. Indeed, Martha Banta's
observation seven years ago about James's notebooks generally, that they
reveal his "access to the writer's workplace" and the "principle of rank
organicism let loose upon the world,"[8] is exemplified to a very high degree in
the "Project of Novel." Our reacting to it as a creative work is salutary, I think,
if only to turn our minds away momentarily from the sort of issue we usually
attend to, such as Waymarsh's name here being "Waymark" or Little Bilham's
being "Burbage," or such matters as Strether's young son having died by a
swimming accident, or else that the "vulgar little article of domestic use"
produced by Mr. Newsome in Hartford or Worcester (not yet Woollett) is
"to be duly specified" (*CN*, 547)—which of course it never is. These issues,
I say, are momentarily put aside if we attend instead just to the way James
now conceives and molds his main character, allows Strether's consciousness
to unfold, then punctuates the Scenario with clusters of dialogue between
Strether and Gostrey, Strether and Chad, Strether and Madame de Vionnet,
simulating in advance and in miniature the picture/scene modulation which
is a hallmark of *The Ambassadors* itself.

If one has ever spent much time studying James's tales, his "Project of
Novel," I would argue, really "wants to" act like a tale, like a nouvelle, and
either cannot quite do it, or else all but does it, depending on your emphasis.
James divides his Scenario into a prologue followed by three numbered
sections of the same length, each corresponding to a successive stage in
Strether's experience and together executing his hero's evolution somewhat
like the Meyer Abrams concept of the "spiral return" proposed by Daniel
Fogel in his 1981 study of James.[9] Such structuring and formal numbering,
together with a spiderlike descent into the web of Strether's mind, is what

8. Martha Banta, " 'There's Surely a Story in It': James's *Notebooks* and the Working Artist,"
*Henry James Review* 9 (1988): 153–64.
9. Daniel Mark Fogel, *Henry James and the Structure of the Romantic Imagination* (Baton
Rouge: Louisiana State University Press, 1981).

makes the Scenario suggestive of a Jamesian tale. The one major ingredient missing, however, is his rich imagery, the highly dominant metaphorical language of James in 1900, the same year, for example, that he penned "The Great Good Place," with its rich abstract language in tandem with its highly charged metaphors and conceits. This lack of such imagery—there is a small amount in the Scenario—is mainly what prevents me from suggesting that "Project of Novel" is to *The Ambassadors* what the Rembrandt sketch, let us say, is to the major oil canvas. What makes me think of the analogy, however, is the obvious parallel of a major artist doing in effect something like a preliminary sketch.

My principal topic remains the germ, and in this Scenario we actually get two statements of it, thus constituting versions three and four in my count. The first and richer of the two is not only in the prologue, but for all intents and purposes it is the prologue, the whole of it, which suggests that, structurally speaking, the prologue stands in relation to the three numbered, untitled sections pretty much as does the Scenario itself to the composed novel. In any case, James now formally identifies the episode as "my starting point" and "the germ of my subject." The incident this time is far more delineated than in 1895. First of all, he carefully evokes the Sunday afternoon garden party and meticulously explains the geography and architecture of the "old houses of the Faubourg St.-Germain," identifying the residence and garden both of McNeill Whistler (here called simply "a friend of mine") and also a very similar house "contiguous" with it in which James himself had spent considerable time. This careful preliminary description, begun in order to convince the publisher that he can reliably "focus the setting," soon gives rise to a cascade of personal associations and memories analogous to the nostalgic mood and ambience out of which the "anecdote" of the older, "distinguished and mature" man's lament to the younger man bursts forth. James reads into the Howells figure the pith and precision of his character's emotion, calling it at one point a sense of seductive European charm that— for an American—"was practically as new, as up-to-that-time unrevealed (as one may say) as it was picturesque and agreeable" (*CN*, 541–42). Gradually he introduces the speech by writing, "Well, this is what the whole thing, as with a slow rush the sense of it came over him, made him say":

> "Oh, you're young, you're blessedly young—be glad of it; be glad of it and
> *live*. Live all you can: it's a mistake not to. It doesn't so much matter what

you do—but live. This place and these impressions, as well as many of
those, for so many days, of So-and So's and So and So's life, that I've been
receiving and that have had their abundant message, make it all come over
me. I see it now. I haven't done so enough before—and now I'm old; I'm,
at any rate, too old for what I see. Oh, I *do* see, at least—I see a lot. It's
too late. It has gone past me. I've lost it. It couldn't, no doubt, have been
different for me—for one's life takes a form and holds one: one lives as one
can. But the point is that you have time. That's the great thing. You're, as I
say, damn you, so luckily, so happily, so hatefully young. Don't be stupid.
Of course I don't dream you are, or I shouldn't be saying these awful things
to you. Don't, at any rate, make my mistake. Live!" (*CN*, 542–43)[10]

Believe it or not, immediately after this passage (as well as the preceding
evocation of setting and memories and associations) James simply writes,
"I amplify and improve a little, but that was the essence and the tone"
(*CN*, 543). These, of course, are the exact words he told himself five years
earlier, after rendering the anecdote in his notebook based on Sturges's
conversation. Clearly, each time Henry James "amplifies and improves a
little" his inch turns into a more extended ell and he guesses still more of
the unseen from the seen. Banta has likened his notebooks to Thoreau's
celebrated journal, and if that is so, I wonder if James's understated "amplify
and improve a little, but that was the essence," might not begin to sound a
bit like Thoreau's famous cryptic observation: "Thus was my first year's life
in the woods completed; and the second year was similar to it." In any case,
he summarizes the germ-episode and concludes his prologue by referring to
the foregoing as the "dropped seed" from which "the real magic of the *right*
things" were "to spring" (*CN*, 543). This is a Jamesian template for genesis,
composition, and, to some extent, nascent interpretation all together.

There is also a briefer second variation of the germ in James's Scenario—
my number four (or your number three if you wish to designate the actual
Sturges conversation with Howells the "urtext," which somehow to me seems
like the wrong thing for people who really care about genesis to do). This
next instance occurs in section 2 of the Scenario because it coordinates

10. James's reiteration of the "too late" theme in all major versions of the germ speech is
likewise anticipated in an earlier notebook entry, February 5, 1895, which begins "What is there
in the idea of *Too late*" (*CN*, 112).

with its midpoint stage in the plot. James refers to it here as the "very special note . . . alluded to in my few preliminary pages" (*CN*, 556)—that is, in the prologue. He speaks again, too, of "do[ing] the occasion and the picture, of evok[ing] the places and influences," and he also speaks of Strether as our "fermenting friend," and of the moment charged with "wonderful intensity . . . a real date" (*CN*, 557). He even returns to the germ speech itself, but this time presents it more briefly and through indirect discourse: "He [Strether] can't, at such a time of day, begin to live—for he feels, besides, with all the rush of the reaction against his past, that he *hasn't* lived" (*CN*, 558), and so on.

There are a number of fascinating issues that engage the James critic when he or she puts down this scenario and thinks about the novel, or vice versa. None of them is really independent of the originating germ because of its extraordinary interconnection with all that occurs in the book it brought forth. Yet one can undoubtedly distinguish between certain ideas that are more or less emphasized in the Scenario and in the novel respectively. For example, James makes a great point of saying he must, and will, "do" Mrs. Newsome in the novel, though she never directly appears; and all readers agree that that is just what he did. On the other hand, the Scenario itself "does" a memorable job of cumulatively summarizing and specifying all the advantages that Strether stands to lose if he sides with Chad and Marie away from Mrs. Newsome and Sarah Pocock, whereas in the novel itself the particularity of that substantial sacrifice has to be mostly inferred by the reader, except for one episode on Chad's balcony—overlooking the Blvd. Malesherbes and the prosperous good life of Paris's right bank—in which Chad, apparently testing the waters for any cupidity in Strether (and finding none), alludes suggestively to all that Strether will have to renounce. Chad is suggestive, yes, but not comprehensive, never exhibiting James's own solidity of specification found in the Scenario. Surely the key here was James's committed point of view: that is, Strether's character as "deputy" throughout the story virtually disallows such specific massing together of his own advantages-in-jeopardy, because Strether has no more fundamental drive for worldly goods than has, say, Merton Densher in *The Wings of the Dove.*

Another interesting feature that shows up when one comes to the Scenario with both the novel and the 1895 notebook entry in mind, simultaneously, is that James is marrying a comedy of manners to the book's melancholia. That is, he continues to speak of Strether as "rueful" and of the proposed work as "the whole comedy, or tragedy, the drama, whatever we call it" (*CN*, 564). As the plot-directed reversals begin to cascade, the second wave of ambassadors arrives, "Waymark" finally gets his second wind with Sarah, Jim Pocock is ready to live all *he* can—these and many other similar elements achieve that Quixote-like suspension referred to earlier, as the comic personality of the book competes with its originating meditative theme of "too late," found back in James's February 1895 notebook. Such competing moods, however, do not change James's hope, at the end of the Scenario, that this work would possess the structure and, one assumes, the beauty of "a rounded medallion, in a series of a dozen hung, with its effect of high relief, on a wall" (*CN*, 575–76). Considering his eventual judgment of the work and its effective twelve-book structure, one must assume that James believed he had indeed crafted some such medallionlike series—despite, for instance, the continuing scholarly dispute about the alleged reversal of chapters 28 and 29 in the first American and New York editions, a debate most recently joined by Jerome McGann. Since the dispute inevitably involves the question of temporal sequence, perhaps its lesson is to remind us that in late James much of the "main" action occurs retrospectively, is recollected in the mind at a sometimes unspecified future moment. McGann's witty hypothesis counteracting the prevailing view regarding which chapter belongs first at least makes us re-appreciate the nonlinear element always present in James's late retrospective narrative method.[11]

The fifth version of the germ is the one that is, I trust, already most familiar to the reader of this essay, and that is, of course, the fully realized episode in the second chapter of Book Fifth of *The Ambassadors*. When a reader examines this powerful moment in the novel itself on the heels of studying the October 1895 notebook entry and then the prologue to the

11. The chapter dispute, that is, has itself taken an entirely new "reversal" by McGann's essay, "Revision, Rewriting, Rereading; or 'An Error [Not] in *The Ambassadors*,'" *American Literature* 64 (March 1992): 95–110, in which he makes a playful, ingenious claim that it was the first English Edition—which James did not use for his Scribner's revision—that has the chapters in the wrong order, whereas the first American Edition—which James did revise from—had the chapter sequence right all along (the magazine text, as mentioned earlier, had omitted chapter 28 altogether). Hence, for McGann, all the editions we used to believe had it "wrong" have been right, and the ones we now think have "corrected" it (including Rosenbaum's Norton Critical Edition, cited in this essay) have it wrong!

1900 Scenario, he or she perforce is struck by the evolving progression of all three versions as well as by the full creative flowering James accomplished in the novel. First, the preliminary ambience of the occasion stressed by James in the Scenario is now extended and distributed over the first chapter of Book Fifth and halfway into the second; Strether is given ample time to imbibe the seductive charm of the visual scene in Gloriani's garden, to let the "rather grey interior" of his mind "drink in for once the sun of a clime not marked in his old geography" (*A*, 120). James follows this with the impact of Strether's introduction to Madame de Vionnet, who impresses him as no one has since his arrival from America except, quite arguably, the transformed Chad himself, who whisks her away almost immediately after Strether receives the full measure of her charming presence, leaving him alone once more with Little Bilham and thus ready to deliver the germ speech.

The speech in *The Ambassadors,* far more than in the Scenario, has the character of a full soliloquy except that Little Bilham's presence, of course, disqualifies it technically as one. James, as the poet says, loads his rift with ore, principally by interlacing the rhetorical stages of the speech with figurative language presumably welling out from Strether because of the emotion and intensity of the moment:

It's not too late for *you,* on any side, and you don't strike me as in danger of missing the train; besides which people can be in general pretty well trusted, of course—with the clock of their freedom ticking so loud as it seems to do here—to keep an eye on the fleeting hour. All the same don't forget that you're young—blessedly young; be glad of it on the contrary and live up to it. Live all you can; it's a mistake not to. It doesn't so much matter what you do in particular, so long as you have your life. If you haven't had that what *have* you had? This place and these impressions—mild as you may find them to wrap a man up so; all my impressions of Chad and of people I've seen at *his* place well, have had their abundant message for me, have just dropped *that* into my mind. I see it now. I haven't done so enough before— and now I'm too old; too old at any rate for what I see. Oh I *do* see, at least; and more than you'd believe or I can express. It's too late. And it's as if the train had fairly waited at the station for me without my having had the gumption to know it was there. Now I hear its faint receding whistle miles and miles down the line. What one loses one loses; make no mistake about that. The affair—I mean the affair of life—couldn't, no doubt, have been different for me; for it's at the best a tin mould, either fluted or embossed, with ornamental excrescences, or else smooth and dreadfully plain, into which, a helpless jelly, one's consciousness is poured—so that one "takes" the form, as the great cook says, and is more or less compactly held by it: one lives in fine as one can. Still, one has the illusion of freedom; therefore don't be, like me, without the memory of that illusion. I was either, at the right time, too stupid or too intelligent to have it; I don't quite know which. Of course at present I'm a case of reaction against the mistake; and the voice of reaction should, no doubt, always be taken with an allowance. But that doesn't affect the point that the right time is now yours. The right time is *any* time that one is still so lucky as to have. You've plenty; that's the great thing; you're, as I say, damn you, so happily and hatefully young. Don't at any rate miss things out of stupidity. Of course I don't take you for a fool, or I shouldn't be addressing you thus awfully. Do what you like so long as you don't make *my* mistake. For it was a mistake. Live! (*A,* 131–32)[12]

Apart from the pacing of this speech (James says, "with full pauses and straight dashes, Strether had so delivered himself" [*A,* 132]) and the iterative use of the word *mistake,* somewhat like incremental repetition in poetry, it is the striking insertion of the metaphors that seems to bind this chapter to the novel as a whole, thus collaborating James's view that the germ stretches out from one end of the book to the other. For example, the train that Strether laments missing, even though it awaited him past departure time, so to speak, is finally "caught" by him later in Book Eleventh (a train he "selected almost at random," says the text [*A,* 302]), when he rides it to the French countryside and eventually chances upon Chad and Madame de Vionnet in an attitude inferring their sexual intimacy, thereby collapsing his own elevated interpretation of what Little Bilham has called their "virtuous attachment." In other words, the train metaphor points directly across the canvas of the novel to its great recognition/meditation scene, which, reminiscent of Isabel Archer's all-night vigil in *The Portrait of a Lady,* might likewise be described with James's language from the preface to *The Portrait*

12. It is noteworthy that this central speech was not substantially revised from either the first American or first English editions, aside from the removal of a few commas in keeping with James's general style in the New York Edition; compare *The Ambassadors* (New York: Harper & Brothers, 1903), 149–50; furthermore, it is at least possible that the metaphorical train's receding "whistle" may be James's punning "signature" for the originating germ-location, so to speak, at the home of James McNeill Whistler.

as "obviously the best thing in the book, but it is only a supreme illustration of the general plan" (*LC*, 1084).

Next, the metaphor of the "great cook" and his "tin mould" for ornamental jellied dishes, although its immediate function is surely to represent the limitations of human agency, is another image that extends across the entire book in both directions, establishing connection with Strether's series of meals that act as benchmarks of his European apprenticeship. First there is his recollection of dining out back home with Mrs. Newsome, which occurs during the excitement of his very different evening dinner in Book Second at his London hotel with Maria Gostrey, whose dress is " 'cut down,' as he believed the term to be, in respect to shoulders and bosom, in a manner quite other than Mrs. Newsome's" (*A*, 42). Then there is the soft, sensual meal in Book Seventh on the left bank with Madame de Vionnet after he runs into her by accident at Notre Dame Cathedral, a meal that marks still greater initiation away from the Puritan tone of his evenings out with Mrs. Newsome and also, to Strether's own surprise, at a considerable distance even from his outing in London with Maria Gostrey. Still later, in Book Eleventh, there is the meal set for him by the hostess at the Cheval Blanc in the rustic village Strether wanders into. He is "hungry," has worked up an "appetite," and is told by the hostess that "she had in fact just laid the cloth for two persons who, unlike Monsieur, had arrived by the river—in a boat of their own." Strether is even offered "a 'bitter' before his repast." The next stage of initiation, then, is the awkward meal he must share with Chad and Marie de Vionnet after he accidentally espies them, "prodigious, a chance in a million," in the boat together, after which all three must sit down to eat (*A*, 308, 310). His "bitter" thus becomes his "repast," so to speak, and all three eventually continue the charade, though thinly, by riding back to the city on the train. No wonder Strether later that evening in meditation thinks of Chad and Marie's make-believe as "disagree[ing] with his spiritual stomach" (*A*, 315).

The tin-mould metaphor functions also, however, as the principal signifier of consciousness and freedom, or, more properly, as both the limitations and felt experiences of human freedom. James chooses the germ speech itself as the repository within the novel to embed the book's central philosophical question, whether or not we act as free agents. Strether is of course a character, not the author, and yet a large number of readers, not without encouragement from James, tend to read this book as in part a kind of spiritual autobiography; that, too, may suggest why the process of composition was comparatively so effortless. Even if we do not identify Strether all that closely with James, we do sense that at least these statements about the nature of consciousness and freedom are unusually authorial. But then again, when Strether goes on to say, "don't be, like me, without the memory of that illusion," we feel we *are* back with the character, with the "mature and distinguished man" who originated, distantly, in Howells. Although this essay is not the place to address the matter, the concept of there being varying degrees of fixed sensibility and consciousness, from plain to ornamental, in tandem with the concept of freedom as illusion—this is an intricately mediating philosophical stance between the traditional competing arguments of freedom and determinism; and it answers precisely to the nuanced position taken by Henry James's brother William James in his philosophical doctrines.[13] What should be stressed in this regard is that Henry James's philosophical "indeterminism," to appropriate William James's term, is given credence not only by the sheer variety of consciousnesses and the positive side of freedom as an actual, functioning illusion, but also by the emphatically "chance" encounters that transpire in the novel, such as Strether's encounter with Marie at Notre Dame or with the couple in the boat at Cheval Blanc at the end of a train "selected almost at random."

What James has done with the germ speech in the novel, then, is to take the all-too-human moment and weave his philosophical, thematic, and character studies into it through a poetics of metaphor and motif, a process suggesting those linked medallions he hoped for in his Scenario to Harper's. Even the metaphor of the clock, whose loud ticking Strether associates with freedom, is implicitly a complex image consistent with these ideas above: for while the clock is rhetorically associated with the free European life, as opposed to New England constriction, perhaps, the selfsame image is psychologically associated with the speaker's feeling that for him it is "too late," which is why the clock ticks so loud. The sense that Strether cannot ultimately transcend his own temperament—which is also the sense in which "the illusion of freedom" sounds its negative side—is captured at the end of the novel in Book Twelfth, when Strether humorously compares himself and

13. See my *Henry James and Pragmatistic Thought: A Study in the Relationship between the Philosophy of William James and the Literary Art of Henry James* (Chapel Hill: University of North Carolina Press, 1974).

his adventure to one of the figures on the clock in Berne, Switzerland, who came out on one side, "jigged along their little course in the public eye," and went back in on the other side (*A*, 344). Like the actual train rides compared to the metaphorical trains, the Berne clock diminishes the expectations of free autonomy proposed by the ticking metaphorical clock. For despite his sense of new personal freedom when he first arrives from America, despite his fermenting declaration to live, despite his cultivating a European appetite, Strether cannot transcend his own temperament, even though his, fortunately, is one greatly embossed and not at all "dreadfully plain." No wonder Emerson in his great bittersweet essay "Experience" denominated temperament one of the "lords of life."

The sixth and seventh versions of the germ reside briefly in two letters to Howells, written almost exactly a year apart. The first, in August 1900, precedes not only the publication but also at least part of the composition of the novel, though it does clearly succeed the "detailed Scenario," since James actually refers to it in the letter as having been "[drawn] up a year ago." Sequentially speaking, perhaps I should call this letter to Howells number five and the novel itself number six, unless, of course, James had already finished composing Book Fifth by the time of this letter, which is quite possible. Whichever be the case, he speaks of the work as "lovely— human, dramatic, international, exquisitely 'pure,' exquisitely everything; only absolutely condemned, from the germ up to be workable in not less than 100,000 words." "From the germ up" insinuates the same sense of ease and frictionless composition found again and again with *The Ambassadors*. Along the same lines, James speaks of himself at that moment as a "Cheerful Internationalist," and again of his work as a "form of Cheer."[14]

The second letter, written a year later, in August 1901, comes after James has completed the novel and sent it off to Harper's. This statement, my number seven, is also the one in which he finally declares to Howells that he was the germ. For the novel

> had its earliest origin in a circumstance mentioned to me—years ago—
> in respect to no less a person than yourself. At Torquay, once, our young
> friend Jon. Sturges came down to spend some days near me, and, lately

---

14. *Henry James Letters; Volume IV, 1895–1916*, ed. Leon Edel (Cambridge: Harvard University Press, 1984), 160.

from Paris, repeated to me five words you had said to him one day on his meeting you during a call at Whistler's. I thought the words charming—you have probably quite forgotten them; and the whole incident suggestive—so far as it was an incident; and, more than this, they presently caused me to see in them the faint vague germ, the mere point of the start, of a subject.[15]

James thereupon expounds in his own way a mysterious paradox about his creative process: that Howells is at once deeply disconnected from the novel while, in another sense, and only after the fact, very much reconnected with it. "My point," he says, "is that it had long before—it had in the very act of striking me as a germ—got away from *you* or anything like you! had become impersonal and independent. Nevertheless," James continues, "your initials figure in my little note; and if you hadn't said the five words to Jonathan, he wouldn't have had them (most sympathetically and interestingly) to relate, and I shouldn't have had them to work in my imagination. The moral is that you are responsible for the whole business."[16] Both sides of this alchemic equation are undoubtedly true. That is, Howells had turned into the "distinguished and mature" literary man almost immediately in James's gestation process. At the same time, James's half-humorous declaration that the moral is that Howells is responsible for it all reaffirms the deep and mysterious sense of life's interconnectedness. Philosophically, it is William James's definition of unity as residing in conjunction, confluence, and ambulation through every intervening part of experience; dramatically, it is one with Strether's lament and defense to Sarah Pocock's accusations that "Everything has come as a sort of indistinguishable part of everything else" (*A*, 279); genetically, it is the recognition that the initials "W. D. H." in his 1895 notebook entry signal an initiating germ whose metamorphosis extended all the way through to the completion of the novel. As for the five words, one imagines they were "Live. Live all you can." More than likely there were other words related to James by Sturges, though probably not too many. And the ones there were James had long ago distilled in his own mind down to these five, before he then began to "amplify and improve a little."[17]

15. Ibid., 199.
16. Ibid.
17. A year later, in 1902, one may still sense the staying power, so to speak, of the "germ" sentiment in a letter from James to Edith Wharton, wherein he tells her that "my desire earnestly,

The eighth and last variation of the germ is found in James's New York Edition preface to *The Ambassadors*, written in 1909. This final reference is, in one sense, the most exuberant commentary yet, primarily because James in rereading his novel was struck afresh by the sheer extent to which the initiating germ permeates the novel from one end to the other. In no other preface does he begin like this: "Nothing is more easy than to state the subject of 'The Ambassadors,' " or "Nothing can exceed the closeness with which the whole fits again into its germ," or "Never can a composition of this sort have sprung straighter from a dropped grain of suggestion," or "never can that grain, developed, overgrown and smothered, have yet lurked more in the mass as an independent particle" (*LC*, 1304–5). And so he takes us still again to Strether's "irrepressible outburst" to Little Bilham in Gloriani's garden on Sunday afternoon, this time rendering the germ speech from bits and combinations of language found in the 1895 notebook, from the prologue to the Scenario, and from the novel itself, although much reduced and hence considerably diminished in size from the novel's extended soliloquy. James reiterates the point that he can remember "no occasion on which, so confronted [with a germ], I had found it of livelier interest to take stock, in this fashion, of suggested wealth." For this reason he concludes, "Fortunately thus I am able to estimate this as, frankly, quite the best, 'all round,' of all my productions" (*LC*, 1305, 1306). The word *fortunately* is the key word here, in part because the germ itself was such a fortunate one, but more importantly because James realized that, given such a quintessentially ideal "seed," had the book composed from it not been so successful, that outcome might have invalidated his conception of his own creative process. One can almost hear the relief, therefore, when James recognizes that, whereas his second best book, *The Portrait of a Lady,* was a "beautiful difficulty," this one, which seemed to write itself from the germ up, was yet, on re-perusal, his best. Indeed, that note of compositional ease simply suffuses this entire preface: at one point he compares the writing process to "the monotony of fine weather," at another point he says that the steps and stages of his "fable"

---

tenderly, intelligently [is] to admonish you while you are young, free, expert, exposed (to illumination) . . . admonish you, I say, in favor of the *American Subject*. There it is round you. Don't pass it by—the immediate, the real, the ours, the yours, the novelist's that it waits for. Take hold of it and keep hold, and let it pull you where it will" (James, *Letters*, vol. 4, 235–36).

placed themselves with such promptness that he himself huffed and puffed "from a good way behind, to catch up with them, breathless and a little flurried, as [I] best could" (*LC*, 1306, 1311).

This preface, of course, addresses a number of other items, mostly technical ones, which have long since been the province of James scholarship and criticism. The most familiar include the necessity to restrict the point of view to Strether as a third-person "register" (together with the comparative drawbacks of first-person narration); the more complicated function of a *ficelle* figure like Maria Gostrey transcending her role; the successful "alternations" of picture and scene; the successful presence, throughout, of the "grace of intensity." And yet, beyond these admittedly important technical considerations, James obviously feels the intense presence of his hero, whose germ speech is now called "melancholy eloquence," who allows James the opportunity to "bite into" the "promise of a hero so mature," and whose fundamental character gives him the "immeasurable" chance to " 'do' a man of imagination" (*LC*, 1306–7). Upon rereading the novel, James sees that the power of this germ's habitat in the depths of Strether's character is what enables the novel both to have " 'led up' to" the melancholy outburst in the garden and, just as important, to have followed through with Strether's "very gropings" to the end. One of James's most perspicacious remarks in this respect is that Strether's irrepressible outburst to Bilham is likewise "the voice of the false position" (*LC*, 1309, 1313). Such an assessment may open up the novel for a critique of Strether by a certain kind of critic so predisposed, yet it equally permits an empathetic approach to him by a very differently minded critic, since a "false position," for the latter, is the human one; and besides, it resides more or less halfway through Strether's adventure and does not necessarily mean to characterize the ending—where the first critic, so to speak, already awaits and says it does. These opposing critical positions, each responding to Strether's decline of Maria Gostrey's proffered love and his decision to leave for home, have solid enough Jamesian justification: the first has the continuity of Strether's deepest unyielding "temperament," the Emersonian lord of life; the second has James's commitment to a dynamic central character, one who can have a bildungsroman experience in middle age, who lives in a William Jamesian world where things are never static but always "in the making." As for James himself, he concludes the preface rejoicing that "the Novel [as a genre] remains still, under the right persuasion, the most independent, most elastic, most prodigious of literary forms" (*LC*, 1321). This has, unmistakably, that same note of "cheer" found in the 1900 letter to Howells written in the midst of the novel's composition. Rereading *The Ambassadors* convinced Henry James that it was indeed a novel "under the right persuasion."

Let me conclude this essay with some reflections about *The Ambassadors* and Jamesian revision—an old topic made new again by several recent scholarly hypotheses.[18] A study of James's various germs for *The Ambassadors* reinforces what the textual evidence already reveals, that he did not feel the need for much revision in the New York Edition since his conception of the novel was never problematic in the way it was, for example, in *The Wings of the Dove*, a novel more extensively revised.[19] But there is a larger sense in which *The Ambassadors* itself perhaps was a "revision." When in his final preface to *The Golden Bowl* James formally addresses the broader issue of revision in his collected writings, he explains that, for him, it generally turned out to be a case not of his painfully having to "re-write" but of less painful "re-vision," that is, his "see[ing] again" directly from his own "rereading."

In the same New York Edition preface, however, he more briefly laments for a second time as the one exception to his revision experience a lingering dissatisfaction with *The American* ("if only one *could* re-write"). This topic he had already addressed, to be sure, in his well-known earlier preface to that novel. Yet now he also expresses gratitude for what he calls "the altogether better literary manners [than *The American*]" of both *The Ambassadors* and *The Golden Bowl* (*LC*, 1332, 1337).[20] What this final allusion to *The American*—written within his preface to *The Golden Bowl*—may tell us is that, in a certain sense, *The Ambassadors* itself was for him a more satisfying

18. For the latest hypotheses on James's textual revision, see Dana Ringuette, "The Self-Forming Subject: Henry James's Pragmatistic Revision," *Mosaic* 23:1 (1990): 11–30; Philip Horne, *Henry James and Revision* (Oxford: Clarendon Press, 1990); Anthony J. Mazzella, "James's Revisions," in *A Companion to Henry James Studies*, ed. Daniel Mark Fogel (Westport, Conn.: Greenwood Press, 1993), 311–33.

19. Compare, for example, the more modest extent of the "Textual Notes" representing James's changes in *The Ambassadors*, that is, pp. 348–54 in Rosenbaum's edition, with that of the more substantial "Textual Variants" in Crowley and Hocks's edition of *The Wings of the Dove*, 423–36.

20. James does not here include *The Wings of the Dove* with his two other major phase novels as possessing "better literary manners," probably because, just as he had found it difficult to compose *The Wings*, he was likewise dissatisfied with its structure, calling it in his preface a "misplaced pivot"; see Crowley and Hocks, *Wings of the Dove*, 16.

"re-seeing" of *The American*, although I rather doubt James realized or intended that purpose when he began composing *The Ambassadors*. That he may have sensed it later is suggested mainly by these few comments from the prefaces and just possibly by the two "lists" of five novels each given to Mrs. George Prothero in 1913 after a request to her by Stark Young (later a distinguished drama critic) for specific guidance from James himself about what novels to read and in what order to read them. In the second list he inserts both *The American* and *The Ambassadors*, neither of which appears in the first list. Furthermore, he calls the second list "the more 'advanced.'" Now, since we know he believed *The Ambassadors* his best work and thought *The American* a flawed novel for which he nonetheless felt strong affection, perhaps he was insinuating in his second list that an "advanced" reader or a "young Texas" man of letters like Stark Young might notice a relationship between *The American* and *The Ambassadors*.[21]

In fact *The Ambassadors* does seem to be a reconception of *The American*. To borrow language from Mark Twain, James's thirty-five-year-old "squatter," Christopher Newman, a westerner, later turns into a fifty-five-year-old "dandy," Lambert Strether, a New Englander. Both undergo their initiations into Parisian and Gallic culture, each with an opposing mixture of disappointment and admiration—Newman more disappointment than admiration, Strether more admiration than disappointment. Each has his male and female confidants, Count Valentin and Mrs. Tristram, Little Bilham and Maria Gostrey, respectively. Perhaps most important, James was able in the later book to disentangle or at least discipline his powerful personal allegiance away from Strether to a degree he never quite could with Newman, so that whereas in the earlier book James allegedly "committed romance" by totally identifying with Newman, later he would instead *portray* a romantic perspective, Strether's, by stepping just the right number of paces away from his "deputy" and treating him with equal measures of criticism and sympathy, much as he had done successfully with Isabel Archer in *The Portrait*

---

21. Crowley and Hocks, *Wings of the Dove*, 456–57; *A*, 411–12. The first list comprises *Roderick Hudson, The Portrait of a Lady, The Princess Casamassima, The Wings of the Dove*, and *The Golden Bowl*; the second, "more 'advanced'" list comprises *The American, The Tragic Muse, The Wings of the Dove, The Ambassadors*, and *The Golden Bowl*. In the same letter James pleads with Mrs. Prothero to have Young read the novels in the "revised and prefaced" New York Edition or else "forfeit half, or more than half, my confidence."

*of a Lady*. To put some of this another way, James was himself patriotically "Howells-like" in *The American*, but in *The Ambassadors* his protagonist originated in Howells himself, and this may have helped free James from being too Howells-like: that is, he would be less chauvinistic, more cosmopolitan than in *The American*. I also believe James in the 1870s had been less critically "distant" from Newman just because he *was* a westerner; James was more used to establishing aesthetic distance from all his New England characters—as evidenced with Rev. Babcock, Newman's traveling companion, in the earlier novel. Returning to the issue of Howells, *The American* is often conveyed by chunks of conversational speech, like a Howells novel (one of the very few criticisms James later made of Howells's narrative method, by the way), whereas *The Ambassadors* uses the compositional layering of Jamesian "picture" and digested "scene" to perfection. Finally, there are certain highly suggestive comparative details and touches, such as Newman's speaking of "wash tubs" and "leather" as his business ventures opposed to Strether's never naming the Woollett "article" (*A*, 48); and there is also Newman's declaration to possess, in a wife, "the best article in the market"[22] opposed to Strether's memorable decline of Maria Gostrey's offer of herself by insisting "Not, out of the whole affair, to have got anything for myself" (*A*, 346). In any event, James's lasting pleasure with *The Ambassadors* never wavers from his first Howellsian "germ," and his eventual choice of it as the best of his novels resonates in the prefaces in counterpoint to *The American,* the problem-laden novel with self-confessed identification and emotional tug. Ultimately, these two books evoke the gifted youth and serene maturity of James the writer, and the various stages of "revision" between them.

What the foregoing examination of James's multiple "germs" for *The Ambassadors* suggests methodologically is that there can be a special excitement in tracing through a series of closely related statements by an author that seem cumulatively to renew, to confirm in spades, if you will, a perspective generally acceptable but perhaps not fully savored. This approach is obviously different from the sort of critical project whose principal task is to rend the veil of cumulative pre-postmodern wisdom, a subversive task I occasionally sense is nowadays too often sought by academia and by

---

22. Henry James, *The American,* ed. Roy Harvey Pearce and Matthew J. Bruccoli (Boston: Houghton Mifflin Co., 1962), 87, 35.

publishers: for withal its aura of novelty and ideological exposé, the result can sometimes reveal an unfortunate predilection, to use Joseph Campbell's distinction, in favor of the celebrity in lieu of the hero. By our locating and revisiting the life instant in Henry James that began *The Ambassadors* and discovering it repeated throughout the history of the novel's making, I believe we can appreciate afresh the extent that Strether, again recurring to Campbell's framework, though not a celebrity does qualify deeply as a hero.

# "There Was Something Mystic about It"

## The Composition of *Sister Carrie* by Dreiser et al.

R I C H A R D   W .   D O W E L L

§   §   §

## I

T HE STORY OF *Sister Carrie* began in June 1899, when Theodore
Dreiser and Jug, his wife of six months, left the hectic pace of New York
City to vacation in bucolic Maumee, Ohio, as the guests of Arthur Henry,
who would inspire the composition of that novel and to whom it would
be appreciatively dedicated. The carefree, pleasure-loving Henry was himself
destined to remain something of a dilettante whose literary enthusiasm far
outdistanced anything he would ever achieve, but for the typically dour, self-
doubting Dreiser, his early influence was vital. Without Henry's ambitions
for himself and for Dreiser, *Sister Carrie* and possibly Dreiser's career as
a novelist might never have become realities. Eventually, after the rupture
of their friendship, Dreiser would ridicule Henry's "vaulting egotism which
caused him to imagine, first, that he was as great a thinker and writer as
had ever appeared; second, that he was at the same time practical, a man of
the world, a man of affairs"; yet, during the summer of 1899, that "vaulting
egotism" was infectious. As Dreiser conceded, Henry was "a dreamer of
dreams, a spinner of fine fancies, a lover of romances that fascinated me by
their very impossibilities."[1]

---

1. Theodore Dreiser, "Rona Murtha," in *A Gallery of Women* (New York: Horace Liveright,
1929), 2:567. In this sketch, based on his acquaintance with Anna Mallon, Dreiser took his
vengeance on Arthur Henry, identified as Winnie Vlasto.

Dreiser and Henry first met in March 1894, when the latter was a twenty-six-year-old editor of the *Toledo Blade* and Dreiser, then twenty-two, was an itinerant reporter working his way to New York City. At the time, Henry could offer Dreiser only temporary employment, but they were quickly drawn together by their literary aspirations. Henry, who had already published a novel, shared some of his poetry and a book of fairy tales, while Dreiser, fresh from a stint as drama critic for the *St. Louis Globe-Democrat,* talked of his desire to become a playwright and perhaps of the operetta he had recently begun, "Jeremiah I."[2] Though Dreiser worked for Henry less than a week, their mutual admiration and dreams of greatness formed the basis of a warm friendship. "If he had been a girl," Dreiser later wrote, recalling that first meeting, "I would have married him, of course. It would have been inevitable. We were intellectual affinities. Our dreams were practically identical."[3]

By November 1894, Dreiser had reached New York, where he soon failed as a reporter for the *World.* He quickly rebounded, however, to initiate, edit, and write much of the copy for a woman's magazine titled *Ev'ry Month,* a small advertising vehicle for the Howley, Haviland music-publishing firm, in which Dreiser's song-writing brother, Paul Dresser, was a partner. One of Dreiser's contributors to *Ev'ry Month* was Arthur Henry, who migrated to New York briefly in early 1897 to pursue a career as a poet. There he found Dreiser frustrated by the restrictions of his editorship. Despite making a good salary, Dreiser lamented, "The things I am able to get the boss to publish that I believe in are very few. The rest must tickle the vanity or cater to the foibles and prejudices of readers. From my standpoint, I am not succeeding." Henry's advice was that Dreiser should stop editing the works of others and start writing the kind of literature he did believe in. "He nagged . . . ," Dreiser recalled, "saying he saw short stories in me." Instead of following Henry's advice immediately, Dreiser turned his attention to freelance magazine feature writing with sufficient success that by 1899 his name appeared in *Who's Who in America.* But again he was feeling restless

2. Theodore Dreiser, *Newspaper Days* (New York: Horace Liveright, 1931), 374. See also Richard Lingeman, "Dreiser's 'Jeremiah I': Found at Last," *Dreiser Studies* 20 (Fall 1989): 2–8; and Ellen Moers, "A 'New' First Novel by Arthur Henry," *Dreiser Newsletter* 4 (Fall 1973): 7–9.
3. Dreiser, *Newspaper Days,* 373.

and unfulfilled. A vacation in Maumee with Arthur Henry seemed the proper anodyne.[4]

In that relaxed atmosphere, Dreiser finally succumbed to Henry's urging that he must attempt some fiction. He began a short story titled "The Shining Slave Makers." "And after every paragraph I blushed for my folly," he confessed to H. L. Mencken in 1916; "it seemed so asinine."[5] Nevertheless, Henry's encouragement kept Dreiser at his task, and within two months, he had completed five stories. Contrary to Dreiser's later accounts, these stories were not sold and published quickly,[6] but their completion did apparently give him enough confidence that when Henry suggested he try a novel, Dreiser was receptive.

With the end of the summer, Dreiser had to return to New York, but by then Henry himself was in need of moral support. He had begun a romantic novel of lost-but-enduring love titled *A Princess of Arcady* and now insisted that Dreiser had to begin one also. They could read each other's manuscripts, offer advice and encouragement, and thereby keep each other going. When Dreiser agreed to undertake a companion venture, Henry accompanied him and Jug east and installed himself in their apartment, sharing the expenses. There, in September 1899, Dreiser took out a sheet of

---

4. Quoted in W. A. Swanberg, *Dreiser* (New York: Charles Scribner's Sons, 1965), 73–74; *Letters of Theodore Dreiser,* ed. Robert H. Elias (Philadelphia: University of Pennsylvania Press, 1959), 1:212.

5. *Letters,* 1:212. Dreiser published "The Shining Slave Makers" in *Ainslee's* in June 1901; it was reprinted as "McEwen of the Shining Slave Makers" in *Free and Other Stories* (New York: Boni and Liveright, 1918).

6. Dreiser in his 1916 account to H. L. Mencken (*Letters,* 1:213) left the impression that his success with these early short stories had encouraged him to attempt *Sister Carrie:* "Later [Arthur Henry] began to ding-dong about a novel. I must write a novel. By then I had written four short stories or five, and sold them all." Dreiser then listed "The Shining Slave Makers," "Butcher Rogaum's Door," "Nigger Jeff," "When the Old Century Was New," and "The World and the Bubble." The facts are that some of these stories were initially rejected and none was sold until after *Sister Carrie* was well underway. The first four were eventually published in 1901, the year after the publication of *Sister Carrie.* The fifth, "The World and the Bubble," has never been identified. For a fuller discussion of the stories preceding the composition of *Sister Carrie,* see Donald Pizer, "A Summer at Maumee," in *Essays Mostly on Periodical Publishing in America: A Collection in Honor of Clarence Gohdes,* ed. James Woodress (Durham: Duke University Press, 1973), 193–204.

yellow paper and randomly wrote "Sister Carrie" at the top. The novel was underway.

## II

Dreiser always maintained that he began *Sister Carrie* without a plan, merely to please Henry. As he told Dorothy Dudley in 1930, "My mind was a blank except for the name. I had no idea who or what she was to be. I have often thought there was something mystic about it, as if I were being used, like a medium." Of course, as a newspaper reporter, magazine editor, and freelance writer, Dreiser had considerable awareness of the literary, philosophical, social, and scientific movements of his day—what Thomas P. Riggio has termed "a reservoir of imaginative resources"—and throughout the composition of the novel he drew liberally upon this fund of knowledge, even to the point of splicing in verbatim passages from George Ade's *Fables in Slang*, Augustin Daly's *Under the Gaslight*, a *New York Times* circular offering work to scab labor during the 1895 Brooklyn streetcar strike, and his own essay "Curious Shifts of the Poor."[7] The use of the George Ade material to flesh out the initial description of the traveling salesman Drouet encouraged a reviewer for the *Syracuse Post Standard* to observe that in composing *Sister*

---

7. Quoted in Dudley, *Forgotten Frontiers: Dreiser and the Land of the Free* (New York: Harrison Smith and Robert Haas, 1932), 160; Riggio, "Notes on the Origins of *Sister Carrie*," *Library Chronicle* 10 (Spring 1979): 8. Source studies of *Sister Carrie* are too numerous and complex to be analyzed individually in this essay; however, a representative sampling would include the following: Lars Ahnebrink, "Dreiser's *Sister Carrie* and Balzac," *Symposium* 7 (November 1953): 306–22; Nancy Warner Barrineau, "Lillian Nordica and *Sister Carrie*," *Dreiser Studies* 20 (Fall 1989): 21–24; Stephen C. Brennan, "*Sister Carrie* and the Tolstoyan Artist," *Research Studies* (Washington State University) 47 (March 1979): 1–16; D. B. Graham, "Dreiser's *Maggie*," *American Literary Realism* 7 (Spring 1974): 169–70; Christopher G. Katope, "*Sister Carrie* and Spencer's First Principles," *American Literature* 41 (March 1969): 64–75; Duane J. MacMillan, "*Sister Carrie*, 'Chapter IV': Theodore Dreiser's 'Tip-of-the-Hat' to Stephen Crane," *Dreiser Newsletter* 10 (Spring 1979): 1–7; Michael J. McDonough, "A Note on Dreiser's Use of the 1895 Brooklyn Trolley Car Strike," *Dreiser Studies* 18 (Spring 1987): 31–34; Robert M. McIlvaine, "A Literary Source for Hurstwood's Last Scene," *Research Studies* (Washington State University) 40 (March 1972): 78–91; Ellen Moers, *Two Dreisers* (New York: Viking, 1969); Donald Pizer, *The Novels of Theodore Dreiser* (Minneapolis: University of Minnesota Press, 1976); and Gary Scharnhorst, "A Possible Source for *Sister Carrie*: Horatio Alger's *Helen Ford*," *Dreiser Newsletter* 9 (Spring 1978): 1–4.

*Carrie,* Dreiser had generously adopted the "principle of absorbing whatever you want, wherever you find it."[8]

Yet, the most fertile sources for *Sister Carrie* were Dreiser's own life and the lives of family members. As biographer Richard Lingeman has pointed out, the name of Dreiser's heroine, a woman who traded on her sexual appeal, can be traced to his own libidinous frustrations as a teenager growing up in Warsaw, Indiana. "The name 'Carrie,' which he wrote automatically at the head of his manuscript, tapped his earliest sexual memories. One of the girls in Warsaw who had figured in his fantasies was named Carrie Tuttle—'Cad' for short." Likewise, Columbia City, Sister Carrie's hometown, was rooted in those adolescent sexual fantasies. Though in the novel he shifted the town to Wisconsin, the Columbia City that Dreiser knew was approximately thirty miles from Warsaw and had gained a measure of notoriety as the place Warsaw's daring young men would go for sexual adventures. Because Dreiser was too young and too poor to go with them, he was left to imagine the "sybaritic delights" available there. As he recalled in *A Hoosier Holiday,* "With an imagination that probably far outran my years, I built up a fancy as to Columbia City which far exceeded its import, of course. To me, it was a kind of Cairo of the Egyptians, with two-horned Hathor in the skies, and what breaths of palms and dulcet quavers of strings and drums I know not."[9]

For the opening chapters of the novel, Dreiser recalled his own early experiences as a job seeker in Chicago, even to the point of making Carrie his exact age: she too was eighteen in August 1889. Like him, she entered Chicago alone by train at night and thrilled to the lights of the city with their promise of excitement and luxury. Once there, Carrie lived in the same neighborhoods Dreiser and his family had, shared his fascination with the street scenes, marveled, as he had, at the city's opulence, and in search of work retraced his steps with the same overwhelming sense of confusion and timidity. Like him, she experienced numerous rebuffs and ultimately was forced to accept employment that was low paying, depressing, and physically demanding. Ultimately, as the young Dreiser also frequently

8. Quoted in Jack Salzman, "Dreiser and Ade: Note on the Text of *Sister Carrie*," *American Literature* 40 (January 1969): 547.

9. Richard Lingeman, *Theodore Dreiser: At the Gates of the City, 1871–1907* (New York: G. P. Putnam's Sons, 1986), 145; Theodore Dreiser, *A Hoosier Holiday* (New York: John Lane, 1916), 276–77.

had under such circumstances, she lost the position. As F. O. Matthiessen has demonstrated, passages describing Carrie's first days in Chicago and those describing Dreiser's own in his autobiography *Dawn* are virtually interchangeable.[10]

Inspired by these bittersweet reminiscences, Dreiser wrote with an "easy pen" until the middle of October, completing nine chapters and arriving at the point where Drouet introduced Carrie to Hurstwood. This seemingly effortless progress through the early stages of the narrative made a lasting impression on Richard Duffy, an editor for *Ainslee's,* who years later could recall Dreiser's supreme confidence: "when once he really got down to writing *[Sister Carrie]* the fecundity of the man was amazing. Every few days he would make the breezy announcement that since he last came in view he had written as many as ten or twenty-thousand words." And because he did write with such speed, Dreiser was most dependent on the editing of Henry and Jug.[11] Henry's revisions of the holograph manuscript were relatively few and generally involved reworking awkward or pretentious passages; however, Jug's contributions were more numerous and substantive. She employed her skills as a former grade-school teacher to correct Dreiser's notoriously poor spelling and grammar and stayed alert for factual inaccuracies, appending to the end of chapter 3 a series of questions such as "When did the word 'drummer' first come into use? Page 4" and "When were large Plate Glass windows first used? Page 6." In addition, Dreiser seemingly depended on Jug for the feminine point of view, particularly during the first thirty-one chapters, when Carrie dominated the action. For example, in chapter 16,

10. F. O. Matthiessen, *Theodore Dreiser* (New York: William Sloane Associates, 1951), 66.
11. Richard Duffy, "When They Were Twenty-One, II—A New York Group of Literary Bohemians," *Bookman* 38 (January 1914): 524. In 1914, Dreiser presented the holograph of *Sister Carrie* to H. L. Mencken, who in turn donated it to the New York Public Library, where it is currently housed in the Manuscripts and Archives Division. The typescript, prepared by Anna Mallon's agency and used by Doubleday, Page typesetters, is part of the Dreiser Collection at the Charles Patterson Van Pelt Library at the University of Pennsylvania. Galleys and page proofs are not extant. For more in-depth analyses of the editing of the holograph and the typescript than this essay will undertake, see James L. W. West III, John C. Berkey, and Alice Winters, "*Sister Carrie:* Manuscript to Print," in *Sister Carrie: The Pennsylvania Edition,* ed. John C. Berkey et al. (Philadelphia: University of Pennsylvania Press, 1981), 503–41; Pizer, *Novels of Theodore Dreiser,* 42–52; and Stephen Brennan, "The Composition of *Sister Carrie:* A Reconsideration," *Dreiser Newsletter* 9 (Fall 1978): 17–23.

Dreiser had written, "On her feet were yellow shoes and in her hands her gloves."[12] Since Carrie was otherwise dressed in blue and white, Jug must have been struck by the garishness of the total outfit as well as the awkwardness of the phrasing. She revised the sentence to read: "Her brown shoes peeped occasionally from beneath her skirt. She carried her gloves in her hand."[13] At times, Jug's suggested changes bordered on censorship as she toned down mild profanity and removed suggestive references to Carrie's body or clothing. She also improved Carrie's spoken English. As a result of Jug's influence, the Carrie that emerged may well have become a bit more refined than the Carrie that Dreiser originally conceived. In all, Jug made well over two hundred editorial changes, a number which suggests that at least during the Chicago section of the novel Dreiser worked closely with her and valued her contributions. Years later, however, after their separation, he sought to minimize her role. As he told Dorothy Dudley, "all she ever wanted to do was to cut out what she called 'the bad parts,' and she hadn't a chance at that. If I learned anything about style from another at this time, I owe it to Henry."[14]

After Dreiser's initial burst of creativity had carried him through nine chapters, he bogged down for almost two months in his effort to develop the relationship between Carrie and Hurstwood. "Then I quit, disgusted," he recalled in a letter to H. L. Mencken. "I thought it was rotten." Part of the problem may have been that by then he had ceased to draw primarily upon his own experiences and was telling the story of his sister Emma. Emma, who signed her letters "Sister Emma," perhaps suggesting the novel's title, was eight years older than Theodore and reportedly the prettiest of the five Dreiser girls. Dreiser himself later described her as "one of the most attractive of all the girls . . . in a showy, erotic way." In 1881, when she was eighteen, the already-promiscuous Emma tired of the small-town environment of Sullivan, Indiana, where the family was then living, and, like Carrie, took the train to

12. *Sister Carrie: The Pennsylvania Edition*, 147. The text of the Pennsylvania Edition, with its nearly two hundred pages of apparatus, is based on the holograph. Hereafter all references to this edition will be cited as *PE*.

13. *Sister Carrie: A Norton Critical Edition*, ed. Donald Pizer (New York: W. W. Norton, 1970), 109. The text of the Norton Critical Edition is based on the 1900 Doubleday, Page edition. Hereafter all references to this edition will be cited as *NCE*.

14. Quoted in Dudley, *Forgotten Frontiers*, 163.

Chicago to make her way alone. Eventually, she became the mistress of an elderly architect who installed her in an apartment that seemed magnificent to the twelve-year-old Theodore. In *Dawn,* he recounts a visit with Emma in the summer of 1884. Amid what he considered luxurious appointments, she appeared to be "prosperous and cheerful." By the following year, she had met and fallen in love with L. A. "Grove" Hopkins, a clerk for the firm of Chapin and Gore, which owned several Chicago saloons. Though Hopkins had a wife and daughter, he and Emma engaged in an affair, meeting at the home of Emma and Theodore's sister Teresa, herself a kept woman. In February 1886, this trysting place was invaded by the police, accompanied by Mrs. Hopkins, who had had her husband trailed by a Pinkerton detective. Within days of this exposure, Hopkins stole $3,500 and some jewelry from his employers and fled with Emma to Montreal. All evidence suggested that the robbery was premeditated and that Emma was a willing participant.[15]

Once in Montreal, Hopkins returned the jewelry and all but $800 and proceeded on with Emma to New York City, where he became involved with the politically corrupt Tammany Hall machine and prospered. At the time of their mother's death in 1890, Emma returned to Chicago "clad in furs and silks and arriving in a carriage."[16] However, by the time Dreiser had worked his way to New York in 1894, she, Hopkins, and their two children were in near poverty. The collapse of Tammany Hall following the Lexow committee investigation had thrown Hopkins out of work and seemingly broken his spirit. In his sullen despair, he had become so abusive and unfaithful to Emma that with Theodore's assistance she abandoned him and secretly moved to another section of the city. Eventually, she married unhappily, grew quite matronly, and devoted the rest of her life to the care of her children.

In mid-December 1899, at Arthur Henry's urging, Dreiser returned to the manuscript to transform the sordid details of the Emma Dreiser–Grove Hopkins affair into Carrie's relationship with Hurstwood, making several changes in the process. For example, the jaunty Drouet was already on

15. *Letters,* 1:213; quoted in Moers, *Two Dreisers,* 79; Theodore Dreiser, *Dawn* (New York: Horace Liveright, 1931), 173. For more specifics of the Emma Dreiser–Grove Hopkins affair, see George Steinbrecher Jr., "Inaccurate Accounts of *Sister Carrie,*" *American Literature* 23 (January 1952): 490–93, and Pizer, *Novels of Theodore Dreiser,* 32–35.

16. Dreiser, *Dawn,* 520.

the scene to replace the aging architect Emma left for Hopkins; the $3,500 Hopkins embezzled was raised to $10,800; the Chapin and Gore saloon became a somewhat more prestigious Chicago establishment, Hannah and Hogg; and Hurstwood was given a son as well as a daughter. Such changes may, in part, have resulted from Dreiser's imperfect knowledge of Hopkins's crime. At the time it occurred, he was a boy of fourteen living in Warsaw, Indiana, and later, in 1894, he probably received a somewhat biased account from Emma. So his information would have been at best vague and perhaps inaccurate. But Dreiser had other reasons to alter the details of his source material. Most importantly, he wanted to demonstrate his deterministic philosophy, specifically the dominance of chance. As he told a St. Louis interviewer shortly after the publication of the novel, "What I desired to do was to show two little beings, or more, playing in and out among the giant legs of circumstance."[17] To this end, Dreiser sought to craft characters whose social positions and moral inclinations would normally preclude their involvement in the events that would engulf them. Thus, "Grove" Hopkins, the lower-middle-class clerk, was transformed into the sartorially resplendent saloon manager, George W. Hurstwood, whose income and three-story "perfectly appointed house" on the fashionable North Side made him "altogether a very acceptable individual of our great American upper class—the first grade below the luxuriously rich" and gave him "greatness in a way" (*PE*, 81, 44, 180). In regard to his affluence and social ease, the Chicago Hurstwood resembled Dreiser's celebrity brother Paul Dresser much more than he did Hopkins.[18]

The circumstances of the embezzlement were also altered to make Hurstwood's guilt ambiguous. Whereas Hopkins's crime was planned and executed with precision, Hurstwood's theft was the culmination of a series of coincidences. On that particular evening, the normally abstemious manager had been drinking because of personal problems with his wife and with Carrie; thus, he more readily yielded to temptation when the cashier uncharacteristically forgot to bank the day's receipts and left the safe unlocked. Seeing the money as a solution to his dilemma, Hurstwood wavered between intent and

17. "Author of 'Sister Carrie' Formerly Was a St. Louisan," *St. Louis Post-Dispatch*, January 26, 1902, p. 4. Reprinted in *NCE*, 458.

18. Scholars who have discussed Dreiser's use of Paul Dresser as the model for Hurstwood include Moers, *Two Dreisers*, 86–89, and Lingeman, *Theodore Dreiser*, 251–52.

fear until the safe accidentally locked while the money was in his possession. In a panic, he fled, completing the crime that would ultimately result in his destruction.

The sexually experienced and generally amoral Emma was replaced by a considerably more innocent and naive Carrie, whose affair with Drouet was an act of desperation accompanied by some moral anguish and whose relationship with Hurstwood was initially based on the assumption that he was a single man. Although Emma was intimately involved in Hopkins's theft, even to the point of assuming an alias, Carrie became the unsuspecting victim of Hurstwood's deception. Upon learning that he was a married man, Carrie, whose tendency was to drift, had made one of her few firm decisions: she would terminate the romance. Then, however, she was duped into boarding the train to Montreal by Hurstwood's assurance that they were merely going to the South Side to visit a badly injured Drouet in the hospital. Thus began a journey destined to lead Carrie to fame and fortune in New York—a journey engineered largely by chance.

Having introduced these moral complexities into his narrative, Dreiser worked on *Sister Carrie* for another six weeks, until late January 1900, and completed eighteen more chapters. Then, at the point where Hurstwood was to embezzle the money, Dreiser stalled again, discouraged by his inability to demonstrate the ambiguity of the manager's guilt. As he later explained to Dorothy Dudley, "I had to quit, it seemed to me the thing was a failure, a total frost. . . . I think I experienced a defeat in the face of Hurstwood's defeat as to Carrie. I took it up once or twice but had to quit. I tried writing stories; thought I had better go back to articles. . . . I had reached the place where Hurstwood robs the safe. I didn't know where I was going; I had lost the thread."[19] And this time Arthur Henry was not available to give Dreiser the needed assurance or to share the monthly rent on the apartment. Henry had temporarily abandoned the novel-writing partnership to pursue an extramarital affair with Anna Mallon, who owned a typing agency and would eventually become Henry's second wife. Dreiser responded to this defection by returning to the psychological and financial security of freelance magazine writing. Toward the end of January, he wrote the editor of *Pearson's Magazine*

---

19. Quoted in Dudley, *Forgotten Frontiers*, 162; see also *Letters*, 1:213, and Robert H. Elias, *Theodore Dreiser: Apostle of Nature*, emended edition (Ithaca: Cornell University Press, 1970), 107.

to propose a trip as far south as Florida to research nine possible articles. Included on this research agenda was a stopover with inventor Elmer Gates, whose Laboratory of Psychology and Psychurgy in Chevy Chase, Maryland, was engaged in experiments in physiological psychology. Dreiser returned to New York in mid-February fascinated by Gates's discoveries, particularly his theory of "anastates" and "katastates," which would be used to help explain Hurstwood's lethargy and physical decline in the second half of the novel.[20]

Shortly thereafter, Henry returned to resume his gadfly role, read the manuscript, and pronounced it good. With this encouragement and the stimulation of his recent visit to Gates's laboratory, Dreiser solved his problem with the robbery episode and pushed into the New York section of *Sister Carrie*, where the narrative again tapped into some very personal memories. The winter of 1894–1895, during which Hurstwood would commit suicide, had been painful for Dreiser himself. Being newly arrived in New York at that time and needing to conserve his funds as he sought work on one of the newspapers, Dreiser had stayed with Emma and Hopkins and thus had had the opportunity to meet and study his beaten, parasitic host. In *Newspaper Days*, Dreiser described Hopkins after the defeat of Tammany Hall as a "dark and shrewd and hawklike person who seemed to be always following me with his eyes." Willing to live off the meager rent Dreiser gave him each week, Hopkins seldom left the apartment and never sought work. "He appeared to be done for, played out," Dreiser recalled. "He had wearied of the game and was drifting."[21]

As hauntingly appropriate as this description is to Hurstwood during the early stages of his decline, Dreiser made little use of the Emma Dreiser–Grove Hopkins story for the New York section of his narrative. Clearly Carrie's spectacular success on the Broadway stage bore no resemblance to the dreary events of Emma's later years, and Hopkins was never reduced to the total destitution Hurstwood experienced. For Carrie's ascent to stardom, Dreiser drew upon his own interest in the theater as well as countless interviews with successful female artists during his days as a freelance journalist.[22] And for Hurstwood's tragic failure, he returned to his own life, not for experiences

20. For a fuller discussion of Elmer Gates's influence on *Sister Carrie*, see Moers, *Two Dreisers*, 160–70, and Lingeman, *Theodore Dreiser*, 261–62.

21. Dreiser, *Newspaper Days*, 435; quoted in Moers, *Two Dreisers*, 30.

22. See Barrineau, "Lillian Nordica and *Sister Carrie*."

that he had actually lived, but for those he had once feared were imminent. During that winter of 1894–1895, as Dreiser had walked the streets in search of a position, he was rudely turned away time and again by office boys who were protecting editors from interruption by job seekers, and each day's failure brought him nearer the end of his limited resources. Soon it became obvious that the city was in the midst of a severe depression, as soup kitchens were being established to sustain the army of unemployed, with whom Dreiser had begun to feel an ominous kinship. Finally one day, overwhelmed and dispirited by the futility of the situation, he found himself seated idly on a park bench staring at the impenetrable office buildings. As he recaptured the moment in *Newspaper Days,* "About me on the benches of the park was, even in this grey, chill December weather, that large company of bums, loafers, tramps, idlers, the flotsam and jetsam of the great city's whirl and strife to be seen there today. I presume I looked at them and then considered myself and these great offices, and it was then that *Hurstwood* was born. The city seemed so huge and cruel."[23]

Even after Dreiser was able to secure a position on the *World* as a space-rate reporter, he could not escape the self-fulfilling fear that he was doomed to fail in an environment too competitive for his modest abilities, that he could never recapture the success he had enjoyed in Chicago, St. Louis, and Pittsburgh. As he later expressed this sense of intimidation, "How was a sniveling scribbler to make his way in such a world? Nothing but chance and luck, as I saw it, could further the average man or lift him out of his rut, and since when had it been proved that I was a favorite of fortune? A crushing sense of incompetence and general inefficiency seemed to settle upon me, and I could not shake it off."[24] It was on this same note of impending doom that Dreiser ushered the transplanted Hurstwood into the brisk New York environment:

> Whatever a man like Hurstwood could be in Chicago, it is very evident that he would be but an inconspicuous drop in an ocean like New York. . . . In Chicago the two roads to distinction were politics and trade. In New York the roads were any one of a half-hundred, and each had been diligently pursued by hundreds, so that celebrities were numerous. The sea was already

23. Dreiser, *Newspaper Days,* 463–64.
24. Ibid., 280–81.

full of whales. A common fish must needs disappear wholly from view—remain unseen. In other words, Hurstwood was nothing. (*PE,* 304–5)

And in the chapters that followed, Dreiser proceeded to visit the horrors of beggary and homelessness, which he had earlier imagined for himself, on Hurstwood, who was also no favorite of fortune.


### III

Recalling the New York section of *Sister Carrie,* Dreiser told Dorothy Dudley that he was paralyzed by his memories of "the *World* days" and forced to abandon the manuscript for a third time. "Somehow I felt unworthy to write all that," he recalled. "It seemed too big, too baffling, don't you know?" In this case, however, Dreiser's memory seems inaccurate, for all evidence suggests that once he returned to his narrative in late February, Dreiser enjoyed a sustained burst of creative energy that carried him through the last half of the novel in little more than a month. In fact, Hurstwood's tragic decline so captured his imagination that the fated ex-manager began to dominate the action, whereas Carrie's spectacular rise from novice chorus girl to star was attributed to some rather outrageous coincidences and treated quite summarily. For many readers, Dreiser's somewhat pro forma handling of Carrie's success has been unconvincing and certainly not indicative of the "emotional greatness" that he claimed for his heroine. For H. L. Mencken, this shift of emphasis to Hurstwood in the second half resulted in a structural weakness that compromised *Sister Carrie*'s stature. As Mencken told Dreiser in 1911, expressing his preference for *Jennie Gerhardt,* "I needn't say that *[Jennie]* seems to me an advance above *Sister Carrie.* Its obvious superiority lies in its better form. You strained (or perhaps broke) the back of *Sister Carrie* when you let Hurstwood lead you away from Carrie. In *Jennie Gerhardt,* there is no such running amuck."[25]

If Dreiser's identification with Hurstwood led him to run amuck structurally, it seems to have chastened him stylistically, for in the New York section of the manuscript, the revisions by Jug and Henry are much less in evidence. The awkward sentences and pretentious diction that had marred

25. Quoted in Dudley, *Forgotten Frontiers,* 162; *Letters,* 1:115.

the earlier chapters virtually disappeared, and the number of intrusive philosophical and historical asides was reduced. What remained was a more simple, direct, and powerful prose. Praising the accuracy and dignity of several scenes in the second half of *Sister Carrie*, particularly Dreiser's handling of Hurstwood's suicide, F. O. Matthiessen noted, "When his mind was most absorbed with what he had to say, the flourishes of the feature-writer fell away, as did also the cumbersome, only half-accurate abstract terms ('affectional,' 'actualities'). Then he could write passages where nothing is striking except the total effect." And that "total effect" is a moving portrait of human suffering, one seldom equaled in American literature. "Perhaps no better word picture of a man's downfall has ever been painted than is to be found within these pages," wrote a *Newark Sunday News* reviewer, describing Hurstwood's decline. "The evolution of the hanger-on, the beggar, the social outcast, here finds its final portrayal."[26]

Over a decade later, Dreiser could still recall the sense of commitment with which he approached the grim events that characterized Hurstwood's last days: "Something prompted me while I was writing to write sincerely. I would come to strange, hard bitter sad facts in my story, for after all it was a story, and I would say shall I put that down and something within the centre of my being would say 'You must! You must! You dare not do otherwise.' "[27] With the last of these "strange, hard bitter sad facts," Hurstwood's death in a Bowery flophouse, Dreiser brought his narrative to an end, concluding it bleakly with the ex-manager's resigned utterance as the gas fumes began to take their toll: " 'What's the use,' he said wearily, as he stretched himself to rest" (*PE*, 499). Then, quite prematurely, as it turned out, Dreiser wrote, "The End. Thursday, March 29–2:53 P.M."

These final chapters were then sent to Henry's mistress, Anna Mallon, whose agency had been preparing the typescript piecemeal, and when they were returned, Dreiser, Jug, and Henry set about giving the narrative what they must have presumed would be its final editing. During this process, however, someone—perhaps Dreiser, who was notoriously indecisive about ending his novels—began to have second thoughts about the conclusion.

26. Matthiessen, *Theodore Dreiser*, 87; "Sister Carrie," *Newark Sunday News*, September 1, 1901, Magazine Section, p. 2.
27. Quoted in Thomas P. Riggio, "Dreiser: Autobiographical Fragment, 1911," *Dreiser Studies* 18 (Spring 1987): 18.

In the penultimate chapter, he had originally reunited Carrie and a minor character, Robert Ames, who was an intellectual inventor often seen by scholars as a spokesman for Dreiser on the evils of materialism. Earlier in the narrative, Ames had shocked Carrie by showing his disdain for wealth; in the final pages, he returned to condemn her selfishness and urge her to make use of her acting talents by serving mankind, and Carrie, flattered by his attention, was inspired to consider his challenge. When they parted, Ames found himself deeply impressed by Carrie's humanity and "wide awake to her beauty"; she in turn had "an irrepressible feeling showing in her eyes" (*PE,* 487). Certainly the reader is tempted to think that Ames might well become the third man in Carrie's life and lead her to a higher plane of fulfillment. This expectation is but slightly discouraged by a following coda in which Dreiser warned that Carrie's interest in Ames would be fleeting and that it was her destiny to be forever driven by the "blind strivings of the human heart" (*PE,* 487).

During the revision process, the reunion between Carrie and Ames was shortened and largely rewritten to eliminate any suggestion of mutual attraction. In this altered version, Ames became more condescending in regard to Carrie's success, and she was primarily puzzled by his admonition that she pursue altruistic ends. As Dreiser notes, "there was nothing responsive between them" (*NCE,* 253), and Carrie found herself wondering "why the one-time keen interest in him was no longer with her" (*NCE,* 354). For his part, Ames concluded the meeting with a summary criticism: "If I were you, I'd change" (*NCE,* 354). Then, following Hurstwood's suicide, Dreiser added several paragraphs tracing Carrie's futile search for happiness. For the novel's final paragraph, he used a revised version of the coda initially written to conclude the reunion between Carrie and Ames. Among the revisions were the sobering additions that Carrie was doomed to "long, alone," and dream of such happiness as she might "never feel" (*NCE,* 369).

During a 1907 interview, Dreiser gave a long-accepted and often-repeated explanation of the revised ending. "When I finished *[Sister Carrie]* I felt that it was not done," he told a reporter for the *New York Herald.* "The narrative, I felt, was finished, but not completed. The problem in my mind was not to round it out with literary grace, but to lead the story to a point, an elevation, where it could be left and yet continue into the future. The story had to stop, and yet I wanted in the final picture to suggest the continuation of Carrie's fate along the lines of established truths." For a time, the ending he sought eluded him. Then, one afternoon, hoping to benefit from a change of scenery, Dreiser visited the Palisades, overlooking the Hudson River. There he relaxed on an overhanging shelf, allowing his ideas free rein. "Two hours passed in a delicious mental drifting. Then suddenly came the inspiration of its own accord. I reached for my note book and pencil and wrote. And when I left the Palisades 'Sister Carrie' was completed."[28]

Manuscript evidence suggests, however, that Dreiser's recollection in this case might have been a bit fanciful, for accompanying the holograph at the New York Public Library are thirteen pages of notes concerning the revision of the ending.[29] Except for the first page, written by Dreiser, these notes are in Jug's hand. Two suggestions for revision stand out: Ames must not be left as a "matrimonial possibility" and the novel's final focus should be on Carrie. Some of the phrasing of these notes eventually found its way into the revised section. Also, the version of the final paragraph ultimately used—a version somewhat more ominous than a draft preserved in Dreiser's hand—was at least transcribed for the typist by Jug. Thus, the revised ending seemingly evolved through several stages and was the result of a collaboration rather than the product of a moment of inspiration amid the natural beauties of the Palisades.

## IV

When the manuscript was ready for submission, Dreiser decided to try the publisher of Mark Twain and William Dean Howells, Harper and Brothers, perhaps because Henry Mills Alden, editor of *Harper's Monthly*, was a sometime reader for that firm. Alden had recently published a couple of Dreiser's freelance pieces, so Dreiser sent *Sister Carrie* to him for preliminary appraisal. Alden complimented the novel personally but advised against sending it to Harper; however, when Dreiser insisted, he forwarded it in early April. As Alden predicted, Harper rejected *Sister Carrie*, telling Dreiser in an evaluation dated May 2, 1900, that the novel was "a superior piece of reportorial realism—of highclass newspaper work" which was factually

28. " 'Sister Carrie': Theodore Dreiser," *New York Herald,* July 7, 1907, Literary and Art Section, p. 2. Reprinted in *NCE,* 432.

29. For an analysis of the notes accompanying the *Sister Carrie* holograph, I am indebted to West, Berkey, and Winters, "*Sister Carrie:* Manuscript to Print," 514–19.

faithful to "a certain below-the-surface life in Chicago of twenty years ago." The Harper reader went on to praise Dreiser's "sympathetic appreciation of the motives" of his characters but felt that his handling of the "continued illicit relations of the heroine" was ultimately wearisome and not sufficiently delicate as to prevent offense to the readers, particularly the feminine readers, "who control the destinies of so many novels." The style was declared "uneven," generally good but "disfigured" by colloquialisms (*PE*, 519).

Alden's reservations and the rejection by Harper apparently convinced Dreiser that *Sister Carrie* in its original form was unpublishable, so once again he enlisted the aid of Arthur Henry to edit out what ultimately became approximately 36,000 words. In later years, Dreiser created the impression that he had taken the primary responsibility for the cuts. Writing historian Louis Filler in 1937, he provided the following scenario: "As for *Sister Carrie* being cut, it happened this way. When I finished the book, I realized it was too long, and I went over it and marked what I thought should come out. Then I consulted with a friend, Arthur Henry, who suggested other cuts, and whenever I agreed with him I cut the book. It was thus shortened to its present length."[30] A study of the typescript, however, suggests that Arthur Henry took the lead in shortening *Sister Carrie*, lightly crossing out passages he wished to see deleted. Dreiser then approved these deletions by decisively retracing Henry's marks with a soft, blunt pencil. The editors of the Pennsylvania Edition of *Sister Carrie* have noted that Dreiser "almost never disagreed with Henry. In only two or three instances in the entire typescript did Dreiser not make a block cut that had been recommended by Henry, and Dreiser erased only a scattered few of Henry's revisions and rewordings" (*PE*, 522).

The primary aim of the cuts was to streamline the narrative by eliminating passages that were repetitive or digressive, particularly if those passages

---

30. Quoted in Pizer, *Novels of Theodore Dreiser*, 48. The chronology of events at this time is a matter of some controversy. For example, Donald Pizer has argued that Dreiser and Henry realized immediately after the novel's composition that it was too long and slow-paced to be published and thus cut the typescript before sending it to Harper and Brothers. Pizer has insisted that there is no evidence to support the contention of the Pennsylvania editors that the major editing took place in response to Harper's rejection. See the introduction to *New Essays on "Sister Carrie,"* ed. Donald Pizer (Cambridge: Cambridge University Press, 1991), 8–9.

were potentially offensive.[31] To this end, the seamier side of Chicago was deemphasized. Some of the shabbier views of the factory district were struck; street toughs who ogled Carrie disappeared; and the factory girls talked a bit less about their tawdry activities of the night before. Particular targets of Henry's pencil were episodes involving sexual exploitation. Twice, while job hunting in Chicago, Carrie was offered positions explicitly contingent upon her sexual cooperation, and once she encountered a theater manager who used his position to seduce applicants. These episodes were cut. The New York section was edited less severely, but here too passages revealing the underside of the theater world were revised or deleted. After such revisions, the intentions of men eyeing Carrie from the front row or sending her lustful notes were not so explicit. Overall, the Chicago and New York that emerged from these excisions were less threatening environments than the ones Dreiser had originally portrayed.

Also modified by the cuts were the characterizations of Carrie, Drouet, and Hurstwood. The original Carrie, for example, had developed into a somewhat more tough-minded, calculating survivor, particularly in the Chicago section of the novel. This quality was most evident in some excised passages following Drouet's decision to leave her after learning of her interest in the more affluent Hurstwood. At this point, Carrie decided to support herself by finding employment. While applying to department stores, she dissembled regarding her lack of experience and was encouraged that her physical appeal gave her an advantage with male employers. At last, at the end of an unrewarding day, Carrie encountered the lecherous manager of a dishonest picture-framing company, who "ogled her most salaciously and . . . tacitly conveyed to her one of the most brazen propositions imaginable—seeking to buy her services and favor for five dollars per week " (*PE*, 259). Though repulsed by the man's appearance and manner, she did not reject his offer; in fact, Carrie felt relieved by the security of a job offer. "She knew that if she took that place," Dreiser had originally written, "it would be to put herself in the way of disagreeable familiarity and solicitation, and she hesitated to think that anything could bring her to it. Still the day had gone by and

31. For more detailed analyses of the consequences of the block cuts from the typescript, see West, Berkey, and Winters, "*Sister Carrie:* Manuscript to Print," 520–22; Pizer, *Novels of Theodore Dreiser,* 48–50; and Richard W. Dowell, "*Sister Carrie* Restored," *Dreiser Newsletter* 12 (Spring 1981): 1–8.

five dollars was five dollars" (*PE*, 259). Then, when Hurstwood intervened and tricked her onto the train bound for Montreal, she was not entirely the passive Carrie that emerged from the editing. Instead, she weighed the relative advantages of staying with him or returning to Chicago without Drouet to support her; she listened to Hurstwood's promise of a "nice home" and "a decent life in another city" (*PE*, 285); and finally she succumbed to the luxury of the Pullman car, the excitement of travel, and the pleasure of a shopping spree in Montreal. With the elimination of these scenes depicting a somewhat aggressive Carrie, as well as passages revealing her self-justification after moral compromises, Dreiser and Henry created a more innocent and drifting heroine.

Also, Drouet's sensuality and duplicity became less explicit through editing, as references to his "desire" were struck and over four hundred words describing his womanizing were deleted. "On his trade pilgrimages," Dreiser had written in the holograph version, "he was like to forget Carrie entirely. She came into his mind when all later divinities were out, or when he was on his way back to Chicago. . . . He would enter Carrie's presence with all the spirit of a lover—away from her would forsake her memory with the ease of the unattached masher, which, after all, he was" (*PE*, 105–6). Also, his promise to marry Carrie after completing a "fictitious real estate deal" was first presented as more clearly a ruse, labeled by Dreiser "a sop to Carrie's matrimonial desires" designed to make her "feel content with her state, the while he winged his merry thoughtless round" (*PE*, 135). Though readers of the revised text have tended to respond rather positively to Drouet's generous good nature and have shared his sense of injury upon learning of Carrie's defection to Hurstwood ("You didn't do me right, Cad" [*PE*, 260]), the fact is that when these words were originally uttered, they had the distinct taint of hypocrisy. All in all, as first conceived by Dreiser, the "old butterfly" had wings that were somewhat more sullied.

The characterization most significantly altered, however, was Hurstwood's. In the holograph, he was presented as a more devious and lustful character who was to a greater extent responsible for his own downfall. He was the blatant hypocrite, maintaining the decorous public life that his managerial position demanded while being a philanderer in private long before meeting Carrie. Dreiser wrote in an excised passage that, compared to Drouet, Hurstwood "saw a trifle more clearly the necessities of our social organization, but he was more unscrupulous in the matter of sinning against it. He did not, as a matter of fact, conduct himself as loosely as Drouet, but it was entirely owing to a respect for his situation. In the actual matter of a decision and a consummation, he was worse than Drouet. He more deliberately set aside the canons of right as he understood them" (*PE*, 106). In his attempt to lure Carrie away from Drouet, Hurstwood was originally driven more explicitly by sexual desire and titillated by the illicit nature of the affair. And once he had Carrie in the hotel in Montreal, he "longed for a complete matrimonial union" (*PE*, 300) after appeasing her with some new outfits. In fact, Hurstwood's conduct prompted Dreiser to expound at some length on the potential doom of men whose "only thought is to obtain pleasure and shun responsibility" (*PE*, 132). During one of the longer philosophical flights deleted, Dreiser foreshadowed Hurstwood's tragic decline in New York:

> When, after error, pain falls as a lash, [adulterous men] do not comprehend that their suffering is due to misbehavior. Many such an individual is so lashed by necessity and law that he falls fainting to the ground, dies hungry in the gutter or rotting in jail and it never once flashes across his mind that he has been lashed only in so far as he has persisted in attempting to trespass the boundaries which necessity sets. (*PE*, 132)

Even in the robbery of the safe, Hurstwood was originally more culpable. As the scene was eventually revised, the fatal irony was that the safe door accidentally locked after Hurstwood had decided *not* to abscond with the money and was in the process of returning it to the proper boxes. In the holograph version, however, the door closed when he had decided to go through with the theft and was in the process of returning the empty money boxes after filling his satchel. Immediately preceding the clicking of the safe, Dreiser had first written two paragraphs that were later removed:

> Could he not get away? What would be the use of remaining? He would never get such a chance again. He emptied the good money into the satchel. There was something fascinating about the soft green stack—the loose silver and gold. He felt sure now that he could not leave that. No, no. He would do it. He would lock the safe before he had time to change his mind.
>
> He went over and restored the empty boxes. Then he pushed the door to for somewhere near the sixth time. He wavered, thinking, putting his hand to his brow. (*PE*, 270–71)

Though Dreiser equivocated slightly in the final line, his original intent was apparently to make Hurstwood's flight from Chicago and decline in New York the results of a much more willful act than they ultimately became.

When Dreiser submitted the *Sister Carrie* typescript to Doubleday, Page and Company later in May 1900, the narrative pace had been quickened, some of the more sordid elements had been removed, and the characters had been made more sympathetic; yet, the novel's publication was far from assured. Doubleday, Page was a relatively new firm which had published naturalist Frank Norris's *McTeague* in 1899; thus, Henry Mills Alden recommended it to Dreiser as a more liberal press that might be willing to take a chance on a novel of *Sister Carrie*'s frank nature. When submitted, the novel was fortuitously assigned to the selfsame Frank Norris, who was also a reader for the firm. Doubtless impressed by its naturalistic qualities, Norris declared *Sister Carrie* a "masterpiece," a must for publication.[32] Immediately, in a letter dated May 28, Norris communicated his enthusiasm to Dreiser: "I said, and it gives me pleasure to repeat it, that it was the best novel I have read in M.S. since I [have] been reading for the firm, and that it pleased me as well as any novel I have read in any form, published or otherwise" (*NCE*, 434). The manuscript was then read by Henry Lanier, senior editor, and Walter Hines Page, junior partner. Both concurred with Norris's recommendation but were somewhat less impressed. Lanier disliked the title and had reservations about Dreiser's Balzacian technique of using actual names in a fictional work; both were concerned about the commonness of the characters. Nevertheless, on June 9, Page wrote Dreiser to congratulate him on "so good a piece of work" (*NCE*, 435) and to set up a meeting for the following day, when Page gave Dreiser a verbal promise to publish *Sister Carrie* in the fall. The senior partner, Frank Doubleday, was abroad at the time.

Assuming that all was well, Dreiser left Henry in New York to continue negotiations with Doubleday, Page and departed for an extended vacation with his in-laws in Missouri. In mid-July, however, the first shot of Dreiser's well-documented battle with his first publisher was fired.[33] Henry informed him in a letter dated July 14 that the firm was dragging its heels on publication

32. Quoted in Dudley, *Forgotten Frontiers*, 168.

33. For a fuller narrative of Dreiser's struggle with Doubleday, Page, see Lingeman, *Theodore Dreiser*, 283–94; Dudley, *Forgotten Frontiers*, 166–84; and James L. W. West III, *A "Sister Carrie" Portfolio* (Charlottesville: University Press of Virginia, 1985), 54–74.

and that Lanier threatened to block the novel unless a "more imposing and pretentious" title was provided and the names of real people were changed (*NCE*, 435–36). Four days later, Norris wrote Henry, suggesting that in view of the growing opposition *Sister Carrie* might prudently be offered to another firm. On July 19, Page wrote Dreiser to voice his concern about the wisdom of publishing a novel whose characters would fail to interest "the great majority of readers" and whose coarseness might jeopardize Dreiser's literary future. He therefore asked that Doubleday, Page be released from its publication agreement (*NCE*, 439–40). That same day, Henry wrote to reveal the primary reason behind this reevaluation of the novel: Frank Doubleday had returned, had branded the novel "immoral and badly written," and wished to renege on the promise to publish it. Presumably, Doubleday disapproved (at least from a commercial standpoint) of Dreiser's allowing Carrie to achieve fame and fortune as an actress despite her many moral compromises and did not wish to associate his press with such cynicism.[34] Though he admitted to Henry in a subsequent conference that he was legally bound to publish *Sister Carrie*, Doubleday warned that if forced to keep the agreement, he "would make no effort to sell it as the more it sold the worse he would feel about it" (*NCE*, 438).

On July 23, Dreiser wrote Henry, enclosing a letter to be typed and forwarded to Page. To Henry, he announced his fatalistic decision to hold Doubleday, Page to its promise, as the widespread knowledge of the novel's forthcoming publication would make rejection at that point humiliating and injurious to his career (*NCE*, 440–43). In his letter to Page, Dreiser did not respond directly to the request that the firm be released from its obligation. Rather, he noted the personal and financial injury he would suffer from an eleventh-hour change of plans and appealed to Doubleday, Page's "keen and

34. Legend has cast Neltje Doubleday, Frank Doubleday's wife, in the role of villain concerning the suppression of *Sister Carrie*. No compelling evidence has been found to validate her complicity, however. Dreiser believed her to be responsible for her husband's antipathy (*Letters*, 2:418, 421), and in support of this belief, Dorothy Dudley presented a dramatic scene, admittedly imagined, in which Neltje Doubleday stormed into the study of her husband, who was "possibly enjoying *Sister Carrie*," to demand that in the name of decency he block its publication. Dudley insisted that in spite of her many philanthropies Neltje Doubleday could not identify with the lives of the lower classes or appreciate Dreiser's compassion for them (*Forgotten Frontiers*, 171–79).

honorable conception of justice and duty." The question of the novel's merit could be answered by public response (*NCE*, 443–45).

When on August 2 Page wrote again to ask for a release, arguing that the publication of a morally questionable novel like *Sister Carrie* would be more injurious to its author in the long run than its rejection, Dreiser, bolstered by Norris and Henry, refused to yield. He voiced his faith in the truthfulness and moral value of the novel and again expressed a willingness to allow the reading public to be the final arbiter: "I feel and I know that what I have seen and what I have heard of the rudeness and bitterness of life are in the eyes and ears of all men justifiable—that the world is greedy for details of how men rise and fall. In the presence of a story which deals with the firm insistence of law, the elements of chance and sub-conscious direction, men will not, I have heart to feel, stand unanimously indifferent" (*NCE*, 449–51). Page on August 15 made one last effort to avoid publication by offering to place *Sister Carrie* with another publisher, but Dreiser apparently did not officially respond to this suggestion. Nor did he budge when, during a final discussion of the matter, Doubleday exploded: "All right! You stand on your legal rights and we'll stand on ours. . . . I see that a man of your stamp will have trouble with any publisher you deal with and it will please me if you never set foot in this office again. We publish one edition as to contract, but we won't do as we would by a book we liked."[35] Thus, after consulting their attorney regarding minimal publication and marketing obligations, Doubleday, Page bowed to the inevitable and drew up a formal contract listing the book's title as "The Flesh and the Spirit." Dreiser signed it on August 20, after writing in "Sister Carrie" as an alternate title.

In early September, Doubleday, Page returned the typescript for required revisions, laying out the particulars in a cover letter from Doubleday bearing the chilly salutation "Dear Sir." He announced that he would yield to Dreiser's preference for "Sister Carrie" as the title but that all references to real people and places had to be removed, as did profanity. Also, passages of questionable taste were identified as those which should be "changed to advantage" (*NCE*, 452). Again Dreiser and Henry went through the typescript, after which it was returned "partly revised." Though they did eliminate many real names, Dreiser argued that some—such as Augustin

---

35. Quoted in Swanberg, *Dreiser,* 90.

Daly, John L. Sullivan, and the restaurant Delmonico—were already common in literature, including literature published by Doubleday, Page, and did not need alteration. He also balked at the excision of mild oaths, such as "damn" and "by God" (*NCE*, 453). On the other hand, Dreiser tended to yield in regard to sexually suggestive passages, and in the process he whitewashed Hurstwood's character even more by eliminating references to women the manager entertained after hours at his saloon and to visits he made to "those more unmentionable resorts of vice—the gilded chambers of shame with which Chicago was then so liberally cursed" (*PE*, 44, 48).

It was perhaps at this time that the poetic chapter titles were handwritten into the typescript by both Dreiser and Henry, though their time of composition and purpose have been debated. The editors of the Pennsylvania Edition speculated that the titles were last-minute additions to compensate for the philosophical passages lost to previous cuts (*PE*, 525, 583). Philip Williams agreed with this timing but suggested that they were Dreiser's final effort to raise the literary level of the novel as a concession to Doubleday, Page. Donald Pizer, on the other hand, has argued that the titles were composed during the major revision of the typescript before it was submitted to publishers and that their "lachrymose" quality reflects Henry's poetic nature and demonstrates his great influence on Dreiser at this time.[36]

Someone apparently made additional revisions on the page proofs, most of which were incidental; some, however, reveal a continuing effort to cleanse *Sister Carrie*. Some of the real names that Dreiser had left unchanged were altered; the word *bastards* was excised from a strike scene (*PE*, 424); the "dingy lavatory" (*PE*, 460) where Hurstwood counted his last ten dollars became a "dingy hall" (*NCE*, 337); and the bogus wedding ceremony in Montreal between Carrie and Hurstwood was shifted to the afternoon of the day of their arrival rather than the day after they had spent a night together in the hotel. As the relationship between Dreiser and his publisher was obviously strained at this point and as neither the galleys nor the page proofs are extant, it is impossible to determine the extent of Dreiser's participation in or approval of these changes.

On November 8, 1900, *Sister Carrie* was published, bearing a dedication to "Arthur Henry whose steadfast ideals and serene devotion to truth and

---

36. Philip Williams, "Chapter Titles of *Sister Carrie*," *American Literature* 36 (November 1964): 359–60; Pizer, *Novels of Theodore Dreiser*, 52.

beauty have served to lighten the purpose and strengthen the method of this volume." The recipient of this generous dedication had predicted that the "story will make all its objectors look small when it gets to the public" (*NCE*, 439); however, the "objectors" gave it little opportunity. Only 1,008 copies were printed, and 450 of these were left unbound. Those which were bound had a dull red cover with small black lettering, "an assassin's edition," Dorothy Dudley described it, "in a country where books have to look expensive in order to be well thought of."[37] Dreiser later claimed that Doubleday suppressed the novel by having all salable copies confined to the firm's basement rather than marketing them, and it is true that *Sister Carrie* was not widely advertised. Copies did, however, find their way into bookstores, and orders were filled. Also, Frank Norris was allowed to send out 127 review copies and conduct an extensive letter-writing campaign in the novel's behalf. He succeeded to the point that its critical reception was generally positive, although sometimes grudgingly so.[38] But commercially, *Sister Carrie* was a failure. The first edition sold only 456 copies and brought Dreiser $68.40 in royalties. As W. A. Swanberg summed up the situation, "The public simply did not want *Sister Carrie* in 1900."[39]

The failure of *Sister Carrie* devastated Dreiser and contributed to a neurasthenic condition that debilitated him for three years.[40] When he returned to the literary world in 1904, however, his faith in *Sister Carrie* had not diminished, and he worked tirelessly to place it with another publisher, purchasing the plates and remaining stock himself in 1906. The following year, B. W. Dodge reissued *Sister Carrie,* and the story of its rise to the stature of American classic began. During this period, Dreiser contemplated further revision;[41] however, he actually made few changes. For the Dodge edition, he rewrote twenty lines to eliminate the plagiarism from George Ade and dropped the dedication to Arthur Henry, with whom he by then

37. Dudley, *Forgotten Frontiers,* 183.

38. Jack Salzman has demonstrated that contrary to legend negative reviews of *Sister Carrie* in 1900 were few in number ("Critical Recognition of *Sister Carrie,* 1900–1907," *Journal of American Studies* 3 [July 1969]: 124–25).

39. Swanberg, *Dreiser,* 92.

40. For details concerning Dreiser's illness, see Richard W. Dowell, introduction to *An Amateur Laborer,* ed. Richard W. Dowell, James L. W. West III, and Neda Westlake (Philadelphia: University of Pennsylvania Press, 1983), xi–xlix.

41. See James L. W. West III, "John Paul Dreiser's Copy of *Sister Carrie,*" *Library Chronicle* 44 (Spring 1979): 85–93, and *Letters,* 1:135.

had quarreled. After that, *Sister Carrie* would be republished without change seven more times in the United States during Dreiser's lifetime. In fact, all editions but one were printed from the altered Doubleday, Page plates.[42]


## V


In 1981, the Pennsylvania Edition challenged the preeminence of the Doubleday, Page text by presenting *Sister Carrie* as Dreiser had initially conceived and written it. Choosing as their copy-text the holograph manuscript before it was submitted to Jug and Henry for revision, the Pennsylvania editors argued that Dreiser's artistic control declined as the novel went through its various editing stages. "In the strictest sense," they insisted, "his authorial function ceased after he inscribed the holograph draft of *Sister Carrie*" (*PE*, 580). From that point on, he took a more passive role, as his collaborators, Anna Mallon's typists, and the Doubleday, Page editors made changes which perhaps improved the prose mechanically and increased the novel's publication potential and marketability but often compromised its narrative power and philosophical focus.

Neither Jug nor Henry fully comprehended Dreiser's artistic intentions, the Pennsylvania editors contended, and thus they introduced revisions and cuts that simplified characterization, weakened the philosophical foundation, and often dissipated the force of Dreiser's Germanic prose. Although Dreiser approved and participated in these changes, he did so because he desperately wanted to see the novel published and because his background as a journalist had conditioned him to readily accept the editing of others. Alterations made during the typing stage were frequently inadvertent and perhaps went unrecognized, whereas those recommended by Doubleday and perhaps accomplished on the page proofs were virtually forced on Dreiser. Thus, the text that emerged was compromised by practical considerations and well-meaning but at times artistically unsound advice.

To re-create the *Sister Carrie* Dreiser intended to write, the Pennsylvania editors rejected the majority of revisions not made in Dreiser's hand and restored most of the deleted passages. Editing by Jug, Henry, and others

---

42. In 1939, when Dreiser was sixty-eight, the Limited Editions Club reset *Sister Carrie* for a deluxe edition but did not alter the text.

was accepted only if it contributed to the clarity or grammatical correctness of the prose. As a result of this restoration, the editors insisted, the prose is more consistently Dreiserian, the philosophical implications are clearer, and the characters have greater complexity and credibility. They become "a fascinating group, motivated by conflicting urges they cannot understand and at the mercy of fates they cannot control" (*PE*, 534). Carrie emerges somewhat tougher and more sexually aware; Drouet becomes more cynical and less appealing; Hurstwood is understood to be more unscrupulous and vulnerable from the beginning; and even Ames has greater warmth. Finally, the Pennsylvania editors returned to the original endings for the final two chapters, feeling that Ames's infatuation with Carrie and Hurstwood's suicide as a conclusion represent Dreiser's independent plan and are more consistent with the novel as a whole. The revised ending seemed "contrived and unnatural—more like clumsy graftings than natural parts of the novel" (*PE*, 585). The cumulative effect of the decisions made by the Pennsylvania editors is "a more balanced and compelling novel, a new and more tragic work of art" (*PE*, 535).

The validity and superiority of the Pennsylvania Edition have not been universally accepted, however. For example, Donald Pizer, one of the edition's severest critics,[43] has challenged the logic of the editorial decisions, arguing that to reject the contributions of Jug and Henry is to ignore Dreiser's lifelong composition practices. Typically Dreiser wrote first drafts that were too long for publication and then sought the help of friends, lovers, secretaries, and editors during the revision process. Also, he had second thoughts about the endings of most of his novels, six of eight, in fact, and usually depended on the advice of others in making the final decision. Thus, the evolution of the Doubleday, Page *Sister Carrie* accurately reflects the collaborative nature of Dreiser's work. In addition, Dreiser had several opportunities during his lifetime to "restore" *Sister Carrie,* had he chosen to do so, but did not.

Though conceding the Pennsylvania Edition's value in making available the composition history of *Sister Carrie,* Pizer has also challenged the artistic superiority of the text, noting that the majority of the cuts represent Henry's

---

43. For further examination of Pizer's views on the Pennsylvania Edition, see his "Self-Censorship and Textual Editing," in *Textual Criticism and Interpretation,* ed. Jerome J. McGann (Chicago: University of Chicago Press, 1985), 156–61, and "Book Reviews: *Sister Carrie,*" *American Literature* 53 (January 1982): 731–37.

attempt to prune out repetition and irrelevancies—work that would have been done by any skilled editor—but that in some instances the revisions also reflect a desire for character consistency. At the outset, having been patterned on Dreiser's sister Emma and her lover Hopkins, Carrie and Hurstwood were conceived as relatively crude, amoral people; however, as the novel progressed and they became projections of Dreiser's own artistic aspirations and fears of failure, their portrayals became increasingly sympathetic. Thus, by lessening Hurstwood's culpability and smoothing out Carrie's rougher edges, particularly in the early stages of the narrative, Dreiser and Henry were not censoring the material but rather attempting to anticipate a more tragic Hurstwood and a more refined Carrie, one who would be credible as a successful actress and seeker of beauty. As Pizer concluded his analysis of the novel's revision, "Behind the ballyhoo attached to the 'discovery' of the 'true' *Sister Carrie,* the Pennsylvania edition is simply not that clearly better or worse than the Doubleday-Page version of 1900. The principal impression of most general readers familiar with the first edition will be, I believe, simply that it is longer."[44]

A final concern for Pizer is the historical validity of the Pennsylvania Edition. The text that emerged in 1900 is the product of the literary climate of that era, Dreiser's bitter struggle with a reluctant publisher, and the tensions in his own life—including perhaps tensions between artistic integrity and a deep desire for financial success. Also, the critical reception of the 1900 version, its initial failure, and its ultimate success played a significant role in the development of twentieth-century American literature. Thus, to replace that text is to compromise the novel's historical and biographical significance. "If we are to read *Sister Carrie* as a novel of 1900," wrote Pizer, "I would prefer to read the novel that emerged out of the personal tensions, conflicting motives, and cultural complexities of that moment and that in eighty years since its publication has accrued a rich public responsiveness and role. I would not care to read a *Carrie* that has in effect been created out of the textual editing controversies and theorizing of the 1960s and 1970s."[45] And so, appropriately enough, the story of *Sister Carrie*'s composition ends for now in controversy.

44. Pizer, "Self-Censorship and Textual Editing," 159.
45. Ibid., 160.

But what of Henry's *Princess of Arcady, Sister Carrie*'s companion novel? According to Dreiser's account to Mencken in 1916, years after the rupture of his friendship with Arthur Henry, that novel also became a cooperative venture. As Dreiser recalled, "Henry's interest in *Sister Carrie* having been so great, his own book was neglected and he could not finish the last chapter. Since he had told it to me so often and I knew exactly what he desired to say, I wrote it. But don't accuse him or me of it in public. It wouldn't be kind, I'm afraid." After its completion, *A Princess of Arcady* was dedicated to Anna Mallon, accepted by Doubleday, Page, and, like *Sister Carrie,* published in 1900. Unlike *Carrie,* it was advertised as a "charming idyll," "a delicate romance," and a "striking contrast to the strenuous and often unpleasant fiction which is so common today."[46]

---

46. *Letters,* 1:214; quoted in Lingeman, *Theodore Dreiser,* 244.

# Building *The House of Mirth*

CANDACE WAID

§   §   §

IN 1902, AFTER READING *The Valley of Decision*, Edith Wharton's two-volume novel set in eighteenth-century Italy, Henry James advised the beginning novelist to devote herself to "the American subject." He insisted: "Don't pass it by—the immediate, the real, the only, the yours, the novelist's that it waits for. *Do New York!*" In his letter to her sister-in-law, Mary Cadwalader Jones, James warned, "she must be tethered in native pastures even if it means confining her to a backyard in New York." As James confessed his desire "to get hold of the little lady and pump the pure essence of my wisdom and experience into her,"[1] Wharton already was at work on a novel set in New York City and the rural estates of Long Island, but this early work, entitled "Disintegration," would remain unfinished. Like her unpublished autobiography, "Life and I," and in some ways like her highly autobiographical unfinished novel, "Literature," "Disintegration" depicts a lonely child who finds solace in the world of books and the lyrical comforts of language. Although not specifically autobiographical, "Disintegration" may have been left unfinished because it offered too painful a portrait of Wharton's own childhood. In 1925, Wharton would recast the story in *The Mother's Recompense* (1925), presenting it from the perspective of the mother rather than the isolated child. In addition, there are strong presentiments in "Disintegration" of *The Custom of the Country* (1913), Wharton's second

---

1. Cited in R. W. B. Lewis, *Edith Wharton: A Biography* (New York: Harper and Row, 1975), 126, from a letter James wrote to Mary Cadwalader Jones in August 1902. As part of his efforts, James tells her he is sending Wharton his *Wings of the Dove*, which he confesses is "rather long winded."

major novel about New York society. This early fragment also contains a striking image that would find its way into *The House of Mirth,* the breakthrough novel about New York society that Wharton would publish in 1905. Mr. Clephane of "Disintegration" tells a sympathetic male friend: "I tell you what it is, if a woman throws you over for a man, you're a man yourself and can face it; but if she throws you over for an income you're no more than an empty purse in the gutter." Like the discarded husband in "Disintegration," Gus Trenor, the sexual predator who tries to entrap the naive heroine of *The House of Mirth,* links female sexual interests to money as he complains that he has been "chuck[ed] in the gutter like an empty purse."[2] This detail is the only trace of "Disintegration" that survives in *The House of Mirth.*

Although some of the names of the characters in the novel began to appear in her notebooks as early as the turn of the century, Wharton actually began to write *The House of Mirth* in 1904. This novel would not only be set in New York; it would, in James's phrase, "do New York." Wharton described her subject, "the immediate, the real," as "fashionable New York"[3] and the novel would be marketed as an insider's critique of New York society. Wharton promised *The House of Mirth* to *Scribner's* before it was completed. With no date set for its publication in either serial or book form, Wharton found herself drifting "between [her] critical dissatisfaction with the work, and the distractions of a busy and hospitable life, full of friends and travel, reading and gardening" (*BG,* 207). Late in 1904, however, Wharton's publisher asked her if her new novel could replace another work which was not yet ready; and overcoming her initial hesitation, she agreed to begin its publication in monthly installments. When *The House of Mirth* began appearing in *Scribner's* magazine in January of 1905, Wharton had completed fewer than 50,000 words of the novel. With her first chapter appearing as she continued to write the novel, Wharton was encouraged by

2. Edith Wharton, *The House of Mirth,* ed. R. W. B. Lewis (New York: New York University Press, 1977), 142. Hereafter cited parenthetically in the text as *HM.* See typescript of the unfinished novel "Disintegration," p. 22, Wharton Collection, Beinecke Rare Book and Manuscript Library, Yale University. Permission to quote from the manuscripts in the Wharton Collection in this essay is gratefully acknowledged.

3. Edith Wharton, *A Backward Glance* (New York: Charles Scribner's Sons, 1985), 206. Hereafter cited parenthetically as *BG.*

the response of an eager reading public and she had what was for her the unusual experience of having readers respond to a work which was still in her hands. Wharton also discovered that in writing for an immutable deadline, a schedule which had been set with the appearance of the first chapters, she gained "what I most lacked—self-confidence." "[B]ent . . . to the discipline of the daily task," Wharton discovered "that inscrutable 'inspiration of the writing table' which Baudelaire, most untrammeled and nerve-racked of geniuses, proclaimed as insistently as Trollope." "It was good," she would write in *A Backward Glance,* "to be turned from a drifting amateur into a professional; but that was nothing compared to the effect on my imagination of systematic daily effort. I was like Saul the son of Kish, who went out to find an ass, and came back with a kingdom: the kingdom of mastery over my tools" (*BG,* 208–9).

By the time *The House of Mirth* reached bookstores in October 1905, it was already a cultural and, in many ways, a social event. Wharton's New York, "real" and "immediate," was for most readers a distant phenomenon; and part of its attraction was the promise proclaimed on the dust jacket (in what Wharton considered to be lurid prose) that "for the first time the veil has been lifted from New York society." Writing to the publisher, Wharton protested forcefully: "I thought that, in the House of Scribner, 'The House of Mirth' was safe from all such Harperesque methods of *réclame.*" In response to her plea to them to "do all you can to stop the spread of that pestilent paragraph, and to efface it from the paper cover of future printings," Scribner's oversaw the immediate removal of the paragraph which made the novel's author "sick at the recollection of it!"[4] Although Wharton disapproved of the selling of her book as an exposé, a marketing strategy which seemed to place her in the popular province of muckrakers and other writers of sensational fiction, in at least one letter responding to comments from an admiring reader she acknowledged that in writing the novel she had indeed lifted a concealing "garment" to expose a formerly hidden aspect of New York life. After thanking her reader for his kind words about the novel, Wharton insisted, "I must protest, & emphatically, against the suggestion that I have 'stripped' New York society. New York society is still amply clad, & the little corner of its garment that I lifted was meant to show only that

4. Lewis, *Edith Wharton: A Biography,* 151.

little atrophied organ—the group of idle and dull people—that exists in any big & wealthy social body."[5]

A best-seller, the first printing was sold out immediately and subsequent printings had difficulty keeping up with the orders. One advertising circular, underlined and saved by Wharton herself, claimed that printers were working day and night to satisfy the demand. *The House of Mirth* sold thirty thousand copies in the first six weeks. In a small pocket diary begun in 1905 and continued through 1906, amidst occasional notations about the weather, Wharton often recorded her sales, apparently pleased by the continued and surprising success of her novel. Writing to Charles Scribner less than a month after the novel's publication in book form, Wharton expressed her delight: "It is a very beautiful thought to me that 80,000 people should want to read 'The House of Mirth,' & if the number should ascend to 100,000 I fear my pleasure would exceed the bounds of decency." Commenting on a publicity photograph, Wharton seems conscious of her new notoriety as she describes her calculated pose, "with my eyes looking down, *trying to look modest?!*" The popular success of Wharton's novel (which was not expected to sell a great deal because it was not a love story) put at least one skeptical editor in the position of re-evaluating his view of the tastes of the American reading public. Less than two months after the novel's appearance in book form, she wrote to Edward Burlingame of Scribner's, using the same biblical allusion she would use nearly thirty years later to describe her experience of learning to be a writer, "I am especially glad to find that you think *[The House of Mirth's]* large circulation a sign of awakening taste in our fellowcountrymen—at least in 100,000 of them. I was afraid that, reversing the experience of Saul and the son of Kish, I had gone out to seek a kingdom and found all the asses!"[6]

Wharton's novel remained at the top of the best-seller list for four months in a year which saw the publication of such works as Upton Sinclair's

---

5. Wharton continues: "If it seems more conspicuous in New York than in an old civilization, it is because the whole social organization with us is so much smaller & less elaborate—& if, as I believe, it is more harmful in its influence, it is because fewer responsibilities attach to money with us than in other societies" (Wharton to William Roscoe Thayer, *The Letters of Edith Wharton*, ed. R. W. B. Lewis and Nancy Lewis [New York: Charles Scribner's Sons, 1988], November 11, 1905, pp. 96–97).

6. *Letters*, November 11, 1905, p. 95; November 23, 1905, p. 98.

masterpiece of muckraking, *The Jungle,* and Thomas Dixon's popular, race-baiting novel, *The Clansman.*[7] As Millicent Bell has shown, even before *The House of Mirth* had become the best and most rapidly selling book in the history of what Wharton herself had begun calling the "House of Scribner," the ambitious author had begun to negotiate new terms, probably based on her hopes that the strong initial response to the serial would be translated into sales of the book. After only three installments had appeared, she confidently wrote her publishers that after "the Enormous Sales of 'The House of Mirth' which I predict for next November you will see my prices leap up!"[8] Later, after her optimistic predictions had been realized, Wharton demonstrated that she was conscious of the market value of a sought-after professional writer. Negotiating the contract for another novel in May of 1905, four months before *The House of Mirth* would appear in book form, she asked for an $8,000 advance and proposed an increase in royalties from 15 percent to 20 percent "if the sale of the [proposed] volume exceeded 10,000." In a humorous swipe at those who were disappointed by the weakness of Lawrence Selden, Wharton promised a hero with new muscle in her next novel, *The Fruit of the Tree.* She warned that her new character would be a manly figure who would insist on higher royalties: "he is going to be a very strong man; so strong that I believe he will break all records. Perhaps in consideration of his strength you will think it not unreasonable to start with a 20% royalty? If you were to refuse, he is so violent that I don't know whether I can answer for the consequences!"[9]

Wharton's first story had appeared in *Scribner's* in 1891 and her first volume of fiction, *The Greater Inclination,* appeared eight years later, in 1899. She would later claim that the appearance of this first volume of fiction "broke the chains which had held me so long in a kind of torpor" (*BG,* 122). This work, which includes a series of stories written after her nervous breakdown, marks the point at which she came to acknowledge her life as

7. Lewis lists these novels in *Edith Wharton: A Biography,* 151. Dixon's *Clansman* rose to even greater prominence as the novel that D. W. Griffith used as the basis for his racist epic, *The Birth of a Nation.*

8. Millicent Bell, "Lady into Author: Edith Wharton and the House of Scribner," *American Quarterly* 9 (1957): 298–300.

9. Cited by Bell from a letter written by Wharton to her publishers on November 22, 1905.

a writer as the greater inclination, an inclination which took precedence over her exhausting and enervating duties as a young society matron. From the outset, Wharton had received a number of positive notices about her fiction, but none had equaled the moment when she went into a British bookstore and was offered *The Greater Inclination,* what she described as her "own firstborn," as "the book of the day!" (*BG*, 124). Viewed for the most part as a writer of stories, Wharton brought out two other collections, *Crucial Instances* (1901) and *The Descent of Man* (1904). Whereas her stories were often ironic and revealed an effort to expose sentimental constructions, her early novellas—*The Touchstone* (1900) and *Sanctuary* (1903)—were carried by elaborate emotional plotting which depended heavily on the traditions of melodrama. In contrast, Wharton's two-volume novel, *The Valley of Decision* (1902), seemed more coldly intellectual, its characters almost overwhelmed by the novel's attention to background and setting. *The Valley of Decision* displayed its author's meticulous research into the history of the cultural life and the powerful intellectual, social, and religious forces shaping eighteenth-century Italy (including such details as the proper dress for nuns going to illicit assignations).[10] In addition to suggesting her deep interest in Italian culture, an interest which continued in such works of nonfiction as *Italian Villas and Their Gardens* (1904) and her less technical and more impressionistic *Italian Backgrounds* (1905), *The Valley of Decision* recalls Wharton's first foray into book writing, her 1897 coauthored treatise on interior decoration entitled *The Decoration of Houses.*

As she looked back on the process of writing *The House of Mirth* in *A Backward Glance,* Wharton would recall that despite the critical and popular success of the novel, she felt that she still did not "yet know how to write a novel; *but I know how to find out how to.*" Continuing her efforts to teach herself how to write a novel, Wharton felt that she wrote the next novels "without the feeling that I had made much progress" and that it was only in the composition of *Ethan Frome* (1911) that she "suddenly felt the artisan's full control of his implements" (*BG*, 209). In a letter to the novelist Robert Grant written in 1907, responding to his comments on *The Fruit of the Tree*

---

10. I am grateful to R. W. B. Lewis for his discussions about Wharton's research and the extent of her attention to historical detail.

(the flawed novel which immediately followed her triumph in *The House of Mirth*), Wharton offered a gendered explanation of what she saw as her problems as a writer:

> I am very much pleased that you like the construction of the book, & more than agree with you that I haven't been able to keep the characters from being, so to speak, mere *building-material*. The fact is that I am beginning to see exactly where my weakest point is.—I conceive my subjects like a man—that is, rather more architectonically & dramatically than most women—& then execute them like a woman; or rather, I sacrifice, to my desire for construction & breadth, the small incidental effects that women have always excelled in, the episodical characterization, I mean. The worst of it is that the fault is congenital & not from the ambition to do big things.

Wharton goes on to ascribe gender to the practice of genres:

> As soon as I look at a subject from the novel-angle I see it in its relation to a larger whole, in all its remotest connections; & I can't help trying to take them all in, at the cost of the smaller realism that I arrive at, I think, better in my short stories. This is the reason why I have always obscurely felt that I didn't know how to write a novel. I feel it more clearly after each attempt, because it is in such contrast to the sense of authority with which I take hold of a short story.[11]

Henry James criticized *The House of Mirth* by calling it "two books and too confused"[12] and he was particularly troubled by what Wharton might have called the "episodical" structure of the second book of the novel. However, this half of the novel (which follows the erratic course of Lily Bart's descent through the layers of society in the final year of her life) in many ways accomplishes the marriage of the short story and the novel as Wharton describes them in her letter to Grant. As Wharton plotted *The House of Mirth*, Lily Bart's story unfolds through "episodical characterization[s]."

11. *Letters*, November 9, 1907, p. 124.
12. Lewis, *Edith Wharton: A Biography*, 153. Lewis quotes a letter written by James to Mary Cadwaller Jones in which James refers to *The House of Mirth* as "Mrs. Wharton's pleasantly palpable hit."

Indeed, although *The House of Mirth* was planned as a novel, its appearance in monthly installments in *Scribner's* magazine underlined its affinity with short fiction and may have led Wharton to think of the individual chapters if not as self-contained entities at least as related episodes of a novel which were destined to appear in segments. While there are only a few of the cliff-hangers that are characteristic of serially published gothic thrillers, such as James's own *Turn of the Screw,* the anticipation of breaks in the narrative no doubt forced her as she was completing the novel to think about the cohesion within the monthly segments, and this, in turn, may have influenced her in the pacing of the book. The plotting of *The House of Mirth* is in many ways dramatic; Wharton, who was translating a play by Suderman at around the same time, was no doubt influenced by the theatrical productions she was attending as she staged the scenes of her novel.[13]

As she prepared the manuscript of *The House of Mirth* for publication, Wharton reread the installments of her novel. With her passion for order, her near worship of classical symmetry, and her admittedly "exorbitant" "theory of what the novel ought to be," she worried about the vagaries of her plot. Beset by great doubts and even greater insecurity about the merit of the work, she rejoiced in a letter from one of her editors at Scribner's, William Crary Brownell, complimenting her on the architecture of the work. "[S]urprised & pleased, & altogether taken aback," Wharton describes herself as unable "decently [to] compose my countenance. . . . I was pleased with bits, myself; but as I go over the proofs the whole thing strikes me as so loosely built, with so many dangling threads, & *cul-de-sacs,* & long dusty stretches, that I had reached the point of wondering how I had ever tried my hand at a long thing—So your seeing a certain amount of architecture in it rejoices me above everything."[14]

If James and others were disappointed by Wharton's plotting of the second half of the novel, they recognized the central and unifying appeal of Lily Bart. James announced with admiration that Lily Bart was "big and true—

---

13. See Cynthia Griffin Wolff, "Lily Bart and the Drama of Femininity," *American Literary History* 6 (1994): 71–87.

14. Quoting Alphonse Daudet's comment on his own sense of inadequacy as a novelist, the woman whom Henry James would later describe as an eagle lamented: "Je rêve d'un aigle, j'accouche d'un colibri [I dream of an eagle, and I give birth to a hummingbird]," *Letters,* August 5, 1905, pp. 94–95.

and very difficult to have *kept* big and true."[15] Part of the balance which Wharton achieves in *The House of Mirth* comes from her powerful sense of her subject. Recalling her fears that New York society and the rich and thoughtless figures who occupy its "house[s] of mirth" might offer too shallow a ground for her novel, she found herself turning her attention to the potential devastation which was part of the legacy of these "irresponsible pleasure-seekers." Answering her own question about whether a topic might be too trivial to merit the detailed scrutiny of a novel, Wharton concluded that "a frivolous society can acquire dramatic significance only through what its frivolity destroys. Its tragic implication lies in its power of debasing of people and ideals. The answer, in short, was my heroine, Lily Bart" (*BG*, 207). Writing the year before *The House of Mirth* appeared, W. L. Courtney in *The Feminine Note in Fiction* praised Wharton's work as an interesting example of the psychological novels associated with Henry James but noted that "no one could describe her as a great novelist."[16] This view changed with the appearance of *The House of Mirth*. In her new novel, Wharton seemed freed from the wooden characters and the morass of detail and furniture of the past which had taken over her earlier novel, *The Valley of Decision*. She achieved an aesthetic breakthrough and even the few critics who persisted in minimizing her talent as a novelist acknowledged that she had become a major figure on the American literary scene. *The House of Mirth* was in many ways the book in which Edith Wharton began to write like Edith Wharton. Aspects of her capacity for sharp wit and social satire had been glimpsed in her short stories, but the incisive prose and sustained analysis in this work established her place not only as one of the best writers in America but also as an important cultural critic.

Whatever Wharton's doubts about her abilities as a writer of fiction, her preservation of the manuscript versions of her novels, stories, and other works through her several changes of permanent residence, including her move from the United States to France, suggests that she valued the documents which tell the story of her development as a writer. It is impossible to

15. Cited by Lewis in *Edith Wharton: A Biography*, 153.

16. W. L. Courtney, *The Feminine Note in Fiction* (London: Chapman and Hall, 1904), xxxiii. For a more detailed discussion of Wharton's place in relation to American literature, see Candace Waid, *Edith Wharton's Letters from the Underworld: Fictions of Women and Writing* (Chapel Hill: University of North Carolina Press, 1991).

say at which point she began to understand that the pages of her manuscripts and other caches of less classifiable yet intriguing scraps and shards would be of interest to posterity—at which point she came to the realization that she would be recognized and remembered for her literary work. As one looks at the care with which she prepared her manuscripts, one can only begin to appreciate the private value they must have held for her. Among these fastidiously kept records of her life as a writer, she preserved her first effort at writing a longer work of fiction, the novella "Fast and Loose," which was begun when she was fourteen and completed early in her fifteenth year. The preservation of this manuscript through the years suggests the importance of writing in Wharton's conception of her life, as well as her lifelong investment in the process and materials of writing.

The manuscripts of *The House of Mirth*, the handwritten original and two typewritten versions, are housed in the Wharton Collection of the Beinecke Rare Book and Manuscript Library of Yale University. R. W. B. Lewis has given the most concise description of the manuscript of *The House of Mirth*, which he describes as having "passed through at least seven stages before it appeared in print":

> There was (1) the original handwritten version, which was itself (2) revised by hand, so extensively that the new handwritten version had to be pasted over the original. There followed (3) a typescript, and this in turn was emended by hand (4), again sometimes so thoroughly that a paste-over was required. . . . Next there was a second typescript (5), this also corrected with obvious care by hand (6). But since the published text varies on page after page from the second typescript (though in most cases only slightly), we can posit (7) a certain re-working in the galley proofs.[17]

Although some sections are missing, most of the manuscript has been carefully preserved.

The manuscript itself seems to reveal aspects of the story of the writing of *The House of Mirth* which Wharton tells in her autobiography. The early chapters of *The House of Mirth*, written in her small, careful hand with many words packed onto the page, seem in their very density to bear the legible

17. R. W. B. Lewis, introduction to *The House of Mirth* (New York: New York University Press, 1977), 330.

trace of her anxiety. This part of the manuscript has spidery markings and carefully inscribed revisions; here, instead of two typescripts of each page, there are occasionally three versions. According to Wharton's later account, the initial anxiety she felt in composing *The House of Mirth* was allayed by the demands of the writing itself, which brought with it increasing confidence and a new awareness of the daily work of her chosen profession. As Wharton began to respond to the pressures of her publisher's schedule, she developed a more efficient method of writing, anticipating and facilitating her practice of extensive revision. Writing in a large hand, Wharton began to compose her prose with only a few words to the line, giving herself space for revision on each page. This method also allowed her to cut out and replace lines in the form of strips with selvage; these strips (with revisions and/or additions) were then pasted in with their edges secured under the severed manuscript. (Part of her method is revealed on the back of a page of the manuscript which shows a single line written over three times in an unsuccessful effort to prepare one of these strips.) The neatly mended manuscript is heavy with the paste and extra paper from this form of rewriting; sometimes a page comprises as many as eight strips and often pages that are too long to conform to the size of the original paper are folded inward.

Although even the uncut pages tend to have some words or phrases marked, the manuscript as a whole appears as a carefully constructed and reconstructed object. The amount of cutting makes it impossible to know the extent and character of all of Wharton's revisions, many of which, as the carefully spliced manuscript suggests, ended up on the cutting room floor: most of the rejected writing does not even appear in the manuscript, even in its deleted form. Looking on the backs of pieces of pasted-in manuscript, one can see evidence of an unimaginative Lily who, without her characteristic, ladylike indirection, tells Trenor what she thinks: " 'Ah,' she burst out, 'You're ignoble!' " Such a line does not appear in chapter 13, where Wharton creates an ominous tone by constructing a complex tissue of allusions which join the threat of sexuality to the scene's ruling specters, poverty and death. The prosaic Lily Bart who would utter such a statement has been consigned (in a fate Lily fears for herself at the end of the novel) to the "refuse-heap" (*HM*, 307).

It is obvious that Wharton reviewed each word of the text several times and that while her revisions become less extensive as the process of publication becomes more fixed and formal, words change between the final typed manuscript and the serial publication in *Scribner's,* just as a few words change and errors are corrected between these installments and the novel's appearance in book form. These changes are consistent with the attention to detail which, as her letters to her publishers suggest, she brought to every phase of the production and marketing of her books, from typesetting to advertising copy. For instance, from time to time, she reminded her publishers that she felt that printer's ornaments were needed in her novels to mark important headings. As she approached books, Wharton was aware of their physical presence, in particular the effects of the typeface and the spacing of margins. Wharton had a strong sense of the visual aesthetic of books, an awareness that apparently antedated her ability to read. As a child she held books in her hands as she declaimed stories of her own invention in the narrative ritual she called "making up"; and, even in this early period, she demonstrated a powerful preference for certain kinds of books. According to *A Backward Glance,* her favorite inspirational work to be used in this childhood ritual was Washington Irving's *Alhambra:* "shaggy volumes, printed in close black characters on rough-edged yellowish pages. . . . There was richness and mystery in the thick black type, a hint of bursting overflowing material in the serried lines and scant margin. To this day I am bored by the sight of widely spaced type, and a little islet of text in a sailless sea of white paper" (*BG,* 34).

Wharton's strong sense of the visual, tactile, and material aspects of her texts, evidenced in the care with which she constructed her manuscripts as well as in her interest in the design of the final published product, may have itself influenced the composition of the novel's plot. Viewed in the context of Wharton's method of composition, one of the most fascinating parts of the novel is the account of the charwoman, Mrs. Haffen, who pieces together the parts of Bertha Dorset's letters after they have been torn into pieces and discarded by Lawrence Selden. In the first version, Wharton continues to paste strips into the manuscript, using the edges of the strips as selvage, but in the typed revision of this passage, she seems to have tried Mrs. Haffen's method of mending letters in *The House of Mirth,* where "the letters had been pieced together with strips of thin paper. Some were in small fragments, the others merely torn in half" (*HM,* 103). Like Mrs. Haffen, who has pasted together the rended letters by placing the parts on thin white strips, Wharton here uses extra blank strips which function like tape to hold together the parts of the typescript from the back.

This method, joining typed lines where there is little selvage, may document Wharton's devotion to the realism of her fiction as well as providing yet another clue that she associated these illicit letters, written by a woman, with her own enterprise as a writer.[18] As she wrote about a character employing a method so similar to the one that she was using in constructing her own severed manuscript, it seems as if she could not resist trying out the technique for mending letters which she has Mrs. Haffen practice in her fiction—as if character and author are influencing each other in their textual reconstruction. It is hardly a coincidence that Wharton appears to have used this particular method for what may have been the first time as she revised the section of typescript which describes this very process. However, this practice of using extra strips for backing was also quite practical for accomplishing the task at hand—the seaming together of typescripts which lacked the selvage she purposefully included between the lines of the handwritten manuscript. The joining of typescript to typescript is relatively rare in this manuscript where extensive revisions to the typed texts continue to take the form of handwritten additions, strips or paragraphs pasted into the clean copy by Wharton herself.

Wharton first called the manuscript that would become *The House of Mirth* "A Moment's Ornament," taking her title from Wordsworth's poem "She Was a Phantom of Delight." The phantom of Wordsworth's lyric offered a compelling version of the ideal of womanhood which nineteenth-century girls and women aspired to, and, as such, it was frequently copied by young women into the moral scrapbooks of religious and social advice which they called commonplace books. Indeed, it is possible and even likely that Wharton would have first read "She Was a Phantom of Delight" in her mother's youthful hand; Wordsworth's poem held a prominent place among the quotations in Lucretia Jones's own commonplace book.[19] This emphasis on the collection of prescriptive quotations is a familiar practice in the world of Lily Bart, who, early in the novel, appeals to Lawrence Selden for moral guidance after disparaging her aunt's faith in "copy-book axioms" (*HM*, 7). Wordsworth's poem, which concludes by describing "A perfect Woman,

18. For an extensive discussion of both Bertha and Lily as figures for the woman writer, see Waid, *Wharton's Letters from the Underworld*, 15–50.

19. Janet Goodwyn, *Edith Wharton: Traveller in the Land of Letters* (London: Macmillan Publishers Ltd., 1990), 57.

nobly planned, / To warn, to comfort, and command; / And yet a Spirit still, and bright / With something of angelic light," begins by introducing the temporal fate of female beauty: "She was a Phantom of delight / When first she gleamed upon my sight; / A lovely Apparition, sent / To be a moment's ornament."

Wharton's investment in alluding to Wordsworth's poem provides a useful example of her aesthetic of revision. Her dedication to clean and precise modern prose is perhaps expressed best near the conclusion of her first book, the nonfiction work *The Decoration of Houses*: "*Tout ce qui n'est pas necessaire est nuisible.* There is a sense in which works of art may be said to endure by virtue of that which is left out of them, and it is this 'tact of omission' which characterizes the master hand."[20] Writing in her autobiography about her acts of revision, Wharton recalled that she and her friend Walter Berry would go on "adjective hunts" across her manuscripts, coming back with "such heavy bags" (*BG*, 116). The opening paragraph of the first version of *The House of Mirth* offers a case in point. In its original form it reads: "Hensley stood still, surprised. In the afternoon rush of Grand Central his eyes had been refreshed by the apparition of a tall & truly tailored figure, with bright hair under a feathered hat." Of course, the name "Hensley" is marked out and replaced by the more allusive Selden, but the most characteristic and sweeping change takes place as adjectives and adverbs are cleaned away and the detailed description of how this striking woman appears to the eye is replaced by a simple phrase that announces "the apparition of Miss Lily Hurst." Wharton's first draft often seems to be spun out with strands of alliteration encumbered by adjectives and adverbs, as in the phrase "tall & truly tailored." These felicitous phrases which appear to come to Wharton as she is composing her first draft are scrutinized and kept only if they meet Wharton's standards for clarity and precision.

The phantom of Wordsworth's poem, what he calls "the lovely apparition," remains in the revised opening of the first typescript, which is still called "A Moment's Ornament": "Selden stood still surprised. In the afternoon rush of the Grand Central Station his eyes had been refreshed by the apparition of Miss Lily Bart." Obviously we can see here an important change from "Hurst"

---

20. Edith Wharton and Ogden Codman Jr., *The Decoration of Houses* (New York: Scribner's, 1897), 198.

to "Bart," a more resonant name for the heroine who will be haunted by the temptation both to be art and to have her beauty bartered in the marriage market. (Wharton's original name for Lily was Juliet, which may have been inspired by Shakespeare's heroine, who takes a sleeping potion and kills herself after a late letter causes her lover to arrive too late.)[21] The second typescript (originally entitled "The Year of the Rose" with the final title *The House of Mirth* added in ink) includes two other significant changes. The opening sentence is streamlined and made more direct, and in the following sentence the word *apparition* is crossed out and replaced by the word *sight.* Identical with the passage in the final typescript, the opening of *The House of Mirth* reads "Selden paused in surprise. In the afternoon rush of the Grand Central Station his eyes had been refreshed by the sight of Miss Lily Bart." The allusion to Wordsworth's poem is visible only if one knows the prehistory of the passage; like the idealized woman of Wordsworth's poem, Lily might be said to "gleam[ . . . ] upon [her admirer's] sight." By replacing *apparition* with *sight,* Wharton emphasizes the fact that a striking woman is being beheld by a man from a particular point of view. From the outset, Miss Lily Bart is a figure who is seen by Selden; and indeed, part of her downfall in the novel results from her status as a figure who attracts attention and who seems destined both to be seen and to inspire speculation (in the various senses of the word).[22] The opening sentences in both the manuscript and the typescript of the novel bear the traces of Wharton's early interest in the language and ideas of Wordsworth's poem, but at the same time the clean lines of the altered opening reveal the aesthetic criteria of Wharton's extensive revisions.

Although Wharton changed the title "A Moment's Ornament," which appears as the heading of the first typescript, its motif still can be detected throughout the manuscript; the word *moment* is important throughout the book, and Wharton pays special attention to it, sometimes writing it in and sometimes crossing it out. For a brief period, in the heading of the second typescript, "A Moment's Ornament" became "The Year of the Rose," before

21. See Waid, *Wharton's Letters from the Underworld,* 39.
22. For a discussion of the financial speculation surrounding Lily, see Wai-Chee Dimock, "Debasing Exchange: Edith Wharton's *The House of Mirth,*" *PMLA* 100 (1985): 783–92; and Wayne W. Westbrook, "Lily—Bartering on the New York Social Exchange in *The House of Mirth,*" *Ball State University Forum* 20 (1979): 59–64.

it in turn was replaced by Wharton's inscription of the words *The House of Mirth*. In the initial title change, the "moment" has become a "year," and the "ornament," with its intimation of objectification, has become a flower, an emblem of the natural as well as the beautiful. Both titles convey important aspects of the novel's concern with the association between female beauty and the temporal. Yet, like the first title, the second title still encompasses only one aspect of the story of Lily Bart as she makes her social descent into death during the final year and a half of her life. Unlike Undine of *The Custom of the Country,* whose allegiance seems clear as she converts the natural into the artificial, Lily Bart is caught between the desire for an art based on artifice and a calling, echoed in her name, to be part of the natural world: to be, in biblical terms, a lily of the field. Although the floral allusion proved inadequate as a description of the work as a whole, the idea behind it is crucial to the unfolding of the novel. *The House of Mirth* tells the story of the efflorescence of a beautiful woman of twenty-nine as she begins to glimpse her own fading, and it concludes with her being cut off just past her moment of full bloom, preserved through what Cynthia Griffin Wolff has characterized as "the beautiful death."[23]

Under the title "The Year of the Rose," characterized further as "A Novel," Wharton included an epigraph from *Richard II:* "A brittle glory shineth in this face — / As brittle as the glory is the face." She deleted this passage when she replaced the title alluding to the physical qualities of Lily Bart with a title referring to the society which would destroy her fragile heroine. When writing under the title "The Year of the Rose," Wharton also experimented with naming the books which in the final version are designated with roman numerals simply as I and II. Book I was promisingly called "The Flower," but she never entered a name for the plucked or perhaps the unplucked and fading rose or Lily of Book II. As Lewis and others have pointed out, both of these titles are inadequate because Wharton's novel was really about the tension between the ornament and the rose. In *The House of Mirth,* the living beauty of nature is transformed into the dead and objectified beauty of an

23. See Lewis, introduction to *The House of Mirth,* for an important discussion of the relationship between Wharton's working titles; Elizabeth Ammons notes the importance of biblical allusions here in *Edith Wharton's Argument with America* (Athens: University of Georgia Press, 1980). See Cynthia Griffin Wolff, "Lily Bart and the Beautiful Death," *American Literature* 46 (1976): 16–40.

ornament. This tension between the natural and the ornamental is a crucial force in the structuring of the novel. While both elements are evident near the end of Book I, as Lily performs in a tableau vivant, by the close of Book II Lily no longer performs as a painting. When she is still what might be called "a phantom of delight," Lily stands in the place of a painted figure "banishing the phantom of [its] dead beauty by the beams of her living grace" (*HM*, 131). In the scene which parallels her previous role as Sir Joshua Reynolds's "Mrs. Lloyd," Lily has become an emblem of stilled life, the central figure in a scene of *nature morte;* laid out on the sheets of her deathbed, she has gone beyond nature to become an object, but even this ornamental status is by definition temporal and temporary.[24]

The title *The House of Mirth* is taken from *Ecclesiastes* 7:4: "The heart of the wise is in the house of mourning; but the heart of fools is in the house of mirth." Although the novel tells the story of the fools, the destructive denizens of New York society, it concludes with a focus on the sacrifice and death of Lily Bart, which leaves the reader (along with Selden and his cousin, Gerty Farish) in "the house of mourning." Wharton claimed that she was always aware of her endings when she first began to write. This was not true for *The Age of Innocence*,[25] but it seems to be at least partially accurate for *The House of Mirth*. At the moment that she affixed this final title to the text and perhaps even earlier in the titles that evoke the temporal and temporary qualities of female beauty, Wharton was aware that her heroine was progressing toward death at the end of the novel. As the book manuscript went to press, Wharton was horrified to discover that without consulting her the publisher had decided to use the passage from *Ecclesiastes* as an epigraph. She wrote to William Crary Brownell at Scribner's: "Even when I sank to the depth of letting the illustrations be put in the book—&, oh, I wish I hadn't now!—I never contemplated a text on the title-page. It was all very well for The Valley, where the verse simply 'constated' a fact, but in this case, where it inculcates a moral, I might be suspected of plagiarizing

24. For a discussion of these terms and scenes, see Waid, *Wharton's Letters from the Underworld.*

25. In one of the outlines for *The Age of Innocence*, Newland Archer marries the Countess Ellen Olenska rather than the paragon of purity, May Welland. This is, of course, reversed in the final version of novel.

from Mrs. Margaret Sangster's beautiful volume, 'Five Days With God.' "[26] In addition to emphasizing her distance from a popular female poet who was concerned with religious themes, Wharton concluded, "I think the title explains itself amply as the tale progresses, & I have taken the liberty of drawing an inexorable blue line through the text."[27]

Unwilling to label her story with a moral, Wharton may also have been opposed to including any epigraph which would limit the resonance of her title. Certainly Wharton's title *The House of Mirth* underlines other important aspects of the text besides those evoked by the religious allusion. Characteristically, in both Wharton's work and her worldview, the description of houses, often the interiors as well as the exteriors of houses, conveys the personalities of her characters. From the publication of her first book, *The Decoration of Houses,* a work coauthored with the architect Ogden Codman in which she intended to rescue interior design from the province of dressmakers and restore it to the realm of architectural forms, Wharton presented houses not only as extensions of the people who lived in them but also as edifices which display the values of the societies which produced them. Even those unaware of the title's biblical source, then, would still understand that Lily Bart passes through a series of houses of mirth, inhabited by fools, on her way to the lower-class boardinghouse that smells of fried food and shows a blistered and dilapidated front to those who pass by on the street. This is the house where Lily dies and Selden gains some measure of final, if still deeply flawed, wisdom. The wisdom which comes from Selden's altering confrontation with Lily's death suggests the terms of the biblical "house of mourning."

Although Wharton chose to excise the epigraph rather than to have it shouted from the title page, the biblical allusion to the wise who dwell in "the house of mourning" is among the unspoken words which shape the language of the ending of the novel. As Selden approaches the bleak boardinghouse, he associates Lily with the single sign of beauty, the window with a flowerpot, rather than the window with a closed shade. Selden comes

26. Wharton refers to her first novel, *The Valley of Decision,* published three years earlier, in 1902.

27. *Letters,* August 5, 1905, pp. 94–95. See also the note describing Margaret Sangster and her poetry.

bearing a "word" for Lily, the mysterious word, never audibly spoken, which in the final line of the novel is described as "the word" that "passed between them . . . which made all clear" (*HM*, 323). In the manuscript version, as he thinks about his reason for not having come the evening before, Selden looks at the outside of Lily's building and full of promise reminds himself, "It was a word for sunrise, not for twilight." The revision of this sentence makes it one of the most powerful lines in the novel as Wharton finds poetry in a shifting of terms. By crossing out and replacing three words and casting the first phrase as a negative statement, Wharton infuses her sentence with profound resonance and narrative power: "It was not a word for twilight, but for the morning." The mention of twilight recalls and turns away from Wordsworth's "phantom of delight," who is said to have the hair and eyes of twilight, yet the most important change alludes to the novel's final title. Instead of saying that Selden's word is "for the sunrise," Wharton reminds her wise readers, the ones who do not have to be reminded by an epigraph, that this word is both "for the morning" and "for the mourning."[28] Aside from its prominent place in the title, "the house of mirth" is never actually mentioned in Wharton's novel. While some readers would be aware of the specific terms of the allusion, others would benefit from the fruitful tension between title and text—a type of narrative provocation employed later by both Joyce and Faulkner.

Wharton's allusion to *Ecclesiastes* in her title might also signal another part of the foundation of *The House of Mirth*, a link between Wharton's representation of Lily's death and the famous death of one of the most resolutely virtuous heroines in the history of the novel, Richardson's Clarissa. In a lengthy postscript to *Clarissa*, Richardson quotes extensively from one of Addison's essays in the *Spectator* on the relative merits of happy and unhappy endings in tragedy. Defending works with unhappy endings, Richardson recalls that historically "those which ended unhappily had always pleased the people, and carried away the prize, in the public disputes of the Stage, from those that ended happily," and he adds: "It can not be supposed, that the Athenians, in this their highest age of taste and politeness, were less humane, less tender-hearted, than we of the present. But they were not *afraid* of being moved, nor *ashamed* of shewing themselves to be so, at the distress they saw

---

28. Manuscript of *The House of Mirth*, 178, Wharton Collection.

well painted and represented. In short, they were of the opinion, with the wisest of men, *That it was better to go to the house of mourning than to the house of mirth;* and had fortitude enough to trust themselves with their own generous grief, because they found their hearts mended by it."[29]

When *The House of Mirth* was dramatized by Clyde Fitch, Wharton attended the New York opening with William Dean Howells, who explained the audience's unfavorable response to the play by remarking, "[W]hat the American public always wants is a tragedy with a happy ending" (*BG*, 147). Just as readers pleaded with Richardson to save his heroine and give his novel a happy ending, Wharton's first readers held out hopes for Lily. (Her fate was anxiously anticipated; one distraught reader sent a telegram to a friend announcing: "Lily Bart is dead.") Wharton's novel, like *Clarissa*, evoked letters asking why there could not have been a romantic resolution which would have allowed its compelling heroine to live. Clarissa, repeatedly referred to in extravagant terms as "the ornament and glory of her Sex" and the "[f]lower of the world,"[30] draws on the same female iconography which inspired Wharton's original titles. Clarissa also designs an elaborate lily (indeed a broken lily) for the coffin that also serves as a writing desk in her final days; like Lily, she spends time writing and settling accounts before she dies. As Wharton imagined the ending of her novel and the death of Lily Bart, she most likely thought of other novels which conclude with the deaths of beautiful and virtuous heroines. Perhaps anticipating her own readers' responses in those recorded by Richardson, Wharton may have found in Richardson's defense of his tragic ending that "it was better to go to the house of mourning than to the house of mirth" a title for her novel about female sacrifice which, like Richardson's, finally focuses on the body of a dead heroine.[31]

The ambiguity surrounding the death of Lily Bart has caused some controversy among critics. In particular, like readers of *Clarissa*, critics have been concerned about whether Lily committed suicide rather than died

29. Samuel Richardson, *Clarissa. Or, The History of a Young Lady,* 8 vols. (3d ed., London, 1751; reprint, New York: AMS Press, 1990), 8:285.

30. *Clarissa,* 8:34, 74.

31. Clarissa leaves detailed instructions for the handling of her body and the viewing of her corpse. Whereas the dead Lily is exposed for anyone to see, Clarissa, allowing only a few exceptions, has planned ahead to keep her coffin closed to the curious.

of an overdose of her sleeping draught or of the weltschmerz to which heroines are so susceptible. Wharton's careful manuscript revisions of Lily's thoughts about the future in these scenes show that Wharton consciously constructed this ambiguity through a series of subtle alterations. The parts of Lily's life which are destined not to take place because of her death tend to be referred to as certainties, while the phrases which suggest her actual fate are framed as possibilities. Revisions in this section of the manuscript reveal Wharton's efforts to sharpen the ambiguity and to maintain a clearly articulated vagueness. As Lily, like the dying Clarissa, puts her accounts in order, the manuscript version suggests the possibility that she might not use her recently acquired money to settle her odious debt to Gus Trenor: "There was the cheque in her desk, for instance—she meant to send it to Trenor the next morning; but when the morning came she might put off doing so, might slip into gradual acquiescence in her debt." In the revised version, the possibility becomes a certainty: "when the morning came she *would* put off doing so, *would* slip into gradual tolerance of her debt."[32]

Imagining her "fall," Lily feels "the countless hands of habit dragging her back into some fresh compromise with fate" (*HM*, 315).[33] This fantasy of the inevitability of her sinking moral courage causes her to desire a conclusion ("If only life could end now—end on this tragic yet sweet vision of lost possibilities" [*HM*, 315]) and at the same time anticipates her desire to take the medication and submerge herself in sleep. Again, as she considers the dangers of going beyond the maximum dosage of her sleeping elixir, the possibility suggested in the word *might* is exchanged for the greater certainty found in the word *would*. Lily is clearly gambling as she raises the dosage, seeing her death as a remote possibility: "But, after all that was but one chance in a hundred, the action of the drug was incalculable, & the addition of a few drops to the regular dose might merely procure her the rest she so desperately needed." Instead of "might merely," her awareness of the dangers seems attenuated in the revised manuscript, which reads: "the addition of a few drops to the regular dose *would probably* do no more than procure her the rest she so desperately needed."[34] Only a few lines later in

32. Manuscript, 164 (my emphasis).
33. Lily is described in the manuscript as feeling "the hundred tentacles of habit tugging" (164) her toward the same conclusion.
34. Manuscript, 169 (my emphasis).

the manuscript, a sentence which begins "She must escape" is broken off and replaced by the assertion "Her mind shrank from the glare of thought . . . , darkness was what she must have at any cost." Lily "escape[s]" finally by shrinking from the "glare of thought"; and through these subtle revisions, as Wharton exchanges the word *might* for the more affirmative word *would*, Lily's role in her own death is left shrouded in a carefully and increasingly crafted obscurity.

Although much of the critical response to *The House of Mirth* was highly complimentary, at least one reviewer was not entirely pleased with the social consciousness which he felt pervaded the novel. In a newspaper article saved by Wharton headlined "Books of the Day: Mrs. Wharton's Latest Novel," the unnamed critic argues that " 'The House of Mirth' would be more of a novel if it were less of a sociological pamphlet." Comparing it to "the report of some committee of one hundred delegated to discover and disclose the cause of our rapidly increasing degeneration," he describes Wharton as "preach[ing] a sermon that relentlessly exposes the depth of degradation into which modern American society has fallen."[35] While the social consciousness of the novel seems rather subtle when compared to the explicitness of some of the politically and sociologically motivated novels of the era, *The House of Mirth* does seem to be reaching toward a more sophisticated analysis of society than is present in Wharton's earlier works. The manuscripts and revisions of the novel reveal that in writing *The House of Mirth* Wharton consciously sought to interweave some of these issues into the fabric of the plot. For example, in scenes which become more obvious as the novel draws to a close, Wharton brings Lily Bart's social ambitions and struggle for survival into focus by associating her both with the working girls (to whom she once played the role of the kind and charitable lady) and with the socially ambitious (yet finally sympathetic) Jew, Simon Rosedale.

Until the concluding chapters of the novel, the working girls of Lily Bart's New York seem to be an unnamed mass, whether as the members of Gerty Farish's club or as the hostile and anonymous workers who surround Lily in the sweatshop where in order to survive she works sewing spangles on

35. "Books of the Day: Mrs. Wharton's Latest Novel," *Contemporary Reviews of The House of Mirth*, Wharton Collection.

hats. Rosedale becomes a more sympathetic figure as Lily's fortunes fall in the second book of the novel; despite his financial success and social gains, he feels compassion for the socially destitute and impoverished Lily. Near the conclusion of the novel, Wharton also introduces the figure of a fallen working girl, Nettie Struther, who has raised herself from the "refuse-heap" (*HM*, 307) and who, like Rosedale, represents the possibility of personal struggle and self-preservation despite seemingly insurmountable forces of social condemnation and adversity. These parts of a social dialectic which overshadow the lives of Rosedale and Nettie Struther—the anti-Semitism of what Wharton elsewhere calls "Old New York" and the poverty that leaves a class of working girls vulnerable to sexual predators—offer clear parallels to Lily Bart's life and question the inevitability of her fate. These forces, introduced during Wharton's complex process of revision, offer important glimpses into her efforts to build powerful social tensions into the structure of *The House of Mirth*.

Early in the novel, during her second visit to Trenor's country home, Bellomont, Lily finds her hostess's manner "unchanged," yet she recognizes "a faint coldness in that of the other ladies." This coldness, an "occasional caustic reference to 'your friends the Wellington Brys,' or to 'the little Jew who has bought the Greiner house—someone told us you knew him Miss Bart,' " shows Lily "that she was in disfavour with that portion of society which, while contributing least to its amusement, has assumed the right to determine what forms that amusement shall take" (*HM*, 127). Initially, the phrase in the manuscript version refers to Rosedale only as the "new man"; this phrase is then crossed out and replaced by a pointedly anti-Semitic reference to "the little Jew." In constructing the foundation for her complex social dialectic, Wharton replaces the "new man"—often a positive characterization in American literature—with a stereotypic epithet. The other outsiders, the Wellington Brys, the nouveau riche couple called the "Welly Brys," are labeled as intrinsically ridiculous in the manuscript on the basis of their name alone. Initially called "the Hamilton Eggles," the correspondingly familiar name "the Ham Eggles" would have recalled their relation to crude acts of consumption.

Rosedale (whose name may link him to women and art by recalling the name of Mrs. Ambrose Dale from "Copy," one of Wharton's rare depictions of a woman novelist) is described in words which echo his name as "a plump rosy man of the blond Jewish type" (*HM*, 12). While Rosedale's coloring may suggest something about his hopes for blending in, his potential for assimilation, his floral name (which links him with Lily) for a brief period in the composition of the novel drew him even closer to the heroine as it echoed "The Year of the Rose." Both the Welly Brys and Rosedale suffer from newness in this old society; their attack on Old New York is made possible by new money. However, Rosedale is not just "new," as Wharton has her social arbiters point out; he is also a Jew. This implication of anti-Semitism is also legible in Lily Bart's early and visceral distaste for the attentions of Rosedale. The reference to "the little Jew" which Wharton introduces into the discourse of the novel is part of the prejudice of a society which already has begun to recognize the unmarried Lily's affinities as a *jeune fille à marier* at the considerable age of twenty-nine with these threateningly "new" or "foreign" outsiders.

Later, as Gerty Farish talks to her cousin Lawrence Selden before the curtain rises on the tableaux vivants at the Welly Brys, Wharton incorporates an extensive addition in script which she pastes onto the typescript. In this late revision, Wharton introduces the plight of the working girls; and however vague and ill defined, the fact that both Lily and Rosedale contribute to this cause suggests their deeper affinities and prefigures Lily's surprising fate. This addition sounds the same prejudicial note audible in the contempt for Lily's "friends" voiced earlier by the society ladies at Bellomont. As Gerty Farish chatters to Selden about Lily's support of a charity to help working girls, she asks: "Did I tell you Lily gave us three hundred dollars? Wasn't it splendid of her? And then she collected a lot of money from her friends—Mrs. Bry gave us five hundred, and Mr. Rosedale gave us a thousand. I do wish Lily were not so nice to Mr. Rosedale, but she says it's no use being rude to him, because he doesn't see the difference" (*HM*, 129). Gerty goes on in this passage to argue that the people who say that Lily is "cold and conceited" have not seen her laughing and talking with the working-class women who are part of Gerty's "Girls' Club." Speaking in the Brys' ballroom, Gerty Farish does not complain about the Welly Brys' new money, but she does underline her allegiance to an older prejudice, the unspoken anti-Semitism which places Rosedale in a different category. Her prejudice is not softened by Rosedale's charitable contribution to the welfare of the working girls—another oppressed group—nor is it diminished by the obvious contrast that Wharton sets up between a gift from a generous figure such as Rosedale and the cost of one of Bertha Dorset's pearls, which according to Gerty would pay for the activities of the "Girls' Club" for an entire year.

By incorporating this extensive passage, which juxtaposes Lily's attitude toward Rosedale with her sympathy for the girls who are less fortunate than herself, Wharton prepares for the conclusion of the novel. Lily never becomes a Jew or even, despite her offer at one point, the wife of a Jew, but she does become a working girl. After Lily has become a wage laborer in a millinery sweatshop and later when she is unemployed, only Rosedale understands her plight and tries to help her; he alone recognizes her life as an act of noble sacrifice. He knows that Lily has not used the social capital that has fallen into her hands in the form of Berea's illicit letters; he knows that she has "the power in [her] hands" (*HM*, 257) to change the ending of her life and the ending of the novel which she inhabits. Just as Rosedale becomes a sympathetic presence as Lily falls down the social ladder, a working girl whom Lily has helped earlier befriends her and brings her home after finding her on a bench in the park. This figure, Nettie Struther, who has married and found a new life after being seduced and abandoned by a man at her work (first designated in the manuscript as a "regular society man"[36] and then in the novel as merely a man who has "seen a great deal of society" [*HM*, 309]), represents the potential for Lily herself to rise from the ruins of her reputation as a fallen woman. Lily's associations with this woman are also ominous, however, since Lily has used the money she gained from the transaction with Gus Trenor, money which has sullied both her reputation and her sense of her own virtue, to send Nettie to the country when she became ill after being abandoned by her unfaithful and unscrupulous lover.

In gratitude for Lily's kindness, Nettie Struther has named her child after a regal character played by an actress who reminded her of Lily. The queen is initially called "Mary Adelia" in the manuscript; but Wharton changes this detail so that the name of the character played by the actress becomes that of the ill-fated and notoriously uncharitable "Mary Anto'nette" (*HM*, 309). In a moment of bitter and intentional wit, Wharton inserts an extra "r" into the baby's name, turning it into "Marry Anto'nette," which might be read as a warning for Lily to marry too, like the fallen Nettie. As Lily Bart imagines herself holding the baby who is named for a stage queen who

---

36. Manuscript, 145.

loses her head, the dying Lily seems fated to cling to a vulnerable identity which is bodied forth in the fantasy of a female infant. Lily, as she imagines holding the female baby, has passed beyond the symbolism of birth into the actuality of death. Like the historical Marie Antoinette, Lily is divided from her conscious mind and left on stage to be viewed as a "stilled" body.

From as early as chapter 13 in Book I, when (in the manuscript version) Lily enters Gus Trenor's "shrouded" house, which "look[s] as if it were waiting for the corpse to be brought down," and the word *corpse* is marked out and replaced with the word *body*,[37] Lily Bart is drawn toward an embodiment which focuses on her sexuality but also leads to death. In this scene of what has been called Gus Trenor's attempt at rape, Lily is vulnerable not only because she lacks a male protector (whether father, brother, or husband), but also because of a related reason—her poverty. Initially in the manuscript version, Trenor tells the entering Lily, "you look a little cold yourself." Underlining the significance of her floral name, which has long been associated with purity, the word *cold* from Trenor's perspective may allude to her sexual temperament, but in Wharton's revision this word is replaced by the word *pinched*, a term which alludes more pointedly to her financial state. Trenor's description of Lily as "pinched" becomes part of the series of allusions which will eventually link Lily's poverty to forebodings of her death: to Trenor's calculating eye, Lily looks "dead-beat."[38] While the earlier shift to the word *body* from the more mortuarial and specific word *corpse* clearly underlines the sexual forces at work in this scene, as the passage progresses, Wharton's carefully shaded revisions seem to acknowledge the shadows of poverty and death. In building and revising *The House of Mirth*, Wharton links the prejudice against Jews with the sexual vulnerability and sacrifice of impoverished women and places both among the destructive social forces that she critiques in her novel. Throughout the versions of the

37. Manuscript, 137.

38. Manuscript, 276–79. Although I have been discussing chapter 13, the final sentence of chapter 12 suggests something of what is to come in the language of the following chapter as Trenor announces: "My wife was dead right to stay away: she says life's too short to spend it in breaking in new people" (p. 135). The sexual nuance in Wharton's use of the idiom "breaking in" is made explicit by her use of the same concept in *The Buccaneers*. In Wharton's final novel, the former Conchita Closson, now a worldly and experienced woman, apologizes for her suggestive speech, telling her American friends: "I forgot you little Puritans weren't broken in yet" (Edith Wharton, *The Buccaneers*, ed. Candace Waid [London: Everyman, J. M. Dent, 1993], 356).

manuscript, by changing words and sometimes phrases, Wharton constructs a novel rich in nuance and subtle in its drive toward increasingly complex narrative connections.

The manuscript of *The House of Mirth* reveals a great deal about Wharton's development as a writer, in particular the ways in which she shaped her drafts into the prose that is characteristic of her best work. *The House of Mirth* is much more than a well-written novel; it is, as the revised manuscript and typescripts reveal, a carefully crafted work of art. Some of the changes in the manuscript of *The House of Mirth* are motivated by Wharton's desire to articulate thematic associations and social commentary. Many of the alterations are what (for want of a better word) might be called tonal. These carefully calibrated shifts in language, which result in Wharton's characteristic clarity of tone, provide the record of a writer with a fine ear. In the early versions of the manuscript, the text is sometimes almost overwhelmed by Wharton's pleasure in alliteration and complex assonance, a tendency which reveals her susceptibility to the lyric qualities of language, but these sonorous sentences are not always preserved. What becomes obvious to a reader of Wharton's manuscripts is that her search for precision of meaning in the individual words often seems to curtail her flights into poetry. This is not to say that Wharton's writing is not lyrical or driven by a sense of poetry, but rather to suggest that sharpness of phrase and clarity were paramount to her in her prose compositions. As we have seen, even in her revisions of the novel's title Wharton worked with an acute sense of what was at stake in her choice of words as she constructed the patterns of meaning that structure the novel.

Although she had published four collections of short stories, two non-fiction volumes about Italy, a book on house decoration, a novella, and a two-volume historical novel, Wharton still referred to herself as a "drifting amateur" as she took up her pen and began to write *The House of Mirth*. *The House of Mirth* was an important book for Edith Wharton. It was not only her first best-selling book, but also the work which she would later claim taught her how to write a novel. With the publication of *The House of Mirth*, Wharton gained a wide audience and became one of the most respected writers of American literature and one of her native country's most forceful and insightful cultural critics. She also began her most productive period as a writer of serious fiction.

# "A Truly American Book"

## Pressing *The Grapes of Wrath*

R O B E R T   D E M O T T

§    §    §

The idea of an art detached from its creator is not only outmoded; it is false.

—Albert Camus

## I

T HERE IS NOTHING detached or slickly objective about John Stein-beck's masterpiece. For its creator, *The Grapes of Wrath* was a thoroughly engaging, utterly consuming novel; it arose from the sympathetic psychic wound brought on by his witnessing the cataclysmic migrant-farm-worker situation in California in the mid-1930s. *The Grapes of Wrath* is a harrowing cry from the heart, and Steinbeck's passionate investment took on a kind of sacramental air: "What some people find in religion a writer may find in his craft . . . a kind of breaking through to glory," he said in 1965.[1] The

This essay, substantially expanded for the present collection, builds upon three earlier versions: the introduction and bridging commentaries to my edition of *Working Days* (1989), the essay " 'Working Days and Hours': Steinbeck's Writing of *The Grapes of Wrath*" (1990), and my introduction to the Penguin Twentieth-Century Classics Series edition of *The Grapes of Wrath* (1992). I thank Elaine Steinbeck, McIntosh and Otis Inc., Viking Penguin, Inc., and *Studies in American Fiction* for permission to quote. I also thank Roy Simmonds and Susan Shillinglaw for generous readings of earlier versions; this version is dedicated to John Ditsky and Pare Lorentz.

1. John Steinbeck, interview by Herbert Kretzmer, in *Conversations with John Steinbeck*, ed. Thomas Fensch (Jackson: University Press of Mississippi, 1988), 95. Hereafter cited parenthetically in the text as *CJS*. Joseph Henry Jackson, "Why Steinbeck Wrote *The Grapes of Wrath*," *Booklets for Bookmen*, no. 1 (New York: Limited Editions Club, 1940), 3, was among the first to suggest that the book issued from Steinbeck's profound shock and "hurt."

pressure of living through the research, creation, publication, reception, and aftermath of this novel—over a span of nearly four years—changed Steinbeck so profoundly that he became a different kind of artist after *The Grapes of Wrath*. But the breakthrough and transformation, the notoriety and glory, and the critical backlash were still in the future when, on June 18, 1938, three weeks or so after starting the final version of *Grapes*, thirty-six-year-old Steinbeck—head full of lament—sang a doleful tune: "If I could do this book properly it would be one of the really fine books and a truly American book. But I am assailed with my own ignorance and inability. I'll just have to work from a background of these. Honesty. If I can keep an honesty it is all I can expect of my poor brain. . . . If I can do that it will be all my lack of genius can produce. For no one else knows my lack of ability the way I do. I am pushing against it all the time."[2]

Pushing against limits was Steinbeck's forte. His first novel, *Cup of Gold* (1929), a swashbuckling historical romance based on the life of the seventeenth-century Welsh buccaneer Henry Morgan, gave no indication that Steinbeck would eventually be capable of producing a graphic novel with the startling originality, magnitude, and compassion of *The Grapes of Wrath*. What transpired in the ten years between the two books is as arresting an example of self-willed artistic growth as we have in American letters, for in the nine volumes of prose (mostly fiction) that Steinbeck produced in that decade, he simply became better and better as a writer. His achievement is especially moving because he did not think of himself as naturally gifted and rarely believed he had ever "arrived" as a writer: "I was not made for success. I find myself with a growing reputation. In many ways it is a terrible thing. . . . Among other things I feel that I have put something over. That this little success of mine is cheating" (*WD*, [1]).

Steinbeck's self-accusations were constant during *Grapes*'s composition, and yet ironically it not only turned out to be a "fine" book, but it also

2. John Steinbeck, *Working Days: The Journals of "The Grapes of Wrath," 1938–1941*, ed. Robert DeMott (New York: Viking, 1989), 29–30. Hereafter cited parenthetically in the text as *WD*. Steinbeck was a fairly scrupulous observer of his own writerly processes and intentions. This private journal records his day-to-day struggles with the composition of the novel and includes additional entries which cover its conflicted aftermath. Entries 2 through 100 complement the public novel; read together, journal and novel provide a twin-voiced, parallel discourse and perhaps one of our most intriguing blow-by-blow accounts of the making of any major twentieth-century American novel.

is generally considered to be the greatest of his seventeen novels. Like other rough-hewn products of American genius—Stowe's *Uncle Tom's Cabin*, Twain's *Adventures of Huckleberry Finn*, Kesey's *One Flew over the Cuckoo's Nest*, and Walker's *The Color Purple* (four "flawed" novels that also humanize America's downtrodden by exposing social ills)—*The Grapes of Wrath* has a home-grown quality: part naturalistic epic, part jeremiad, part captivity narrative, part road novel, part transcendental gospel. Steinbeck's aggressive mixture of native philosophy, New Deal politics, blue-collar radicalism, working-class characters, folk wisdom, and homespun literary form—all set to a jazzy, rhythmic style, bold, improvisational form, and nervy, raw dialogue—gave the novel its "American" qualities, its fusion of experience and discourse. Even the novel's title, taken from Julia Ward Howe's "Battle Hymn of the Republic," was clearly in the American grain: "[I]t is a march and this book is a kind of march . . . in our own revolutionary tradition," Steinbeck announced on September 10, 1938, to Elizabeth Otis, his literary agent and confidante.[3]

After its composition from late May through late October, 1938, *The Grapes of Wrath* passed from the 751-page typescript prepared by his wife, Carol, to published novel in record time—four months. In March 1939, when Steinbeck received copies from one of three advance printings, he told Pascal Covici, his editor at Viking Press, that he was "immensely pleased with them" (*SLL*, 182). The novel's impressive physical and aesthetic appearance was the result of its imposing size (619 pages) and Elmer Hader's striking dust-jacket illustration of the Joads looking out on a lush California valley. And partly true to Steinbeck's insistence that *The Grapes of Wrath* be "keyed into the American scene," Covici had Viking print the first page of the words and music from the "Battle Hymn" inside the book's front and rear covers in an attempt (unsuccessfully, it turned out) to deflect accusations of Communism against the book and its author. In gratitude for their assistance, Steinbeck had dedicated the novel to Carol and to Thomas Edwards Collins, a government-relief-camp specialist (their roles will be examined below).

Given his emotional commitment to the California migrant laborers' situation, Steinbeck refused to write a book cynically calculated to court commercial success. "Funny how mean and little books become in the face of such tragedies," he confessed to Otis (*SLL,* 159). It was doubly ironic, then, that shortly after its official publication date, April 14, 1939, spurred by the nearly ninety reviews (mostly positive) that appeared in newspapers, magazines, and literary journals between April and June, *The Grapes of Wrath* went to the top of best-seller lists and stayed there for most of the year, selling 428,900 copies in hardcover at $2.75 each. *The Grapes of Wrath* won the 1940 Pulitzer Prize (Steinbeck gave the $1,000 prize to a Monterey friend and fellow writer Ritch Lovejoy). By 1941, when the Sun Dial Press issued a cloth reprint for a dollar, the publisher announced that over 543,000 copies of *Grapes* had already been sold. It eventually became the cornerstone of Steinbeck's 1962 Nobel Prize award and proved itself to be among the most enduring works of fiction by any American author. In spite of the flaws its critics perceive—frequent sentimentality, flat characterizations, heavy-handed symbolism, and unconvincing dialogue—or perhaps because of them (general readers tend to embrace the book's mystic soul and are less troubled by its imperfect body), *The Grapes of Wrath,* during the past half century, has sold more than fourteen million copies.[4] It has, in short, emphatically entered both the American consciousness and the American conscience.

   *Grapes* has also had a charmed life on screen and stage. Steinbeck sold the novel's film rights for $75,000 to producer Darryl F. Zanuck. Then Nunnally Johnson scripted a film version, directed by John Ford and released in 1940, which, though truncated, was nonetheless memorably paced, photographed, and acted, especially by Henry Fonda as Tom Joad, Jane Darwell as Ma, and John Carradine as Jim Casy. (A "hard, straight picture . . . that looks and feels like a documentary film and . . . has a hard, truthful ring," Steinbeck reported after seeing its Hollywood preview [*SLL,* 195].) A few years ago, Frank Galati faithfully adapted the novel for his Chicago-based Steppenwolf Company, whose Broadway production won a Tony Award as Best Play in 1990. Ike Sallas, the hero of Ken Kesey's latest novel, *Sailor Song* (1992), prizes the novel and places it among his collection of classic American books—"the essential heavies," he calls them—a status the book clearly holds worldwide, for *The Grapes of Wrath* has also been translated into over thirty

---

   4. William Strachan, a former senior editor at Viking Penguin, provided sales information to me in a March 1985 letter. According to the novelist's widow, Elaine Steinbeck, *Grapes* still sells 100,000 paperback copies each year.

languages. It seems that Steinbeck's words continue, in Warren French's apt phrase, "the education of the heart."[5]

All this public fanfare and hoopla has overshadowed the private history of the novel's background and creation. The story of the novel's making is an intriguing and dramatic one in itself, full of some of the same twists and turns, travails, triumphs, and ironies that characterize the Joad family's journey to the Promised Land. While Steinbeck's puritanical doubts about his ability to carry out the plan of his ambitious novel surface repeatedly in his daily journal, he rarely questioned the risks involved in bringing his whole sensibility—the leverage of his entire heart—to bear upon its writing. Like another populist manifesto of the American spirit, Whitman's *Leaves of Grass,* Steinbeck's novel had a complicated, tumultuous growth. *The Grapes of Wrath* was the product of Steinbeck's increasing immersion in the "matter of the migrants," which required a zigzag walk before he discovered the proper means of doing the topic justice. In one way or another, from August 1936, when Steinbeck told Louis Paul he had discovered a subject "like nothing in the world" (*SLL*, 129), through October 1939, when he resolved privately to put behind him "that part of my life that made the *Grapes*" (*WD*, 106), the migrant issue, which had wounded him deeply, was the central obsession of this obsessive writer.

First, he produced a seven-part series of newspaper articles, "The Harvest Gypsies"; then he worked on an unfinished novel, "The Oklahomans," and on a completed, but destroyed, satire, "L'Affaire Lettuceberg"; and finally—in a five-month stretch in 1938—he wrote *The Grapes of Wrath.* Each version of the story shared a fixed core of elements: on one side, the entrenched power, wealth, authority, and consequent tyranny of California's industrialized agricultural system (symbolized by Associated Farmers, Inc.), which produced flagrant violations of the migrants' civil and human rights and ensured their continuing peonage through threats, reprisals, and violence; on the other side, the powerlessness, poverty, victimization, and fear of the nomadic American migrants whose willingness to work, desire to retain their dignity, and wish to settle land of their own were kept alive by their

5. Warren French, *John Steinbeck's Fiction Revisited* (New York: Twayne Publishers, 1994), 75. See Robert B. Harmon, *"The Grapes of Wrath": A Fifty Year Bibliographic Survey* (San Jose: Steinbeck Research Center/San Jose State University, 1989), 15–32, for a handy list of translations of *Grapes.*

innate resilience and resourcefulness and by the democratic benefits of the government sanitary camps. From the moment he entered the fray, Steinbeck had no doubt that the presence of the migrants would change the fabric of California life, though he had little foresight about what his own role in that change would be (or, for that matter, what changes would be wrought in him). His purpose was avowedly humanitarian and partisan; he wanted to be an effective advocate, but he did not want to appear presumptuous: "Every effort I can bring to bear is and has been at the call of the common working people to the end that they may eat what they raise, use what they produce, and in every way and in completeness share in the works of their hands and their heads," he declared unequivocally to *San Francisco News* columnist John Barry (*WD*, 152).

## II

*The Grapes of Wrath*'s communal vision began in the fire of Steinbeck's own labor, but the flames were fanned by numerous people. Few major American novels are more indebted to the generosity of others than *Grapes* is. Before continuing this narrative of the novel's genesis and growth, it will be necessary to sketch the chief benefactors, especially Carol Steinbeck and Tom Collins, both of whom had significant impact on Steinbeck's work. Carol Henning Steinbeck, his outgoing first wife (they married in 1930), was far more politically radical than John, and she actively supported members of northern California's local fugitive agricultural labor movement before he did.[6] Carol was an energetic, talented person in her own right, and she agreed to relinquish a career of her own in favor of helping to manage her husband's. Their partnership and marriage were smoother and more egalitarian in the struggling years of Steinbeck's career; with the enormous success—and pressures—brought first by the runaway best-seller *Of Mice and Men* (1937), and then by *The Grapes of Wrath*, their situation became more tenuous and volatile. Carol Steinbeck was an extremely strong-willed,

6. Contrary to popular belief, Steinbeck was never a Marxist or a member of the Communist party. According to his biographer, Steinbeck was not interested in doctrinaire political theories at this point of his career. See Jackson J. Benson, "The Background to the Composition of *The Grapes of Wrath*," in *Critical Essays on Steinbeck's "The Grapes of Wrath,"* ed. John Ditsky (Boston: G. K. Hall, 1989), 52–53.

demonstrative person, and she was often frustrated and resentful and some-times jealous; her husband, inordinately shy, was frequently beleaguered, confused, and demanding. In the late 1930s, whenever he was writing daily, which was much of the time, Carol handled—but didn't always like—most of the routine domestic duties. She also shielded her husband as much as possible from unwarranted disruptions and intrusions, and oversaw some of the financial arrangements between Steinbeck and his literary agents, an increasingly large job. "Carol does so much," Steinbeck admitted on August 2, 1938 (*WD*, 50).

Carol also served as John's cultural envoy and stand-in. In January 1938, on a trip to New York City to attend a performance of George S. Kaufman's long-running Broadway production of *Of Mice and Men*, she met with docu-mentary filmmaker Pare Lorentz and arranged his first visit to the Steinbecks' home in Los Gatos, California, to discuss a joint Steinbeck/Lorentz movie version of *In Dubious Battle* (which was never made) and a private showing of *The Plow That Broke the Plains* (1936) and *The River* (1937). These pioneering documentary films, made by Lorentz for President Franklin D. Roosevelt's New Deal–inspired Resettlement Administration (forerunner of the Farm Security Administration [FSA]), dealt with human displacement and natural erosion caused by storms in the Dust Bowl and floods in the Mississippi Valley—themes that were, of course, close to Steinbeck's heart. After their initial meeting, Lorentz became an extremely important figure in the novelist's life, providing everything from practical advice on politics to spirited artistic cheerleading.

Carol left her stamp on *The Grapes of Wrath* in many ways. As Steinbeck told Otis, Carol's time was "too valuable to do purely stenographic work" (*SLL*, 171), but she did type the manuscript, which was a formidable task in itself because her husband could cram fifty-five or more lines of his spidery hand on a single page of his outsized ledger book. She began typing from the early part of the holograph manuscript while her husband was still writing its latter sections, and she sometimes smoothed and edited the text as she went along, serving in the early stages as a rigorous critical commentator (after typing 300 pages, she confessed to Otis that she had lost "all sense of proportion" and felt unfit "to judge it at all"). In a brilliant and justly celebrated stroke, on September 2, Carol chose the novel's title from Howe's "Battle Hymn of the Republic," perhaps inspired by her hearing of Lorentz's radio drama, *Ecce Homo!*, which ends with a martial version of Howe's song.[7] Steinbeck was impressed with the "looks of it—marvelous title. The book has being at last"; he considered it "Carol's best title so far" (*SLL*, 171). ("Tell Carol she is a whiz at picking titles and she has done it again with the new one," his drama agent, Annie Laurie Williams, exulted.) Her role as facilitator is recorded permanently in one half of the novel's dedication: "To CAROL who willed it." On February 23, 1939, Steinbeck told Pascal Covici at Viking that he had given Carol the holograph manuscript of *The Grapes of Wrath*: "You see I feel that this is Carol's book" (*SLL*, 180).[8]

Eventually, Carol's brittle efficiency, brusque managerial style, and violent mood swings seemed to cause more problems than they solved. She, too, was exhausted by the novel's completion and at her wit's end over its histrionic reception. Steinbeck told Otis on June 22, 1939, "The telephone never stops ringing, telegrams all the time, fifty to seventy-five letters a day all wanting something. People who won't take no for an answer sending books to be signed. . . . Something has to be worked out or I am finished writing. I went south to work and I came back to find Carol just about hysterical. She had been pushed beyond endurance" (*SLL*, 185). His willful involvement with a much younger woman, a Hollywood singer named Gwyndolyn Conger, whom he met in mid-1939 and who quickly came to represent everything Steinbeck felt romantically lacking in Carol, signaled the beginning of the end of their marriage. They separated rancorously in 1941 and divorced two years later.

The second part of the novel's dedication—"To TOM who lived it"—refers to Tom Collins, the novelist's chief source of accurate migrant information. Collins not only put Steinbeck in touch with people like the Joads and Jim Casy, but he also served as Steinbeck's real-life prototype for the character Jim Rawley, the manager of the Weedpatch government camp, which became an oasis of relief for the harried Joads and is featured in chapters 22 through 26 of *The Grapes of Wrath*. The Weedpatch camp is an accurate rendering of Collins's Arvin camp. Steinbeck portrayed Collins with photographic

---

7. See also Pare Lorentz, *FDR's Moviemaker: Memoirs and Scripts* (Reno: University of Nevada Press, 1992), 121. Jackson, "Why Steinbeck Wrote *The Grapes of Wrath*," 10–11, was first to note the impact of Lorentz's work on Steinbeck's novel.

8. In 1954, Carol sold the manuscript to Clifton Waller Barrett through book dealer John Howell of San Francisco. The typescript was presented to the Library of Congress in 1941 by Frank J. Hogan, a lawyer and book collector.

accuracy in chapter 22: "A little man dressed all in white stood behind [Ma Joad]—a man with a thin, brown, lined face and merry eyes. He was as lean as a picket. His white clean clothes were frayed at the seams."9 Steinbeck also caught Collins's effective interpersonal technique in Jim Rawley's wearing frayed clothes and in his winning over Ma Joad by the simple request of a cup of her coffee (*GW,* 416).

An intrepid, idealistic, and exceptionally compassionate man, Collins was the manager of a model Region IX FSA camp, located in Kern County, at the southern end of California's Central Valley. The twenty-acre Arvin Sanitary Camp was one of several proposed demonstration tent camps intended to provide humane, clean, and democratic—but temporary— living conditions for ninety-six families at a time from the growing army of migrant workers entering California from the lower Midwest's Dust Bowl region. (More than two dozen camps were planned in 1935 by the Resettlement Administration; by 1940, with New Deal budgets slashed by conservatives in Congress, only fifteen were actually completed or under construction.) Collins possessed a genius for camp administration and was widely respected throughout California. Labor historian Anne Loftis calls Collins a "hands on" administrator.10 Collins had the right mix of fanaticism, vision, and tactfulness. He and Steinbeck, both New Deal Democrats, hit it off immediately. One of the many legends that grew up around *The Grapes of Wrath* purported that Steinbeck traveled with a migrant family all the way from Oklahoma to California; that never happened, though he and Carol did follow Route 66 on a car trip from Chicago to Los Gatos in 1937. Actually, Tom Collins was the novelist's companion on several grueling research trips made from 1936 to 1938 to investigate field conditions in the Central Valley.

Fortunately, Collins was a punctual and voluminous report writer (a plan to publish his reports eventually fell through [*WD,* lii–liii]). His colorful

9. John Steinbeck, *The Grapes of Wrath* (New York: Viking, 1939; reprint, New York: Penguin Books, Twentieth Century Classics Series, 1992), 415 (page references are the same for both editions). Hereafter cited parenthetically in the text as *GW.* Unlike the portrait of Collins in Rawley, the equation between other historical human beings and fictional characters is blurred and conjectural. Most of the major characters that eventually came to populate *Grapes* were probably composite creations of historical antecedents. See Benson, "Background to the Composition," 52–53.

10. Anne Loftis, "Steinbeck and the Federal Migrant Camps," *San Jose Studies* 16 (Winter 1990): 80.

weekly accounts of the workers' activities, diets, entertainments, beliefs, music, and observations provided Steinbeck with a ready documentary supplement to his own researches. Collins guided Steinbeck through the intricacies of the agricultural labor scene, put him in direct contact with migrant families, and permitted him to incorporate "great gobs" of information into his own writing. "Letter from Tom. . . . He is so good. I need this stuff. It is exact and just the thing that will be used against me if I am wrong," Steinbeck noted on June 24, 1938 (*WD*, 33).

In 1939, at Steinbeck's recommendation, Collins worked as a well-paid technical advisor to John Ford's Twentieth Century–Fox production of *The Grapes of Wrath* ("Tom will howl his head off if they get out of hand," Steinbeck told Elizabeth Otis). And later—probably spurred by the success of both novel and film—Collins himself (under the pseudonym Windsor Drake) wrote an autobiographical/fictional memoir, to which Steinbeck, who appears as a character, added a foreword: "Windsor and I traveled together, sat in the ditches with the migrant workers, lived and ate with them. We heard a thousand miseries and a thousand jokes. We ate fried dough and sow belly, worked with the sick and the hungry, listened to complaints and little triumphs."[11] The book was accepted but never reached print because the publisher reneged on the deal. After that, Collins resigned from the FSA, and he and Steinbeck passed out of each other's lives.

Clearly, Steinbeck had a knack for associating himself with gifted, far-sighted, generous people, many of whom helped provide the context of *The Grapes of Wrath*. George West, chief editorial writer for the progressive Scripps-Howard newspaper the *San Francisco News,* instigated Steinbeck's initial investigations of the migrant-labor situation. Frederick R. Soule, the enlightened regional information advisor at the San Francisco office of the FSA, and his assistant Helen Horn (who later, as Helen Hosmer, directed the Simon Lubin Society) provided statistics and documents for Steinbeck's seven-part series on migrants in the *News* and otherwise opened official doors for Steinbeck that might have stayed closed. Soule's colleague Eric Thomsen, regional director of the FSA office in San Francisco, personally escorted Steinbeck to the Central Valley and introduced him to Tom Collins

11. John Steinbeck, foreword to *Bringing in the Sheaves,* by Windsor Drake [Thomas Collins], in Jackson J. Benson, " 'To Tom Who Lived It': John Steinbeck and the Man from Weedpatch," *Journal of Modern Literature* 5 (April 1976): 213.

at the Arvin camp for the first time. Indeed, as Jackson Benson was quick to recognize, in an unintentional and ultimately ironic way the federal government underwrote part of Steinbeck's research and smoothed the path of this first major written account of the deplorable California agricultural situation.[12]

## III

Not counting the scotched plan to edit and publish Tom Collins's reports, an abandoned play laid in "a squatter's camp in Kern County," and a warm-up essay published in *The Nation* called "Dubious Battle in California" and intended to "give a mild idea" of the civil war brewing under his "nose," Steinbeck's first lengthy excursion into the migrants' problems was published in the liberal, pro-labor *San Francisco News*. His series "The Harvest Gypsies," produced at West's invitation, formed the foundation of Steinbeck's concern for a long time to come, raised issues and initiated forces, gave him a working vocabulary with which to understand current events, and furthered his position as a reliable interpreter. This stage resulted from the notoriety caused by his recently published strike novel, *In Dubious Battle* (1936), after which Steinbeck found—often against his will—that he was fast becoming considered a spokesman for the contemporary agricultural labor situation in a state that was primarily promanagement. This was ironic because while *In Dubious Battle* exposed the capitalist dynamics of corporate farming, it took no side for or against labor, preferring instead to see the fruit strike as a symbol of "man's eternal, bitter warfare with himself" (*SLL*, 98).

The articles in "The Harvest Gypsies," peppered with Dorothea Lange's graphic photographs of migrants, appeared from October 5 to 12, 1936. Steinbeck's gritty reports detailed the plan of California's feudal agricultural industry. The pieces introduced the antagonists, underscored the anachronistic rift between the Okie agrarian past and the mechanized California present, explained the economic background and insidious effects of the labor issue, examined the deplorable migrant living conditions, and exposed the unconscionable practices of the interlocking conglomerate of corporation farms. (These elements remained central to the core and texture of *The*

12. Benson, " 'To Tom Who Lived It,' " 184.

*Grapes of Wrath.*) Primarily, though, Steinbeck's eye was on the "nomadic, poverty-stricken harvesters," the "150,000 homeless migrants" who were "gypsies by force of circumstance," as he announced in his opening piece: "And so they move, frantically, with starvation close behind them. And in this series of articles we shall try to see how they live and what kind of people they are, what their living standard is, what is done for them, and what their problems and needs are. For while California has been successful in its use of migrant labor, it is gradually building a human structure which will certainly change the state, and may, if handled with the inhumanity and stupidity that have characterized the past, destroy the present system of agricultural economics."[13]

Although Steinbeck later admitted that he was taken "over completely, heart and soul" by the "fine, brave people," he still maintained a measured style to promote understanding and intelligent solutions. Steinbeck's articles are full of case studies, chilling factual statistics, and an unsettling catalogue of human woes (illness, incapacitation, persecution, death) observed from close contact with field workers he had met. In the spirit of advocacy journalism, Steinbeck concluded with prophetic recommendations for alleviating the problem with federal aid and local support; this in turn would create subsistence farms, establish a migratory labor board, encourage unionization, and punish terrorism. When they were published in 1936 and again when they were reprinted in 1938 as a twenty-five-cent pamphlet called *Their Blood Is Strong* by the nonprofit Simon J. Lubin Society (which sold 10,000 copies in four printings), Steinbeck's articles solidified his credibility—both in and out of the migrant camps—as a serious commentator in a league with sociologist Carey McWilliams and Paul Taylor, Dorothea Lange's husband, two other influential, respected investigators.[14]

Steinbeck understood that the migrants wouldn't disappear, even though California officials hoped they would. He also knew that the subject he had dipped into reached further than he had imagined and was beginning to present itself as a possible novel. Consequently, Steinbeck built on his *News*

13. *The Harvest Gypsies: On the Road to "The Grapes of Wrath,"* ed. Charles Wollenberg (Berkeley: Heyday Books, 1988), 19.

14. The text of *Their Blood Is Strong,* which includes an additional entry, "Epilogue: Spring 1938," is reprinted in Warren French, ed., *A Companion to "The Grapes of Wrath"* (New York: Viking, 1963), 53–92.

pieces and on at least one more month-long field trip with Tom Collins in October and November of 1937. In Steinbeck's old panel truck (a pie delivery wagon in its former life), they started from Gridley, where Collins was managing a new camp, but then roamed California from Stockton to Needles, wherever migrants were gathered to work.[15] His purpose was to gather more research for his next version, the "big" book of fiction which had apparently been on his mind for most of that year, and which Steinbeck and Collins had obviously discussed. (In an undated letter probably written in the spring of 1937, he said to Collins, "You know of course my plans for the long novel dealing with the migrant" [*WD*, lii].) A letter to Elizabeth Otis, written on January 27, 1937, indicates he had been wrestling with this version since the previous winter: "The new book has struck a bad snag. . . . The subject is so huge it scares me to death." Several months later, in an interview in the *Los Gatos Mail-News*, Steinbeck publicly claimed for the first time that he had started a book whose topic was the Dust Bowl refugees, the "Oklahomans." Though he was "reluctant to discuss the characters and plot," he said it was "one third complete and will be about 1000 pages in length."[16] Given his comment to Otis in January and the fact that he traveled a good deal that year (including a trip with Carol to the Soviet Union), three hundred pages of completed manuscript at this point may have been wishful thinking on his part, or it may have represented the total number of pages of Collins's reports and his own research notes (which have never been found) he had accumulated during the year. If nothing else, the interview announced his proprietary attention to the material, about which he was known to have been protective and, as Horace Bristol later learned, even secretive.

15. The probable destinations and routes of Steinbeck's and Collins's 1937 travels inside California are provided in Benson, " 'To Tom Who Lived It,' " 183–85, and in his "Background to the Composition," 64–65.

16. Dorothy Steel, " 'Oklahomans' Topic of Steinbeck," *Los Gatos Mail-News*, November 4, 1937, p. 1. Susan Shillinglaw, "Local Newspapers Report on 'The Oklahomans,' " *Steinbeck Newsletter* 2 (Fall 1988): 4, rightly notes the "unconvincing" tone and sanitized political view (emphasizing the migrants' upward social mobility) that emerges in this conservative interview and in the next one, with Louis Walther. She wonders whether Steinbeck wasn't making a "bid for hometown favor at a time when he feared reprisal from the Associated Farmers and law enforcement officers?" To make things more confusing—or more interesting—Joseph Henry Jackson, "John Steinbeck, A Portrait," *Saturday Review of Literature* 16 (September 25, 1937): 18, claimed Steinbeck was working on "three related longer novels" during 1937.

In a second interview, with journalist Louis Walther, published January 8, 1938, in the *San Jose Mercury Herald,* he apparently had not progressed much, if at all. After hitting several "snags," he was working on a "rather long novel" allegedly called "The Oklahomans," which was "still a long way from finished." Steinbeck, generally guarded with interviewers, revealed enough to Walther to indicate his novel's focus was the salutary, irrepressible character of the "southern dust bowl immigrants" who, he believed, would profoundly alter the tenor of life in California. "Their coming here now is going to change things almost as much as did the coming of the first American settlers." Furthermore, "The Californian doesn't know what he does want. The Oklahoman knows just exactly what he wants. He wants a piece of land. And he goes after it and gets it" (*CJS,* 11–12). In *The Grapes of Wrath,* Steinbeck did not relinquish his land-hunger theme, or his belief that the migrants formed a specific phalanx group within the large national mass movement of the 1930s, but he certainly dropped his somewhat condescending, imperious, and naive tone in favor of a more inevitably tragic one.

As nearly as can be determined, between January and March 1938 Steinbeck quietly stopped work on this manuscript Walther had named "The Oklahomans." Steinbeck never mentioned it again by name, the manuscript has never been found, and his boasts of three hundred completed pages aside, it is doubtful that he had actually written a substantial amount of it at all. In the first entry of *Working Days,* on February 7[?], 1938, he mentioned having written "ten pages" of an otherwise unidentified book: "You pages . . . are the dribble cup—you are the cloth to wipe up the vomit. Maybe I can get these fears and disgusts on you and then burn you up. Then maybe I won't be so haunted" (6). And six weeks later, on March 23, 1938, he again told Elizabeth Otis: "I've been writing on the novel but I've had to destroy it several times. I don't seem to know any more about writing a novel than I did ten years ago. You'd think I would learn. I suppose I could dash it off but I want this one to be a pretty good one. There's another difficulty too. I'm trying to write history while it is happening and I don't want to be wrong" (*SLL,* 162). These troubled comments in early 1938 have long been thought to refer to the beginnings of "L'Affaire Lettuceberg" (discussed below), but it is far more likely that they refer to his difficulties in writing one or more avatars of the Oklahomans book, the Ur–*Grapes of Wrath,* which had, after more than a year and a couple of starts and stops, not yet found its proper impetus or creative urgency and in fact may have blown up in his face following his interview in the *San Jose Mercury Herald*. But in mulling over, rehearsing, and living with the subject of this "long novel dealing with the migrant" for so long ("I've been three years on the material," he told critic Harry T. Moore in July), Steinbeck was staking his claim to that imaginative territory, repeatedly experimenting with a way to fictionalize material that was until then the stuff of contemporary reportage. The general chapters in *Grapes* would be especially influenced by his long rehearsal.

Actually, the migrant situation had worsened, and along with it Steinbeck's capacity for anger and his need for direct involvement had grown. The workers' misery was increasing in the winter of 1938, especially in Visalia and Nipomo, where thousands of families were marooned by floods. From Los Gatos, Steinbeck wrote Otis in February:

> I must go over into the interior valleys. There are about five thousand families starving to death over there, not just hungry but actually starving. The government is trying to feed them and get medical attention to them with the fascist group of utilities and banks and huge growers sabotoging the thing all along the line. . . . In one tent there are twenty people quarantined for smallpox and two of the women are to have babies in that tent this week. I've tied into the thing from the first and I must get down there and see it and see if I can't do something to help knock these murderers on the heads. . . . They think that if these people are allowed to live in camps with proper sanitary facilities, they will organize and that is the bugbear of the large landowner and the corporation farmer. The states and counties will give them nothing because they are outsiders. But the crops of any part of this state could not be harvested without these outsiders. I'm pretty mad about it. (*SLL*, 158)

In late February and early March 1938 Steinbeck witnessed these deplorable conditions firsthand at Visalia, where, after three weeks of steady rain, "the water is a foot deep in the tents and the children are up on the beds and there is no food and no fire, and the county has taken off all the nurses because 'the problem is so great that we can't do anything about it.' So they do nothing," he informed Otis on March 7, 1938 (*SLL*, 161). In the company of *Life* magazine photographer Horace Bristol, Tom Collins, and other FSA personnel, Steinbeck worked day and night for nearly two weeks, sometimes dropping in the mud from exhaustion, to help relieve the people's misery, though of course no aid seemed adequate. Steinbeck was supposed to be writing an article with Bristol for *Life* magazine, but what he encountered was so devastating, he told Otis, that he was utterly transfixed by the "staggering" conditions; the "suffering" was so great that objective reporting would only falsify the moment.[17] Suddenly, Steinbeck realized that the issue was not as simple as portraying the "naive directness" of the migrants' desire for land. Indeed, the cauldron of his own soul was beginning to boil with anger, frustration, and impotence. Apparently neither the "Oklahomans" version nor the proposed article could adequately redress the injustices he had recently witnessed. "When I wrote *The Grapes of Wrath*," he declared in a 1952 Voice of America radio interview, "I was filled . . . with certain angers . . . at people who were doing injustices to other people" (quoted in *WD*, xxxiii).

In his work as a novelist, Steinbeck often experienced a delayed reaction to piercing events. Perhaps as early as February—but certainly no later than early April ("New book goes very fast but I am afraid it is pretty lousy. I don't care much," he told Otis on April 26, 1938)—through approximately mid-May 1938, Steinbeck worked at the third stage of his effort, and produced "L'Affaire Lettuceberg." With this abortive—but necessary—sidetrack venture, Steinbeck's migrant subject matter took its most drastic turn, inspired by an ugly event in Salinas, California, his hometown, two years earlier. In September 1936 Steinbeck had encountered the vicious clash between workers and growers in a lettuce strike—"there are riots in Salinas and killings in the streets of that dear little town where I was born," he told novelist George Albee (*SLL*, 132). The strike was smashed with "fascist" terrorism, including gas bombings, shootings, and strict lock-

---

17. After Visalia, Steinbeck pulled back from his work with Bristol, preferring instead to throw his efforts into his own fictional version, which he was beginning to conceive in tragic terms and which he knew would require his undivided attention. This led to hard feelings on the photographer's part (*WD*, lv–lvi). Bristol's Visalia photographs, with some captions from *The Grapes of Wrath*, turned up in *Life* on June 5, 1939, pp. 66–67, and again on February 19, 1940, pp. 10–11, where they were used to show the authenticity of John Ford's cinematic version of the novel. For a different, more suspicious, view of Steinbeck's motives concerning Bristol and the meaning of the Visalia experience, and for a discussion of his allegiances and affinities with journalism, see William Howarth, "The Mother of Literature: Journalism and *The Grapes of Wrath*," in *New Essays on "The Grapes of Wrath,"* ed. David Wyatt (New York: Cambridge University Press, 1990), 71–99.

outs, and recollections of the workers' defeat and the systematic violation of their civil rights festered in Steinbeck for more than a year. "I am treasonable enough not to believe in the liberty of a man or a group to exploit, torment, or slaughter other men or groups. I believe in the despotism of human life and happiness against the liberty of money and possessions," he said in a 1937 statement for the League of American Writers.[18]

Perhaps as early as the first week of February 1938, and no later than the first week of April, galvanized by reports of the worsening conditions in Visalia and Nipomo, Steinbeck felt the urgent need to do something direct in retaliation. He never became what committed activists would consider fully radicalized (his writings stemmed more from his own feelings and humane sensibility than from the persuasiveness of the Left's economic and social ideas), but by putting his pen to the service of this cause, he was stepping as close to being a firebrand as he ever would. He launched into "L'Affaire Lettuceberg," a vituperative satire aimed at attacking the leading citizens of Salinas, a cabal of organizers called "the committee of seven," who foment the army of armed vigilantes (a thousand strong) recruited from the common populace of Salinas—clerks, service-station operators, shopkeepers. "L'Affaire" was a detour from his main concern for the migrant workers, already recorded in "The Harvest Gypsies" and adumbrated in the "Oklahoman" rehearsals. In fact, "L'Affaire" wasn't "literary" at all; rather, it was a "vulgar" tract concocted to do a specific job. Sometime in early May 1938 Steinbeck, who had already written approximately 60,000 words (and was aiming for 10,000 more), confessed to Annie Laurie Williams: "I'll have the first draft of this book done in about two weeks. . . . And it is a vicious book, a mean book. I don't know whether it will be any good at all. It might well be very lousy but it has a lot of poison in it that I had to get out of my system and this is a good way to do it" (quoted in *WD*, xxxix).

18. John Steinbeck, letter in *Writers Take Sides: Letters about the War in Spain from 418 American Authors* (New York: League of American Writers, 1938), 57. The Salinas lettuce strike extended from September 4 to November 3, 1936, and was especially violent. (It is still considered the Salinas Valley's worst agricultural strike.) Less certain is whether Steinbeck actually went to Salinas to investigate events for himself or viewed the battle from a distance, either from Los Gatos or from the site(s) of his field research. The strike was a nationally covered event, so plenty of information was available in newspapers, especially the *San Francisco Chronicle*. In any case, the labor situation was so "tense" throughout California that Steinbeck felt the *News* might not print "The Harvest Gypsies" after all (*SLL*, 132).

Shortly after that prediction, however, Steinbeck wrote again to Otis and to his publisher, Pascal Covici (who had already announced the publication of "L'Affaire"), to inform them that he would not be delivering the manuscript they expected:

> This is going to be a hard letter to write. . . . this book is finished and it is a bad book and I must get rid of it. It can't be printed. It is bad because it isn't honest. Oh! these incidents all happened but—I'm not telling as much of the truth about them as I know. In satire you have to restrict the picture and I just can't do satire. . . . I know, you could sell possibly 30,000 copies. I know that a great many people would think they liked the book. I myself have built up a hole-proof argument on how and why I liked it. I can't beat the argument but I don't like the book. And I would be doing Pat [Covici] a greater injury in letting him print it than I would by destroying it. Not once in the writing of it have I felt the curious warm pleasure that comes when work is going well. My whole work drive has been aimed at making people understand each other and then I deliberately write this book the aim of which is to cause hatred through partial understanding. My father would have called it a smart-alec book. It was full of tricks to make people ridiculous. If I can't do better I have slipped badly. And that I won't admit, yet. (quoted in *WD*, xl–xli)

Urged on by Carol, who hated "L'Affaire," Steinbeck made the right move. On May 24, 1938, Annie Laurie Williams, speaking for the staff at McIntosh and Otis literary agents, replied: "I admire you for having the courage of your convictions and know you would feel better if you could have heard what Elizabeth and Pat both said when they read your letter. . . . [W]e all admire you more than ever for sticking by your instincts about your work" (quoted in *WD*, lv).

## IV

Steinbeck rebounded immediately and hit the ground running. Traditionally, he did not work weekends or holidays, so he probably took off Memorial Day weekend, which means that—judging from the fact that he wrote the "turtle episode," or the third chapter (*WD*, 20), on Tuesday, May 31, and calculating backwards from there at 2,000 words per day—he began *The Grapes of Wrath* on Wednesday, May 25, and certainly no later than

Thursday, May 26. His conscience squared, his integrity restored, Steinbeck quickly embarked on the longest sustained writing job of his career. Ridding himself of poison by passing through a "bad" book proved beneficial, he told Otis on June 1, 1938: " . . . it is a nice thing to be working and believing in my work again. I hope I can keep the drive. . . . I only feel whole and well when it is this way" (*SLL,* 167). Naturally, his partisanship for the workers and his sense of indignation at California's labor situation carried over, but they were given a more articulate and believable shape.

From the moment Steinbeck struck the first lines of the new novel to paper—"To the red country and part of the gray country of Oklahoma, the last rains came gently, and they did not cut the scarred earth. The plows crossed and recrossed the rivulet marks"[19]—through the winter of 1939, when the last of the corrections and editorial details were negotiated— "I meant, Pat, to print *all all all* the verses of the Battle Hymn. They're all pertinent and they're all exciting. And the music if you can," he chastised (*SLL,* 175)—*The Grapes of Wrath* was a task which fully commanded Steinbeck's artistic energy and attention. Everything he had written earlier— from his 1936 *Nation* article, through "Starvation under the Orange Trees," an impassioned April 1938 essay that functioned as the epilogue to *Their Blood Is Strong,* and even through "Breakfast," a poignant short story/sketch included in his short story collection *The Long Valley* (1938)—became grist for his final attempt. "For the first time I am working on a book that is not limited and that will take every bit of experience and thought and feeling that I have," he claimed on June 11, 1938 (*WD,* 26).

From his numerous field travels with Collins, and from countless hours of talking to migrant people, working beside them, listening to them, and sharing their problems, Steinbeck summoned all the concrete details of human form, language, and landscape that ensure artistic verisimilitude, as

19. "The Grapes of Wrath," autograph manuscript, 1938, page 1, Item 6239, John Steinbeck Collection, Clifton Waller Barrett Library, Manuscripts Division, Special Collections Department, University of Virginia Library, Charlottesville, Virginia. Pagination given here refers to Steinbeck's handwritten numerals at the top right- or top left-hand side of each page, not to the numbers printed on each ledger page. To be precise, Steinbeck's first words on the paper were "New Start," superposed over "Big Writing." This referred to his new start after "L'Affaire" and the fact that Carol made him promise to write in larger and more legible script to make her typing job easier.

well as the subtler, imaginative nuances of dialect, idiosyncratic tics, habits, and gestures that animate fictional characterization and would make his "people . . . intensely alive the whole time" (*WD*, 40).[20] From the outset in creating the Joad family to occupy the narrative chapters of *The Grapes of Wrath*, Steinbeck endowed his novel with a specific human context, a felt emotional quality, and a capacious dramatic dimension his earlier versions lacked: "Begin the detailed description of the family I am to live with. Must take time in the description, detail, detail, looks, clothes, gestures. . . . We have to know these people. Know their looks and their nature," he reminded himself on June 17 (*WD*, 29). Most importantly, by deliberately conceiving the Joads as "an over-essence of people," Steinbeck elevated the entire history of the migrant struggle into the realm of art and joined the mythic westering journey with latently heroic characters, according to this key notation on June 30: "Yesterday . . . I went over the whole of the book in my head—fixed on the last scene, huge and symbolic, toward which the whole story moves. And that was a good thing, for it was a reunderstanding of the dignity of the effort and the mightyness of the theme. I feel very small and inadequate and incapable but I grew again to love the story which is so much greater than I am. To love and admire the people who are so much stronger and purer and braver than I am" (*WD*, 36). His transformation of Rose of Sharon from "silly pregnant" teenager to mysterious madonna figure in the novel's final scene was not only long prepared for in his imagination, but became, in a sense, the novel's alpha and omega, at once its point of departure and its finale.

20. Part of Steinbeck's expertise was knowing how to employ his generative sources. He returned frequently for inspiration and material to Tom Collins's reports. For instance, in a section called "Bits of Migrant Wisdom," noted in the "Kern Migratory Labor Camp Report for week ending May 2, 1936," Collins records a heated discussion with two women about how best to cut down on the extravagant use of toilet paper. Steinbeck saw the humor in the account of "the great toilet paper scandal" (*WD*, 71) and utilized some of the original material on September 13 for chapter 22 of *Grapes*: "Hardly put a roll out 'fore it's gone. . . . One lady says we oughta have a little bell that rings ever' time the roll turns oncet. Then we could count how many ever'body takes" (430). See Benson, " 'To Tom Who Lived It,' " 174–79, for more examples of the kind of detailed material and observations Collins incorporated in his reports, and Martha Heasley Cox, "Fact into Fiction in *The Grapes of Wrath*: The Weedpatch and Arvin Camps," in *John Steinbeck: East and West*, ed. Tetsumaro Hayashi, Yasuo Hashiguchi, and Richard F. Peterson, Steinbeck Monograph Series, no. 8 (Muncie, Ind.: Ball State University/Steinbeck Society of America, 1978), 18–19, for other parallels not developed in Benson.

It is a critical commonplace that many American authors, often with little in the way of a shared novelistic tradition to emulate, or finding that established fictional models don't suit their sensibilities, forge their own way by synthesizing their personal vision and experience with a variety of cultural forms and literary styles. Steinbeck was no exception. To execute *The Grapes of Wrath* he drew on the jump-cut technique of John Dos Passos's *U.S.A.* trilogy (1937), the narrative tempo of Pare Lorentz's radio drama *Ecce Homo!*, the sequential quality of Lorentz's films *The Plow That Broke the Plains* (1936) and *The River* (1937), the stark visual effects of Dorothea Lange's photographs of Dust Bowl Oklahoma and California migrant life, the timbre of the Greek epics, the rhythms of the King James Bible, the refrains of American folk music, and the biological impetus of his and Edward F. Ricketts's ecological phalanx, or group-man, theory, in which an aggregate group of individuals acts according to a single purpose, and in so doing, their identity as a group organism transcends individual personalities. Steinbeck's imagination transformed these resources, especially Old and New Testament themes, parallels, and inversions, into his own holistic structure, his own individual signature. Malcolm Cowley's claim that a "whole literature is summarized in this book and much of it is carried to a new level of excellence" is especially pertinent and underscores the capacious dimension of the novel.[21]

If Steinbeck's artistic influences were disparate, his conception of the novel's structure was uniform in its growth. The epic scale and technical plan of *Grapes* apparently crystallized between May 15 and May 25, 1938. During that fertile transitional moment the organizational design of the novel clearly established itself in Steinbeck's mind. Unlike William Faulkner, say, Steinbeck was not an elite literary practitioner or formal innovator, but he still achieved in *Grapes* a compelling combination of individual style, visual realism, and rambunctious, symphonic form that was at once accessible and experimental, documentarian and fictive, expository and lyrical. He anticipated almost precisely the novel's length and the amount of time it would take to complete it. He apparently did not work from a formal outline (at least no written one has ever turned up); rather, he sketched out the novel

---

21. Malcolm Cowley, *Think Back on Us . . . A Contemporary Chronicle of the 1930s*, ed. Henry Dan Piper (Carbondale: Southern Illinois University Press, 1967), 350.

in his head in aggregate first (he appears to have assembled a nearly complete list of potential topics for his intercalary, or general, chapters by the time he started writing), followed by a brief planning session each day, or every few days if he happened to be working on a long chapter, such as chapter 20.[22] On August 18, he noted: "Now away from the daily life and into the book. I read a couple of chapters to company last night and could see the whole thing clearly. Also it doesn't sound bad. Today is going to take a long time. I have to get on the line of my family again. The outline of today will carry over some days. Must get it straight, must get it clear and straight" (*WD*, 58). Sticking to his outline became increasingly important, because this chapter, continually disrupted by intrusions, took him from August 18 to September 3 to complete. When it was finished, Steinbeck scrawled at the bottom of manuscript page 109, "long son of a bitch too."

In early July 1938 Steinbeck confided to Harry T. Moore that he was employing what was for him a "new method" of fictional technique which purposefully combined a suitably elastic form and elevated style to express the far-reaching tragedy of the migrant drama.[23] Influenced by Tolstoy's construction in *War and Peace*—which Steinbeck told Merle Danford a few months later was his favorite "literary creation" (*CJS*, 23)—he devised for *The Grapes of Wrath* a contrapuntal structure, alternating in the thirty chapters between short lyrical ones of exposition and background pertinent to the migrants as a group (Chapters 1, 3, 5, 7, 9, 11, 12, 14, 15, 17, 19, 21, 23, 25, 27, 29) and the long narrative chapters of the Joad family's dramatic exodus to California (all the other chapters). Steinbeck structured his novel by juxtaposition. His "particular" chapters are the slow-paced and lengthy

22. Steinbeck's autograph manuscript and his published novel both have thirty chapters in exactly the same sequence, though the former begins with an alternating system of roman and arabic numerals (to indicate general and narrative chapters, respectively), then shifts to arabic numbers at manuscript page 29. Uniform numbering of chapters 1–30 first took place on the typescript and may have been Carol's suggestion. Chapter 20 in the typescript and in the published novel was originally chapter 8 of Book II of the autograph manuscript. Roy S. Simmonds, "The Original Manuscript," *San Jose Studies* 16 (Winter 1990): 131–32, brings some order to Steinbeck's "chaotic" numbering by providing a handy appendix that compares the text of the manuscript with Viking's first edition.

23. John Steinbeck to Harry T. Moore, July 6, 1938. Moore, working on *The Novels of John Steinbeck: A First Critical Study* (Chicago: Normandie House, 1939), had written Steinbeck for "information for a critique of some kind" (*WD*, 38).

narrative chapters that embody traditional characterization and advance the dramatic plot, while his jazzy, rapid-fire "interchapters" work at another level of recognition by expressing an atemporal, universal, synoptic view of the migrant condition. As he composed chapters 5 and 6, for instance, Steinbeck reminded himself that, for maximum effect, "I want the reader to be able to keep [the general and particular chapters] separate in his mind" (*WD*, 23–24). In fact, his "general" or intercalary chapters ("pace changers," Steinbeck called them), were expressly designed to "hit the reader below the belt. With the rhythms and symbols of poetry one can get into a reader—open him up and while he is open introduce things on an intellectual level which he would not or could not receive unless he were opened up," as Steinbeck revealed to Columbia undergraduate Herbert Sturz in 1953.[24]

*The Grapes of Wrath* is an engaged novel with a partisan posture and many complex voices and passionate prose styles: "No other American novel has succeeded in forging and making instrumental so many prose styles," Peter Lisca believes.[25] Except for *Grapes*'s unflinching treatment of the Great Depression's climatic, social, and economic conditions, and those non-teleologically inspired interchapters which serve to halt the slide of his characters' emotions toward sentimentality, there is nothing cynically distanced about it, nothing coolly modernist, in the way we have come to understand the elite literary implications of that term in the past seventy-five years. (*The Grapes of Wrath* is in some ways an old-fashioned novel, even down to its curious avoidance of human sexuality.) It is not narrated

24. John Steinbeck to Herbert Sturz, February 10, 1953. Mr. Sturz kindly provided me with a photocopy of Steinbeck's autograph original before donating it to the Rare Book Room of the B. Davis Schwartz Library of Long Island University at Greenvale, New York. The letter was published in the *New York Times* on August 6, 1990, and again in Phyllis T. Dircks, "Steinbeck's Statement on the Inner Chapters of *The Grapes of Wrath*," *Steinbeck Quarterly* 24 (Summer–Fall 1991): 91–92.

25. Peter Lisca, *The Wide World of John Steinbeck* (New Brunswick, N.J.: Rutgers University Press, 1958), 164. In their Bakhtinian study, Louis Owens and Hector Torres, "Dialogic Structure and Levels of Discourse in Steinbeck's *The Grapes of Wrath*," *Arizona Quarterly* 45 (Winter 1989): 77, put it another way: "Steinbeck shows no interest in substituting one 'monologic' voice for another. Instead . . . he creates a text in which no single voice speaks with final authority: the endings of neither the Joad chapters, nor the interchapters, nor the novel as a whole can be taken as final narrative closures. Rather, these endings foreground Steinbeck's complex view of the subject and subjects of his novel and the complex levels of discourse contained within it."

from the first-person point of view, yet the language has a consistently catchy eyewitness quality about it; and the vivid biblical, empirical, poetical, cinematic, and folk styles Steinbeck employed demonstrate the remarkable tonal and visual acuity of his ear and eye. Passages like this one, written on September 22, come from a place far deeper than the intellect, come from the visceral center of the writer's being:

> There is a crime here that goes beyond denunciation. There is a sorrow here that weeping cannot symbolize. There is a failure here that topples all our success. The fertile earth, the straight tree arrows, the sturdy trunks, and the ripe fruit. And children dying of pellagra must die because a profit cannot be taken from an orange. . . . and in the eyes of the people there is the failure; and in the eyes of the hungry there is a growing wrath. In the souls of the people the grapes of wrath are filling and growing heavy, growing heavy for the vintage. (*GW*, 477)

The tempo of this passage—one of the most striking in *Grapes*—indicates the importance of musical and harmonic analogies to the novel. Steinbeck told Merle Armitage on February 17, 1939, that in "composition, in movement, in tone and in scope," *The Grapes of Wrath* is "symphonic."[26] Steinbeck's covenant was with his own radical sense of the fiction-making process, not with a well-made linear formula. Indeed, his fusion of intimate narrative and panoramic editorial chapters enforces a dialogic concert. Chapters, styles, voices all speak to each other, set up resonances, send echoes back and forth—point and counterpoint, strophe and antistrophe—as in a huge symphony whose total tonal and spatial impression far surpasses the sum of its discrete and sometimes dissonant parts. It should come as no surprise that Steinbeck listened almost religiously to classical music either before or during his writing sessions. Tchaikovsky's ballet *The Swan Lake*, Stravinsky's "very fine" *Symphony of Psalms*, and Beethoven's symphonies and sonatas created a mood conducive to writing and established a rhythm

---

26. Quoted in Robert DeMott, " 'Working Days and Hours': Steinbeck's Writing of *The Grapes of Wrath*," *Studies in American Fiction* 18 (Spring 1990): 14. In a letter to Otis (*Letters to Elizabeth: A Selection of Letters from John Steinbeck to Elizabeth Otis*, ed. Florian J. Shasky and Susan F. Riggs [San Francisco: Book Club of California, 1978], 11), Steinbeck claimed that he employed "the mathematics of musical composition in writing" *Grapes*.

for the day's work. For instance, on June 21, in preparation for writing chapter 9, the short interchapter about the migrants deciding which, if any, of their belongings they can take west, Steinbeck played *The Swan,* "because there too is the loss of a loved thing of the past" (*WD,* 31). And when he didn't have the record player going, he contented himself with the chug and whir of the washing machine.

Steinbeck's novel belongs to that vital class of fictions whose shape issues not from an ideal blueprint of aesthetic propriety, but from the generative urgency of their authors' experience ("It *had* to be written," Stanley Kunitz said in *Wilson Library Bulletin* in October 1939). Steinbeck's direct involvement with the plight of hundreds of thousands of Dust Bowl migrants in the latter half of the 1930s created his obsessive urge to tell their story honestly but also movingly. "This must be a good book," he wrote on June 10, 1938. "It simply must. I haven't any choice. It must be far and away the best thing I have ever attempted—slow but sure, piling detail on detail until a picture and an experience emerge. Until the whole throbbing thing emerges" (*WD,* 25). Making his audience see and feel that living picture was paramount. "I am not writing a satisfying story," he claimed to Pascal Covici on January 16, 1939: "I've done my damndest to rip a reader's nerves to rags, I don't want him satisfied. . . . I tried to write this book the way lives are being lived not the way books are written. . . . Throughout I've tried to make the reader participate in the actuality, what he takes from it will be scaled entirely on his own depth or hollowness. There are five layers in this book, a reader will find as many as he can and he won't find more than he has in himself" (*SLL,* 178–79). Steinbeck's participatory aesthetic was based on a circle of complicity which linked "the trinity" of writer, text, and reader to ensure maximum affective impact. On June 7, 1938, as he completed chapter 5, for instance, he kept his eye steadily on target: "Today's work is the overtone of the tractors, the men who run them, the men they displace, the sound of them, the smell of them. I've got to get this over. Got to because this one's tone is very important—this is the eviction sound and the tonal reason for movement. Must do it well" (*WD,* 23).

As he said, Steinbeck conceived his novel on five simultaneous levels of existence, ranging from socioeconomic determinism to transcendent spirituality. Louis Owens explains how biblical parallels illuminate four of Steinbeck's layers: "On one level it is the story of a family's struggle for survival in the Promised Land. . . . On another level it is the story of a people's struggle, the migrants'. On a third level it is the story of a nation, America. On still another level, through . . . the allusions to Christ and those to the Israelites and Exodus, it becomes the story of mankind's quest for profound comprehension of his commitment to his fellow man and to the earth he inhabits."[27] Thus Steinbeck pushed back the normative boundaries of traditional mimetic fiction and redefined the proletarian form. Like most significant American novels, *The Grapes of Wrath* does not offer codified social solutions. Even though it privileges a particular section of the white American migrant labor scene (Steinbeck ignores the problems of the nonwhite migrant workers—Filipino, Chinese, Japanese, and Mexican—who made up a large percentage of California's agricultural labor force, according to Carey McWilliams's 1939 sociological study, *Factories in the Field*), his book—if the testimony of the late Cesar Chavez is any indication—still speaks to the universal experience of human disenfranchisement, still looks toward an authentic human ecology. In this sense it is both a hermeneutical and a heuristic text. At every level *The Grapes of Wrath* enacts the process of its author's belief and embodies the shape of his faith, as in this ringing synthesis from chapter 14: "The last clear definite function of man—muscles aching to work, minds aching to create beyond the single need—this is man. To build a wall, to build a house, a dam, and in the wall and house and dam to put something of Manself, and to Manself take back something of the wall, the house, the dam; to take hard muscles from the lifting, to take the clear lines and form from conceiving. For man, unlike any other thing organic or inorganic in the universe, grows beyond his work, walks up the stairs of his concepts, emerges ahead of his accomplishments" (*GW*, 204).

## V

John Steinbeck lived to write. He believed it was redemptive, transformative work. Each day, as early as possible, but generally no later than 11:15 A.M., he brewed a pot of "ranch" coffee (clarified with a raw egg) and sequestered himself in the eight-by-eight-foot work room of "Arroyo del Ajo" ("Garlic Gulch"), the house he and Carol built in 1936 on Greenwood

---

27. Louis Owens, *The Grapes of Wrath: Trouble in the Promised Land* (Boston: Twayne Publishers, 1989), 45.

Lane in Los Gatos: "Just big enough for a bed and a desk and a gun rack and a little book case. I like to sleep in the room I work in," he confided to George Albee (*SLL*, 133). In his study, or some days out on their porch deck or in their guest cottage, he warmed up religiously with letters to Otis or Covici and an all-important entry in his working journal to give him "the opening use of words every day" (*WD*, 38). Thus, Steinbeck created a disciplined working rhythm and what he called a "unity feeling"—a sense of continuity and cohabitation with his material that made "it easy and fun to work" (*WD*, 27). "Let the damn book go three hundred thousand words if it wants to. This is my life. Why should I want to finish my own life? The confidence is on me again. I can feel it. It's stopping work that does the damage," he wrote on July 7, 1938 (*WD*, 39). Ideally, for a few hours each day, the world Steinbeck created took precedence over the one in which he lived. Because, for an artist, both worlds can be considered "real," at times during 1938 Steinbeck didn't know where one began and the other left off; walking back into the domestic world from the world of imagination was not always a smooth shift for him (or for Carol). His work demanded his attention so completely that he finally refused to dissipate his energy in extraliterary pursuits: "I won't do any of these public things. Can't. It isn't my nature and I won't be stampeded. And so the stand must be made and I must keep out of politics," he promised himself, though he continually worried about the migrant situation in California and news of Nazi/Fascist advances in Eastern Europe, which contributed to the book's edginess, its sense of doom.

But as the summer wore on, emerging ahead of his accomplishments seemed an insurmountable task for Steinbeck because, besides losing the "threads" that tied him to his characters, he was low on patience and had lost his sense of humor. "Was ever a book written under greater difficulty?" (*WD*, 63), he moaned. Nearly every day brought unsolicited requests for his name, his money, and his time, including unscheduled visitors, unanticipated disruptions and reversals. Domestic and conjugal relations with Carol were often strained (Steinbeck apparently remained mostly celibate when he was deeply immersed in his writing [*WD*, 34]). Houseguests trooped to Los Gatos all summer, including his sisters, Beth Ainsworth and Mary Dekker, and longtime friends Carlton Sheffield, George and Gail Mors, Ed Ricketts, Ritch and Tal Lovejoy, plus new celebrity acquaintances Wallace Ford and Broderick Crawford (stars of the recently closed New York Drama Critics Circle Award–winning play, *Of Mice and Men*), Charlie Chaplin, and Pare

Lorentz. As if that weren't enough to erode the novelist's composure, the Steinbecks' tiny house on Greenwood Lane was besieged with the noise of neighborhood building and boisterous activity, which nearly drove them to distraction. By midsummer, hoping for permanent sanctuary, they decided to buy the secluded Biddle Ranch, a forty-seven-acre spread on Brush Road in the Santa Cruz Mountains above Los Gatos. Even though it was the most "beautiful" location they had seen (*WD*, 42), its original homestead was in disrepair, so besides buying the land they would also have to build a new house, and that too became a source of added distractions. The Steinbecks didn't move there until November 1938, a month after the novel was finished (final typing of the manuscript and corrections of the typescript and galley proofs took place at the Biddle Ranch from November 1938 to early February 1939), but preparations for the purchase ate a great deal of Steinbeck's time and energy from mid-July onward.

August proved the most embattled period. Early in the month—on the third—Steinbeck noted in his journal, "There are now four things or five rather to write through—throat, bankruptcy, Pare, ranch, and the book. If I get this book done it will be remarkable" (*WD*, 51). His litany of woes included Carol's tonsillectomy, which incapacitated her; the bankruptcy of Steinbeck's publisher, Covici-Friede, which threatened the end of their current income and posed an uncertain publishing future for the novel he was writing; Pare Lorentz's arrangements for making a film version of *In Dubious Battle;* the purchase of the Biddle Ranch, which they both wanted badly; and the book itself, still untitled (and therefore without "being"), which seemed more recalcitrant than ever. By mid-August, roughly halfway through the novel, Steinbeck took stock of his situation: the Viking Press had bought his contract, hired Pat Covici as a senior editor as part of the deal, and planned a first printing of 15,000 copies for Steinbeck's collection of short stories, *The Long Valley;* a string of famous houseguests had either just departed or were about to arrive; and he and Carol had closed on the Biddle property for $10,500. On August 16, in the middle of what he called a "Bad Lazy Time," he lamented: "Demoralization complete and seemingly unbeatable. So many things happening that I can't not be interested. . . . All this is more excitement than our whole lives put together. All crowded into a month. My many weaknesses are beginning to show their heads. I simply must get this thing out of my system. I'm not a writer. I've been fooling myself and other people. . . . This success will ruin me as sure as hell. It probably won't last and that will be all right" (*WD*, 56). Four days later, on August 20, Lorentz, the newly appointed director of the United States Film Service, arrived for the weekend. His visit broke Steinbeck's depression and logjam. They discussed further a full-length movie of *In Dubious Battle*, then rushed off to visit Chaplin at Pebble Beach, where they stayed up all night drinking and talking about the state of America.[28] Though their film project would ultimately fall through, Steinbeck was encouraged by Lorentz's optimism about the country at large and his prediction that Steinbeck's "monumental" book would be one of "the greatest novels of the age." Steinbeck doggedly kept up his daily stint (he aimed for 2,000 words at each sitting, some days managing as few as 800, some days, when the juices were flowing, as many as 2,200) through what Carol called the "interminable details and minor crises" of August and September (*WD*, 17–18).

That Steinbeck lost only four or five working days during that entire stretch points up just how deeply he augmented his talent with discipline and hard work. Where his characters use tools to elevate work to a dignified level, Steinbeck turned to his "comfortable and comforting" pen, an instrument that became an "extension" of the best part of himself: "Work is the only good thing," he claimed on July 6, 1938 (*WD*, 39). For Steinbeck, writing was a means of textual habitation, a way of living in the world he created. He wrote books methodically the way other people built houses, word by word, sentence by sentence. His act of composing was also self-creation, a way of fulfilling his emotional and psychological dream of belonging by being at home, by living in the architectural spaces created by his imagination. In fact, this creative, interior, or "architextual" level of engagement is the elusive, unacknowledged fifth layer of Steinbeck's novel.

Although Steinbeck insisted on effacing his own presence in *The Grapes of Wrath* (*SLL*, 180–81), the fact remains that it is a very personal book, rooted in his own compulsion. Aspects of Steinbeck's life bore directly on manuscript decisions. During his planning session on July 13, admittedly confused by the increasing lure of owning the Biddle Ranch—"I want that ranch"

---

28. Part of Steinbeck's cryptic entry for August 23, 1938, reads: "Pare came over the weekend. Big time. Carol sprained her ankle q.t. Went down to the peninsula with Pare and spent the night at Chaplin's place. Talked all night" (*WD*, 59). Lorentz, *FDR's Moviemaker*, 117–19, recalls the excursion to Chaplin's house in more vivid style and provides details that indicate that pressure from writing the novel made relations between the Steinbecks not just tense but nearly callous.

(*WD*, 42)—he decided to write chapter 14, the general chapter on Manself, which became one of the most important theoretical chapters and perhaps the most significant summation of organismal philosophy Steinbeck had yet written. The first half includes the paean to the universal human capacity for creation. The second half expresses the core of Steinbeck's mature phalanx theory, his belief in the possibility of the creation of an aggregate, dynamic "We" from distinct, myriad selves (*GW*, 206). The summary quality of this chapter suggests that Steinbeck intended to use it later as a kind of climactic crescendo (he ended up using chapter 25). Instead he inserted the Manself chapter at the midpoint of the novel for several reasons: its dithyrambic tone and heightened language reawakened his flagging interest; its optimistic, theoretical bias restored focus and clarity to the narrative line; its extolment of creativity, based on humanity's willingness to "suffer and die for a concept" (*GW*, 205), provided an immediate reminder that his own compositional process could be endured for the sake of the cause he espoused; and its concern for families who had lost their land and homes may have partly assuaged his guilt, if not his sense of irony, as he was about to make the biggest property purchase of his life. Furthermore, the "plodding" pace of Steinbeck's writing schedule informed the slow, "crawling" movement of the Joads' journey, while the harried beat of his own life gave the proper "feel" and tone to his beleaguered characters. Their unsavory weaknesses and vanities, their struggle for survival, their unsuspecting heroism are Steinbeck's as well. If *The Grapes of Wrath* praises the honorableness of labor and ratifies the obsessive quest for a home it is because the author himself felt that these twin acts called into being the most committed, the most empathetic, the most resourceful qualities of the human psyche.

By early October, Steinbeck, rebuked often by his wife, roused himself from another bout of "self indulgence" and "foolishness" to mount the final drive (*WD*, 81). Like a gift, the last five chapters of the novel came to him so abundantly that he had more material than he could use (Rose of Sharon was to contract measles, which in turn would cause the death of her infant). On Wednesday, October 5, and again on Friday, October 7, he planned chapter 26:

> And my story is coming better. I see it better. Ma's crossing with the clerk, and then Tom's going out—meeting Casy, trying to move the men in the camp. Arrest and beating. Return in secret. Move. Cotton—flood. And the end—Tom comes back. Stolen things. Must go. Be Around. Birth.

And the rising waters. And the starving man. And the end. What more? (*WD*, 82–83)

This leisurelyness must go on although the tempo gets faster the details must be as slow. Today the hiding of Tom and the scene with his mother. The cut in wages. Tom has to go. Getting together. The drop to starvation level of the wages. The trapped quality. Must get it in—Difficulty of getting clean. No soap. No money to buy soap. Then peaches. The rush of workers and the fight for the peaches. Fight to get them. Must get this all in. There's so damned much in this book already. I must keep it coming. . . . (*WD*, 84)

Here the full force of Steinbeck's experience at Visalia eight months earlier came into play, prompting his metamorphosis from right-minded competency to inspired vision. What Steinbeck had witnessed in that "heartbreaking" sea of mud and debris called forth every ounce of his moral indignation, social anger, and empathy, which in turn profoundly affected his novel's climax. His internal wounding opened the floodgates of his affection, created *The Grapes of Wrath*'s compelling justification, provided its haunting spiritual urgency, and rooted it in the deepest wellsprings of democratic fellow-feeling. In the same way that rain floods the novel's concluding chapters, so the memory of Steinbeck's cataclysmic experience, his compensation for the futility and impotency of Visalia, pervades the ending of the book; its ominous emotional climate is charged by a terrible beauty symbolized by Rose of Sharon's gratuitous act of sharing her breast with a starving stranger. "It must be an accident, it must be a stranger, and it must be quick," Steinbeck instructed Covici. "To build this stranger into the structure of the book would be to warp the whole meaning of the book. The fact that the Joads don't know him, don't care about him, have no ties to him—that is the emphasis. The giving of the breast has no more sentiment than the giving of a piece of bread" (*SLL*, 178). This prophetic final tableau scene—often decried and misunderstood, but for that no less subversively erotic, mysteriously indeterminate—refuses to fade from view; before the apocalypse occurs, before everything is lost in otherness, Steinbeck suggests, *all* gestures must pass from self to world, from flesh to word, from communication to communion. It was the perfect ending for his book.[29]

29. Martha Heasley Cox, "The Conclusion of *The Grapes of Wrath*: Steinbeck's Conception and Execution," *San Jose Studies* 1 (November 1975): 73–81, was the first to see the novel's

Steinbeck's participation at Visalia also empowered his transformation of Tom Joad, the slowly awakening disciple of Jim Casy. Tom's acceptance of the crucified preacher's gospel of social presence occurs just as the deluge is about to begin: "Wherever they's a fight so hungry people can eat, I'll be there. Wherever they's a cop beatin' up a guy, I'll be there. If Casy knowed, why, I'll be in the way guys yell when they're mad an'—I'll be in the way kids laugh when they're hungry an' they know supper's ready. An' when our folks eat the stuff they raise an' live in the houses they build—why, I'll be there. See? God, I'm talkin' like Casy. Comes of thinkin' about him so much. Seems like I can see him sometimes" (*GW,* 572).

In one of those uncanny transferences artists can make in moments of extreme exhaustion or receptivity, Steinbeck not only believed that his fictive alter ego, Tom Joad, floated above *The Grapes of Wrath*'s "last pages . . . like a spirit," but also imagined that Joad actually entered the novelist's work space, the private chamber of his room: " 'Tom! Tom! Tom!' I know. It wasn't him. Yes, I think I can go on now. In fact, I feel stronger. Much stronger. Funny where the energy comes from. Now to work, only now it isn't work any more," he recorded in his journal on October 20 (*WD,* 91). With that breakthrough—at once a visitation and a benediction—Steinbeck arrived at the intersection of novel and journal, that luminous point, that fifth layer of involvement, where the life of the writer merges with his created world. He entered the architecture of his own novel, and, however briefly, lived in its fictive space, where, like Tom Joad, Steinbeck discovered it was no longer necessary to lead people toward a distant new Eden or illusory Promised Land; rather, the most heroic action was simply to learn to be present, to inhabit the "wherever" fully and at once.

The terms of his complex investment fulfilled, Steinbeck needed only a few more days to finish his novel. Around noon on Wednesday, October 26, 1938, feeling "so dizzy" he could "hardly see the page" (*WD,* 93), he completed the last 775 words of the novel; at the bottom of the concluding manuscript page, Steinbeck, whose writing was normally tiny, scrawled in letters an inch and a half high "END#."[30] It should have been cause for wild celebrating, but

ending positively in light of Steinbeck's stated intentions in the as-yet-unpublished "Diary of a Book" (later titled *Working Days*).

30. "The Grapes of Wrath," autograph manuscript, 165.

between bouts of bone-weary tiredness and nervous exhaustion, Steinbeck felt only numbness and perhaps some of the mysterious satisfaction that comes from having transformed the weight of his whole life into the new book. In *The Grapes of Wrath* the multiple streams of subjective experience, amelioration, graphic realism, biblical themes, and symbolic forms gather to create the "truly American book" Steinbeck had planned. "Finished this day," his final journal entry concluded simply, "and I hope to God it's good" (*WD*, 93).

## VI

In 1963 Steinbeck told Caskie Stinnett: "I wrote *The Grapes of Wrath* in one hundred days, but many years of preparation preceded it. I take a hell of a long time to get started. The actual writing is the last process" (*CJS*, 87–88). Though Steinbeck made 99 entries in his daily journal, and actually wrote the novel in 93 sittings, it was his way of saying that *The Grapes of Wrath* was an intuited whole which embodied the form of his devotion. The entire 200,000-word manuscript took up 165 handwritten pages (plus one smaller sheet) of a 12" × 18" lined ledger book. When he was hot, Steinbeck wrote fast, paying little or no attention to proper spelling, punctuation, or paragraphing. On top of that his script was so small he was capable of cramming over 1,300 words on a single oversized ledger sheet (page 156 of the manuscript is the equivalent of four pages of the Viking text). In short, the novel was written with remarkably preordained motion and directed passion; the relative cleanness and clarity of the holograph manuscript is awesome. To British scholar Roy S. Simmonds it displays a "phenomenal" unity of purpose, an example of "spontaneous prose" created long before Kerouac's *On the Road*.[31]

In one instance Steinbeck inserted an unnumbered sheet between pages 87 and 88 of the manuscript. This contained three short bridge passages (totaling approximately 500 words) to explain Noah Joad's abandonment at the Colorado River. There is also a very ungainly passage of 159 words, originally intended to be part of chapter 21, which one of the Steinbecks wisely canceled when proofreading the typescript:

---

31. Simmonds, "The Original Manuscript," 129.

Once the Germans in their hordes came to the rich margin of Rome;
and they came timidly, saying 'we have been driven, give us land.' And the
Romans armed the frontier and built forts against the hordes of need/ .
~~And the Romans armed the frontier~~ And the legions patrolled the borders,
cased in metal, armed with the best steel. And the barbarians came, naked,
across the border, humbly, humbly. They received the swords in their breasts
and marched on; and their dead bore down the swords and the barbarians
marched on and took the land. And they were driven by their need, and
they conquered with their need. In battle the women fought in the line, and
the yellow-haired children lay in the grass with knives to ham-string the
legionaries, to snick through the hamstrings of the horses. But the legions
had no needs, no wills, no force. And the best trained, best armed troops
in the world went down before the hordes of need.[32]

Not in the manuscript or in the typescript, but in the galleys of the Viking
text, a passage of 82 words was later added to chapter 26 and one of 228
words designed for effective pacing was added to chapter 30. Otherwise,
the emendations are neither major nor substantive—often just changes in
syntax, punctuation, paragraphing, spelling, and names (the family that
shares the flooding boxcar with the Joads at novel's end were called the
Hamills in manuscript, but Steinbeck changed that to the Wainwrights
in Carol's typescript). Page after page went essentially unmodified from
autograph manuscript to typescript to published novel. Though Steinbeck
severely doubted his own artistic ability, and in fact wavered sometimes in
regard to such niceties as chapter divisions (he originally conceived the novel
in three parts), in writing this novel he was creating with the full potency of
his imaginative powers. His ability to execute a work of its magnitude places
him among the premier creative talents of his time. From the vantage point
of history, the venture stands as one of those happy occasions when a writer
simply wrote better than he thought he could.

Steinbeck had completely lost sight of the novel's effectiveness and had
little grasp on its potential popularity, so he warned Covici and the Viking
Press against a large first printing. Viking ignored him and spent $10,000

---

32. This passage appears on p. 110 of the autograph manuscript and, in its canceled form, on
p. 462 of the typescript of *The Grapes of Wrath*, Item MMC-1713, Box 1, Manuscripts Division,
Library of Congress.

on publicity and printed an initial run of 50,000 copies. After recuperating in San Francisco from the stress of writing the book, the Steinbecks moved to their new Brush Road mountain home. It was still under construction, so they camped awhile in the old homestead, where Carol finished the huge typescript, and together they made "routine" final corrections. After Covici had read 400 pages of the typescript on a visit to Los Gatos in late October (*WD*, 91), he badgered Steinbeck for his own copy of the manuscript; Steinbeck gave in and sent the first two chapters to him on November 29. The whole of Carol's cleanly typed copy, which was actually only the second draft of the book (*SLL*, 171), was sent to his New York agents on December 7, 1938, roughly six months after Steinbeck had started the novel. Elizabeth Otis visited Los Gatos in late December to smooth out some of Steinbeck's rough language, like the dozen or so appearances of the words *fuck, shit, screw,* and *fat ass,* which were the chief offenders. They reached a workable compromise: Steinbeck agreed to change only those words "which Carol and Elizabeth said stopped the reader's mind"; beyond that, "those readers who are insulted by normal events or language mean nothing to me," he told Covici on January 3, 1939 (*SLL*, 175). The novel's enthusiastic reception at Viking was spoiled by the wrangling that ensued over the controversial Rose of Sharon ending, which the firm wanted Steinbeck to change, not only to make it more "integral" to the plot, but also because it seemed larcenously close to de Maupassant's tale "Iddyle" (1884). On January 16, 1939, Steinbeck fired back:

> I am sorry but I cannot change that ending. . . . The giving of the breast has no more sentiment than the giving of a piece of bread. I'm sorry if that doesn't get over. It will maybe. I've been on this design and balance for a long time and I think I know how I want it. And if I'm wrong, I'm alone in my wrongness. As for the Maupassant story, I've never read it but I can't see that it makes much difference. There are no new stories and I wouldn't like them if there were. The incident of the earth mother feeding by the breast is older than literature. You know that I have never been touchy about changes, but I have too many thousands of hours on this book, every incident has been too carefully chosen and its weight judged and fitted. The balance is there. (*SLL*, 178)

The entire postwriting flurry, including answering the persistent marginal queries on the typescript posed by a copy editor (whose initials were DZ), proofreading the galleys, and fending off Viking's requests for public appear-ances, struck the novelist, by then suffering from sciatica and tonsillitis, as anticlimactic: "[D]o you really think we've lost a single reader by refusing to do the usual things? By not speaking at luncheons do you think I've lost sales? I don't. And if it were true I'd rather lose that kind of readers" (*SLL*, 181).

Steinbeck may not have been interested in the promotional activities surrounding his book, but plenty of other people were. *The Grapes of Wrath* was widely and favorably reviewed, and its fidelity to fact, its degree of social realism were discussed and debated in the popular press when it was first published. It has been praised by the Left as a triumph of proletarian writing, nominated by critics and reviewers alike as "The Great American Novel," given historical significance by Senator Robert M. La Follette's inquiries into California's tyrannical farm labor conditions, and validated by Carey McWilliams, whose own great work, *Factories in the Fields,* is the classic so-ciological counterpart to Steinbeck's novel. But *The Grapes of Wrath* has also been attacked by elitist scholars as sentimental, unconvincing, and inartistic; banned repeatedly by school boards and libraries for its rebellious theme and frank language; and denounced by right-wing ministers, corporate farmers, and politicians as communistic, immoral, degrading, warped, and untruthful. The Associated Farmers mounted a smear campaign to discredit the book and its author, who often felt his life was in danger. Rebuttals intended to whitewash the Okie situation, such as *Of Human Kindness,* written by Steinbeck's Los Gatos neighbor Ruth Comfort Mitchell, had no impact whatsoever.

Since it was published, *The Grapes of Wrath* has been steadily studied and analyzed by literary critics, scholars, historians, and creative writers. It is no exaggeration to say that, during the past half century, few American novels have attracted such passionate attacks and equally passionate defenses. It seems hard to believe that critics are all reading the same novel. Philip Rahv's complaint in the *Partisan Review* (Spring 1939) that "the novel is far too didactic and long-winded" and "fails on the test of craftsmanship" should be weighed against Charles Angoff's assessment in the *North American Review* (Summer 1939) that it is "momentous, monumental, and memorable," and an example of "the highest art." This dialectic still characterizes the novel's critical reception. In a 1989 speech, critic Leslie Fiedler attacked the novel as "maudlin, sentimental, and overblown"; a month later, in a review, novelist William Kennedy praised it for standing "tall . . . a mighty, mighty book."[33]

If the past fifty years have seen little consensus about the exact nature of the novel's achievement, at least contemporary analysts treat the book as a legitimate work of fiction rather than as a propagandistic tract. No matter which lens *Grapes* is viewed through, its textual richness, its many layers of action, language, and characterization continue to pay enormous dividends. As John Ditsky discovered, "the Joads are still in motion, and their vehicle with them."[34] Academic theories to the contrary, reading remains a subjective act, and perhaps the only sure thing about *The Grapes of Wrath* is its capacity to elicit powerful audience responses. This of course was Steinbeck's intention from the first. "I don't think *The Grapes of Wrath* is obscure in what it tries to say, " he claimed in 1955. "Its structure is very carefully worked out. . . . Just read it, don't count it!"[35]

As a result of shifting political emphases, the enlightened recommendations of the La Follette Committee (that the National Labor Relations Act include farm workers), the effects of loosening or abolishing some labor laws (such as California's discriminatory "anti-migrant" law, established in 1901, which was struck down by the Supreme Court in 1941 in a decision *The Grapes of Wrath* helped bring about), the creation of compulsory military service, and the inevitable recruitment of migrant families into defense-plant

33. Leslie Fiedler, "Looking Back after 50 Years," *San Jose Studies* 16 (Winter 1990): 55; William Kennedy, " 'My Work Is No Good,' " *New York Times Book Review,* April 9, 1989, 44–45. Contemporary reviews by Philip Rahv and Charles Angoff are available in John Ditsky, ed., *Critical Essays on Steinbeck's "The Grapes of Wrath"* (Boston: G. K. Hall, 1989), 30–31, 33–35. See Ray Lewis White, "*The Grapes of Wrath* and the Critics of 1939," *Resources for American Literary Study* 13 (Autumn 1983): 134–63, for a compilation of 108 annotated contemporary reviews. Harmon, *Fifty Year Bibliographic Survey,* 37–152, lists 844 reviews and scholarly articles on *Grapes*.

34. Ditsky, introduction to *Critical Essays,* 15. Ditsky's introduction is the most exhaustive overview of *Grapes* criticism since Lisca undertook a survey for the Viking Critical Library edition, *The Grapes of Wrath: Text and Criticism* (New York: Viking, 1972), 695–707 (Lisca is currently revising the book). Ditsky updated his overview in "*The Grapes of Wrath* at Fifty: The Critical Perspective," in *The Grapes of Wrath: A Special Issue,* ed. Susan Shillinglaw, *San Jose Studies* 16 (Winter 1990): 46–53.

35. John Steinbeck, "A Letter on Criticism," *Colorado Quarterly* 4 (Autumn 1955): 53; reprinted in *Steinbeck and His Critics: A Record of Twenty-five Years,* ed. E. W. Tedlock and C. V. Wicker (Albuquerque: University of New Mexico Press, 1957), 53.

and shipyard jobs caused by the booming economy of World War II that signaled the beginning of their successful assimilation (California growers soon complained of an acute shortage of seasonal labor), the particular set of epochal conditions that crystallized Steinbeck's awareness in the first place passed from his view.[36] Like other momentous American novels that embody the bitter, often tragic, transition from one way of life to another, *The Grapes of Wrath* possessed, among its other attributes, perfect timing. Its appearance permanently changed the literary geography of the United States.

It also changed Steinbeck permanently. Many "have speculated," Jackson Benson writes, "about what happened to change Steinbeck after *The Grapes of Wrath*. One answer is that what happened was the writing of the novel itself."[37] Writing 260,000 words in a single year "finished" him, he told Lawrence Clark Powell on January 24, 1939. After his long siege with the "matter of the migrants" ("I don't know whether there is anything left of me," he confided in October 1939), his "will to death" was so "strengthened" that by the end of the thirties he was sick of writing proletarian fiction, so he decided to quit it. This was a decision many critics and reviewers held against him for the rest of his life; they wanted him to write *The Grapes of Wrath* over and over again, which he refused to do. "The process of writing a book is the process of outgrowing it," he told Herbert Sturz. "Disciplinary criticism comes too late. You aren't going to write that one again anyway. When you start another—the horizons have receded and you are just as cold and frightened as you were with the first one."[38]

The unabated sales, the frenzied public clamor, and the vicious personal attacks over *The Grapes of Wrath* confirmed Steinbeck's worst fears about the fruits of success and pushed the tension between the Steinbecks to the breaking point, a situation exacerbated by his romance with Gwyn

36. Information in this paragraph is gleaned from Philip Brooks, "Notes on Rare Books," *New York Times Book Review*, February 1, 1942, 22; Walter J. Stein, *California and the Dust Bowl Migrants* (Westport, Conn.: Greenwood Press, 1973), 279–81; James N. Gregory, *American Exodus: The Dust Bowl Migration and the Okie Culture in California* (New York: Oxford University Press, 1989), 172–73; and Dick Meister and Anne Loftis, *A Long Time Coming: The Struggle to Unionize America's Farm Workers* (New York: Macmillan, 1977).

37. Jackson J. Benson, *The True Adventures of John Steinbeck, Writer* (New York: Viking, 1984), 392.

38. John Steinbeck to Herbert Sturz, February 10, 1953; also Dircks, "Steinbeck's Statement on the Inner Chapters," 92.

Conger (they were married from 1943 to 1948) and his repeated absence on trips to Hollywood and Mexico. By the early 1940s, "finishing off a complete revolution" and having "worked the novel" as far as he could "take it" (*SLL*, 193–94), Steinbeck was no longer content to be the man— or the artist—he had once been. Steinbeck's change from social realist to metafictionist was not caused by a bankruptcy of talent, a change of venue, or a failure of honesty. Rather, it was the backlash from an unprecedented and unanticipated success, a repugnant "posterity." "I have always wondered why no author has survived a best-seller," he told John Rice in a June 1939 interview. "Now I know. The publicity and fan-fare are just as bad as they would be for a boxer. One gets self-conscious and that's the end of one's writing" (*CJS*, 15). His new writing lacked the aggressive bite of his late 1930s fiction, but it had the virtue of being different and varied. After 1940 much of his important work centered on explorations of a new topic—the implications of individual choice and imaginative consciousness. A prophetic postmodernist, Steinbeck's subject in *Sea of Cortez* (1941), *Cannery Row* (1945), *East of Eden* (1952), *Sweet Thursday* (1954), *The Winter of Our Discontent* (1961), and *Journal of a Novel* (1969) was the creative process itself, the epistemological dance of the law of thought and the law of things.

The Grapes of Wrath remains among the most wrenching fictional indict-ments of the myth of California as a promised land. Ironically, as John Steinbeck composed this novel that tested a social group's capacity for survival in a hostile world, he was himself unraveled. As a consequence, the particular angle of vision, the vital signature, the moral indignation, that made his art exemplary in the first place could never be repeated with the same integrated force. Once his name became inseparably linked with the title of his most famous novel, Steinbeck could never escape the influence of his earlier life, but thankfully, it is tempting to say, neither can we. Wherever human beings dream of a dignified and free society in which they can harvest the fruits of their own labor, *The Grapes of Wrath*'s voice can still be heard. Every strong novel redefines our conception of the genre's dimensions and reorders our awareness of its possibilities. As a tale of dashed illusions, inhuman suffering, and betrayed promises—all strung on a gossamer thread of hope—*The Grapes of Wrath* not only sums up the depression era's socially conscious art, but, beyond that, with its emotional urgency, evocative power, and sustained drama, has few peers in American fiction in general.

# The Making of *Delta Wedding,* or Doing "Something Diarmuid Thought I Could Do"

ALBERT J. DEVLIN

§  §  §

## I

A S WITH SO MANY American novels of distinction, *Delta Wedding* was the result of a convergence of artistic ambition, fortuitous event, and literary background. Eudora Welty remarked once that "novels have long fuses that run way back."[1] Her agent, Diarmuid Russell, may have lit the fuse to her first novel, but the combustible material was Welty's own—her achieved success in the short story and the dramatized themes that continued to interest her; her acute appreciation of Virginia Woolf's modernist aesthetic and her own desire, however hesitant, to accomplish a lyrical novel; her inheritance of the literary tradition of "the Southern family romance"; and a deep, if rather specialized, interest in the Mississippi Delta and its people. These were the natural and personal materials of her novel, but they were shaped in part by external circumstance—by a literary marketplace that demanded a novel from even the most successful story writer; by the adroit, and timely, urging of a literary agent to transform an unsalable story, "The Delta Cousins," into a novel; and by the ironies of a wartime economy that on the one hand might refuse a story as too long, but on the other was hospitable to a novel-length treatment of much the same material. These and other sources may tell a plausible and perhaps engaging story of composition, but Eudora Welty will always have

---

1. Eudora Welty, *Conversations with Eudora Welty,* ed. Peggy Whitman Prenshaw (Jackson: University Press of Mississippi, 1984), 256. Hereafter cited parenthetically in the text as *CEW.*

the last word in this endeavor: "What we know about writing the novel *is* the novel."[2]

## II

The making of Eudora Welty's first novel is a tale whose plot may be thicker than her story of the waning of plantation life in the Mississippi Delta. It includes the author's self-image as a born short-story writer, her accidental bowing to requests that she undertake a novel, her exposure to the Delta by her friend John Robinson, to whom the book is dedicated, and, most obliquely, her probing for a humane order in cruel, unscrupulous days, for *Delta Wedding* was written in wartime and published in 1946. No one, I think, has understood better the sole law of Welty's imaginative life than her friend Elizabeth Bowen: "It has been necessary for her to evolve for herself her own language, and to arrive, each time she writes, at a new form. With her, nothing comes out of stock, and it has been impossible for her to remain static."[3] In *Delta Wedding* the main elements of this new form are the canons of literary modernism that Welty derived in part, at least, from Virginia Woolf and the more homely conventions of "the Southern family romance." Their fusion would lead Welty to reveal her own identity with new daring and precision. Few journal reviewers of *Delta Wedding* recognized either the passion or the danger of this arrival; but over the years Bowen's prediction has been realized: "I should like to think that *Delta Wedding* may, in time, come to be recognized as a classic."[4]

Welty's long-awaited novel takes place in September 1923 in the Mississippi Delta, and has for plot, if such it is, the equivocal marriage of a plantation belle and the local overseer. The whole tribe of Fairchilds, including aunts and great-aunts and myriad black retainers, regrets Dabney Fairchild's "wildness" for Troy Flavin, the laconic overseer of Shellmound, but their dismay

---

2. Eudora Welty, "Words into Fiction" (1965), in *The Eye of the Story: Selected Essays and Reviews* (New York: Random House, 1978), 137. Hereafter cited parenthetically in the text as "WF."

3. Elizabeth Bowen, review of *The Golden Apples*, by Eudora Welty, *Books of Today* (London), September 1950, 2.

4. Elizabeth Bowen, review of *Delta Wedding*, by Eudora Welty, *The Tatler and Bystander* (London), August 6, 1947, 183.

remains an undertone of gibe and jest rather than confrontation with the hill man from Tishomingo County. The novel takes little more than a week's time and ends with the return of the Flavins from their honeymoon in New Orleans. (Their sighting of a streetcar named Desire is one of those serendipitous moments that make of writers as different as Eudora Welty and Tennessee Williams a spectatorial company.) The wedding ceremony itself occurs in a brief sentence and may confirm the suspicion of one character that "nothing really so very much, happened,"[5] after all, at Shellmound. It is a sign of Welty's poise and playful self-assurance that this sly description of lyrical practice is spoken by "little Robbie Reid," the fugitive wife of George Fairchild, whose literary instincts are less than sharply honed. This and other evidence of subtle presentation meet and are paradoxically interwoven in a book that Welty claims to have written almost by chance. Nonetheless, this "most ill-planned or unplanned of books,"[6] as Welty has always described *Delta Wedding*, marks her first maturity in a career that has made her preeminent, or nearly so, among the most important writers of her time.

The brief career of Katherine Mansfield held, or so Elizabeth Bowen thought, a parable of artistic striving and development: "It is with maturity that the really searching ordeal of the writer begins. Maturity, remember, must last a long time. And it must not be confused with single perfections, such as [Katherine Mansfield] had accomplished without yet having solved her abiding problems."[7] I reminded Miss Welty of these lines in 1986, when Peggy Prenshaw and I interviewed the writer at her home in Jackson, Mississippi. Her agreement with Bowen's profile of maturity was swift and intuitive: "That's marvelous. No escaping it once you've got it. . . . It's just the very seed of things, isn't it? The very core" ("ACEW," 7–8). "Single perfections" and "abiding problems," I thought at the time, rather aptly described Welty's own situation as she approached the writing of *Delta Wedding*, a

5. Eudora Welty, *Delta Wedding* (New York: Harcourt, Brace and Company, 1946), 190. Further quotations are from this edition and are cited parenthetically in the text as *DW*. See Noel Polk, *Eudora Welty: A Bibliography of Her Work* (Jackson: University Press of Mississippi, 1994), 46–59, for the printing history of *Delta Wedding*.

6. Eudora Welty, "A Conversation with Eudora Welty" (1986), with Albert J. Devlin and Peggy Whitman Prenshaw, in *Welty: A Life in Literature*, ed. Albert J. Devlin (Jackson: University Press of Mississippi, 1987), 9. Hereafter cited parenthetically in the text as "ACEW."

7. Elizabeth Bowen, introduction to *Stories by Katherine Mansfield* (New York: Vintage Books, 1956), vi.

book much on my mind. Welty's "single perfections," like those of her ally Katherine Mansfield, were admired for their refinement of sensibility; but their aesthetic matrix was little understood, and Welty's daring experiments often seemed to place her characters in the most obscure relation with the world. This apparent divorce from reality (and its furtive twin, the innate errancy of language) is an abiding problem of literary modernism itself, as Welty surely realized; but it constituted for her a unique set of compositional challenges that eventuated in the Delta narrative of the Fairchild clan. The fullness of their dwindling life, Welty may have sensed in late 1943, held "the key" to her own maturity and development.

## III

At the end of 1943, Eudora Welty was a thirty-four-year-old professional writer living at the family home in Jackson. Her first publication in 1936 in *Manuscript* had set a pattern of stories appearing in small magazines and academic quarterlies (especially the *Southern Review* of Cleanth Brooks and Robert Penn Warren) that paid little in specie or in fame. Welty fortuitously acquired her agent, Diarmuid Russell, in June 1940, and he quickly set about exposing his client's work to a national audience. By the year's end, Russell had placed "A Worn Path" and "Powerhouse" with the *Atlantic Monthly;* and in the following three years, he arranged contracts with Doubleday, Doran, and Harcourt, Brace to publish two collections of stories and the novella *The Robber Bridegroom.* Between 1940 and 1943, recognition for Welty included stints at Bread Loaf and Yaddo (where she continued her friendship with Katherine Anne Porter, an early advocate of her stories at the *Southern Review*), three successive O'Henry awards, including two "firsts," a Guggenheim fellowship, invitations by *Saturday Review* and *Mademoiselle* to contribute to their special southern numbers, and further appearances in national magazines. More importantly, Welty had bucked the "novel first" rule of commercial publishing with collections in 1941 and 1943 and a novella steeped in Mississippi fantasy in the intervening year.[8]

8. See Michael Kreyling, *Author and Agent: Eudora Welty and Diarmuid Russell* (New York: Farrar, Straus and Giroux, 1991), 32–54. Hereafter cited parenthetically in the text as *AA.* I am indebted to Kreyling for his supplying new information on Welty's literary career, and especially for his astute description of the Welty–Russell correspondence, 1940–1973. At present, this

The first six months of Russell's agency confirmed how hard it was for Welty to crack the national magazines and press—an effort that antedates Russell's good offices by at least four or five years. *Collier's, Good Housekeeping, Harper's Bazaar, Harper's Magazine, Mademoiselle,* and *The New Yorker,* a well-hedged sending list by any measure, all returned the classic story "Why I Live at the P.O." in 1940 (*AA,* 39). Plans for a collection proceeded in tandem with single-story submissions, but the larger project was rebuffed as well, until Doubleday was sufficiently prodded by the editor John Woodburn to accept the collection *A Curtain of Green* in January 1941.

Amid the periodic disappointment of submission and return was predictable evidence that commercial publishing little understood the logic of Welty's creative process. Welty's stories were thought "obscure" by "the miserable crew of editors," as Russell reported in September 1940; and invariably the collection could not be considered "except in connection with a novel" (*AA,* 39). This familiar caveat raised troubling questions for Welty about the privilege of the novel form itself. Not without wavering and self-doubt at this time did Welty accept the truth of her own interior logic and the irrelevance of that imposed by the marketplace. For the time being, she would be content to write in the "fine security" of such astute readers as Katherine Anne Porter and Diarmuid Russell, son of the Irish visionary A.E. "I can wait and wait," Welty assured Russell in November 1940, "for time does not seem to press very closely down here. It is just in the city that it prods and presses . . . and acts important" (*AA,* 50–51). Writing "South," Welty seemed to say, would allow her the leisure to follow each story "to its pure & final & clear form" (*AA,* 70). This same leisure would also help to relieve the tension between novel and story that had been greatly exacerbated in the North; the pivotal text in fostering more cordial relations between the two is the unpublished story "The Delta Cousins." Completed in late 1943 in the one draft version that survives (or is available for study), the story would lead Welty by seeming magic into the unfamiliar and spacious Delta of the novel.[9]

---

important collection is being processed by the State Department of Archives and History in Jackson, Mississippi.

9. Welty dated "The Delta Cousins" 1942, but the Welty–Russell correspondence, as cited in Kreyling, *Author and Agent,* establishes early November 1943 as the most probable date of the story's first "completion."

## IV

In November 1943, Welty mailed a carbon of "The Delta Cousins" to her friend John Robinson, who had lived near Greenwood in the Delta and introduced Welty to this singular land. The typescript came with a prescient warning, in Welty's hand, that agent and editors would soon repeat: "—it's mighty long." Diarmuid Russell suggested that Welty make cuts to satisfy the restraints of wartime publishing, or that she consider the present thirty-six pages to be "Chapter Two of a novel."[10] A year earlier, Russell thought that another story ("At the Landing") might be expanded, but Welty resisted at the time, and wisely so: "I don't think it would take a novel—just a better story" (*AA*, 96–97). As Welty continued to ponder "The Delta Cousins" in late 1943, especially its forbidding length, she used revealing terms to describe the unruly process of composition: it was "like one of those jinxed pots that cooks more & more pudding" (*AA*, 104). In December 1944, Welty sent a revised draft of the story to Russell, which is not available for study, if it is extant; and in January she could not predict the effect of the new year upon her bubbling materials: "Spring is going to make me wonder and ponder" (*AA*, 111), she told Russell, about a story that apparently would not agree to be shorter.

As metaphors of creativity, the magic pot of folklore and the persuasion of spring link the evolution of Welty's first novel with forces involuntary and magical, and with a sending schedule as timely as the seasons. Between these early and seemingly offhand metaphors and Welty's first considered description of her writing process, there is firm tonal and conceptual agreement: what the writer knows, Welty confirmed in 1955, is that "the word comes surest out of too much, not too little," and that the ground of composition is always "a growing maze of possibilities" that proves the writer's freedom.[11] As the story went forward in early 1945, the rival claims of genre would lose whatever rigidity they had acquired. In revision, "The Delta Cousins" was indeed the protean text described by the ever-sanguine Diarmuid Russell.

---

10. See Charles T. Bunting, " 'The Interior World': An Interview with Eudora Welty" (1972), in *Conversations with Eudora Welty*, 47. Welty repeated similar descriptions of Russell's advice in at least two other interviews in the 1970s and 1980s, although Russell's correspondence is not quoted to this effect in *Author and Agent*.

11. Eudora Welty, "How I Write," *Virginia Quarterly Review* 31 (1955): 245–46.

The longish story that Welty mailed to John Robinson lacked a solid core of vision needed to give the half-dozen or so episodes their proper inevitability. Still they are engaging as compositional units, and they help to explain Welty's gravitation to the form of the novel.[12] Laura Kimball's adventures with her Shelton cousins evolve thematically from Welty's treatment of childhood in "The Winds" (1942). In writing that very personal story, Welty explained that she meant to convey "a feeling of cycles" as a manifestation of "life & change" overtaking the young protagonist (AA, 71). Especially with her cousin India does the nine-year-old Laura encounter the same transformations of life. Their tutor is an old beekeeper wearing "a silvery veil" who takes the girls on a river excursion to a faraway house in the woods. Its emanation of danger and allurement is compounded when Richard "touch[ed] his trousers and a little old fish seemed to come out."[13] In the novel, the marital theme would link sexual initiation with the bride, Dabney, rather than her young sister and cousin; and thus the doting beekeeper did not survive revision. But this archaic traveler with "a green stick" had been useful to Welty. His wanderings helped her to map the more primitive reaches of the Delta and to realize the true aesthetic dimension of the "quiet" house in the woods. In Delta Wedding it would be named and historicized and attached to the pervasive theme of marriage.

Laura Kimball is the proverbial motherless child who is drawn to the Sheltons' abundant family life. The black retainers of Delta Wedding have not yet been deployed, nor has Welty designed the many branchings of the Fairchild family tree; but the shape of clan is unmistakable. Uncle Tatum is the titular head of the family, and his wife, Mim, is a fainting, "breathless" consort who is pregnant once again. Their many children and relatives and friends are devoted to gaiety and carry few "burdens" ("DC," 8). But the present occasion is dimmed for Uncle Raymond, Tatum's younger brother

12. See Michael Kreyling, Eudora Welty's Achievement of Order (Baton Rouge: Louisiana State University Press, 1980), 55–61, and Suzanne Marrs, ed., The Welty Collection: A Guide to the Eudora Welty Manuscripts and Documents at the Mississippi Department of Archives and History (Jackson: University Press of Mississippi, 1988), 9–13, for cogent discussions of Welty's revision of "The Delta Cousins."

13. Eudora Welty, "The Delta Cousins," The Eudora Welty Collection, Series 4, Mississippi Department of Archives and History, Jackson, p. 26. Hereafter cited parenthetically in the text as "DC." Passages from "The Delta Cousins" are quoted by the permission of Russell & Volkening as agents of the author.

from Memphis, whose "wife has left him" ("DC," 26). This is India's secret, and the novel will expand her revelation into a major episode. "The Delta Cousins" ends with a family picnic "on the banks of the Sunflower River" that has Welty thinking again about "cycles" and their underlying unity: "Cotton was everywhere, as far as the sky—the snow white fields. They rolled on and on. It was endless. The wheels rolled but nothing changed" ("DC," 35). *Delta Wedding* will end on much the same epiphanic note, but only after Welty has subjected the Fairchild way of life to a sterner fatality than is present in the story.

Aesthetic discourse and the facts of narrative often fuse in Welty's fiction to produce texts that bespeak their own dynamics. Embedded in "The Delta Cousins" is Welty's essential configuration of the daring performer, the prudent watcher, and the hint of revelation. The discourse begins when Laura is greeted by her headlong kin. Always "rushing, chasing, flying," her cousins "were in reality the sensations of life and they knew it." As portentous as the Delta itself, they attract and frighten Laura in equal measure: "At any moment she might expose her ignorance—at any moment she might learn everything" ("DC," 7–8). The problematics of Laura's witness—her timidity and fear of exposure, and her guarding of emotion "from the contamination even of thought" ("DC," 14–15)—are comprehended by the failure of language itself. "People were each one more than they were said to be," Laura realizes: "Could all ever be told" of Raymond, or of India, or of the heart's mysterious "need" ("DC," 30–31)? When Dabney pulls this secret and precocious reader from beneath the bed and makes a disapproving face at Laura, Welty reveals the gap between aesthetic discourse and the uses of everyday life.

Attentive readers of "A Memory," "The Key," and especially "A Still Moment"—stories that Welty published between 1937 and 1942—would have found the aesthetics of "The Delta Cousins" to be familiar. What the historical figures of "A Still Moment" had wanted "was simply *all*."[14] Their desire "to brood above the entire and passionate life of the wide world, to become its rightful part" (*CS*, 191), touches the same elusive unity of being that Laura salutes from the passing Delta train: "When the day lengthened, a pink light

14. Eudora Welty, "A Still Moment," in *The Collected Stories of Eudora Welty* (New York: Harcourt Brace Jovanovich, 1980), 196. Further quotations of the collected short fiction are from this edition and are cited parenthetically in the text as *CS*.

lay over the cotton, and the last rich note of a song seemed to be hanging in the air. She stretched her arm out the window," as if to touch the radiance of the twilight ("DC," 2). Welty's revision of "The Delta Cousins" may have been prompted in part by Laura Kimball's own astonishing sensitivity. In *Delta Wedding* Laura McRaven would still cherish the "anticipation" ("DC," 36) of her cousins; but the aesthetic "duties" would be parceled out, as it were, among the many Fairchilds, and the nine-year-old prodigy relieved of her implausible sensitivity.[15]

The modernist aesthetic embedded in "The Delta Cousins" did not change in essentials as the story overspread its original form. Nor, I should say, had this aesthetic changed greatly since the time of "A Memory" (1937), when Eudora Welty exposed another young girl to unruly forces that might in a moment reveal "everything" to her. Welty knew early the nature of her desire and its inherent problematics, which she often distilled into the stories of *A Curtain of Green* (1941) and *The Wide Net* (1943). "The Delta Cousins" is notable for locating this process in a place that was unfamiliar to Welty, but whose resources she was undoubtedly testing. In the novel, the Mississippi Delta is fully realized, and with it Eudora Welty began to touch the core of her identity as a writer. The amplitude and capaciousness of the Delta and the form of the novel must have seemed perfectly complementary to Welty, whose imagination was challenged to perform more difficult feats of self-disclosure.

## V

John Robinson is a key figure in Welty's turning from the small-town setting of earlier stories to the relatively unfamiliar Delta. It was this "Delta expert" (as Welty deemed Robinson in 1945) who "introduced" Welty to his unique homeplace, and it was to him that she mailed her most personal response while he was stationed abroad in the service: "The Delta Cousins," in late 1943, and then "chapter by chapter" the novel-in-progress. It was his family that Welty visited during the war, and it was they who opened "old diaries" to her, giving Welty "a feeling of the background of the Delta" ("ACEW," 9–10) and perhaps also the shape of the Fairchild family tree, with its profusion of Civil War dead. Eudora Welty's relationship with John

---

15. See Kreyling, *Achievement of Order,* 56, 61.

Robinson (an aspiring writer himself) in the 1940s has been described as "serious" by Michael Kreyling (*AA*, 111), and it may speak poignantly to her special cherishing of the Delta kin.

At a point not easily marked, this apparent personal investment merges with a public image of the Delta well known to Mississippians of Welty's generation. For the writer David Cohn, no claim was too grand or fervent to describe his Delta homeplace in 1935. "Here are no hills, no rocks, no thin earth barely hiding the stones beneath, but pure soil endlessly deep, dark and sweet, dripping fatness."[16] Three years later, the Federal Writers' Project found much the same bounty: "Fed through countless eons" by the flooding of the river, the flat, "unending" fields of the Mississippi Delta have "a fertility equaling that of the Nile." The people of privilege in the Delta were no less unique than their surroundings. "Settled on land as unstable as it is productive," the planter "has evolved an active yet irresponsible way of life." The Delta, or so the compilers of *Mississippi: A Guide to the Magnolia State*, opined, "is more than a distinct geographical unit—it is also a way of life."[17]

Welty too was charmed by the Delta. A wedding there "couldn't be compressed into one day," she mirthfully told an interviewer who asked about the "time span" of *Delta Wedding* (*CEW*, 47); and to another, Dick Cavett, she explained that its people were "richer, had so much, did so much" more, than other Mississippians.[18] The natural bounty of the Delta and its enchanting folkways seemed to contain "all" for Welty's surrogate receptors. At Shellmound they live avidly on the plane of sensibility, and in the more "blissful" reaches of the novel, they seem to partake of the mythical Delta itself. "Drenched" in the astonishing "whiteness" of the moon, Dabney is awakened and drawn to "her window" in a prefiguring of marital love: "The whole leafy structure of the outside world seemed agitated and rustled. . . . The cotton like the rolling breath of sleep overflowed the fields. Out into it, if she were married, she would walk now—her bare foot touch[ing] . . . the roof, the chimney, the window of her husband, the solid house. Draw me in, she whispered, draw me in" (*DW*, 89–90).

16. David L. Cohn, *Where I Was Born and Raised, Part One*, 1935 (Boston: Houghton Mifflin, 1948), 26.

17. *Mississippi: A Guide to the Magnolia State*, Federal Writers' Project of the Works Progress Administration, American Guide Series (New York: Viking, 1938), 315, 2–3.

18. Eudora Welty, interview by Dick Cavett, *The Dick Cavett Show*, Public Broadcasting System, May 24, 1978.

The metaphorical window through which Dabney passes in desire, and before her Laura Kimball, is a device that Welty used earlier in "A Memory" and with a foreboding effect quite pertinent to *Delta Wedding*. "I had made small frames with my fingers, to look out at everything," the narrator recalls in describing the summer of her first love, as well as a nervous habit of composition instilled by recent "painting lessons" (*CS*, 75). Amid her reverie, the frame of a small beach—one that Welty knew as a child in Jackson— fills not with radiance or bliss but vulgar sporting bathers who displace the young girl's "timeless" (*CS*, 77) dream of love. From her own vantage point in the early 1940s, Welty knew that the "charmed life" (*DW*, 166) of the Fairchilds had vanished as well. Their defining moment of modernity may be fixed rather precisely in October 1944, as Welty, coincidentally, pondered the fate of "The Delta Cousins." Of the mythical Delta, *Business Week* reported that "mechanical cotton pickers [had] moved onto a 28-acre field . . . near Clarksdale, Miss., to harvest what is believed to be the first commercial cotton acreage ever raised entirely by machinery."[19]

For the Sheltons and the Fairchilds, the past is merely "a private, dull matter" soon "forgotten" ("DC," 8; *DW*, 15). But these words, repeated in story and novel alike, promise only extinction for blithe Shellmound. Shellmound is not Poynton or even Pointz Hall, at least not architecturally, but it shares with these more famous literary houses the same fatality. The antagonist is modern history itself; and whether specified by Henry James in the atomizing will of individuals, or by Virginia Woolf in that of nations, it is the same ravaging force that Welty observed in the Delta attacking the polity of the Fairchilds. Her eye had been trained along modernist lines to watch for the assault; and Welty, ever the good photographer, knew exactly when to open the shutter. In framing *Delta Wedding*, she selected 1923, "between the acts," as it were, of the two world wars. The latest of these calamities provided a memorable punctuation in August 1945, as Welty completed revision of the novel. With its "countless eons" of formation, the Delta mocked the fragility of human life and culture, and it undermined such blissful images as Dabney's love trailing upon the night. The element of fatality made a modernist image of the Delta, and its spaciousness, in turn, helped to make a novelist of Welty.

19. "Mechanical Crop," *Business Week,* October 21, 1944, 54, 57.

## VI

"Now I have something hard for you to do," Welty wrote to her new agent in June 1940: "I have a collection—a collection of short stories by an unknown writer who doesn't ever want to write a novel first." "Please," she continued, "do not tell me that I will have to write a novel. I do not see why if you enjoy writing short stories and cannot even think in the form of a novel you should be driven away . . . and made to slave at something you do not like and do badly" (*AA*, 34). By late autumn, Russell could report only that both Viking and Reynal & Hitchcock had refused the collection, and with the familiar inquiry about a novel. Welty's mood approached resignation: "It may be that I will try a novel some time soon," Welty told Russell, "since the lack seems to make such a difference." She added as hopeful ballast that "the natural thing for me to do [is] what I can within a lesser space. I suspect that that comes from my being a female, and is permanent" (*AA*, 49). In the rather gloomy atmosphere of late 1940, Russell repeated the advice that had first gained Welty's trust: "Only by following your own path can you get anywhere," he cautioned. He went on, however, to describe the "real value" of writing a novel: "[It] is an arduous piece of work that demands concentration and hard work and this is good for everybody. Short stories can be written while one is under an influence. Novels [can]not and because of this more effort and more discipline is demanded" (*AA*, 50). In effect, the agent was adroitly telling his new client, "Now I have something hard for you to do."

This exchange has considerable foreground in Welty's career. Her first editors at *Manuscript* began the refrain in 1936 by asking Welty if she were not at work on a novel. Their friendly question was repeated, or so it probably seemed to Welty, by every editor in New York or Boston who wrote to applaud a new story or to keep in touch. It was posed in 1939 by no less a luminary than Ford Madox Ford, who had recommended Welty's collection to American and English editors of his wide acquaintance. "Is there, by the bye," he asked urbanely, "any reason why you shouldn't write a novel?"[20] By late 1940, Welty's perplexity and irritation had coalesced

---

20. Ford Madox Ford, letter to Eudora Welty, May 25, 1939, The Eudora Welty Collection. The imagery of the novel inquiry helps to map Welty's early relations with commercial publishing. Harold Strauss of Covici-Friede, who admired Welty's first published story, "Death of a Traveling Salesman," wrote to Welty on May 13, 1936, to say that she "owe[d] it to herself to undertake a

around the privilege of the novel as defined by the marketplace. Rather precisely does Welty's allusion to slave labor and her melancholy attachment of gender to genre measure the coercion that she saw threatening the joy of writing. Russell himself may have underscored this attachment by seeming to cast the novel in a metaphor of masculine creativity. The impasse was partially relieved in January 1941, when Doubleday purchased *A Curtain of Green;* but Russell's challenge remained, and so did Welty's seeming inability to "think in the form of a novel." There is no evidence that Welty undertook at this time any strenuous or even deliberate measures to meet the challenge of novel writing. Instead, she drafted a long, difficult story in late 1940 that became the occasion for a rather special kind of novelistic thought. The "great days" of territorial Mississippi was the setting of this story, and the "dazzling" (*AA*, 52) appeal of Welty's new Mississippi materials undoubtedly helped to temper the writer's disappointments in the marketplace.

In January 1941, Welty was still "writing away" at the new story in her imagination, and she regretted having sent the draft of "First Love" to Russell prematurely. For his part, Russell thought her conception "magnificent," but he found traces of Welty's ever-familiar "obscurity" (*AA*, 60), or so it seemed, in her treatment of Aaron Burr's daring sojourn in the Mississippi Territory. The unseasonable cold that marked Burr's arrival in Natchez in January 1807 was especially troubling to author and agent; and it led Welty to reexamine the aesthetic function of that "bitterest winter of them all" (*CS*, 153). The "trouble," she soon realized, was that "everything [in the story's meteorological scheme] carried the burden of being so many things at once." But that difficulty, Welty knew, was a good omen: "I take as a sign that there is a good story possible, when there seem to be numbers of other stories being written in writing [the original one], when every word that is put down will be carrying along with it all these things that are floating around it" (*AA*, 58). "Don't think I have delusions of grandeur about my little stories" (*AA*, 58), Welty added, with coy approval, one thinks, of their growing length and difficulty.

---

novel." Two weeks later, on May 27, Strauss advised Welty that "it is quite impossible to publish a volume of stories by a relatively unknown author" and that she should "tackle a full-length novel" (letters in The Eudora Welty Collection).

"First Love" remained a story, but Welty had also described a kind of "unwritten novel" in her letter to Russell. Its form was loose and fluid, with one "story" emerging naturally from another without the prodding of any undue causality. The fullness of the narrative was concentrated poetically in "every word," rather than laid out in linear fashion. Thus was fictional time attenuated to keep to the speedy and unpredictable curve of subjectivity. The ambitious center of "First Love" was the story's historic weather. This medium Welty used deftly to project the entangled public and personal life of Natchez and to give formal design to the story itself.

Welty's "unwritten novel" is, of course, a none-too-subtle citation of Virginia Woolf. In January 1920, Woolf described "a new form for a new novel" that soon resulted in *Jacob's Room* (1922). "Suppose," she puzzled in her diary, "one thing should open out of another—as in An Unwritten Novel—only not for 10 pages but 200 or so—doesn't that give the looseness & lightness I want?"[21] In April 1944, Welty reviewed Woolf's posthumous collection, *A Haunted House and Other Short Stories*. Most telling in the volume, she thought, was the story entitled "An Unwritten Novel." Published first in July 1920, it follows the same pliant method described in Woolf's diary entry. An unnamed writer attempts to reach the hidden life of a stranger sitting opposite her in a railway car. As emotion, sensation, gesture, incident, climax, and anticlimax evolve, the story surmises a provisional life for the still unknown, and unknowable, woman. "Here," Welty says, "like a technique of a technique, is Woolf writing before her own eyes."[22]

"She was the one who opened the door" (*CEW*, 75). In 1972 Welty paid full tribute to Woolf for her instructive framing of the aesthetic object. But in 1944, as Welty pondered her Delta materials, Woolf in all likelihood played a more strategic role for the reluctant novelist.[23] The fluid modality of the "unwritten novel" that Welty described in "First Love" was reconfirmed in

21. *The Diary of Virginia Woolf*, ed. Anne Olivier Belle, 5 vols. (New York: Harcourt Brace Jovanovich, 1977–1984), 2:13.

22. Eudora Welty, "Mirrors for Reality," review of *A Haunted House and Other Short Stories* (1944), by Virginia Woolf, *New York Times Book Review*, April 16, 1944, 3.

23. See Albert J. Devlin, "Meeting the World in *Delta Wedding*," in *Critical Essays on Eudora Welty*, ed. W. Craig Turner and Lee Emling Harding (Boston: G. K. Hall & Co., 1989), 90–109, for citation of Welty's review of *A Haunted House* and discussion of its relation to Welty's literary situation in 1944. In 1991 Kreyling pointed astutely to Welty's emphasis upon "An Unwritten Novel" in the review (*Author and Agent*, 108–9).

theory and practice by Woolf's own projective text. Its center of composition, as Welty described in the review, was precisely the same "growing maze of possibilities" that defined the "space" of the short-story writer. In effect, this "lesser space" could expand and contract for Welty within the form of the novel, and with no diminishment either of the writer's freedom or of the mysterious object of fiction itself. Welty's earlier attempts at novel writing, especially in the late 1930s, had been undertaken, or so Katherine Anne Porter thought, "laboriously, dutifully, [Welty] youthfully thinking herself perhaps in the wrong to refuse."[24] The textual evidence of *Delta Wedding* points instead to a more brisk, assured, and satisfying process of composition, especially in early 1945, and to the presence of a sympathetic audience. In our interview, Miss Welty recalled sending the novel-in-progress to John Robinson as a form of entertainment. She also laughed to think that in writing *Delta Wedding,* she had done "something Diarmuid thought I could do" ("ACEW," 9). With commercial laws relaxed, and a compatible audience in view, Welty revealed how natural it was for her to "think in the form of a novel."

## VII

In January 1944, Russell sent "The Delta Cousins" to the *Atlantic Monthly,* and for much of the remaining year cuts were informally negotiated by agent, author, and the prospective publisher, Edward Weeks (*AA,* 106–7). No irony can better catch the seemingly fortuitous writing of *Delta Wedding* than the author's reply to wartime rationing of print. The natural short-story writer did not prune the offending 3,000 words from "The Delta Cousins," as Weeks required, and as she had apparently tried to do; but she wrote a full-length novel instead. And as if to further ironize Weeks's original advice, Welty also published a serialized version of *Delta Wedding* in the *Atlantic* shortly before book publication. The sketchy evidence indicates that, intermittently in 1944, Welty continued to revise "The Delta Cousins," with scant economizing— but no stroke was more crucial than the holograph revision on page 12 of the

24. Katherine Anne Porter, introduction to *A Curtain of Green* (1941), by Eudora Welty; reprinted in *Selected Stories of Eudora Welty* (New York: Random House, 1954). The assessment of Welty's novelistic mischances may bespeak the prolonged composition of *Ship of Fools* (1962), which was problematic as early as 1941, when Porter wrote the introduction for *A Curtain of Green.*

ribbon typescript: Uncle Raymond would return to Memphis, Welty added in pencil above the line, "as soon as the wedding was over." This revision, which does not appear on the carbon sent to John Robinson in late 1943, cannot be dated precisely; but the presumptive evidence of the typescripts is that it shows an early stage of Welty's tinkering with "The Delta Cousins"—before, that is, the "pot" began to boil seriously.[25] Her brief and perhaps at first casual allusion to marriage gave Welty the vehicle needed to expand *and* contract her Delta materials.

On February 20, 1945, Welty wrote to Russell to say that she had returned from a visit to the Delta and was about to resume work on "The Delta Cousins." One critical stimulus at this time, as Suzanne Marrs has recently confirmed,[26] was her reading of the family diaries that Miss Welty noted in our 1986 interview. Two weeks later, on March 9, Welty was "marrying off the girl," as the "jinxed pot" continued to boil. On March 19, she estimated to Russell that the typescript "must be 100 pp. long by now," and on March 27 Welty was "still doing" her story.[27] For a short-story writer ill practiced in plot-making, the Delta wedding was nothing less than manna. Not only did it have a built-in calendar that gave extension and division of time, but it also had great potential for obscuring its passage amid the Fairchilds' ceaseless talk and frantic efforts to marry Dabney in cotton-picking time. The proper "approach" to the "Unwritten Novel," Virginia Woolf thought, required that "scarcely a brick . . . be seen."[28] Rather archly does Welty practice this same deception when Ellen confuses the

25. The ribbon typescript of "The Delta Cousins" in The Eudora Welty Collection shows corrections and brief additions in ink, type, and pencil. The carbon, which was mailed to John Robinson on November 5, 1943, shows changes only in ink. The notations in pencil appear to be the latest changes in the ribbon typescript. They include the important reference on p. 12 to a wedding, but Welty's treatment of "The Delta Cousins" at this time is more accurately described as correction than revision.

26. Suzanne Marrs, " 'The Treasure Most Dearly Regarded': Memory and Imagination in *Delta Wedding*," *Southern Literary Journal* 25 (1993): 86.

27. As the project continued, Welty reported, on June 12, 1945, that she had delivered ninety pages of revised typescript of "Shellmound," as the novel was known at this time, to Russell and the *Atlantic Monthly.* Welty continued to revise/retype the remaining text amid debilitating summer heat and worry over her brother's safety in the Pacific theater. By late August–early September 1945, she had completed typing the final draft and said rather wearily that "she had learned much from the doing." (Information from the unpublished Welty–Russell correspondence supplied by Michael Kreyling.)

28. *Diary of Virginia Woolf,* 2:13.

calendar of events, and the reader too for a time: "I was hoping we'd get somebody in the family could keep track of time," she frets artlessly, after Troy fails to correct her own "mixed up" (*DW*, 109) dating of the rehearsal supper.

I am aware of no extant notes or intermediate drafts of *Delta Wedding*. It was Welty's practice in revising, as she has said, "to tear up as I go . . . , so I won't have these things reproaching me . . . , and also so nobody else can read them" (*CEW*, 244). But still a rather sharp writerly image of Welty in 1945 can be seen in her own correspondence. A year earlier, in March, when she was still considering cuts to "The Delta Cousins," Welty told Russell: "Any day I may get [the story] down on the floor, which is the best way, and cut it with scissors and pin it this way and that and squint at it" (*AA*, 106). Welty has changed compositional metaphors on Woolf, but the final seamless order of *Delta Wedding* reveals the same strenuous effort to hide any trace of construction.

While squinting at her Delta novel, Welty may have noticed how prolific a "putter-inner" the short-story writer had become. She once solved the problem of having to give plausible speech to historical figures by using a deaf and mute interlocutor—in the story "First Love." But no such reserve hindered Welty in giving speech to the unfamiliar Deltans, or in re-creating their houses and histories. The single house of the Sheltons was set at "the edge of country" ("DC," 4) and had little of the plantation ethos. In *Delta Wedding* it evolved into three distinctive houses, set amid vast cotton fields, which trace the Fairchild settlement from the early nineteenth century until the present. Marmion, as it is named in the novel, closely resembles the haunt of the beeman Richard, but the "castle-like house" (*DW*, 122) is given a tragic family history that has left it vacant since 1890. Even by the spacious standards of plantation fiction, *Delta Wedding* is an unusually well furnished novel. The six principal days of the wedding are filled with songs, rhymes, riddles, games, laughter, tears, teasing, grieving, tantrums, vaunting, memories, dreams, potions, ubiquitous Negroes, and children flying from one adventure to another. "All the company in the world" (*DW*, 135) arrives daily from Memphis and elsewhere, and they join the three generations of Fairchilds living at Shellmound to make this the most clamorous household in Mississippi. Through it all, the drone of the compress is a reminder of "the infinity of the Delta" (*DW*, 77), which knows nothing of Fairchilds or of weddings.

The wedding also allowed Welty to concentrate the narrative. The days of preparation, from Laura's arrival on Monday, September 10, to the rehearsal supper on Friday, build novelistic suspense only to release it with the anticlimactic report that "Mr. Rondo married Dabney and Troy" (*DW,* 214). Suspense in *Delta Wedding* accrues not from linearity, but from precipitous moments of vision such as those Ellen and Dabney experience at the primitive margins of the Delta. To Ellen, the "lost girl" in the woods seems to prefigure her daughter's own exposure in marriage (*DW,* 68–72); and to Dabney, the "silence" of the whirlpool in the nearby Yazoo bespeaks the ominous, endless web of creation (*DW,* 122–23). Such portentous "moments of being," Welty said in reviewing *A Haunted House,* were the palpable "reflections of the abstract world of the spirit, the matter that mirrored the reality." The reality in each case is a penetrating subjectivity that saturates the narrative with the transforming rite of the wedding.

Ellen Fairchild is Welty's most astute, if unwitting, expositor of the "unwritten novel." It is she who confuses the days of the week to create the illusion of seamless narrative, and it is she who identifies the time-defying function of the Yellow Dog train. Orrin, the oldest Fairchild son, is the first to recount the near accident on Dry Creek trestle shortly before Laura's arrival. "Here's the way it was," he tells his city cousin:

> The whole family but Papa and Mama . . . went fishing in Drowning Lake. It will be two weeks ago Sunday. And so coming home we walked the track. . . . On the trestle Maureen danced and caught her foot. . . . Uncle George kneeled down and went to work on Maureen's foot, and the train came. He hadn't got Maureen's foot loose, so he didn't jump either. The rest of us did jump, and the Dog stopped just before it hit them and ground them all to pieces. (*DW,* 19)

Orrin ends by assuring his listeners that "it was cloudy, or we would have remembered it was time for the Dog" (*DW,* 23).

By filtering this seriocomic episode through India, Shelley, Roy, Dabney, Robbie, and especially Ellen, Welty permits Orrin's sparse, original narration to gain lyric amplitude and authority, until Ellen definitively marks its importance for her family, and the novel itself: "That near-calamity on the trestle was nearer than she had realized to the heart of much that had happened in her family lately." It was, we know, the occasion for Dabney's sudden engagement to Troy, and for George's separation from his imploring wife, Robbie Reid. And it is close also to the heart of Welty's daring aesthetic discourse, as Ellen hints in a superb summertime metaphor. She likens the recurring episode of the Yellow Dog train to "the sheet lightning of summer [that] plays in the whole heaven but presently . . . concentrates in one place, throbbing like a nerve in the sky" (*DW,* 157). As in the writing of "First Love," Welty has centered her lyrical narrative in an episode that "carried the burden of being so many things at once."

## VIII

The Delta wedding opened a vein of subjectivity that is the root and form of the "unwritten novel." But marriage is also a staple of American plantation fiction, a species of historical romance that is pertinent to *Delta Wedding*—however troubling Welty may find it on theoretical grounds, and however little attention she may have paid the literature itself. About the Civil War, which shaped the most important conventions of this popular form, Welty feels only revulsion. "I just hate it, all those hideous battles and the terrible loss. I never have read *Gone with the Wind*" ("ACEW," 20), she confessed in 1986. In much the same dissenting voice, Welty once informed William Buckley that she was "not a bit interested in preserving the home of Jefferson Davis" (*CEW,* 104). And to John Crowe Ransom's equivocal praise of *Delta Wedding* as "one of the last novels in the tradition of the old South," Welty demurred respectfully and said that she could not think of herself "as writing out of any special tradition."[29] Of the term *old South* itself, she was as wary as her distant relative William Hines Page; for each of these skeptical southerners, it had "a connotation of something unreal and not quite straightforward" (*CEW,* 82). Nonetheless, Welty's relation to the practice and ideology of "the Southern family romance" (as Richard King has aptly termed it) is more complicated than the writer may realize, and it contains elements more revealing and constructive than her predictable spurning of its memorializing intention. Welty writes in the aftermath of plantation romance, and especially in its marital grounding is this literature pertinent to the aesthetics of *Delta Wedding*.

29. John Crowe Ransom, "Delta Fiction," review of *Delta Wedding,* by Eudora Welty, *Kenyon Review* 8 (1946): 507.

The first plantation writers in the 1820s and 1830s—George Tucker and John Pendleton Kennedy—established marriage as a convention of the genre, and later romancers used it routinely to structure their domestic plots and give them political heft, as the times required. To assert moral character, to define regional values, and especially to mend the tattered national fabric were normative functions that marriage supplied to writers of northern and southern bias throughout the nineteenth century. That the politics of marriage also quenched the romantic desire of readers of all political stripe may help to explain the appeal of the form long after its original ideological uses had ceased. It is a striking lesson to elitists (if any remain) that the popular-domestic-polemical crux of plantation writing should prove so acutely sensitive to the nuances of cultural crisis. Whether writing North or South, the romancers of the nineteenth century perceived the intrinsic flaws of the plantation economy, and even in the most prosperous of times they foresaw its demise. Their historical sense was cast in retrospection, and it was always poised to discover "the hugest fallacy" of slavery, as Henry James put it at Richmond.

Welty's special place in this tradition is often obscured by her dissenting voice. The "charmed life" of Shellmound, with its own funereal name and antecedents, repeats the plantation writer's awareness of the historically endangered edifice. And closely related to this knowledge is Welty's use of the indigenous marital theme, which helped to center her own reluctant novelistic thinking. Welty rejected outright neither the well-tested polemics of marriage, nor its sentimental, domestic paradigms; instead she redeployed them to effect a more complicated narrative and to project her own deepest aesthetic concerns. These concerns led unerringly to the tableau of George Fairchild on Dry Creek trestle and to Ellen's dawning awareness of the importance of this maritally constructed moment. These pivotal characters are named Raymond and Mim in "The Delta Cousins," and it was there that Welty began to devise their roles in the culminating aesthetic discourse of *Delta Wedding*.

## IX

Uncle Raymond is a clear antecedent for George Fairchild. He is on a three-day visit from Memphis, and he has recently lost his wife, an unnamed runaway in the story. He receives adoring glances from his niece

Laura Kimball, who thinks him "a prince," and from the Sheltons generally, who put this "most loved" kin "above all" ("DC," 12). Ellen Fairchild's antecedence is also clear in "The Delta Cousins." Aunt Mim is mother to a large plantation family and wife to Uncle Tatum, a model for the boisterous Battle Fairchild. She is pregnant again, rather wearily so, and seems miscast among the exuberant Sheltons. At this stage, however, she is remote in sensitivity from the "town-loving, book-loving" (*DW,* 217) Ellen Fairchild, whose displacement from Virginia is a kind of narrative privilege. Neither does Mim join the family picnic on the Sunflower River; nor is she entrusted with very much of the story's burden of sensibility. A brief exception to this unpromising start is found in a scene that hints both at Ellen's more intense consciousness and at her later rapport with George Fairchild.

Pausing to rest in the dining room, Mim is "astonished" by the revelation of her family in all of their "absorbed, intent" lives. Uncle Raymond jumps to his feet and offers his chair to Mim, "like a prince offering his seat at blackjack to a princess." The scene itself, if not Welty's curious figure of a gambler, is retained in *Delta Wedding* (21); but even Raymond's gallantry cannot prolong the vision of his sister-in-law: "Aunt Mim's brown eyes blinked, opened and tried to see again, but the curtain had come together and all went on without her once more" ("DC," 10–12). This brief awareness exploits a layering of realities that Virginia Woolf, predictably, described as a special challenge to the lyrical writer. What is broken suddenly for Mim is the hold of "non-being"—that "great part of every day," Woolf thought, that "is not lived consciously." But "behind" this curtain of the ordinary, the mundane, are such acute "moments of being" as Mim's vision of her family as "immensely alive." Virginia Woolf and Eudora Welty knew that "the real novelist can somehow convey both sorts of being,"[30] but neither writer ever doubted the elusiveness of this unity. For her part, Woolf often confessed failure; and Welty succeeded, if she did, only by writing dangerously "on the sharp edge of experiment."[31]

Welty finished typing the revised script of *Delta Wedding* in late August or early September 1945. Several of the more important revisions were made

---

30. Virginia Woolf, "A Sketch of the Past" (1939–1940), in *Virginia Woolf: Moments of Being,* ed. Jeanne Schulkind, 2d ed. (London: Hogarth Press, 1985), 70–73.

31. Eudora Welty, "How I Write," 246.

to preserve the portentous quality of the Yellow Dog episode. Welty omitted Ellen's memory of a family scene following the "trestle commotion," and she also canceled some of her later rumination about the irony of its effects upon Dabney and Robbie (see typescript pages 148–49 and 157–58). By the time Welty delivered the typescript to Harcourt, Brace, of course, the character of Ellen Fairchild was complete in essentials, although Welty continued to polish it after copyediting.[32] In chapter 3, as noted earlier, Ellen is surprised to find a beautiful young girl loitering in the woods. In part, at least, Welty's intention was to expose Ellen to a radiance that she often "hoped for" (*DW*, 71) in the world; but when her speech dulls the encounter—" 'You can come live at Sue Ellen's, girl,' she said. 'You can help look after her—all her children are boys' "—Welty cancels the offending passage, which sounds more like Aunt Mim. Welty cut a similar passage in chapter 4 in which Ellen gossips peevishly with Aunt Tempe, her flighty sister-in-law from Memphis: "It does look like what we women wish our lives away on, here at Shellmound, is always just the very thing that's impossible! Just the four that two and two won't make."[33] Undoubtedly Welty heard bathos (and prolixity) in each passage and knew that it would violate the decorum of Ellen's character. Welty made other telling revisions of Ellen's character after the typescript had been copyedited, and still others (especially of Troy's character) after the galleys were printed, for which she incurred a sizable penalty.

George Fairchild needed less touching up in the typescript. His studied apartness reflects modernist sources well known to the writer: the theory and

32. The typescript setting copy of *Delta Wedding* shows typed revisions, holograph revisions in blue and black ink, holograph revisions in pencil, and pasted-over and inserted pages. One such insert, p. 31A, may reflect an earlier stage of planning before Welty decided to leave Marmion unoccupied after the death of James Fairchild in 1890. In a note on p. 114, the copyeditor cited an inconsistency in this design, which Welty solved by substituting the Grove for Marmion on p. 31A. "Shellmound" was a working title for *Delta Wedding*, as a letter from Welty to Russell in mid-June 1945 indicates. Polk claims that the title was unchanged in early September 1945, when the full text was delivered to Harcourt, Brace and to *Atlantic Monthly* (*Eudora Welty: A Bibliography*, 50). Shellmound, however, was not Welty's only name for the Fairchild plantation. Before Shellmound it was called "Fairburnie," whose ten characters would have permitted easy substitution of "Shellmound" in the typescript setting copy.

33. Eudora Welty, "Delta Wedding," typescript setting copy, 1945, The Eudora Welty Collection, Series 4, pp. 64, 101. Passages from the setting copy are quoted by the permission of Russell & Volkening as agents of the author.

practice of Virginia Woolf, especially in *Jacob's Room*, and the more recent model of Elizabeth Bowen, from whom Welty said that she had "learned" ("ACEW," 7). Typically George Fairchild is seen in "half-light" or "blurred profile," has few speeches, and is cast in retrospective action by family myth and storytelling. His familiar pipe, which Laura hides and later returns as a gift, has traveled easily from the nearby "Delta Cousins," where it was first bartered for love; and before that, from the distant room of Jacob Flanders, where it helped to bring out another artfully concealed young man. Only by such "hints" (such "biographemes," as Barthes would say) can character be treated in the novel, or so Woolf surmised in her first extended attempt at lyrical narrative.

Equally pertinent to Welty's obscuring technique is Elizabeth Bowen's "rule" that no character designed to mystify, as George Fairchild is, "should be allowed to enter the *seeing* class."[34] Thus, Laura thinks, "it was right" that her uncle should "stand apart" (*DW*, 75) from the intimate life of Shellmound. The same logic of mystery and reserve operates in "The Delta Cousins," and so does a complementary one of prophecy and exposure. As the family picnic begins, Raymond is seen in the wagon "sitting all in white with his collar open and his tall throat bared—as if something wonderful might happen to him tonight. . . . Maurine, now in all contrariness tame as a pigeon, squatted at his foot" ("DC," 36). Precisely when this tableau was restaged on the trestle, one cannot say; but surely it was, and with a significant twist of the "wonderful." But Raymond's profile is also turned to the past in Welty's writing, and it may be the kind of instance that the writer had in mind in 1978 when she said that novels "especially have long fuses that run way back" (*CEW*, 256). To Welty's astute genetic image may be added the irony of the fuse of *Delta Wedding* leading to another unsalable story, entitled "The Key," that was also entangled with an attempt at a novel.

In 1937 Cleanth Brooks of the *Southern Review* was probably the first of at least five editors to reject "The Key" before it was claimed by *Harper's Bazaar* in March 1941, and then, in part at least, because Welty's stock had risen with the sale of *A Curtain of Green* in January. For its collective title, Welty and Russell had first favored "The Key and Other Stories"; and in March 1941 Welty told her agent that the story was closely related to a

34. Elizabeth Bowen, "Notes on Writing a Novel," *Orion* 2 (1945): 24.

1938 experiment in the novel entitled "The Cheated" (*AA*, 63–66).[35] Welty's partiality for "The Key" may hinge upon the loitering young man of the story who seems to be planning his own "unwritten novel" in Yellow Leaf, Mississippi.

"The Key" is set in a tiny train station where Albert and Ellie Morgan begin a long-delayed wedding trip to Niagara Falls. Only belatedly does a young man who watches them closely realize that they are "Deaf and dumb!"—as the other, less sensitive watchers in the waiting room put it. The action consists of nothing more than a key dropped by the stranger, which is seized by Albert as a "sign" of "happiness" hitherto missed in life. The plot is a rather deliberate servant of Welty's aesthetics, and with it the drama of Woolf's story "An Unwritten Novel" is reconstituted in Yellow Leaf, Mississippi: the acute observer, a stranger who "might have been . . . a gambler," as Welty thought Raymond, the functionally barred couple who deflects his gaze, and the railway station as a place of waiting for disclosure. Especially poignant for Welty, as it was for Woolf, is the danger occasioned by the observer's own exposure. " 'Take care,' you wanted to say to him," the nearby narrator warns about this "salamander in the fire" (*CS*, 30). Passages tending to essay further reveal the young man's predicament and perhaps also traces of the novelistic intention that Welty once harbored for "The Key": "You felt some apprehension that he would never express whatever might be the desire of his life in being young and strong, in standing apart in compassion, in making any intuitive present or sacrifice, or in any way of action at all—not because there was too much in the world demanding his strength, but because he was too deeply aware" (*CS*, 33). The story ends with the Morgans having missed their train and the young man giving Ellie a second key with the printed legend "Star Hotel, Room 2." He leaves the station "abruptly"; and "besides the simple compassion in his regard, a look both restless and weary, . . . you could

---

35. In 1938 Welty submitted the partial draft of a novel entitled "The Cheated" to Houghton Mifflin—for which she received an "A" in their fellowship contest but not the final award. What must have been a promising but ill-focused story can be surmised from Robert Linscott's September 17, 1938, letter to Welty (in The Eudora Welty Collection), in which he critiques the manuscript. In 1941 Welty told Russell that "The Cheated" ("about ninety pages") and the story "The Key" were interrelated (*Author and Agent*, 20). Marrs reports Welty's belief that "she may have thrown this novel away" (*The Welty Collection*, 164).

see that he despised and saw the uselessness of the thing he had done"
(*CS*, 37).

   In a brief narrative that resisted sale almost as firmly as did the Morgans
their disclosure, Welty began the rather prolonged imagining of George
Fairchild and his problematic address of the aesthetic object. The apartness
and compassion of the unnamed stranger, "his joy and his despair" (*CS*,
33), are the poles of an aesthetic desire that impels George Fairchild to
make his own "intuitive present or sacrifice" to life itself. Perhaps it was a
poster in the waiting room at Yellow Leaf that hinted at the form it would
take: "A wall poster, dirty with time, showing an old-fashioned locomotive
about to crash into an open touring car filled with women in veils" (*CS*,
30). Reconfigured as the Yellow Dog train, this image of mayhem would be
seized by the Fairchilds for general family hilarity, while Ellen alone would
discern the true "harm" that it entails.


                                       X


   The presence of a wartime culture in Welty's most productive years is
seldom cited in accounts of the writer's career. Rather savagely, for example,
did Diana Trilling charge Welty in 1943 with disloyalty on the home front. As
a southern book with a penchant for primitivism and mythmaking, Welty's
collection *The Wide Net* was especially assailable in Trilling's well-known
column in the *Nation*. But the sharpest critique of all arose from the perilous
nature of the times. Especially in "these days," Trilling warned repeatedly in
1943, "to be soft with words and sentiments is to be irresponsible with
ideas and eventually dangerous." By turning her "gifted" eye from the
outer world to some illusory dreamscape, Welty had evaded the "moral-
intellectual" duty of the writer of fiction when culture itself is threatened.[36]
*Delta Wedding* fared no better when this self-defined "liberal Northern
reader" reviewed Welty's "narcissistic Southern fantasy" a few years later
in the *Nation*.


   36. Welty replied to Diana Trilling's review of *The Wide Net* by telling Russell that Trilling
"says all the things about me I always say about Carson McCullers! So I get slapped right back"
(*Author and Agent*, 101). For a contextualizing treatment of Trilling's review, see Albert J. Devlin,
*Eudora Welty's Chronicle: A Story of Mississippi Life* (Jackson: University Press of Mississippi,
1983), 42–44.

Welty might have answered that fantasy was precisely her way of entering modern history. In fact, years later she said as much in a paper read to the Mississippi Historical Society in Jackson. It "was by no accident," Welty explained, that in writing *The Robber Bridegroom* (1942) she made "local history and the legend and the fairy tale into working equivalents."[37] Embedded in that antic text, which Faulkner admired, is a Turnerian dynamic that hints at the rapid transformation of the old southwestern frontier into something distinctively modern. Alfred Kazin's astute review of *The Robber Bridegroom* cited Welty's "joy" in claiming her native sources. She avoided the usual dullness of historical romance and gave instead "the lost fabulous innocence of our departed frontier," and at a time, Kazin thought, when Americans were being "driven back . . . upon the past" to confirm their identity.[38] A "liberal Northern reader" himself, Kazin understood that Welty's frontier fantasy had created a usable memory of the "enchanted" American past.

During the war years, Welty often worried about the safety of her brothers and friends who were in the service and, more speculatively, of the world itself. She wrote to Russell on August 13, 1945, to report the nearly completed revision of *Delta Wedding* and to express her fear in the aftermath of the bombing of Japan: "I am one of those that tremble about the universe," she confessed. "In an H. G. Wells story, the scientists could have the bombs accidentally fall on their own heads and somebody would say, better that their secret died with them" (*AA*, 112). Welty also trembled for the artist, whose freedom was invariably trimmed in wartime. She was hesitant, for example, to publish "First Love" in 1941 for fear that Aaron Burr's vaunting might be thought "pro-fascist." The pure artist in Welty hated for "that fever to creep into what we think of books or music, because eventually it will leave nothing to be itself" (*AA*, 76). Such aversion to the "fever" of world politics may also help to contextualize one of Welty's few sharp recorded memories of her planning *Delta Wedding*.

A writer who usually shuns research, or at least its revelation, Welty recalls searching "the almanac" for an "uneventful" year in the Delta as setting for her novel. She required a time "that would allow [her] to concentrate on the people without any undue outside influences," such as "war" or

37. Eudora Welty, "Fairy Tale of the Natchez Trace" (1975), in *The Eye of the Story*, 31.

38. Alfred Kazin, "An Enchanted World in America," review of *The Robber Bridegroom*, by Eudora Welty, *New York Herald Tribune Books*, October 25, 1942, sec. 8, p. 19.

"flood" or "fire" (*CEW*, 49–50, 81–82, and "ACEW," 9). This is valuable lore, to which I shall return, but one effect of Welty's repeated story of choosing a benign year (1923, that is) has been to screen *Delta Wedding* from its wartime environment of composition—not a surprising strategy for a writer such as Welty who distrusts the topical. Still, in its own refined way, *Delta Wedding* echoes Welty's considered response to the bristling historical present, especially the bombing of Pearl Harbor, which she shared with Diarmuid Russell in late December 1941:

> It is true, it must be, that it is the outrage to the world spirit . . . that we feel above the viciousness of each single thing, and all seems to be in the solemn shadow of this violation—no, in the shadow of this spirit to which the violation is done, which is still as powerful as ever and in being denied is the more irrevocably defined. All this must take place in each heart—how strong our heart must be that nothing has ever been too much. (*AA*, 81)

This I take to be a virtual blueprint for Welty's framing of the threat to Shellmound and its defense in the "strong" contemplative "heart" of George Fairchild, who is exposed to the "violation" of the world itself. War, "the outrage to the world spirit," must be bracketed within the complex set of motives that led Welty to test her hope for "the universe" in writing *Delta Wedding*. Much of her optimism, I think, was invested in the interpretative vision of reason that Ellen Fairchild brings to the novel.

## XI

Ellen's first challenge is posed by Robbie Reid, who is a late, bedraggled wedding guest at Shellmound. "Caught in marriage," Robbie "had at first looked for one of two blows, or magic touches, to fall—unnerving change or beautiful transformation. . . . But even now—unless the old bugaboo of pregnancy counted—there was no eventuality" (*DW*, 144). Fighting the possessive Fairchilds for George's love and devotion is the only truth that Robbie knows, and she clutches it tightly while approaching the plantation. Ellen's subsequent plea makes a single discourse of the textual and the cultural. "There's a fight *in* us, already," she tells Robbie, "*in* people on this earth, not between us, and there is a fight in Georgie too. It's part of being alive." The "fight is over things, not over people": "Things like the truth, and what you owe people" (*DW*, 163). Does not Ellen's plea echo a fractious world order that "will leave nothing to be itself," including the family; and does she not refer this perennial trouble to the single "heart," for which "nothing has ever been too much"? The public note apparent in these lines is no more than a seepage from the deadly war years, but it was exceptional for Welty nonetheless, and it may mark a point in her career where the overbearing world decisively tested the reserve of her modernist temper. More than anything else, the "poky" (*DW*, 88) Yellow Dog train may have helped Welty to keep her composure.

The episode of the Yellow Dog train is a wonderful piece of homemade aesthetics. It perfectly catches the accent of a glimmering, floundering, mysterious universe and the act of vision that makes it whole. Woven into the episode is the unpredictable shape of life itself. The sky turns cloudy and obscures the family's accounting of the Dog; the proverbial bad seed Maureen releases the sweetness of her Uncle George; the close-knit Fairchilds jump from the trestle to save their separate skins; and the lethal train is halted by the engineer Mr. Doolittle, who is a sleepy imitation of his martial namesake. (Before Welty selected the more topical name Doolittle, with its heroic associations of World War II, the engineer had been the prosaic "Mr. Matthews" in the typescript.) At the center is George Fairchild, the "lover and protector" (*DW*, 212) of the family; but this moment, as Ellen knows, springs from something other than "explainable, Fairchild impulse" (*DW*, 221). "Things—just things, in the outside world," George regarded "with a passion which held him so still that it resembled indifference." Neither Dabney's wedding nor Robbie's "anguish," Ellen senses, had "affected him greatly," but "a flower, a horse running, a color . . . , and, yes, shock, physical danger . . . roused something in him that was immense contemplation, motionless pity, indifference" (*DW*, 186). In his present intensity, human relations fall away as George Fairchild forages in the universe to possess its "*all*." His exposure on the trestle is the essential posture of the artist, and his shielding of the "crazy child" Maureen (vocally barred as were the Morgans by their disability) is the "intuitive present or sacrifice" that eludes the young man of "The Key."

The "fuse" running through Welty's career leads irresistibly to the trestle—or, as Virginia Woolf would have put it, to "the narrow bridge of art." Her well-known trope for the artist's lonely and dangerous outpost is the title also of a 1927 essay in which Woolf repeated her call for a new kind of novel infused "with the exaltation of poetry," and in imagistic terms that prefigure rather closely George Fairchild's own rapt attention to the world. "We long," Woolf said, "for ideas, for dreams, for imaginations, for poetry"[39] in the novels we read. In *Delta Wedding* the conventions of plantation romance and Welty's modernity are no less intimately bound than the homely Dry Creek trestle and its more cosmopolitan counterpart, "the narrow bridge of art." These fusions are the "new form" that Welty "arrived at" in her first novel. They tell especially of her daring reach across national-aesthetic boundaries to realize the full impersonality of the old plantation image. Such difficult work of literary restoration was undertaken by many of Eudora Welty's southern modernist peers, and it is the primary basis for the easy writerly company that Welty keeps with all of them.

## XII

The literary plantation is also extremely helpful in focusing what Elizabeth Bowen meant by the writer's solving her "abiding problems." At the time, they probably seemed as fresh and inviting to Eudora Welty as did each new day of writing; but if inference can be made from her own considered phrasing, they would seem to turn upon the familiar modernist predicament of the artist's being "too deeply aware" ever to make her defining formal gesture. The "beautiful difficulty" (as Henry James put it, and the evidence is strong that Welty read his dense theoretical *Prefaces* with great attention) that Welty faced in writing *Delta Wedding* was to solve this problem by incorporating the solitary passion of George Fairchild into the vocative circle of Shellmound, and the world at large. Once again the conventions of plantation romance proved an ally for Welty in achieving her own balanced vision in the novel.

The feminization of the nineteenth-century literary plantation is a core convention of the genre that Welty adapted to her own special ends. It strikes the historic note of matriarchy at Shellmound, suffuses the several marital plots, and contextualizes the aesthetic function of Ellen Fairchild, who continued, as it were, to "show" Welty around the Delta. Throughout the novel, matriarchy glares at George in hope that he will achieve the cultural

---

39. Virginia Woolf, "The Narrow Bridge of Art" (1927), in *Collected Essays*, 4 vols. (New York: Harcourt, Brace & World, 1967), 2:225.

dreams of the family—as their lover, savior, and scapegoat too. He demurs on the trestle and in his rapture embraces the entire "adorable" world. But this impersonal love is subject nonetheless to the heart's paradoxical need—the "near-fatality" on the trestle leads Troy and Dabney to marry and Robbie Reid to protest her husband's "indifference" by running away. In each case—and they reconstitute the familiar Weltian poles of love and separateness—Shellmound is destabilized by intruders who have penetrated its most intimate union. Robbie's "wifely ferocity" is especially intriguing in light of the feminizing conventions of plantation writing. In crying for George "to come back from his danger as a favor to her," Robbie adopts the hated "Fairchild mask" (*DW,* 146) of special pleading. She too is denied on the trestle, but as Ellen realizes, little Robbie is the unassailable "proof" of George's vision: "To all their eyes shallow, unworthy, she was his love; it was her ordinary face that was looking at him through the lovely and magic veil" (*DW,* 222). The historicized, leveling face of marriage is here made transparent by a love that comprehends the ordinary and the ecstatic. The historicity of the marital image is thus refocused by Welty, not to argue a region's or a nation's politics, but to give temporal balance and grounding to those of the novel.

Traces of the conventional role of the plantation mistress appear in Ellen's domestic efficiency, but Welty has redesigned this figure as well to wear the laurels of the Fairchilds. After the wedding ceremony, Ellen's attention is focused on George, until "all at once she saw into his mind as if he had come dancing out of it leaving it unlocked, laughingly inviting her to the unexpected intimacy." She realizes in turn that his acts would spring always "from long, dark, previous, abstract thought and direct apprehension. . . . It was *inevitable* that George, with this mind, should stand on the trestle" (*DW,* 221). Since the time of "A Memory," such exposure has been a marking characteristic of Welty's aesthetic design and of her simultaneous effort to connect the several orders of perception. For Welty has stressed in essay and interview that "direct apprehension," the "so-called raw material" of experience, requires for its completion an "act of human understanding"— one rendered formally by the artist's changing of "words into fiction" ("WF," 136). Welty's fusion of act and interpretation is expressed in the waning moments of the wedding celebration. As George advances toward Ellen, he seems to her "infinitely simple and infinitely complex . . . but at the same time . . . very finite . . . wholly singular and dear" (*DW,* 222). In penetrating, or in being admitted to her brother-in-law's portentous mind, Ellen "take[s] hold" of mystery in the most "practical" way ("WF," 137). She is an unassuming domestic poet, and hers is the historic voice of the novel speaking through the timeless family of Shellmound Plantation. In late 1940, when Welty heard all too often the discouraging word *obscurity*, she passionately described herself to her agent as "one of those who believe that to communicate is the hope and purpose and the impulse . . . of all that is written and done." To write "clear and unobscured" (*AA*, 49) prose without compromising her vision was always Eudora Welty's goal, and in the character of Ellen Fairchild it found its first substantial incarnation.

## XIII

It is not surprising that Welty's identity would form around the fusion of act and consciousness as the model of artistic perception. This was what Henry James meant by "experience conditioned" in the novel, and it was a fixture of his thought and practice by 1890. Its emotional and cognitive elements were crucially refashioned by G. E. Moore in the famous sixth chapter of *Principia Ethica* (1903), and they were absorbed thereafter by Katherine Mansfield, Virginia Woolf, E. M. Forster, Elizabeth Bowen, and Katherine Anne Porter, to cite the primary antecedents of Eudora Welty. Behind all of them, of course, is the Kantian "judgment of taste" which *"cannot be other than subjective."* But what is finally more revealing of Welty's identity than its precise structure (although its definition has not preoccupied her critics) is the way that it has enacted her literary career. If "it was *inevitable*" that George Fairchild would stand on the trestle, then the same curious necessity may apply to the writing of *Delta Wedding*.

Nowhere in the textual or tributary data is there any evidence of a defining moment when "The Delta Cousins" became a novel. Welty has said that her usual practice was to "tear up" as she revised, so perhaps any transformational evidence was erased in this way (*CEW*, 28). Or perhaps a bundle of notes and drafts is still buried in "a trunk full of stuff" (*CEW*, 81) that Welty has not shared with the Department of Archives and History in Jackson, where her papers are kept. Welty's otherwise revealing correspondence with Diarmuid Russell is also blank in this regard. Apparently it ceased for a time in early 1945 (from March 27 to June 12), when the story was rapidly becoming a novel. What textual evidence exists, or has been supplied by

Welty, consists of the beginning (or perhaps near beginning) and end of her project, as the typescripts of "The Delta Cousins" and the novel reveal. The working middle is absent from view, as Welty probably intended it to be.

The net effect of the evidence is to reinforce, or at least not refute, Welty's familiar story of the "accidental" writing of *Delta Wedding*. Not surprisingly, Welty has said that her second novel began in much the same way: *Losing Battles* (1970) "started out to be short and farcical, but as the people became dearer to me—it changed" (*CEW*, 31). Such a creation myth is compatible with Welty's view of herself as a short-story writer, and this in turn is compatible with two of Welty's favored metaphors of creativity: the magic pot of folklore "that cooks more & more pudding" and the long-running fuse of the novel. These metaphors of abundance and continuity hold fundamental truths for Welty about her own aesthetic process, and the movement of the world at large. They also promise to give compositional heft to the term *accidental*.

The magic pot of folklore reflects Welty's belief that "the word comes surest out of too much, not too little" and the corollary truth, as written by Shelley Fairchild (the eldest daughter) in her diary, that trouble "is old" and, "like the magic pudding pot," there "is nothing to stop it running over" (*DW*, 85). The writer and the ceaseless production of history meet in this rather homely vessel to form what Welty once called the "center of [her] concentration" (*AA*, 90). Throughout her career, "choice after choice" was made in this most personal space, as Welty attempted to follow the "allurement" of each story to "its pure & final & clear form" (*AA*, 70). But the speed and mystery of the process and her own absorption often led Welty to adopt the creative mask of the Fairchilds: "They were *compelled*" (*DW*, 15). Whether the persuasion was of "spring," or of "demon[s]," or simply "dreamy afternoons" spent wandering along the old Natchez Trace, the effect of Welty's self-revealing imagery was to cast a spell upon the writer in her exposure to the world. Feeling "a sensitivity to all that was near," and it was often a "hurting intensity" (*DW*, 80) caused by the "real distortion" of need, and then "writing fast" from a limitless core of vision is the sum and the shape of Welty's aesthetic identity (*AA*, 78–79). In some obscure way, Eudora Welty seems to have realized that the "unwritten" form of the novel could express this identity and that "the outrage" of the times required its amplitude. The "accidental" writing of *Delta Wedding* is something more inevitable and determined than that coy, apologetic term usually denotes.

The long-running fuse is a second metaphor of creativity, and it too probably arises from memories of childhood—not Welty's avid reading of folktales, but her "devotion" to "the movies," where the slowly burning fuse lit by a Saturday villain was a staple of the films of Welty's youth.[40] The "long fuses" that Welty affixed to novels point again to an irresistible act of creation. The fuse that ignites *Delta Wedding* is nothing less than the accruing force and continuity of the career itself. Its arch- or inner-story is Welty's own fervent desire to reveal her identity, and in terms that require ever more daring narrative acts. In the early aestheticized stories, in "The Delta Cousins," and then in the novel-made-supple, the expression of Welty's identity compelled a relative measuring of the world's capacity for "harm" or trouble and of the countervailing power of the "perception we all carry in us of the beauty of order imposed" ("WF," 144). Seen in this way, the attraction of George and Ellen Fairchild is the climax of a long discourse in which the stabilization of word and world is realized as the shape of Welty's hopeful identity. That this mature possession of the aesthetic self should reach back into childhood for its defining metaphors is still another mark of the wholeness of the career.

## XIV

Willa Cather once wrote of a special time "in a writer's development when his 'life line' and the line of his personal endeavor meet." Such a maturing occurred for Welty during the writing of *Delta Wedding;* and with the perspective of some fifty years, it is becoming clearer how the force of world history and of Welty's evolving career met to give the novel shape and moral dimension. Fifty years have also passed since literary modernism could be described as a vital, art-producing reality; and with this perspective, too, *Delta Wedding* emerges more clearly as an instance of the writer's historical positioning. In retrospect, it would be naive to think that Welty was anything less than profoundly affected by the distortion of the early 1940s, or that her desire for self-revelation was not a consequential, dominant motive of writing. Nor can this positioning be separated from the species of modernist

---

40. Eudora Welty, *One Writer's Beginnings* (Cambridge: Harvard University Press, 1984), 36–37.

ideology that circulated among Welty's predecessors in the lyrical mode. Their felicitous reach of sensibility is felt in each shading of *Delta Wedding*, and so too are their characteristic limits and evasions. What these may be in *Delta Wedding* is a fair question to ask, especially now that the compositional history of the novel has been told with some reserve and care, or so I should like to think.

At first glance, Welty's repeated description of her search for a benign year in the Delta seems inoffensive enough as a statement of scene setting; and to my knowledge, it has always been received in such practical, workaday terms. But it may have added dimension as well. Its effect, if not intention, has been to obscure Welty's deft substitution of temporal frames, as the condensed threat of the war years is transposed to a seemingly more peaceful time in the Delta. Welty's gain is one of distance from the historical present, a safer second glance, as it were, at "the outrage to the world spirit." It is one thing to write a novel in wartime, quite another to write a war novel and thereby swell the ranks of historical fiction, or so Welty might have explained her backward-moving chronicity in *Delta Wedding*. But however strategic her choice of 1923, however well it cleared a place and time for the telling of her "family story," it measures ideologically the canons of Welty's historicity and the urgency of her aesthetic design.

For the numerically dominant race of the Delta, the early 1920s was not a time of relative calm but profound disruption of family and custom, as thousands of blacks left their deeply impoverished, racially segregated homeland for the North. Their migration, resisted illegally in parts of the Delta, dismantles any idea of a cultural lull, however apt it may be for Welty's intention. Basic cultural knowledge is suppressed in *Delta Wedding*; and this fact of composition cannot be altered by counting black faces at Shellmound, of which naturally there are many, or by citing the subversive case of a black worker's insolence (*DW*, 195–97). Nor is it productive *to dwell* upon such apparent lacunae, as do those who belabor Conrad's imperial ethnography in *Heart of Darkness*. Conrad and Welty had similar urgent business to conduct in their adopted locales, and it seemed to require of them certain efficiencies of scale. The price of Welty's projecting her identity onto the unfamiliar Delta was the gentling and simplifying of its social reality in 1923. Such an act arises principally from Welty's aesthetics, and it leads beyond the question of race into the broader modernist culture of *Delta Wedding*.

That culture, as interpreted by previous writers, led Welty to shield the Fairchilds from overt historical pressure at the same time that the passing of their way of life was being prophesied by the text. The gap that appears is the defining one of sensibility, and at the most crucial points in the novel, it is occupied by Ellen Fairchild. Neither her domestic lens nor her unwitting analysis of literary technique diminishes her authority in *Delta Wedding*. She is constituted as a rationalizing presence who displaces conflict from the world stage to the solitary human heart, which she valorizes as the only hope of correction. History itself is diminished as a primary category of experience, and fiction too is relieved of any need to act *"as a means"* (as G. E. Moore put it). The subjectivity of Ellen Fairchild is conceived, then, and moves within the expanding and constricting space of Welty's modernity. To test the efficacy of "human understanding" against the present "outrage" is the urgent mission that Welty gave to Ellen Fairchild, and it allowed neither of them any unbridled wandering in the field of Delta history.

The closing pages of *Delta Wedding* reflect this concentration of purpose by gathering the family for another strategic picnic. Troy and Dabney have returned from their honeymoon to begin a new life at Marmion, and George and Robbie are set to return to Memphis; but for this last magical night, the Fairchilds are suspended in the "starry" Delta, which seems an ally against time itself. The far site of the picnic is reached by wagons, not cars, on account of "the tangles and brambles," and the route follows "the old track" across the river to Marmion. Not surprisingly, the regressive journey leads to an essentializing vision, as expressed by Laura and Ellen. "It's the same river, Memphis and New Orleans," Laura answers Dabney, who had fooled the family by going south for her honeymoon. And to this precocious statement of philosophic unity, Ellen adds resonance by lapsing into the "rhythm" of "the repeating fields, the repeating cycles of season and her own life." As she realizes, "there was something in the monotony itself that was beautiful. . . . One moment told you the great things, one moment was enough for you to know the greatest thing" (*DW,* 240).

Much of the talk that follows is about change—about modernizing Delta agriculture and George's reclaiming the Grove from its resident spinsters. But these changes are absorbed as well into the "still moment" of Welty's conclusion, and more specifically into Ellen's affirmation of the human understanding. There the extension and the multiplicity of history form an abridged, recurring order that Laura again ratifies: "I've seen it all afore," she tells India, "It's all happened afore" (*DW*, 241). Welty's intention is to equip the modern historical consciousness with a secularized faith that "there is a coherence in things, a stability; something . . . immune from change," or so thinks Mrs. Ramsay in *To the Lighthouse*. "Of such moments," she and Ellen know, "the thing is made that remains for ever after."[41] Neither is this transcendent order the same "narcissistic Southern fantasy" that Diana Trilling found in *Delta Wedding;* nor is it the bristling field of history that Welty knew as a citizen in the early 1940s. Rather, it is the consciousness of history rendered as a "moment" from which "the greatest thing" arises. For Welty this entity was nothing less than the power of the mind to retain its identity and cultural relations amid "outrage." It was this loving reassurance that she sent to John Robinson "chapter by chapter."

*Delta Wedding* is notable for the "conscious, supervised artistry" (in Lionel Trilling's words) used to test the preservative power of the modern literary mind. Of course, such claims of moral authority as Welty may have implied in writing *Delta Wedding* are discounted today in many critical quarters, and for reasons that are only confirmed by Welty's selective framing of the cultural scene. It is clear too that genetic criticism, founded as it is upon the drama of authorial self-disclosure, is deplored in the same elite quarters. But the present critical moment, which is variously post-modern, post-cultural, post-historical, post-southern, and now post-theory, is itself no less relativized than Welty's own compositional moment in the 1940s. However limited her social categories may seem, Welty built a compelling argument for the redemptive power of the literary mind as the magical pot overbrimmed with history. That a humane conception of life for which she probed in *Delta Wedding* should rest finally in the serenity of art is both a modernist marker and the distinctive signature of Eudora Welty herself. Its appeal to successive audiences, including present-day readers, cannot be doubted.

41. See Louise Westling, *Sacred Groves and Ravaged Gardens: The Fiction of Eudora Welty, Carson McCullers, and Flannery O'Connor* (Athens: University of Georgia Press, 1985), 65–93, for an alert discussion of the Woolf-Welty "interdependence."

# The Early Composition History of *Catch-22*

JAMES NAGEL

§  §  §

IN 1978, THE *Wilson Quarterly* conducted a survey of professors of American literature to determine the most important novels published after World War II. To be sure, the result was a most impressive list, but Joseph Heller's *Catch-22* was ranked first.[1] Its position in this survey indicates the esteem and seriousness with which literary scholars have come to regard Heller's first novel since it appeared in October 1961. Only two months later, on December 7, 1961, Heller took obvious pleasure in writing to the dean of the College of Arts and Letters at the University of Notre Dame that "*Catch-22* is already being discussed in literature courses at Harvard, Brown, and two universities here in New York City."[2] Since Heller had taught for two years in the Department of English at Pennsylvania State University, he was fully conversant with the academy, with both its genuine intellectual stimulation and its professional excesses. Indeed, in the early stages of planning *Catch-22,* Heller had planned a satiric scene in which Major Major "meets an old drunk at an MLA convention who was ruined by a man who said he liked Henry James."[3] In another section Major Major "was from the winter wheat fields of Vermont and a former teacher of English. Made the mistake of

1. See Richard Ohmann, "The Shaping of a Canon: U.S. Fiction, 1960–1975," *Critical Inquiry* 10:1 (1983): 206.

2. See Joseph Heller's letter to Dean Sheedy (December 7, 1961), in the Heller Manuscripts at Goldfarb Library, Brandeis University. Unless otherwise indicated, all manuscript references are to this collection. I am grateful to Joseph Heller for permission to quote from these documents.

3. Joseph Heller, planning document. Prior to actually beginning the composition of the novel, Heller wrote hundreds of note cards and manuscript pages on which he proposed scenes, defined

stating publicly that he did not like Henry James," and there is a suggestion that Major Major "never realized that Proust and Henry James were the same man." Although these comments did not survive to the final version of the novel, no one would have enjoyed the satire more than Heller's former colleagues in the academy.

Beyond its high regard in universities throughout the world, *Catch-22* has become an enormous commercial success as well, selling well over ten million copies in just the first two decades after it was published. Such enormous popularity seems to have come as something of a surprise to both author and publisher, since Simon and Schuster is reported to have ordered a first printing of only 4,000 copies. The financial arrangements, too, suggest modest expectations for all concerned; Heller's advance for the novel was only $1,500, $750 upon signing the contract and another $750 when the manuscript was delivered.[4] Nor did the novel enjoy immediate success: it did not make the best-seller list in hardbound and did not become an international sensation until the paperback edition was released. Some of the attention paid to the novel was surely due to its satiric treatment of war and to the escalating antiwar feeling throughout the 1960s, what Pearl K. Bell labeled "that passionately antiwar decade and its nay-saying, antinomian, black-comic Zeitgeist."[5]

It was a fortuitous coincidence, for nowhere in the *Catch-22* materials is there any reference to the Vietnam War or anything like it, although the novel and the manuscripts resonate with antiwar sentiments, including a notation Heller recorded in 1955 that Douglas MacArthur, in his seventy-fifth-birthday speech, urged "people to let their leaders know that they will

---

characters, organized the chronology, and outlined the structure of the novel. Unfortunately, such documents are not sequentially numbered and are not organized into a discrete unit, making precise reference to them problematic. I will, therefore, minimize documentation to them in routine cases. Similarly, in composing his manuscripts, Heller frequently deleted sections, started over (using a new numbering scheme), moved material, or otherwise revised in such a way that reference to specific manuscript page numbers is all but useless. Indeed, Heller interspersed numbered pages with lettered pages, sometimes going through the alphabet twice in a given chapter before returning to numbered pages once again.

4. On early sales, see William Hogan, "*Catch-22*: A Sleeper That's Catching On," *San Francisco Chronicle*, May 3, 1962, p. 39; on financial arrangements, Chet Flippo, "Checking in with Joseph Heller," *Rolling Stone*, April 16, 1981, pp. 51–52.

5. Pearl K. Bell, "Heller's Trial by Tedium," *The New Leader*, October 28, 1974, p. 17.

refuse to fight wars."[6] But even without the Vietnam War, *Catch-22* would have been notable on purely artistic grounds, for writers and literary scholars quickly responded to its robust wit, devastating satire, and complex satiric method that hearkened to the eighteenth century as well as to the twentieth. John Steinbeck, for example, wrote to Heller in July of 1963 to say that he felt peace had become as ridiculous as war and that he found the novel "great" for both its attitude and its writing. Among others, James Jones, himself the author of a highly regarded war novel, wrote to Simon and Schuster to express his sense of awe at the conflict of tragedy and comedy in the book, finding it "delightful" and "disturbing." Perhaps illustrative of the broad appeal of the novel, actor Tony Curtis wrote to Heller as early as 1962 expressing an interest in doing the movie and calling himself Yossarian.[7]

Despite the enormous popularity of Heller's first novel, and the volume of critical attention it has received in the three decades since it was published, relatively little attention has been paid to the composition history of *Catch-22*, even though the record of the growth of the manuscripts reveals a great deal about the development of the central themes and devices as the concept grew over the years.[8] Of particular importance are the early notes and drafts of the manuscript, for they are enormously detailed and complex, often direct in stating Heller's objectives and reservations about what he was doing with his material. Heller's memories of the beginning of his first novel have been recorded many times in interviews, always with the same basic story:

> I was lying in bed in my four room apartment on the West Side when suddenly this line came to me: "It was love at first sight. The first time he saw the chaplain 'Someone' fell madly in love with him." I didn't have the name Yossarian. The chaplain wasn't necessarily an army chaplain—he could have been a *prison* chaplain. But as soon as the opening sentence was available, the book began to evolve clearly in my mind, even most of the particulars—the tone, the form, many of the characters, including some I

---

6. This document is on file in the Heller Manuscripts.

7. John Steinbeck, letter to Joseph Heller, July 1, 1963, Heller Manuscripts. The letter from James Jones is also in this file. Tony Curtis to Joseph Heller, October 16, 1962, Heller Manuscripts.

8. Indeed, three recent books on Heller's fiction ignore the composition history of his work. See Robert Merrill, *Joseph Heller* (Boston: Twayne, 1987); Stephen W. Potts, *Catch-22: Antiheroic Antinovel* (Boston: Twayne, 1989); David Seed, *The Fiction of Joseph Heller: Against the Grain* (New York: St. Martin's Press, 1989).

eventually couldn't use. All of this took place within an hour and a half. It got me so excited that I did what the cliché says you're supposed to do: I jumped out of bed and paced the floor. That morning I went to my job at the advertising agency and wrote out the first chapter in long hand. Before the end of the week, I had typed it out and sent it to Candida Donadio, my agent. One year later, after much planning, I began chapter two.[9]

The idea was to offer it as the first chapter of a book, and, as a result, it appeared as "Catch-18" in *New World Writing* later that year.[10]

Precisely when the original composition of the novel began has been a matter of some confusion, since Heller has indicated both 1953 and 1955 as the starting dates for the novel, probably referring to different stages in the development of the concept. There are indications in the manuscript, however, that Heller started working on the idea in 1953, trying out many different approaches to the novel before he arrived at the strategy used in the first chapter that was published two years later. By this time Heller had drafted hundreds of note cards outlining virtually every character and incident in the novel along with pages of sketches, conversations, time schemes, and the development of various themes.[11] It is clear that by 1955 he had a first chapter to publish but did not have a major section of the novel completed until 1957, when he submitted it to Robert Gottlieb at Simon and Schuster. Gottlieb was only twenty-six at the time, and a junior editor, but he expressed his interest in the project, made some suggestions, and Heller signed a contract the following year. It took him three more years to complete work on the novel. After publication in late 1961, Heller became an international sensation, and Robert Gottlieb became editor-in-chief of Alfred A. Knopf.

9. Joseph Heller, quoted in George Plimpton, "How It Happened," *New York Times Book Review,* October 6, 1974, p. 3.

10. See Heller's comments in Richard B. Sale, "An Interview in New York with Joseph Heller," *Studies in the Novel* 4 (1972): 63–74. Joseph Heller, "Catch-18," *New World Writing* 7 (April 1955): 204–14.

11. About the beginning date of the book's composition, see Sale, p. 67, where Heller suggests that he started the novel in 1955, and Josh Greenfeld, "22 Was Funnier than 14," *New York Times Book Review,* March 3, 1968, 1, where 1953 is given as the beginning date. Some of my comments about the note-card stage of development were previously published, in somewhat different form, in "The *Catch-22* Note Cards," *Critical Essays on Joseph Heller,* ed. James Nagel (Boston: G. K. Hall, 1984), 51–61 (reprinted from *Studies in the Novel* 8 [1976]: 394–405).

The initial composition of *Catch-22* is important in several senses. On the simplest, perhaps the most important, level, it records the process of invention of one of the most remarkable novels of the twentieth century. It is no inconsequential body of papers that will reveal the process of significant creation at work, and the manuscripts clearly show Heller suggesting ideas to himself, discarding them, outlining possible structures for the shape of his narrative, trying out absurd conversations that underscore important themes. There is much to be learned about both characters and themes in material that was never published, for the manuscripts often are clear about motivations for various actions that are unclear in the novel, why Yossarian went into the hospital with a false liver ailment, for example. In many instances scenes and speeches in the manuscripts elucidate an episode in the published novel. A world of biographical reference in the manuscripts is largely lost in the published novel (in which the setting and the names of characters were changed): references to the places and people Heller knew during his service in the Army Air Corps in World War II, depictions of some of the men in his unit, some of the notable events that preoccupied them during the summer of 1944. These various documents, written in Heller's hand, provide an invaluable guide to understanding the composition and meaning of a monumental contemporary novel.

One point that should be made at the inception of any discussion of the stages of composition of Heller's first novel is that from beginning to end the title of the book was "Catch-18," a title with somewhat richer thematic overtones than "Catch-22." The early drafts of the novel, particularly the sketches and note cards, have a somewhat more "Jewish" emphasis than does the published novel. In Judaism, "eighteen" is a significant number in that the eighteenth letter of the Hebrew alphabet, "chai," means "living" or "life." Eighteen thus has a meaning for Jews that it does not have for other people: the *Mishnah* promotes eighteen as the ideal age for men to marry, and Jews often give personal gifts or charitable contributions in units of eighteen. Thematically, the title "Catch-18" would thus contain a subtle reference to the injunction in the *Torah* to choose life, a principle endorsed by Yossarian at the end of the novel when he deserts.[12]

---

12. On the significance of the number *18,* see Melvin J. Friedman, "Something Jewish Happened: Some Thoughts about Joseph Heller's *Good as Gold,*" in *Critical Essays on Joseph Heller,* 196.

It is also clear that the title was changed not because Heller had second thoughts but because a few weeks before the scheduled printing of the novel, Heller's publisher learned that Leon Uris, who had earlier written *Exodus,* was coming out with a novel entitled *Mila-18.* A change had to be made, and there was discussion of using "Catch-11" in that the duplication of the digit 1 would parallel the structural use of the repetition of scenes. But "11" was rejected because of the movie *Ocean's Eleven* and the now familiar concern for using a number already current in the public imagination.[13] Then Heller found a new title he liked, "Catch-14," and on January 29, 1961, he wrote to his publisher in defense of it: "The name of the book is now CATCH-14. (Forty-eight hours after you resign yourself to the change, you'll find yourself almost preferring this new number. It has the same bland and nondescript significance of the original. It is far enough away from Uris for the book to establish an identity of its own, I believe, yet close enough to the original title to still benefit from the word of mouth publicity we have been giving it.)" For whatever reason, and legend has it that Robert Gottlieb did not find "14" to be a funny number, the title was finally changed once again, this time to "Catch-22," recapturing the concept of repetition. Since the central device of the novel is *déjà vu,* with nearly every crucial scene, until the conclusion, coming back a second time, the title was once again coordinate with the organizational schema of the narrative. As Heller remarked, "the soldier in white comes back a second time, the dying soldier sees everything twice, the chaplain thinks that everything that happens has happened once before. For that reason the two 2's struck me as being very appropriate to the novel."[14] On this logic, and a decidedly accidental series of events, the phrase "catch-22," rather than "catch-18," became the term for bureaucratic impasse the world over.

It did so, however, only because readers found in the novel something they felt was important, a level of humor that was painfully resonant of

13. For the discussion of the change of title from "Catch-18" to "Catch-11" to "Catch-22," see Ken Barnard, "Joseph Heller Tells How *Catch-18* Became *Catch-22* and Why He Was Afraid of Airplanes," *Detroit News Sunday Magazine,* September 13, 1970, pp. 18–19, 24, 27–28, 30, 65.

14. Heller's letters to Alfred A. Knopf are on deposit in the Heller Manuscripts. See Barnard, "Joseph Heller Tells," 24. Although the manuscript of the novel was entitled "Catch-18" for nearly the entire period of composition, I will refer to the manuscript materials as the "Catch-22" manuscripts unless I specifically wish to indicate the chapter entitled "Catch-18" or the story published under that title.

their own experience, a grim reality that, in the 1960s, seemed all too close
to current events. But even these aspects of the novel would not have had
much impact were it not for the craft of the book, an artistry won through
years of Heller's meticulous attention to the details of his novel. Indeed, one
of the remarkable aspects of the writing of *Catch-22* is that Heller seems
not to have discarded anything from the very beginning of composition,
as though he somehow knew even from the start what a sensation his first
attempt at extended fiction would be. As a result, the *Catch-22* manuscripts
contain literally thousands of pages of materials, note cards, early sketches,
drafts of scenes, outlines of chapters, detailed lists of the appearance of each
character in each chapter, outlines of thematic progressions, chronologies in
which the events of the novel are measured against actual events in 1944,
and hundreds of other pages dealing with proposed scenes and characters.
They constitute a truly remarkable creative record, one unmatched in the
papers of any other important American novel.

One of the most fascinating stages in the growth of the manuscript is a
collection of note cards on which Heller, writing at his desk at work, planned
the structure of the novel before composition and then analyzed its contents
after the first complete draft.[15] The most important of these is a group
of thirty-seven cards, written in Heller's hand, headed "CHAPTER CARDS
(outlines for chapters before they were written.)" Based on what Heller has
said in a letter, these cards would have been assembled in 1953, at the earliest
stage of composition, two years before the "sudden inspiration" that resulted
in "Catch-18."[16]

Perhaps the most striking feature of these cards, especially in light of the
frequent charges that the novel is "unstructured," "disorganized," or even

15. On Heller's writing at his desk at work, see Alden Whitman, "Something Always Happens
on the Way to the Office: An Interview with Joseph Heller," *Pages* 1 (1976): 77. My comments
here closely follow those in "The *Catch-22* Note Cards," 51–61. The note cards are lined, 5"
× 8" Kardex cards of a type used by the Remington Rand office Heller worked in during the
composition of the novel. Heller's comments on the cards are variously in blue, red, and black
ink, with occasional pencil notations. The variations in ink would suggest that the planning
progressed slowly, during which the implements on Heller's desk changed. The cards might also
suggest that some of the planning work was done in the office, whereas Heller has indicated
that the writing of the novel was done at home, in the evenings, whenever he felt like it. He did
not rush, and the development of the novel was stretched over eight years.

16. Joseph Heller, letter to author, March 13, 1974, p. 2, Heller Manuscripts.

"chaotic," is the detail of the initial plan. Not only are the main events in each chapter suggested, but characters are named and described, and such matters as structure, chronology, and various themes (including sex and "catch-18") are set into a complex pattern. Other cards indicate the relationships among events, with key sentences written in. A typical card, about twelfth from the beginning,[17] treats the characters and events for what was projected to be a single chapter:

1. Cathcart's background & ambition. Puzzled by _____ de Coverley.
2. Hasn't a chance of becoming a general. Ex-corporal Wintergreen, who evaluates his work, also wants to be a general.
3. For another, there already was a general, Dreedle.
4. ↑Tries to have Chaplain say prayer at briefing.↑
5. Description of General Dreedle. His Nurse.
6. Dreedle's quarrel with Moodis [*sic*].
7. Snowden's secret revealed in argument with Davis.
8. Dreedle brings girl to briefing.
9. Groaning. Dreedle orders Korf shot.
10. That was the mission in which Yossarian lost his balls.

The section of the published novel that relates to these items now comprises much of chapters 19 ("Colonel Cathcart") and 21 ("General Dreedle"), with chapter 20 ("Corporal Whitcomb"), unrelated to these matters, interspersed between them. Thus the ten items on the card resulted in roughly twenty-one pages of the novel.[18]

The business of Colonel Cathcart's background and ambition now begins in chapter 19 with a description of him as a "slick, successful, slipshod, unhappy man of thirty-six who lumbered when he walked and wanted to be a general" (*Catch*, 185). These matters cover a bit over two pages and

17. Given the disorganized state of the Heller manuscripts, it is difficult now to determine the precise order of the cards and even, in some cases, whether a given card was written before or after the initial draft. All references to the numbers and groups of cards are therefore based on my own judgment of the most likely function of the cards when they were written. Heller's comments to me in conversation about the manuscripts has guided my judgment, but even he was unable to remember precise details after a lapse of many years.

18. Joseph Heller, *Catch-22* (New York: Simon and Schuster, 1961), 185–92, 206–20. Hereafter cited parenthetically in the text as *Catch*.

then give way to item 4 on the card, "Tries to have Chaplain say prayer at briefing." To demonstrate how closely Heller worked with the note cards, this item had directional arrows pointing up on both sides of it, and, indeed, in execution the matter listed was moved forward in the chapter. This move underscores the logical relationship between the two concerns: "Colonel Cathcart wanted to be a general so desperately he was willing to try anything, even religion . . ." (*Catch*, 187). The idea develops systematically: Cathcart is impressed by a photograph in *The Saturday Evening Post* of a colonel who has his chaplain conduct prayers before each mission and he reasons, "maybe if we say prayers, they'll put my picture in *The Saturday Evening Post*" (*Catch*, 188). The humor of the situation progresses as Cathcart's thinking begins to take shape in his conversation with the chaplain:

> "Now, I want you to give a lot of thought to the kind of prayers we're going to say. . . . I don't want any of this kingdom of God or Valley of Death stuff. That's all too negative. What are you making such a sour face for?"
>
> "I'm sorry, sir," the chaplain stammered. "I happened to be thinking of the Twenty-third Psalm just as you said that."
>
> "How does that one go?"
>
> "That's the one you were just referring to, sir. 'The Lord is my shepherd I——.' "
>
> "That's the one I was just referring to. It's out. What else have you got?"
> (*Catch*, 189)

Cathcart's logic leads him to an admission that "I'd like to keep away from the subject of religion altogether if we can" and to the true object of his desires: "Why can't we all pray for something good, like a tighter bomb pattern?" (*Catch*, 190). But the plan for prayers is abandoned altogether when the chaplain reveals that the enlisted men do not have a separate God, as Cathcart had assumed, and that excluding them from prayer meetings might antagonize God and result in even looser bomb patterns. Cathcart concludes "the hell with it, then" (*Catch*, 193). Thus the first item on Heller's note card and the elevated matter regarding prayer grew to make up all of chapter 19. The secondary notions of each of these items were moved: Cathcart's puzzlement at _____ de Coverley was delayed to chapter 21, and the revelation that Milo is now the mess officer was placed earlier, in chapter 13, when Major _____ de Coverley promotes him out of a desire for fresh eggs.

The remaining items on the card became chapter 21, "General Dreedle." This chapter presents two main issues: the first is the string of obstructions to Cathcart's promotion to general, one of which is General Dreedle; the second is General Dreedle himself. In the novel, the chapter develops the topics equally. The balance is enriching: the ambitious colonel trying to get promoted contrasts the entrenched general trying to preserve what he has. Cathcart's problems in the novel reflect precisely what Heller listed as items 2 and 3 on his note card:

> Actually, Colonel Cathcart did not have a chance in hell of becoming a general. For one thing, there was ex-P.F.C. Wintergreen, who also wanted to be a general and who always distorted, destroyed, rejected or misdirected any correspondence by, for, or about Colonel Cathcart that might do him credit. For another, there already was a general, General Dreedle, who knew that General Peckem was after his job but did not know how to stop him. (*Catch*, 212)

Heller demoted Wintergreen from "ex-corporal" in the notes to "ex-P.F.C." in the novel. General Peckem, called P. P. Peckenhammer throughout the note cards and the manuscript, has been added as a further complication.

The business of General Dreedle, note card items 5 through 9, now occupies the last half of the chapter (*Catch*, 212–20) with only minor alterations from the notes. "Moodis" is changed to "Moodus"; in the incident of the "groaning" at the staff meeting, Dreedle orders Major Danby, not "Korf," shot for "moaning" (*Catch*, 218). Two items are not treated: the business of Snowden's secret was saved for the conclusion of the novel (*Catch*, 430), where it becomes climactic of the *déjà vu* technique and the most powerful scene in the novel. Placed where it is now, the further revelation of Snowden's secret, that man is matter, emphasizes the theme of mortality just when Yossarian is most concerned with death and survival.

The second idea not treated, relating to Yossarian's castration, Heller later rejected in manuscript revision. The incident of Yossarian's wound was ultimately moved to chapter 26: Aarfy, called "Aarky" throughout the note cards, gets lost on the mission to Ferrara and, before McWatt can seize control of the plane, flies back into the flak and the plane is hit. Yossarian's wound in the novel is in his thigh, but his first assessment follows the suggestion of the note card:

He was unable to move. Then he realized he was sopping wet. He looked down at his crotch with a sinking, sick sensation. A wild crimson blot was crawling rapidly along his shirt front like an enormous sea monster rising to devour him. He was hit! . . . A second solid jolt struck the plane. Yossarian shuddered with revulsion at the queer sight of his wound and screamed at Aarfy for help.

"I lost my balls! I lost my balls! . . . I said I lost my balls! Can't you hear me? I'm wounded in the groin!" (*Catch,* 283–84)

Heller changed a terrible reality to an understandable confusion that represents a normal fear in war. In its revised state the idea unites the sexual theme with the dangers of war and the destructive insensitivity of Aarfy. Yossarian's wound also serves the plot in getting him back into the hospital, where the themes of absurdity, bureaucracy, and insanity are explored: Nurse Cramer insists to Yossarian that his leg is "certainly . . . not your leg! . . . That leg belongs to the U.S. government" (*Catch,* 286). It would have been difficult to make this conversation humorous if Yossarian had been castrated. Nonetheless, the relationship of the published novel to the suggestions on the note card reveals that although Heller continued the creative process throughout the composition and revision of his book, the final product is remarkably consistent with his initial conception. The central tone, the key events, the characters (although often with changed names), and the underlying themes are essentially what Heller recorded on a note card eight years prior to the publication of the novel.

Another note card of particular interest is one entitled "Night of Horrors" in the notes and the manuscript chapter derived from it but "The Eternal City" in the published novel. The card contains seven entries, the first four of which concern matters not eventually made part of the chapter. These have to do with the discovery of penicillin (which Yossarian apparently needs for syphilis), Yossarian's attempts to get the drug through Nurse Duckett, and the acquisition of it by "Aarky." The discovery by Yossarian that the old man in the whorehouse is dead, and that the girls have been driven out of the apartment by the vagaries of "catch-18," thus would have been the result of his search for a cure. He has come to the apartment in Rome to see Aarky. The villain in this episode turns out to be Milo, as item 7 explains: "Milo is exposed as the source of penicillen [*sic*], tricking both Aarky & Yossarian, and as the man who infected the girl to create a demand for his new wonder drug. Yossarian breaks with him." This concept, finally rejected, would have been an interesting but perhaps unnecessary further development of Milo's corruption. It would also have been an overt expression of Yossarian's underlying values, one not in the novel because Milo simply leaves Yossarian in Rome out of a desire to make money from the traffic in illegal tobacco.

This idea and all but one of the other suggestions on the card were finally abandoned or subordinated to what appears as item 5: "Yossarian finally walks through the streets of Rome witnessing various horrors, among them the maid, who has been thrown from the window by Aarky." It is this concept that ultimately became the heart of "The Eternal City" (*Catch*, 396–410). Yossarian, in Rome to look for Nately's whore's kid sister, in an attempt to keep her from a life of prostitution, discovers a nightmare world. In the novel Milo shares these generous motives until he learns of the smuggling of illegal tobacco (*Catch*, 402). What emerges in the chapter is Yossarian's "night of horrors," his surrealistic walk through Rome at night, in which greed, violence, corruption, insanity, and death, prime themes throughout the novel, converge on his consciousness from all sides, and he is arrested for being AWOL.

There are numerous other note cards as intriguing and significant as these two and several individual ideas that were developed or abandoned after their first conception in the notes. That Snowden will be killed on the mission to Avignon, that in response Yossarian will parade in the nude and sit naked in a tree during the funeral, are all established on a card entitled "Ferrara." An example of the kind of minor detail that Heller frequently changed is the suggestion on this card that when Yossarian is awarded his medal, still standing naked in formation, "Dreedle orders a zoot suit for him." Another such revision concerns what is finally chapter 30, "Dunbar" (*Catch*, 324–33), but is called "McAdam" in the notes. (The name "McAdam," of course, was later changed to "McWatt.") The two most dramatic events of the chapter are here suggested: McAdam dives low over the beach, slicing Kid Sampson in half, and then commits suicide. The note card indicates an indefinite "man" as the victim and also suggests that "McAdam kills himself & Daneeker," which was revised, but the main focus of the published chapter is all there. This card also contains a fascinating suggestion: "Nurse Cramer's family tree traced back to include all known villains in History. She completes the line by being a registered Republican who doesn't drink, smoke, fornicate, or lust consciously & [is] guiltless of similar crimes."

An entry for chapter 40, entitled "Catch-18" in the notes, reads "in the morning, Cathcart sends for Yossarian and offers him his deal. Big Brother has been watching Yossarian." The concluding phrase makes explicit an underlying thematic allusion to George Orwell's *1984*, one now more subtly beneath the action of the novel. The same card contains the suggestion that Nately's whore will stab Yossarian as he leaves Cathcart's office, which occurs in the novel, and that she will shout "olé" as she plunges the knife in, which does not.

The note for the final chapter, "Yossarian," contains not only plot suggestions but some interpretive remarks as well. There is a good deal of interest in Yossarian's mortality: "Yossarian is dying, true, but he has about 35 years to live." Another provocative entry, one rejected, suggests that "Among other things, he really does have chronic liver trouble. Condition is malignant & would have killed him if it had not been discovered." It is fortuitous that this idea was changed, for Yossarian's trips to the hospital are now linked to his protest against the absurdity of the war and his personal quest for survival; to add to those ideas the serendipitous saving of his life through the discovery of his cancer in a military hospital he has falsely entered would have been to compound too many levels of irony. Perhaps the most important comments on this note card are those relating to the thematic significance of Yossarian's refusal of Cathcart's deal. In the note card, Yossarian discusses the ethics of the deal and his alternatives with an English deserter: "Easiest would be to go home or fly more missions. Hardest would be for him to fight for identity without sacrificing moral responsibility." The following entry reads "He chooses the last, after all dangers are pointed out to him."

In the novel, the English deserter has been replaced by Major Danby, who, since he does not appear in the preliminary notes, would seem to be a late invention. The conception of the "fight for identity" has been altered: Yossarian says, "I've been fighting all along to save my country. Now I'm going to fight a little to save myself. The country's not in danger any more, but I am" (*Catch*, 435). The "identity" motif has been submerged into the "survival" theme, one centered on Yossarian's physical and moral survival. Thus Yossarian can now claim, "I'm not running away from my responsibilities. I'm running to them" (*Catch*, 440). In thematic terms, this change is among the most important ideas in the preliminary note cards. What is remarkable about them as a group, however, is how closely they correspond to what Heller eventually published some eight years later. It is a dramatic testimony to the clarity of his initial conception, for, although there were many early changes and deletions, along with alterations in the final version of the manuscript, the finished product is well described by the note cards Heller developed in his advertising office, shaping and defining and trying out his idea in miniature before he actually wrote the first draft.

In addition to the note cards, Heller also worked on a number of other documents prior to writing the first full draft of his novel. One group of these that is particularly important is composed of "plans," outlines, sketches, brief exchanges of dialogue, summaries of the role of a character, ideas for plot developments, checklists on which Heller indicated that a certain idea had or had not been included in the first draft. These pages, somewhat more than a hundred, allowed Heller more room than did the note cards to expand on concepts and outlines, although to some extent they serve the same function. For example, on the sheet for "Catch-18" Heller recorded his ideas for the permutations of that concept:

> A. Censoring letters
> B. Increases Wintergreen's punishment
> C. Colonel must request transfer
> D. Sanity in soldier
> E. Drives girls out
> F. Will send Nately Back
> G. Deal With Yossarian.[19]

Heller had thus decided before he began writing that the matter of "catch-18" would occur at least seven times in the novel. Further, as the outline indicates, the general direction of the recurrence progresses from humor to tragedy, from the business of having Wintergreen dig holes to contain the dirt created from previous holes to the final matter of Yossarian's being trapped in a moral dilemma in which his self-respect and his very life are seriously threatened.

19. These sheets are not organized or numbered in any coherent fashion, suggesting that they were written at various times and not as a discrete stage of composition. Some pages are not numbered, while others begin the numbering or lettering scheme all over again. The "Catch-18" sheet is numbered 17, which is crossed out, and renumbered 15. The letters on the outline are enclosed in circles, which I do not indicate in my text.

Some of Heller's notations to himself reveal a considerable interpretive intelligence. On a page about Corporal Snark, Milo's first chef in the novel and the character who poisons the squadron with soap in the mashed potatoes to prove that the men have no taste (*Catch,* 63), Heller records his comments about this relatively minor character. It is clear that Snark is to be thematically opposed to Milo in that Snark cooks for the "art" of his craft and Milo is interested only in the commercial aspects of food. Heller wrote that Snark "would like to forge within the smithy of his soul the uncreated soufflés of the world." Another entry is particularly ironic: "Spots the significance of Milo's enterprises. An egg, in case the critics have missed it, is a symbol of creation. A hard-boiled egg is the symbol of the creative process frozen. A scrambled egg is the symbol of creation scrambled. A powdered egg is the symbol of the creative process pulverized—destroyed." No one reading through Heller's plans would doubt that he gave extraordinary attention to every detail of his novel, including the role and thematic impact of every character in every scene. This pertains even in instances in which Heller did not follow his suggestions, as with some of his ideas for Snowden: "Snowden's innards are loathsome things brought up through a crack in the earth. . . . Snowden's luggage in the bedroom at the enlisted men's apartment . . . Snowden's secret is that they are out to kill Yossarian." These ideas, particularly the last, are not implemented in the novel, nor are such related plans as the notion that General Eisenhower and Harry Truman want Yossarian dead.

One of the documents deals with the war novel that Yossarian and Dunbar struggle to write, a matter suggested on a note card and developed in Heller's plans but not incorporated into the final novel. The note cards contained two suggestions that relate to this document: one entry, item 7, suggests that "Yossarian & Dunbar write novel, although Jew won't conform & they still lack a radical" and the second, item 10, indicates a "parody of Hemingway in introduction of attempt to assemble cast for war novel." In the brief sketches derived from the note-card entries, Heller wrote a half-page developing each idea, the first of which, entitled "Perfect Plot," begins

> now they had just about everything to make a perfect plot for a best-selling war novel. They had a fairy, they had a slav named Florik from the slums, an Irishman, a thinker with a Phd, a cynic who believed in nothing, a husband who's [*sic*] wife had sent him a Dear John letter, a clean-cut

young lad who was doomed to die. They had everything there but the sensitive Jew, and that was enough to turn them against the whole race. They had a Jew but there was just nothing they could do with him. He was healthy, handsome, rugged, and strong, and if anybody else in the ward wanted to make something out of anything he could have taken them in turn, anybody but Yossarian, who didn't want to make anything out of anything. All he cared about was women and there was just nothing in the world you could do with a Jew like that.[20]

Several matters are of interest in the paragraph, including the suggestion that Yossarian is Jewish, an idea buttressed by Heller's comments in a letter in 1974.[21] That Yossarian and Dunbar would be writing a novel about war would be thematically awkward in the context of the progressive immediacy of danger and death. The writing of fiction implies remoteness, the vantage of the observer, more than direct involvement. Heller's idea that an outfit with an ethnic distribution would somehow parody Hemingway seems confused, since Hemingway never wrote any novels along those lines. The parody would seem better directed at some of the popular war movies that circulated in the 1950s. Another important dimension to this scene is that Yossarian and Dunbar are in the hospital, implying either that they are ill or wounded or, more likely, that they are feigning illness to escape hazardous duty, a ruse that runs throughout the novel.

Another Heller document, however, explores alternative reasons why Yossarian wants to go into the hospital. On a page entitled "Conspiracy to Murder Him," Heller outlined some thoughts about Yossarian's growing preoccupation with death:

Grows aware of it with Snowden's death. They were all shooting at him, and when they hit someone else it was a case of mistaken identity. They wanted him dead, there was no doubt about it and there was no doubt that it was all part of a gigantic conspiracy. . . . Colonel Cathcart wanted him dead.

20. This entry is on a sheet entitled "Hospital." For a more detailed transcription of Heller's paragraphs, see James Nagel, "Two Brief Manuscript Sketches: Heller's *Catch-22*," *Modern Fiction Studies* 20 (1974): 221–24.

21. Joseph Heller, letter to Daniel Walden. I have read this letter but do not have a copy. In it Heller says that he always thought of Yossarian as Jewish. However, in other places Heller has said directly that he wanted Yossarian to be without ethnic identity.

> General Dreedle wanted him dead. . . . Eisenhower and Harry S Truman
> wanted him dead. It was the one thing upon which even the enemies were
> agreed. Hitler wanted him dead because he was Assyrian, Stalin wanted
> him dead because he wasn't. Mussolini wanted him dead because he was
> Mussolini, and Tojo wanted him dead because he was short and far away
> and couldn't make himself understood. . . . The only safe place for him in
> the whole world was in the hospital, because in the hospital nobody seemed
> to care whether he lived or died.

This material has genuine comic potential, even in Heller's brief outline of
it, although it makes Yossarian's fear of death somewhat more paranoiac
than in the novel, where his continuous proximity to death is a matter of
circumstance rather than malevolence. Heller's decision not to develop this
idea was part of a general pattern of excision of references to real persons.
Without the resonance of the names, the humor of the passage is greatly
diminished.

Several of the other sketches Heller worked on are also intriguing documents, including a page on which Yossarian, Orr, and Hungry Joe all move
the bomb line before the mission to Bologna. This page, entitled "Rebukes
Yossarian for moving bomb line," contains dialogue in which Clevinger
argues with his obtuse good sense that Yossarian was unfair to the others in
moving the line on the map. In the following paragraph the plot thickened
in a way it does not in the novel:

> It was another clear night filled with bright yellow stars he knew he might
> never see again. Moving the bomb line was not fair to the other men in
> the squadron, men like Orr, who tiptoed out into the darkness and moved
> the bomb line up an inch, and like Hungry Joe, who moved it up another
> inch, and the steady stream of all the others, each one moving it one inch
> so that it was up over Sweden when daylight glowed.

Yossarian alone is culpable in the novel, but this passage establishes the
universality of his apprehension in a manner that may have enriched this
motif. On the other hand, Heller's ultimate rejection of a scene in which
Yossarian explains to the chaplain how much he enjoyed touching Snowden's
torn flesh and organs, and how he rubbed blood over himself to impress
everyone back at the base, was wisely deleted. In this sketch Heller seems to

have been exploring the possibilities of his material, developing ideas before discarding them. The obvious thematic incongruence of Yossarian being pleased by the very death that transforms him would have considerably weakened the Snowden scenes.

There are other related documents that seem to have been written at this stage, after the note cards but before the first draft of the novel. Heller was obviously very concerned about the chronology of the action, not only that it progress in accord with certain key scenes but that these events be consistent with the history of the actual war. At one point he constructed a detailed outline of events in the European theater from 1943 to 1945. He begins in 1943 with the landings in Sicily on June 11 and follows with the Anzio landings in January of 1944, the Normandy invasion on June 6, and the stabilization of German forces in Italy (which necessitated the bombing of transportation lines). He did a separate page on events in Italy between May and August of 1944 (the period of his own bombing missions), outlining the objective of the Italian campaign ("tie down Germans; gain air bases near S. Germany") and the stalemate in southern Italy that delayed the Allied advance. He particularly notes the taking of Rome on June 4, 1944, D-Day two days later, and the victories in Pisa and Florence. His broad outline continues through 1945 and the Battle of the Bulge, the advance of the Russians on the eastern front, the execution of Mussolini, the crossing of the Po, and the fall of Berlin on May 3.

With the historical facts clear, he worked on the chronological outline of his own narrative, using the closest paper large enough to contain his detailed notations, the blotter on his desk. On this document Heller recorded not only the general events of the novel but, within a grid crossing time values with characters, the action for each character at the time of the central events. Heller's chart would then tell him, as he worked on a given scene, what all of the characters were doing. For example, the entries indicate that when Yossarian is wounded he comes into contact with Nurse Duckett and gets psychoanalyzed by Major Sanderson, Dunbar cracks his head in the hospital, Nately refuses to enter the hospital, Aarky gets lost on the mission, Orr has a flat tire, the Soldier in White reappears, and the old man of the Roman brothel continues to be a mystery. Reading the chart down, Heller could follow the activities of any character he chose; reading it across, he could coordinate their activities and keep a complex chronology straight. In this he did not entirely succeed, but, given the intricate time structure of the novel, he needed a method of organizing the complex events.[22]

At some point Heller constructed other documents that also clarify the actions of the characters and the key themes of the novel. Taking their interaction in the plot apart, he meticulously recorded the progression of events involving each character. These documents cover nearly a hundred pages and reveal the painstaking care and detailed attention that Heller gave to the structure of his fiction. Many of these entries contain humorous ideas not in, or submerged in, the novel, one being that Major Major "was from the winter wheat fields of Vermont and a former teacher of English. Made the mistake of stating publicly that he did not like Henry James." Another entry explores the idea that "Rome was a sort of school for sexual experience." Other entries explore the "Night of Horrors," later changed to "The Eternal City," and others the concept of free enterprise. One outline reveals Heller's plan for the ending, which begins "Yossarian is wounded, recovers, and continues flying combat missions until he completes seventy." The emphasis is on Nately's whore, how she tries to stab him when he tells her of Nately's death. That sketch takes him through to the end:

> Yossarian can lend himself obediently to all Colonel Cathcart's designs and lose his life; he can accept Colonel Cathcart's proposition and lose his character. Or, he can desert, and risk losing both when he is eventually apprehended, as he knows he will probably be. There is no way he can re-main a citizen in good standing without falling victim to one dishonorable scheme or another of his legal superior.
>
> In the end, he runs off, closely pursued by Nately's mistress, the embod-iment of danger and of a violent conscience that will never leave him in peace.

As these comments indicate, Heller often gave his ideas critical substance even before he wrote the scenes, acting as creative writer and interpreter simultaneously in a manner rarely equaled for detail and insight in American fiction.

---

22. For copies of Heller's blotter, I am indebted to Colonel Frederick Kiley of the United States Air Force, who was generous with both his time and materials when I spoke with him in Washington, D.C. Kiley used the blotter for the cover of his book *A 'Catch-22' Casebook*, ed. Frederick Kiley and Walter McDonald (New York: Crowell, 1973).

The most important manuscript of *Catch-22* is a handwritten draft a good deal longer than, but essentially the same as, the published novel. It is complete save for the first chapter, which was published separately as "Catch-18" in *New World Writing* in 1955, and for chapter 9, which is simply missing from this draft although present in the typescript. This manuscript displays the additions, deletions, insertions, typeovers, misspellings, and informal punctuation of the type normally found in first drafts.[23] It is essentially handwritten, although there are paragraphs and occasionally pages that are typed, indicating, perhaps, some revision simultaneous to the initial composition. Two chapters of the manuscript do not appear in the novel (as a result the numbers of the chapters are different in each case) and hundreds of brief passages were deleted. Indeed, Heller's revisions consisted more of deletion and addition than of alterations in scenes. The pages are numbered sequentially by chapter, although as other pages were inserted, varying numbering and lettering schemes were used to keep order so that pages frequently have several numbers or letters on them. As was true on the note cards, many of the names of characters differ in the manuscript from the novel: Aarfy appears consistently as Aarky; Peckem is known throughout the manuscript as P. P. Peckenhammer. Nately is a more important character in the manuscript than in the novel, and an entire chapter about his family was deleted. One important character in the manuscript, Rosoff, does not appear at all in the novel. But the central point is that Heller's first draft remains remarkably close to what he outlined in his note cards and to the published novel.

There are other matters in the early composition stages that are significant. One of them is that the location of Yossarian's base throughout the note cards and manuscript is Corsica, where Heller himself had been stationed. Pianosa was not introduced until the manuscript and even the typescript had been completed. The manuscript is more detailed than the novel in describing

23. I will use the term *manuscript* to designate the handwritten draft of the novel, distinct from the *typescript*. Some of the pages of the manuscript have been typed and inserted; some paragraphs were typed with handwriting following, suggesting a revision during the process of composition. In my quotations I will attempt to represent the manuscript accurately, adding only periods to end sentences (sometimes on the manuscript it is not clear if there is a period or not). Throughout my transcriptions, [ ] will be used for editorial interpolations, < > to indicate additions made to the text, and {} to denote deletions by Heller.

features of the setting, since Heller had been to Corsica himself and knew the topography intimately; there is no evidence that he ever visited Pianosa. Yossarian's unit in the manuscript is also Heller's old outfit, the Twelfth Air Force, whereas in the novel it is the Twenty-seventh, a nonexistent unit. In the manuscript there is a much more "literary" frame of reference than in the final novel, and Yossarian is compared to Ahasuerus, Gulliver, and Samson Agonistes, reflecting Heller's graduate training in literature. The manuscript is also somewhat more sexually explicit than the published version, as in the scene in which Daneeka shows the newlyweds how to make love. In the manuscript Daneeka says, "I showed them how penetration was accomplished and explained its importance to impregnation." This reference was dropped in the final draft. In a similar vein, the manuscript has more scatological dialogue, so that when Milo maneuvers a package of dates away from his friend, "Yossarian always did things properly, too, and he gave Milo the package of pitted dates and told him to shove his personal note up his ass." This passage, and this tone, did not survive to publication (*Catch*, 64).

Another area of frequent revision is the final paragraphs of the chapters, which show a great deal of revision, more than any other section of the manuscript. For example, in the first draft the last paragraph of chapter 7, which concludes a section on Milo's complex investment schemes, reads

> the only one complaining was Milo. And the only ones who were happy, as it turned out, were Milo and the grinning thief, for by the time McWatt returned to his tent another bedsheet was gone, along with the sweet tooth and a brand new pair of red polka dot pajamas sent him with love by a wealthy sister-in-law who despised him for what he had been told was his birthday.

Heller crossed all of that out in his manuscript and substituted "but Yossarian still didn't understand." By the time the novel appeared the passage had become

> but Yossarian still didn't understand either how Milo could buy eggs in Malta for seven cents apiece and sell them at a profit in Pianosa for five cents (*Catch*, 66),

which better conveys the absurd humor.

One way in which the manuscript differs from the novel is that there are more passages of interpretive comment in the first draft, such as a comment in chapter 2 about the Texan. In the manuscript the narrator says

> that's what was wrong with the Texan, not that he never ended kneeding [his jowls], but that he overflowed with goodwill and brought the whole ward down trying to cheer it up. He was depressing. He was worse than a missionary or an uncle. <The Texan> {He} wanted everybody in the <ward> {hospital} to be happy. He was really very sick.

In the novel this passage has been reduced in a manner typical of Heller's changes:

> The Texan wanted everybody in the ward to be happy but Yossarian and Dunbar. He was really very sick. (*Catch*, 16)

In shortening this passage, Heller also changed its impact, making the Texan's illness ambiguous. The manuscript implies that his unrestrained ebullience and goodwill are so out of keeping with reality as to be pathological; the novel seems to suggest that because he does not want Yossarian and Dunbar to be happy there must be something wrong with him.

Another expository assertion of theme originally opened chapter 3:

> Colonel Cathcart wanted fifty missions, and he was dead serious about them. Yossarian had one mission, and he was dead serious about that. His mission was to keep alive. His mission was to keep alive as long as he could, for he had decided to live forever or die in the attempt. Yossarian was a towering one hundred and ninety-two pounds of firm bone and tender flesh, and he worshipped the whole bloody mess so much that he would have lain down his life to preserve it. Yossarian was no stranger to heroism. He had courage. He had as much courage as anyone he'd ever met. He had courage enough to be a coward, and that's exactly what he was, a hero.

This assessment of Yossarian's character is the kind of comment reserved for the other characters in the published novel, with Yossarian's role revealed dramatically. Heller deleted this passage and presented the idea with the remark that Yossarian "had decided to live forever or die in the attempt, and his only mission each time he went up was to come down alive" (*Catch*,

29), a more concise formulation. Heller made scores of alterations in the manuscript along these lines, nearly always with the result of reducing expository comment, compressing a scene without losing the effect, or clarifying the motivation of one of the characters.

Occasionally Heller's original ideas were abstract and the revisions concrete and specific, lending realistic detail where there had been only generality. For example, in chapter 3 Heller had written a passage about

> General Peckenhammer's directive requiring all tents in the Mediterranean Theatre of Operations to be pitched with entrances facing back proudly toward the future along imaginary parallel lines projected perpendicular to the chain of events that had made the present inevitable.

In terms of the setting of the novel, always very specific, this passage makes little sense and is not humorous. Whatever philosophical value there might be in these abstractions, they do not comment in any important way on Yossarian's situation, nor does the deterministic suggestion carry much thematic weight since if circumstances are inevitable there is little point in protesting against them. Heller's revision works better: it is clear that General Dreedle is angry about

> General Peckem's recent directive requiring all tents in the Mediterranean theater of operations to be pitched along parallel lines with entrances facing back proudly toward the Washington Monument. (*Catch*, 26)

This version is more deeply comic, with its absurd patriotism motivated by Peckem's unbridled ambition. Dreedle's anger has more to do with his struggle for power with Peckem than with whether the directive makes any sense, although "to General Dreedle, who ran a fighting outfit, it seemed a lot of crap." On another level it also parodies the regimentation of all aspects of military life.

Some passages had an element of humor but were deleted anyway in the revision of the first draft. In the published novel, "Yossarian shot skeet, but never hit any. Appleby shot skeet and never missed" (*Catch*, 35). Heller does not do much with this business, although the passage reinforces the general idea that Appleby is capable and very competitive, whereas Yossarian is mediocre and not at all competitive. In the manuscript, however, Heller made more extensive comment:

Yossarian couldn't shoot a skeet to save his ass. The only time Yossarian ever shot a skeet was the time he discharged his shotgun accidentally and shot a whole box full of skeet right out of Appleby's hands ten minutes before the firing was scheduled to begin. Appleby, one of those who never missed, was impressed profoundly.

This incident makes Yossarian's innocence somewhat more dangerous than in the novel, and it also gives Appleby a more generous spirit.[24] The joke in the manuscript surpasses that in the novel, but it comes at the cost of making Yossarian a dangerous threat. In the final version he is essentially a life-affirming character fighting for survival in a hostile and threatening world.

Another important revision relates to the conclusion of chapter 8, which contains the scene known as "Clevinger's Trial," an intense and shocking section in which Clevinger appears before the Action Board for such crimes as "mopery," "breaking ranks while in formation," and "listening to classical music" (*Catch*, 74). The board consists of Lieutenant Scheisskopf, Major Metcalf, and a "bloated colonel with the big fat mustache." What disturbs Clevinger is not only that he is presumed guilty, in fact *must* be guilty or he would never have been charged, but that he senses the intense hatred of his superior officers. In the novel, that point is emphasized in the conclusion, in which Clevinger realizes that nowhere in the world, not even in Nazi Germany, "were there men who hated him more" (*Catch*, 80). This conclusion is sharp and effective, perhaps the best final line in any of the chapters. It is also a major improvement over what Heller had originally written, which was that

> these were men who were on his side, who pledged allegiance to the same flag. It was a ruinous, shattering encounter, for that was the one thing Clevinger had not learned at Harvard, how to hate, and the one thing Yossarian could not teach him. They were not the enemy soldiers he had enlisted to fight, yet he was the enemy they had enlisted to fight, and it gave them the decisive advantage in whatever incomprehensible struggle they had plunged themselves into against him.

24. There is a suggestion in the deleted dialogue that Havermeyer and Appleby discuss the incident and agree that Yossarian shot the gun on purpose, which would change the attitude of Appleby.

Although there may be elements of tragic wisdom in this insight, its verbosity diffuses the impact of the shorter and more pointed conclusion. Here, as in many instances, Heller demonstrated his considerable skill at revision, making the concluding paragraph in the novel much better than that in the first draft.

Many of Heller's deletions from the manuscript are essentially compressions retaining the same basic themes and the same attributes of character. The reductions thus have the effect of leaving some matters unstated but nonetheless consistent with the passages that appear in the published version. For example, chapter 8 of the novel begins "not even Clevinger understood how Milo could do that, and Clevinger knew everything," referring to Milo's ability to sell eggs for less than he pays for them and still make a profit. The manuscript went on to detail various categories of what Clevinger knew:

> Clevinger knew who was fighting the war and why, who had started the war and when, who would pay for the war and how, and why the war had to be one [won] and by whom, even though winning the war would mean giving everything back to the same sinful people of poise, power, and pretension all over the world who had helped get it started in the first place, just so they could fuck things up all over again with a brand new one that would make it necessary for Yossarian to dump his wet, warm blood out still one more time in <senseless> {meaningless} payment for their headstrong and supercilious blunders. It would all go back to them by default, for they were the only ones willing enough to work full time at getting, keeping, and misusing authority.

In addition to unnecessarily elaborating on an idea inherent in the events, this passage introduces an element of futility in both the war itself and Yossarian's protest. Since everything will revert to its original condition even if the Allies win the war, every level of the action is absurd. In the conclusion of the published novel, Yossarian takes a rather different stance, stating, "I've been fighting all along to save my country." He clearly feels that it does make a difference who wins; that conflict having been resolved, however, he now must devote himself to saving both his life and his integrity, which explains his desertion. The final portion of the deleted passage, a protest against oligarchy and a call for political activism, remains only by implication.

Some of Heller's deletions constitute a pattern that, in effect, diminishes the role of characters or themes. For example, the triumvirate of Scheisskopf, his wife, and the accommodating Dori Duz is more important in the manuscript than in the novel. Many passages involving Yossarian and Dori Duz were deleted in chapter 8, for example, most dealing with Yossarian's lust and her capacity to tantalize him. In another section Dori replaces Mrs. Scheisskopf in bed so that the wife can go out on the town with *Buddenbrooks* looking for someone interesting "to shack up with." Despite the humor in these passages, Dori has less moment than Mrs. Scheisskopf, and Heller diminished her role appropriately in the novel.

Mrs. Scheisskopf gets more attention in the manuscripts than in the published version. Much of what was cut about her, however, contained generalized comments about women that would have introduced tangential issues, and Heller wisely deleted them. For example, he originally wrote in chapter 8 that

> like all married women who have been denied the essential childhood advantages of a broken home and a tenement environment, she yearned to be a slut with lovers by the thousand. Unlike all married women, she had the vision, courage, and intelligence to make a gallant try.

Although this passage would have provided a plausible explanation for her promiscuity, it would have done so in a school of red herrings. So, too, a related section Heller deleted. He originally wrote that

> she was pleasant and confused, with a misplaced sex urge located some-where in her frontal lobe in the unyielding nut of some trite and treasured neurosis in which only she had any curiosity. She was the sort who in olden times would undoubtedly have run off with her colored chauffeur. What stopped her from doing it now was her colored chauffeur. He couldn't stand her. He found her too bourgeois.

Beyond the humor in the etiology of her insatiable desire, there are again unfortunate racial and socioeconomic implications in the chauffeur business that had to be deleted. It seems probable that Heller, unfailingly liberal and humane in his personal views, was initially inspired by some stereotypic comic strategies that, upon reflection, were inconsistent with the themes he was developing.

The role of Scheisskopf in this chapter was also reduced somewhat, al-though not fundamentally altered. There was originally more of his obsession with marching and winning parades, with the men being forced to drill in the dead of night with their feet wrapped in burlap bags to muffle the sound. Heller's style in some of this material took on an anomalous tone:

> Not a human voice was distinguishable throughout the whole clandestine operation; in place of the usual drill commands, Lieutenant Scheisskopf substituted the sigh of a marsh hen, the plash of a bullfrog, and the whir of quails' wings on a slumbrous Friday afternoon.

The rhapsodic mood of the passage is inconsistent with the inhumane, even unhuman, ambition of Scheisskopf, who cares nothing for the men in his unit and would gladly nail them in formation if it would help win the weekly prize in the Sunday parades.

Heller also deleted a good deal of material from chapter 10, which deals with an array of matters starting with Clevinger's death in a cloud, the Grand Conspiracy of Lowery Field, and ex-P.F.C. Wintergreen's devotion to digging holes in Colorado, and proceeding through to the ominously escalating number of missions required in Pianosa. There was originally a good deal more elaboration on Wintergreen's prodigious digging, with several pages detailing how he would dig until he could find the match, thrown by a Lieutenant Tatlock (who did not survive to the published novel), at the bottom of a hole. All of this proceeds from the fact that "it was ex-P.F.C. Wintergreen's military specialty to keep digging and filling up [pits] in punishment for going AWOL every time he had the chance." There was much elaboration in the manuscript on all of this, even to the point that "Staff Sergeants Bell and Nerdlinger set up a bookmaking stand several yards away and gave odds to all comers on how long it would take him to find each match."

Two other deleted passages in chapter 10 of the manuscript are of particular interest, including one that explains why Milo chose his own squadron to bomb and strafe after he convinced the Germans to conduct the war on a businesslike basis:

> Actually, Milo bombed all five squadrons in the Group that night, and the air field, bomb dump, and repair hangars as well. But his own squadron was the only one built close enough to the abandoned railroad ditch for the men to {take shelter there} seek safety there and be machine gunned repeatedly

by the planes floating in over the leafy trees blooming in luxuriant silhouette against the hard, cold, <spectral> {ivory} moon.

The diffusion of Milo's attack in this passage to the entire Group generates rather different values than the more focused raid on the squadron in the novel, in which the danger and threat to life are immediate and devastating.

But a more important passage was cut from this chapter, one that deals with Yossarian's mental condition as it relates to the Snowden scene. A three-page section in the manuscript was deleted that develops some of the causes of Yossarian's "insanity" as seen by others, in this case Sergeant Towser:

> Yossarian had gone crazy twice, in Sergeant Towser's estimation. The symptoms began subtly with a morbid hallucination about a dead man in his tent right after the mission to Orvieto, where the dead man in his tent was really killed, and erupted disgracefully into outright insanity on at least two occasions with which Sergeant Towser was personally familiar, first on the mission to Avignon, when Snowden was killed in the rear of his plane, and again shortly afterward when Yossarian's close friend Clevinger {was} <had been> lost in that mysterious cloud.

What is explicitly clear here is that Yossarian is "insane" only because Towser is insensitive to Yossarian's grieving for a lost friend, to his remorse for the death of a man he did not know, to his feelings about the horrible death of Snowden, and to his general sense of the immediacy of death in their lives. There are further explanations in the deleted sections clarifying the point that Yossarian initially discarded his clothes because they were covered with Snowden's blood and that Yossarian's subsequent retreat into the hospital was occasioned by Clevinger's death. In the published novel this event supports other interpretations: for example, that Yossarian took off his uniform to indicate his rejection of his military role.

This section continues from Towser's point of view, and, since Towser works in Major Major's office, it deals with Yossarian's vigorous attempts to confront his commanding officer. A related passage, also deleted, explores Towser's memories of Mudd, the dead man who lives in Yossarian's tent: "He looked exactly like $E=MC^2$ to Sergeant Towser because he had traveled faster than the speed of light, moving swiftly enough to go away even before he had come and say so long even before he had time to say hello." There is more of this on Mudd, including a scene in which Yossarian returns from a mission to discover that the man in his tent has been killed, and all of these passages were deleted. The effect is that the novel now says little about the details of the Mudd incident or the background of how Yossarian came to walk around naked. A perceptive reader has a sense of the motivational line, but it is not as definite as in Heller's first draft.

One incident that Heller revised rather substantially is the Glorious Loyalty Oath Crusade in chapter 11, an obvious parody of the American loyalty statements of the 1950s and not of military practice in World War II. In the manuscript this crusade targets Communists in the squadron and is not, as in the novel, simply an attempt by Captain Black to discredit Major Major. In the manuscript Black several times asserts that his duty as intelligence officer requires him to identify Communists and to prevent them from examining the bombsights in the planes. Heller repeatedly deleted references to Communism in this section. He also somewhat softened the inconvenience caused to the men by the crusade. He cut out a passage in which the men had to get up at midnight for morning missions and at dawn for afternoon flights because of the necessity to sign so many oaths.

Heller made literally thousands of revisions of this kind as he worked and reworked his material, drawing nearer to publication. In some cases entire chapters were deleted, one involving a calisthenics instructor named Rosoff, who in many ways duplicated Scheisskopf in his excessive zeal for regimentation, and another in which Nately writes home to his father, which shifted some attention away from the theater of war and toward the United States. Many references to actual persons were dropped, including prominent military figures, and the names of men in Heller's unit were changed to avoid any chance of libel suits. But the fact remains that, over the nine years of composition of the novel, the central characters, themes, and incidents that Heller had initially planned in the early stages of the novel remained essentially intact, and in these documents resides one of the most complete, and fascinating, records of the growth of an American classic.

# The Western American Context of
## *One Flew over the Cuckoo's Nest*

STEPHEN L. TANNER

§   §   §

O CCASIONALLY A literary work captivates a large audience by vividly embodying the fears and desires that flow just beneath the level of articulation. Such a work evokes a pleasure of recognition; readers are confirmed in a knowledge of their society that they scarcely knew they possessed. Through such an accomplishment the artist brings into focus social and cultural tendencies that before had been only partially discerned by the general public. *One Flew over the Cuckoo's Nest* is such a work. Written between the summer of 1960 and the spring of 1961, the novel preceded the counterculture movement of the succeeding decade, with its disruption of universities, opposition to the war in Vietnam, back-to-nature revolt against established authority and revered technology, and often indecorous rejection of what it viewed as the affluent complacency of the fifties. Yet the book prophetically contained the essence of this social-cultural turmoil. More importantly, it dramatically articulated the nation's queasy suspicion that its valued tradition of self-reliant individualism was being eroded by institutionalized conformity and dehumanizing technology.

The novel is further distinguished by having succeeded also as a play and a film. The play, adapted by Dale Wasserman, was produced in 1963 and revived in 1971. The 1975 film, produced by Michael Douglas and Saul Zaentz and directed by Milos Forman, won six Academy Awards. Moreover, the novel has frequently been used as a text in a wide variety of disciplines: literature, psychology, sociology, medicine, law, and others. After thirty years, it continues in one printing after another to entertain readers and prompt commentary.

291

That any novel should have so extensive a literary-cultural impact is unusual. The fact that it was the author's first published novel makes the case even more remarkable. Did Kesey suspect as he created the story while a creative writing student at Stanford that it would touch such a responsive chord in so many readers? His own answer is no. In a 1983 interview, he said he completed the manuscript, turned it over to Malcolm Cowley, his teacher and also an editor at Viking, and returned to his home in Oregon to proceed directly to writing another novel. "When the reviews came out and as time went by, I realized that I had written a great book. But that didn't occur to me when I was writing it. I had no idea it would be taken like it was." Later in the same interview, when asked what interested him about himself, he said, "It's 'Why me?' What is it about me, my family, my father, this part of the country that caused it to be me who wrote *Cuckoo's Nest*? It is not something I set out to do. It's as though all the angels got together and said, 'Okay, here's the message that America desperately needs. Now, let's pick him to do it.' "[1] Perhaps Kesey would not have accomplished what he did if he had consciously set out to do it. The pressure of such objectives would have been debilitating. He once wrote to his friend Ken Babbs, "The first book one writes is a noisemaker, a play with no pressure, and it may sometimes have that free-swinging song of the cells."[2]

What follows is an attempt to identify some of the elements which generated that "free-swinging song of the cells." I will also try to answer Kesey's own question "Why me?," to explain in some measure what it was about him, his family, his father, and his part of the country that caused him to write *Cuckoo's Nest*.

The Kesey Collection at the University of Oregon contains a 411-page final typescript of the novel and an earlier, typed version of 406 pages with holograph revisions, most of them minor editing changes. In addition there are 37 pages of miscellaneous fragments. The most important of these are three pages of the first draft of the novel's opening scene, which are included in *One Flew over the Cuckoo's Nest: Text and Criticism*, edited by John C. Pratt. This edition also includes a two-page sample of the few extant pages of the

---

1. Quoted in Peter O. Whitmer, "Ken Kesey's Search for the American Frontier," *Saturday Review*, May–June 1983, 26, 27.

2. Quoted in John C. Pratt, ed., *One Flew over the Cuckoo's Nest: Text and Criticism* (New York: Viking, 1973), vii.

first draft showing how extensive Kesey's revisions were. More than seven pages of the miscellaneous fragments are stream-of-consciousness pencil scribblings on unlined paper, where Kesey registered the effects of some pills a nurse had brought him during a government-sponsored drug test in which he was a volunteer participant. He recorded his perceptions over a three-hour period, the handwriting becoming larger and more sprawling, the impressions more surrealistic. Such experiments with hallucinogens must have influenced his creation of Bromden's hallucinations. Most of the random manuscript pages, however, are of little use because they are inconsecutive and without recognizable relation to the finished novel.

In an undated letter to his friend Ken Babbs,[3] Kesey says that while he and his family were on a trip to Oregon, a friend who had a grudge against him broke into the small building behind his house in Palo Alto and burned his manuscripts. Some of the *Cuckoo's Nest* material may have been destroyed at that time. In any case, to understand the creation of the novel, we must rely on letters, interviews, related manuscripts, and biographical information.

## I

*One Flew over the Cuckoo's Nest* is a product of the American West, specifically of two locations along the Pacific coast: the environs of Eugene, Oregon, and of San Francisco, California. The first was the location of his childhood and formal education; the second was the location where his informal education was catalyzed by other creative minds and by the social-cultural-artistic ferment of that area in the late fifties, particularly the Beat phenomenon.

It is significant that in asking "Why me?" Kesey should mention in particular his family, his father, and his part of the country. These are primary elements in shaping his early development and in turn the products of his imagination. His family along both paternal and maternal lines were farmers and ranchers, the kind of people he described in his second novel, *Sometimes a Great Notion,* as "a stringy-muscled brood of restless and stubborn west-walkers." In the case of Kesey's family the westward migration was from Tennessee and Arkansas to Texas and New Mexico, then to Colorado, where

3. Kesey Collection, University of Oregon, Eugene.

Ken was born, and finally to Oregon. This family line was imbued with traits and values characteristic of the rural West: family ties were strong, physical strength and self-reliance were prized, outdoor activities such as hunting and fishing were an integral part of life, Protestant Christianity informed the rules of behavior, and the pleasures of vernacular talk and storytelling colored daily intercourse.

At family gatherings at his grandfather's farm, Kesey competed with his brother and his cousins in racing, wrestling, boxing, and anything that needed proving. And he absorbed the idiom of vernacular anecdote with its homely but vivid figures of speech. These experiences had lasting effects. The physical competition continued for Kesey in the form of football and wrestling in high school, college, and beyond. At the time he was writing *Cuckoo's Nest*, he was trying to qualify for the Olympic wrestling team at San Francisco's Olympic Club. Use of the region's vernacular persists in Kesey's talk and writing, in his tendency to communicate in anecdote and trope. The country Protestantism, particularly that of his grandmother Smith, left an indelible impression. In 1972 he said, "I'm a hard shell Baptist, born and raised, and though I thought I had left it I found it in myself at every turn, this basic, orthodox Christianity."[4]

This family background registers clearly in *Cuckoo's Nest*—in the strength, self-reliance, and competitiveness of the hero; in the style of the prose and the language used; in the emphasis on harmony with nature; and in the Christian imagery. Kesey's father was a sort of hero for him, a strong, independent sort of cowboy figure that he likened to John Wayne. Fred Kesey loved the outdoors and brought his sons onto the rivers and into the woods with him from an early age. Ken's hunting and fishing experiences were an important part of his youth, richly nourishing the wellsprings of his imagination. He and his father were strong-willed and their relationship was not without conflict, but Ken retained great admiration for his father, who died in 1969. He said that his father believed a time comes when a son should whip his father. It is an important and delicate matter. "A boy has to *know* he can best his father, and his father has to present him the opportunity." It has to be done in the right way and at the right time. "My

4. Quoted in Linda Gaboriau, "Ken Kesey: Summing up the '60s; Sizing up the '70s," *Crawdaddy*, no. 19 (December 1972): 38.

father's a wise man and he gave me the chance. Perhaps this is a father's most significant duty."[5]

Father-son relationships—more precisely, the absence of satisfactory father-son relationships—are a crucial matter in *Cuckoo's Nest*. Bromden tells McMurphy, "My Papa was a full Chief and his name was Tee Ah Milla-toona. That means The-Pine-That-Stands-Tallest-on-the-Mountain. . . . He was real big when I was a kid."[6] But the Combine (Bromden's term for technologized society) diminished his size, and the loss of strength and self-respect that resulted for his son is a principal reason for Bromden's withdrawal from reality in a mental ward. McMurphy, acting as a surrogate father, incites Bromden to exert his strength, and Bromden eventually bests this symbolic father by lifting the control panel, which McMurphy had failed to budge, and bashing it through the window. Kesey once described his father as "a kind of big, rebellious cowboy who never did fit in."[7] The description, of course, aptly fits McMurphy as well. Obviously, Kesey had reason to single out his father as he questioned himself about the sources of the novel.

The last element mentioned specifically in his "Why me?" question is his part of the country, western Oregon. It is the natural landscape of that region, with its evergreen forests, clear rivers, and seacoast, that forms the norm of health and sanity in the book's central conflict. Bromden is a representative natural man who has been alienated from that environment and whose sanity depends on his reestablishing broken connections. His recovery is marked in stages by a renewed capacity to sense the world of nature. It reaches a climax or epiphany on a fishing boat off the Oregon coast with a cosmic blending of nature and laughter. In readily perceived ways, the novel's regional setting has much to do with its distinctive achievement, and it is likely that recent ecological approaches to literary criticism will further delineate relationships between the book's themes and methods and Kesey's environmentally shaped values and frames of reference. Gilbert

5. Quoted in Gordon Lish, "What the Hell You Looking in Here for, Daisy Mae?" *Genesis West* 2:5 (1963): 27.

6. Ken Kesey, *One Flew over the Cuckoo's Nest* (New York: New American Library, 1962), 186. Hereafter cited parenthetically in the text as *CN*.

7. Ken Kesey, "Excerpts Recorded from an Informal Address by Mr. Kesey to the Parents at Crystal Springs School in Hillsborough, California, Presented under the Auspices of the Chrysalis West Foundation," *Genesis West*, 3:1–2 (1965): 40.

Porter perceptively observes that many of the experiences that stimulated Kesey's creativity occurred in California—in creative writing seminars at Stanford, in the interactions of the Perry Lane student community near Stanford, and in his experiences as an aide in the psychiatric wards of the Menlo Park hospital—"but in the transmutation of experience into art, Kesey relocated his world in Oregon, where familiar landmarks provided some stabilizing boundaries for a microcosm psychically out of kilter. Kesey's California experiences suggested a mental ward, but his roots in the Oregon outdoors suggested reality."[8] The history and culture of the Northwest, which constitute a distinctive outlook on American life, permeate the novel just as the region's landscape does.

Another aspect of Kesey's youth in Oregon that helps explain the creation of *Cuckoo's Nest* is his reading and the interests that prompted it and were generated by it. From an early age, he was fascinated by fantasy, by any hint of exciting and mysterious things just beyond the reach of ordinary experience. He read a good deal as a boy, but until high school that reading was mostly comic books, Westerns, and science fiction—comic books such as *Superman, Batman,* and *Captain Marvel;* authors like Zane Grey, Edgar Rice Burroughs, and Jules Verne. This reading was the beginning of a quest, a manifestation of that perennial appetite for transcendent consciousness, a yearning instinctive in most everyone but especially acute in Kesey. He once mentioned this search in an interview. As a boy he had sent for some decals of *Batman* comic-book characters. The package arrived containing a bonus, a small book of magic. This sparked an interest in magic that led him on to ventriloquism and then hypnotism. "And from hypnotism into dope. But it's always been the same trip, the same kind of search."[9] It was this desire that enticed him, after he had written two novels, to seek beyond writing—through experiments with electronic media and further experiments with drugs—new forms of consciousness and artistic expression.

He treats the same kind of yearning in an unpublished essay in which he tells of walking as a boy with his dog across the endless rolling prairies

8. Gilbert Porter, *One Flew over the Cuckoo's Nest: Rising to Heroism* (Boston: Twayne, 1989), 32.

9. Quoted in Gaboriau, "Ken Kesey: Summing up the 60s," 37.

near La Junta, Colorado, his birthplace. When he heard a far-off rumbling coming out of the clouds, he thought it was a herd of wild horses one grandpa or the other had told him about—"with teeth like rows of barbwire and eyes like polished steel balls an' breath that'd peel paint." When he told his mother about it, she said, "It's just thunder, honeybun. You was only imagining you saw horses." As a man looking back he asks, "But why, Mama, is it *just* thunder?" And he wonders as he drives across Colorado "What would still roam these prairies if the old creatures had been allowed to breed and prosper, if they hadn't been decimated by that crippler of the imagination: *only.*" He suggests that fact and fiction blend well and both are essential in presenting "the True Happening of the moment." Merely to report as a camera does is just touching the surface, like panning the stream instead of digging for the vein. "The vein lies under the topsoil of external reality: it is not hidden. We've known of it for ages, this vein, but it has been put down so long by *just,* disparaged so long by *only,* that we have neglected its development." He suggests that mining the vein has many advantages. In writing, for example, "it can mean that as much emphasis can be placed on hyperbole, metaphor, simile, or *fantasy* as on actual events." He concludes, "In the vast seas between red and white blood corpuscles Captain Nemo still secretly pilots his Nautilus, this white-haired scourge of Oppression and Warfare. Why not give him his head? Or through the dense growth of neurons, Lou Wetzel stalks the Zane Grey Indians, silent as moss until he strikes with a chilling war whoop. Why not let him stalk?"[10] Such attitudes are undoubtedly behind the claim by the narrator of *Cuckoo's Nest* that what he tells is "the truth even if it didn't happen" (*CN,* 8).

Comic books, Westerns, and science fiction—these popular genres captured Kesey's fancy and stimulated his imagination in ways he would later take seriously. "A single *Batman* comicbook is more honest than a whole volume of *Time* magazines," he once told an interviewer.[11] He recognized in these popular forms vital American myths that could be employed in serious literature the same way Joyce had made use of classic myths. *Cuckoo's Nest* is informed by the mythology of American popular culture.

10. Ken Kesey, "A Big Motherfucker," 16–18, Kesey Collection.
11. Lish, "What the Hell You Looking," 20.

## II

At the University of Oregon, Kesey was a sort of campus wonder-boy. He involved himself in athletics, theater, and fraternity life. He majored in communications and took courses in creative writing. It was a period of the kind of growth and discovery one would expect when a singularly bright, curious, but relatively uncultured mind is exposed to a university environment, when an emerging charismatic personality is exposed to a wider variety of people and social opportunities. But no matter how stimulating his experiences as an undergraduate may have been, they were not as life-transforming as his experiences as a graduate student at Stanford.

A Woodrow Wilson fellowship enabled him to enter Stanford's creative writing program in 1958. It was a highly regarded program with distinguished writer-teachers such as Wallace Stegner, Richard Scowcroft, Malcolm Cowley, and Frank O'Connor. Perhaps even more important in shaping Kesey's writing skills was the group of students with whom he associated and shared manuscripts and commentary. Among that group were Larry McMurtry, Wendell Berry, Robert Stone, Tillie Olsen, Ed McClanahan, and others whose writing later achieved varying degrees of acclaim. Kesey has likened them to the Green Bay Packers under Vince Lombardi. In addition to the wealth of talent, the seminars were distinguished by a generous spirit of useful critique. Young writers can be hard on each other, quick to give and take offense. However, Kesey's experience with his classmates was positive and resulted in a number of lasting friendships.

An important one of those friendships, and one that clearly illustrates the kind of stimulation they provided, is the one with Ken Babbs. They met in a seminar during Kesey's first semester at Stanford, and during the next few years, while Babbs was in military service, they engaged in a correspondence deliberately intended to provide opportunity for writing practice and mutual evaluation. In a letter to Babbs written while Kesey was working in a mental institution and writing *Cuckoo's Nest,* he suggests that they continue their letters as a way of helping each other,

> because I fog in and forget sometimes that I'm a damn good writer with potential of becoming a great one. Publishing house set-backs slow me down, could stop me and dry me up like a fallen fig. I doubt work that I should know is good. It is more important sometimes to point out the good than it is to distinguish the bad; you're certain of the old standby Bad,

no one needs point that out all the time. But you're forever uncertain of the Good.[12]

In the next sentence, he says he is going to send Babbs sections of the *Cuckoo's Nest* manuscript. The quoted passage is interesting in several ways. The fog image brings to mind his narrator's struggle with fog, an intriguing parallel. The publishing house setbacks refer to his attempts to publish "Zoo," his novel about the Beat culture of San Francisco's North Beach, which had won the Saxton Prize at Stanford but was never published. Clearly, at this point in the creation of *Cuckoo's Nest*, Kesey felt a need to firm up his confidence. He wanted a reader's responses and suggestions, but only if they were encouraging. He must have known intuitively the book's strengths and didn't want criticism that whittled them away; he needed reinforcing praise.

He had to send the manuscript to Vietnam, where Babbs was stationed. Babbs annotated it and wrote a long letter of suggestions, including these:

> I don't like the word, the Combine. You're trying to give a name to something that has no name. It's an emotion, a complacency, and a dulling of the senses that we're fighting, and to try and shut all these things into a box and give it a title is taking an easy gambit that isn't there to be had. . . . Throw away the thought that the opponent is real, that it exists. Everyone that reads with any intelligence knows what you're writing about, you don't have to give it a label.

He praised the hero and agreed that individual strength is more important than group action. "All I can say is do him bigger and better and finer, and you'll make everything and everyone else in the book as big and as fine." But again he counseled Kesey not to make the opposing force tangible or specific: "Forget about having the chief name something the Combine, keep it nameless. Don't sum up this total fight into the Big Nurse."[13]

This is reasonable advice and touches upon the principal risk Kesey took in simplifying the forces of good and evil and embodying them in a specific hero and villain. Some critics have shared Babbs's point of view, but the general public has responded positively to the comic-book and Western-showdown

---

12. Kesey to Ken Babbs, undated, Kesey Collection.
13. Babbs to Kesey, February 12, 1961, Kesey Collection.

simplicity of the book's principal conflicts. In this respect, the novel is a tour de force, an unabashed and skillful use of the appeals characteristic of popular literature and culture.

Kesey was confident enough in his aims that he could resist the advice of a best friend but unsure enough about how he had realized them to be fortified by that friend's praise. Babbs assured him in the same letter that the book had the ingredients of success. "The writing is good, at times rough, but like all your stuff it swings with the wild rhythms of hot life, raw life, good life, and I move out with it, and that's the power of the book for me." He suggested that Kesey might not meet great success for ten or twelve years, but it was coming. The novel appeared in print exactly one year later, and Kesey took satisfaction some months before then in playfully teasing Babbs about his success: "When I got the telegram, direct from Malcolm Cowley, no less, I thought about calling you and rubbing the salt of my fortune into your already smarting literary wounds, but thought better of it when I realized how much more acute the sting would be upon receiving the published book. Unannounced, like an angel of derision swooping down to harass you."[14] But of course he couldn't wait until the book was out before sharing his excitement with Babbs. Perhaps implied in the letter is both Kesey's trust in his own genius and an expression of gratitude for his friend's interest and encouragement.

What Kesey learned from teachers that helped him in creating the novel is difficult to determine with any precision. When asked in 1963 if he had learned anything in his creative writing classes at Stanford, he said he had learned a lot from Malcolm Cowley. What was it he learned? "Well, before Cowley, I studied with James Hall at Oregon. He taught me how *good* writing can be. Cowley taught me how good a writer *I* could be."[15] Cowley had been a visiting teacher during the time Kesey was at work on the novel, 1960–1961, and therefore was the teacher who offered suggestions specifically about *Cuckoo's Nest*. Unfortunately, those annotations and suggestions were not preserved.

Before the seminar with Cowley, Kesey had been taught by Wallace Stegner. His debt to Stegner is problematical. When Gordon Lish asked him

---

14. Kesey to Babbs, undated, Kesey Collection.
15. Lish, "What the Hell You Looking," 25.

what he had learned from Stegner, Kesey replied, "Just never to teach in college," explaining this answer by suggesting that Stegner's writing had been adversely affected by the academic life. "A man becomes *accustomed* to having two hundred people gather every day at one o'clock giving him all of their attention—because he's clever, good-looking, famous, and has a beautiful voice."[16] The sour tone here could have had several sources; maybe it was jealousy or a sense of competition. Stegner was one of the leading writers associated with the West, and Kesey, as westerner, would inevitably be measured against him. But more likely it was a clash of values. Kesey would become a guru of the counterculture or youth-cult movement, a psychedelic impresario in the transition from Beats to Hippies. Stegner was to write critically of that movement. The Bohemianism Kesey was absorbing on Perry Lane and in North Beach probably alienated him from the academic establishment Stegner seemed to represent. Cowley, in contrast, was not an academic—he taught creative writing but was not a full-time professor— and was more sympathetic to the Beat writers Kesey was discovering. Kesey read Kerouac's *On the Road* three times before arriving at Stanford, "hoping to sign on in some way, to join that joyous voyage, like thousands of other volunteers inspired by the same book, and its vision, and, of course, its incomparable hero."[17] Cowley had read the manuscript of *On the Road* while at Viking. He plugged it to his publisher and mentioned it favorably in *The Literary Situation* in 1954, three years before it was published.[18]

One item in the Kesey Collection suggests a certain friction between Kesey and Stegner. It is a chastisement from Stegner that might be related to the clash of perspectives just mentioned. Kesey submitted a paper titled "On Why I Am Not Writing My Last Term Paper." It was one of those things students write when they want to justify failing to complete an assignment by claiming it was not challenging or meaningful enough. Kesey argued that he should be writing a novel instead of doing academic exercises. Stegner would have none of that. His annotation chides Kesey, saying the paper is merely self-expression, which is really self-indulgence. "Now go write that novel, but don't for God's sake let it turn into self-expression."

16. Ibid., 24–25.
17. Ken Kesey, "The Day after Superman Died," *Esquire*, October 1979, 54.
18. Bruce Cook, *The Beat Generation* (New York: Scribner's, 1971), 66.

But regardless of how this reprimand was taken or how Kesey disliked what he viewed as an academic quality in Stegner's writing, there is evidence that he learned from him. According to Kesey's wife, Faye Kesey, both Stegner and Richard Scowcroft played influential roles in Kesey's first year at Stanford. And in letters to Babbs, Kesey acknowledges that Stegner had been right in his emphasis on point of view.[19] Under the stimulus of Stegner, Kesey became preoccupied with point of view, and his first two novels are distinctive in their experimental narrative technique.

Stegner, as far as I know, has not written about his association with Kesey. Malcolm Cowley has. In an essay titled "Kesey at Stanford," he tells of meeting Kesey in his seminar in the fall of 1960. Kesey was not officially enrolled, but as a matter of courtesy, former students were invited to attend. According to Cowley, the class was distinguished and class members developed good relations in discussing each other's work. Cowley's description of the "stolid and self-assured" Kesey resembles Kesey's description of McMurphy: "He had the build of a plunging halfback, with big shoulders and a neck like the stump of a Douglas fir." Kesey read from the manuscript in class and showed the whole thing to Cowley for his critique. Cowley insists that he contributed nothing: "the book is Kesey's from first to last. Probably I pointed out passages that didn't 'work,' that failed to produce a desired effect on the reader. Certainly I asked questions, and some of these may have helped to clarify Kesey's notions of how to go about solving his narrative problems, but the solutions were always his own." John C. Pratt tells us that Cowley discovered rhyme in certain passages, and Kesey made it more explicit in revision. The first drafts seemed to Cowley to have been written rapidly, as evidenced by misspellings and typing errors. Later Kesey would edit with some care. "He had his visions, but he didn't have the fatal notion of some Beat writers, that the first hasty account of a vision was a sacred text not to be tampered with. He revised, he made deletions and additions; he was working with readers in mind."[20] Although Cowley didn't share McMurphy's theory of psychotherapy, he was impressed with the manuscript and was undoubtedly instrumental in its acceptance by Viking. The Cowley connection

19. Faye Kesey, interview by author, Pleasant Hill, Oregon, June 14, 1980; Pratt, *Cuckoo's Nest: Text and Criticism*, 338.

20. Malcolm Cowley, "Kesey at Stanford," in Michael Strelow, ed., *Kesey* (Eugene, Ore.: Northwest Review Books, 1977), 2, 3; Pratt, *Cuckoo's Nest: Text and Criticism*, x.

is one of the elements of chance and good fortune in the concatenation of circumstances resulting in the novel's success.

## III

Kesey's life was radically transformed when he moved into Perry Lane and began making excursions to North Beach, just forty miles away. Perry Lane, which no longer exists, was a neighborhood of small cottages housing a rather Bohemian community of students. The story is familiar, told most colorfully by Tom Wolfe in *The Electric Kool-Aid Acid Test.* Kesey grew a beard; began playing the guitar and singing folk songs; read about jazz and drugs; wrote a novel about what was happening in North Beach; volunteered for government-sponsored drug experiments at the Menlo Park Veterans Administration hospital; began, along with friends, conducting drug experiments of his own; took a job as an aide in the psychiatric ward of the hospital; and so on. Repeating as little as possible of the published information about this time in Kesey's life, I wish to provide some new information and to reexamine what is already known as it relates directly to the genesis of *Cuckoo's Nest.*

Kesey has publicly acknowledged his debt to Jack Kerouac a number of times, and he became close friends with Neal Cassady, the model for a main character in *On the Road.* Although the Cassady friendship profoundly influenced Kesey's later activities, it had nothing to do with *Cuckoo's Nest,* which was completed before the two met. It was the spirit of Kerouac's book rather than the literary method that attracted Kesey. He considered Kerouac a reporter rather than a novelist, and he wasn't trying to be a reporter. Kerouac developed a technique of writing "without consciousness" and in "The Essentials of Spontaneous Prose" attacked the idea that revision is important and necessary. He compared the writer to a jazz saxophonist releasing an unrevised flow. Kesey used a similar method in dictating his drug experiences and in freewriting as he planned his novels. But his novels were planned. His working notes for *Sometimes a Great Notion* and "One Lane," an unpublished novel, reveal his self-consciousness about themes and about methods for conveying them. His courses in film and television scriptwriting at the University of Oregon had required him to design his objectives, and he retained the habit. Moreover, his mind has a philosophical quality and is naturally inclined to discover concepts and themes in even commonplace events.

More frequently mentioned in the letters and tapes in the Kesey Collection than *On the Road* is William S. Burroughs's *Naked Lunch*. In lending his copy to Babbs, he called it his "most prized possession." He greatly admired Burroughs's ability to capture the carnal and psychic throb of human experience. Burroughs says near the end of *Naked Lunch*, "There is only one thing a writer can write about; *what is in front of his senses at the moment of writing*. . . . I am a recording instrument. . . . I do not presume to impose 'story' 'plot' 'continuity.' . . . Insofaras I succeed in Direct recording of certain areas of psychic process I may have limited function. . . . I am not an entertainer." As with Kerouac's "spontaneous prose," Kesey adopted the method only in a modified form. Tony Tanner has suggested that Bromden's paranoid fantasies are "a very Burroughs-like vision."[21] And Burroughs's funny, carnival-pitchman style may have contributed something to the creation of McMurphy, who is frequently likened to a carnival pitchman.

There is much in *Cuckoo's Nest* that derived from the Beats, who advocated a return to nature and a revolt against the machine, attitudes that are paramount in the novel. Bromden's Combine is really a tag for the corporate, technical-industrial, suburban values that alienated the Beat generation. Perhaps prompted by or perhaps simply concurrent with critiques by the serious media in the fifties and books like David Riesman's *The Lonely Crowd* (1952), William H. Whyte's *The Organization Man* (1956), and John Kenneth Galbraith's *The Affluent Society* (1958), the Beats viewed America as inhabited by a lonely crowd of gray-flannel-clad organization men, offering its affluence only to those who were willing to pay the price of strict conformity. Kesey accepted these premises but offered an alternative to the Beats' rebellion, which lacked definite shape and direction and was little more than withdrawal from the mainstream. Kesey's is an activist response that adumbrates the counterculture strategies of the following decade.

The Beat movement was urban; Kesey's roots were rural. This accounts for why he embraced some Beat attitudes and ignored others. His family and regional tradition of self-assertive action prevented his accepting Beat passivity and withdrawal. He told Gordon Lish, "I get weary of people who

21. William S. Burroughs, *Naked Lunch* (New York: Grove, 1959), 221; Tony Tanner, *City of Words: American Fiction, 1950–1970* (London: Jonathan Capps, 1971), 376.

use pessimism to avoid being responsible for all the problems in our culture. A man who says, we're on the road to disaster, is seldom trying to wrench the wheel away from the driver." He prefers the troublemaker who tries to make things better. In a letter to Babbs written while he was on duty at the hospital, Kesey tells of being called upstairs to listen to a tape about the brainwashing of Korean War prisoners: "It was most enlightening, especially in terms of the book I'm writing. It had a lot to do with the 'Code of Conduct.' Remember it? We used to ridicule it upstairs in the ROTC office at Stanford? Well, I'm becoming very square or something—but I'm beginning to believe the code has a lot to it, a lot about strength. Strength is the key. We need strong men."[22] McMurphy, of course, meets the need for strong men.

Allen Ginsberg claimed that "the first serious experimentation with altered states of consciousness came with the Beats using pot and peyote."[23] He had written *Howl* under the influence of drugs—peyote, amphetamines, Dexedrine. Kesey, who says he wrote parts of *Cuckoo's Nest* under the influence of peyote, was introduced to drugs by the Beat culture. In volunteering for experiments with mind-altering drugs, he was following the lead of the Beats' curiosity about how such substances might affect artistic creation.

In a way, Kesey's attraction to the Beats was an attraction to the American tradition of romantic idealism—New England transcendentalism filtered through Whitman to writers like Kerouac and Ginsberg. Whitman had added a coarse, fleshy, vulgar element—the glorification of the body and sex. The Beats carried this impulse even further. Kesey was attracted to the idealism and readily embraced the earthiness, which was compatible with his western-small-town, locker-room background. *Cuckoo's Nest* is informed by American transcendentalism's preoccupation with nature and self-reliance, but it is couched in earthy, ribald language and action. While Beat writing and behavior affected the curious and impressionable Kesey forcefully, his strong personality shaped by western individualism caused him to gradually filter that influence and retain only what suited his own distinctive purposes. The stages in this process are apparent in his unpublished writing.

The novel "Zoo" is specifically about North Beach. It echoes Kerouac in its descriptions of wine drinking, drug addicts, jazz musicians, stupid

---

22. Lish, "What the Hell You Looking," 29; Kesey to Babbs, undated, Kesey Collection.
23. Cook, *Beat Generation*, 103.

and brutal police, interracial marriages, poverty-level Bohemian living, cars scarred by frantic miles on the highway, and talk of nihilism and Zen. It displays the same adolescent fascination with unconventional behavior as *On the Road,* but it artistically shapes autobiographical experience in the interests of theme in a way that book fails to do. The main character in "Zoo" is torn between his attraction to a new way of life in North Beach and his rural Oregon roots. In Kesey's first two novels, "End of Autumn" and "Zoo"—both unpublished—the Oregon roots prevail. In his life following the writing of those novels, however, the new lifestyle in California prevailed until, after serving six months in prison on a marijuana charge, he returned to a farm in Oregon.

So "Zoo" constitutes one stage in his absorption of the Beat influence. An unpublished short story in the Kesey Collection titled "The Kicking Party" reflects another. The setting is a psychiatric ward. The patients wonder why Abel Cramer is an inmate. The paranoids say, "Plotting, the bastard is, plotting to undermine the whole system with his evil laugh and sinful stories!" The head nurse watches him "through her protective glass shield from her sterilized isolation booth." He is talking to "a group of enraptured patients," telling "one of his heightened, hilarious stories of jazz days or junk days or juice days." Here is the basic situation of *Cuckoo's Nest,* but with interesting differences. Cramer is described as "this fabled handsome stud-with-goatee." He is a beatnik with a history of drug and jazz obsession. Moreover, he is mentally disturbed and haunted with the fear of madness. At this point on the road to *Cuckoo's Nest,* the charismatic laugher (McMurphy) and the patient on the brink of insanity (Bromden) are combined in the same person (Cramer), and that person has been created from a world Kesey had merely visited and read about. The turning point came when he precipitated from this solution two characters, a hero of event and a hero of consciousness, both of whom had their source in the life and culture of his own region. Music remained important, but it too was transformed: from jazz, which Kesey had just discovered, to the country-flavored tunes Kesey had grown up with. In short, Kesey was greatly stimulated by his encounter with the Beats but had to get most of that influence out of his system before he achieved the originality of *Cuckoo's Nest* and *Sometimes a Great Notion.*

What did Kerouac think of *Cuckoo's Nest?* In the Kesey Collection is a letter from Kerouac to Tom Ginsberg at Viking written October 19, 1961. Kerouac, who had read an advance copy of the novel, praises it highly but, perhaps because of his own autobiographical approach to writing, is convinced that the author must be the Columbia Gorge Indian himself, who used "Kesey," perhaps his wife's name, to avoid being identified with the "deafmute" hero. He says the author is certainly right about the Combine and praises the way he captures the American lingo. Kerouac even senses the flavor of "real western Indian talk" in the narration. His understanding of narrative personae was no more reliable, it seems, than his knowledge of Native American speech.

## IV

Six months after his first volunteer drug experiment, Kesey was working as a psychiatric aide. Both his introduction to mind-altering drugs and his work as an aide were primary experiences in the inception of *Cuckoo's Nest.* As he once put it, "In the antiseptic wilderness of the Menlo Park VA Hospital, I cleared a space and rigged a runway and waited for my muse to take the controls."[24] He expected the hospital work to supply subject matter and hoped the drugs would inspire new awareness and perspective. The first expectation was fully realized. The matter of drug-induced inspiration is more complicated.

In his own essay on the origins of the novel, "Who Flew over What?" in *Kesey's Garage Sale,* Kesey says that McMurphy was fictional but "inspired by the tragic longing of the real men I worked with on the ward." He described some of these men in a letter to Babbs. Their resemblance to the patients in the novel is obvious. He cultivated an empathy with these men and tried, through drugs, to glimpse their perspective: "I studied inmates as they daily wove intricate and very accurate schizophrenic commentaries of the disaster of their environment, and had found that merely by ingesting a tiny potion I could toss word salad with the nuttiest of them, had discovered that if I plied my consciousness with enough of the proper chemical it was impossible to preconceive, and when preconception is fenced out, truth is liable to occur."[25] He even persuaded a friend in electronics to rig an apparatus and give him a dose of electric-shock therapy so he could write authoritatively about it.

24. Quoted in Pratt, *Cuckoo's Nest: Text and Criticism,* x.

25. Ken Kesey, "Who Flew over What?" *Kesey's Garage Sale* (New York: Viking, 1973), 7; quoted in Pratt, *Cuckoo's Nest: Text and Criticism,* 340–45, xl.

His sympathetic interest in the plight of patients is revealed in a one-sheet summary in the Kesey Collection headed "Be a good story." He notes that a patient had shown up the night before, having left Brentwood Hospital. "Make it a newer hospital, with better facilities and food," Kesey notes to himself. The man had hopped a freight to Oakland in cold weather and gone three days without food. Arriving at the wrong hospital, he had walked to a new one. His feet were blistered and he was hungry and exhausted. Why had he done it? "Because they didn't treat him like a human down there. A man will go through a great deal of physical torment and punishment and cold and hunger—to be afforded at least human dignity."

Also in the collection is a taped conversation in which Kesey and another man who had worked in the same hospital compare their experiences. They agree about the white nurses. They found them hard, tough, trying to prove something. The black nurses were kinder. Kesey tells of working in the geriatrics section and getting in a scuffle with a black aide over the treatment of a patient known as Old Moses. For someone acquainted with the novel, the conversation resonates familiarly.

How realistic is Kesey's portrayal of a psychiatric ward? He worked just as an aide for a relatively short time, and he was not writing as a reporter. His narrator, after all, fades in and out of hallucination, and Kesey was aiming for truths independent of literal accuracy. The question may not even be a fair or useful one to ask. But of course it has been asked, and the answers are varied. John Pratt quotes a British psychiatrist practicing in Canada who provides a list of what he considers the novel's distortions and misrepresentations of psychiatric-hospital care.[26] On the other hand, there are letters in the Kesey Collection from two psychiatrists who find the novel's portrayal of mental care accurate and who wish to quote from it and confer with Kesey on reforms in psychiatric practice. One expresses surprise that Kesey had developed such a remarkable insight in so short a time. "I was in this racket a lot longer than that," he says, "before I realized what was really significant and actually taking place."

A question more relevant to the genesis of the novel and to understanding the process of literary creation is this: what does the novel owe to drug

26. John C. Pratt, "On Editing Kesey: Confessions of a Straight Man," in Strelow, ed., *Kesey,* 10–11.

inspiration? Kesey has said on a number of occasions that the inspiration for his Indian narrator came to him while he was under the influence of peyote. One interviewer provides this quote from a December 1971 conversation: "I was flying on peyote, really strung out there, when this Indian came to me. I knew nothing about Indians, had no Indians on my mind, had nothing that an Indian could ever grab onto, yet this Indian came to me. It was the peyote, then, couldn't be anything else. The Indian came straight out from the drug itself."[27] This claim, in one version or another, is the most widely known item of information about the writing of the novel. Kesey also makes the claim in "Who Flew over What?" and insists that it was not simply a matter of peyote being naturally associated with Indians. Bromden was, he insists, an inspiration from outside his experience. This claim merits careful examination for at least two reasons. First, it is linked to the longstanding question of whether artistic creativity can be enhanced by chemical stimulants. And second, it is Kesey's prime example of the creative benefits of mind-altering drugs.

I suggest that this claim should not be taken at face value. To begin with, Kesey is, or once was, temperamentally inclined to a certain credulity in matters of paranormal experience, as is evidenced in the search or quest already mentioned. His imagination has been captured by everything from the *I Ching* to mysteries of a lost pyramid—anything that offers awareness beyond the commonplace. He was very serious about his experiments with drugs and strongly desired to make discoveries. He has likened his volunteering for such experiments to Neil Armstong's volunteering to go to the moon or Lewis and Clark's willingness to explore the West.[28] He used a good deal of the money earned by *Cuckoo's Nest* to finance attempts to find new forms of expression beyond writing through the use of drugs and electronic equipment. "Who Flew over What?" was written during his Merry Prankster era. He needed an example of drug inspiration to justify the Prankster activities and to confirm to himself that he was on the right track. In other words, the assertion that Bromden was the exclusive product of peyote may be an exaggeration generated by an intense desire that it be true.

27. Quoted in E. D. Webber, "Keepin' on the Bounce: A Study of Ken Kesey as a Distinctively American Novelist," 144, unpublished thesis, no date or place, Kesey Collection.

28. See Jeff Barnard, "Psychedelic Pioneer Values Family Most of All," *Provo (Utah) Herald,* February 19, 1990, B3, and Whitmer, "Ken Kesey's Search," 26.

In "Who Flew over What?" Kesey says that he wrote the first three pages of *Cuckoo's Nest* after swallowing eight little cactus plants. "These pages," he asserts, "remained almost completely unchanged through the numerous rewrites the book went through, and from this first spring I drew all the passion and perception the narrator spoke with during the ten months' writing that followed." Pratt includes these pages in the background section of his critical edition of the novel, noting that by the final version "Kesey made significant revisions, especially after he had decided upon the novel's point of view."[29] It is true that the germ of the narration is apparent in these first pages, but it is also clear that Kesey has again overstated his case.

There is ample reason why Kesey might have selected an Indian for his narrator. He had, in fact, known Indians—or at least observed them—and reflected upon their victimization. On one of the tapes he talks about having played on a football team with an Indian, and about an Indian employed by his father's dairy company. He describes an Indian with lipstick all over his face, his cowboy shirt splattered with blood. He told Gordon Lish of an Indian in a logging camp who went berserk and attacked with a knife a diesel truck traveling down a highway built on what had been his grandfather's land.[30] He wrote a story at the University of Oregon titled "The Avocados," which tells of two University of Oregon students in Los Angeles. In the company of two Mexican girls, they encounter two Klamath Indians, both World War II veterans. One of them, in a wheelchair, is used once in a while in movies when a classic Indian chief face is needed. The other wrestles occasionally. They make prickly pear wine. Once they were going to save and go back to Oregon. "Now," one of them says, "I hear they screwed all the Klamath Indians." The students drop the girls and drive off to see the city with the Indians. The girls are like avocados: soft on the outside but hard inside. The Indians are like a prickly pear cactus: repellent on the outside but sweet inside.

The most obvious intimation of Bromden in Kesey's early writing is the main character of "Sunset at Celilo," a script he wrote for a radio and television writing course. Jim Smith, a Celilo Indian, returns after five years in the army. "He is from a small tribe of poor but happy people who have

29. Pratt, *Cuckoo's Nest: Text and Criticism*, 333.
30. Lish, "What the Hell You Looking," 19.

lived on the Columbia for years and fished for salmon at the Celilo Falls for a living." The government has given permission for a dam at the Dalles. The tribe has been paid $28 million, which has been spent recklessly on television sets, expensive furnishings, and Cadillacs. Jim tries to arouse the tribe and threatens to dynamite the dam, but eventually realizes his efforts are hopeless. In a note to Dean Stark, his teacher, Kesey points out that the story is based on fact and the dam will soon be completed.

These examples show that Kesey had considerable experience with Indians from which to draw upon in his creation of his narrator, that Kesey was exaggerating his faith in drug inspiration when he described the sudden, inexplicable appearance of Bromden. On other occasions he has explained more convincingly that drugs do not provide new ideas or information but simply anesthetize inhibitions and preconceptions and thus allow the imagination a certain temporary freedom and fluidity. When asked once whether drugs had anything to do with the lyrical and fantastic descriptions in *Cuckoo's Nest,* he answered, "Yes, but *drugs* didn't create those descriptions any more than Joyce's *eyeglasses* created *Ulysses.* They merely help one to see the paper more clearly."[31]

V

Kesey's stimulating new experiences during his first two years in California clearly had much to do with the genesis of *Cuckoo's Nest.* But the substance of the novel—its principal tone, language, imagery, and comic vision—derives from frontier attitudes and traditions that he inherited from his family and picked up in his region. In demonstrating the indispensability of humor for combating the negative aspects of an increasingly urban and technological society, the novel reasserts the vitality of certain distinctive patterns in American humor, particularly those of nineteenth-century frontier humor. It not only demonstrates these varieties of American humor but also celebrates them. The novel brings patterns of frontier humor to bear on the urban, technological society of mid-twentieth-century America. The humor of *Cuckoo's Nest* is both an example of and a tribute to a distinctive and persistent rural, vernacular tradition in American humor. Part of the reason

---

31. Ibid., 24.

for the book's popularity is our enduring affection for the unsophisticated, unpretentious, but self-reliant folk humor that evolved along America's shifting western boundaries.

Some confusion about Kesey as a humorist resulted from his role as a counterculture hero and drug guru during California's psychedelic revolution in the early sixties. He was labeled a "black humorist," a term that enjoyed considerable currency in the sixties but has faded from the critical lexicon because it was difficult to define, indiscriminately applied, and eventually mistaken for a racial term. In the late sixties, trying to make sense of black humor as a concept, Hamlin Hill identified its tone as "belligerent, pugnacious, nihilistic." As humor moves into the black zone, he observed, it heads for the irrational and valueless, not seeking the sympathetic alliance of the audience but deliberately insulting and alienating it. He quoted Lennie Bruce as defining the creed: "Everything is rotten—mother is rotten, God is rotten, the flag is rotten."[32]

The year after *Cuckoo's Nest* appeared, Hill had characterized modern American humor as Janus-faced. One face, he wrote, looks upon the native strain rooted in the preceding century, which affirms the values of "common sense, self-reliance, and a kind of predictability in the world." The protagonist of this variety of humor "faces an *external* reality with gusto and exuberance," said Hill. "Even when he launches forth into his version of fantasy, the tall tale, he is based solidly upon the exaggeration of actual reality, not upon nightmare, hysteria, or delusion." Hill labeled the other strain the "dementia praecox school." The antihero of this humor is neurotically concerned with an inner space of nightmare and delusion where unreliability and irrationality abound. Clearly Hill had in mind the trend in modern urban humor to dramatize a sense of inadequacy, impotence, and defeat before the complexities and destructive potential of our century. Its protagonists are repressed, squeamish, and hypersensitive. Their individuality and self-confidence have been compromised by life in a depersonalized mass society. Thus, in Hill's view, modern American humor "releases itself in both the hearty guffaw and the neurotic giggle; it reacts to both the bang and the whimper."[33]

---

32. Hamlin Hill, "Black Humor: Its Causes and Cures," *Colorado Quarterly* 17 (1968): 59.
33. Hamlin Hill, "Modern American Humor: The Janus Laugh," *College English* 25 (1963): 171, 176.

Hill's essays are helpful in clarifying Kesey's relation to the varieties of American humor. Although the principal subject matter of *Cuckoo's Nest* is dementia praecox and its narrator begins his story in a nightmarish state of neurotic fantasy and delusion, the novel is clearly founded upon the values of self-reliance and commonsense harmony with nature. Its victory is that of sanity over insanity, strength over neurotic victimization, and nature over misguided technology. McMurphy's initial exchanges with Harding are confrontations between "the hearty guffaw and the neurotic giggle." McMurphy is the bang, Harding the whimper. Ultimately, of course, McMurphy's earthy, noncerebral humor vanquishes Harding's cynical, intellectual, and timid attempts at wit.

Similarly, although Kesey used techniques associated with so-called black comedy, particularly during the period following *Cuckoo's Nest* and *Sometimes a Great Notion,* when he turned from writing to escapades with the Merry Pranksters, he never espoused the attitudes underlying that kind of humor. He gained notoriety within the California counterculture, but his roots were in rural Oregon and a family heritage of western-American values and vernacular stories. He has never strayed far from those roots. His fellow drug guru, Timothy Leary, who had no particular affinity for such roots, noted this a few years ago when he said of Kesey, "I have always seen him as very Protestant and quite moralistic, and quite American in a puritanical way. And basically untrustworthy, since he is always going to end up with a Bible in his hand, sooner or later." Mark Twain once said, "Humor must not professedly teach, and it must not professedly preach, but it must do both if it would live forever. By forever, I mean thirty years."[34] *Cuckoo's Nest* has met that thirty-year criterion, and its humor is largely Twain's variety in source, method, and purpose.

Recognizing the pitfalls in delineating sources and influences in humor, I want to demonstrate the links between *Cuckoo's Nest* and what, for convenience, I call frontier humor. By this term I mean the indigenous, largely vernacular tradition of humor whose development during the nineteenth century has been described by scholars such are Constance Rourke, Bernard DeVoto, Walter Blair, Hamlin Hill, M. Thomas Inge, James Cox, and Kenneth

---

34. Timothy Leary, quoted in Peter O. Whitmer, with Bruce VanWyngarden, *Aquarius Revisited* (New York: Macmillan, 1987), 11; Mark Twain, quoted in E. B. and Katherine S. White, *A Subtreasury of American Humor* (New York: Coward-McCann, 1941), xxii.

Lynn. The critical literature generated by the novel has identified some of its
similarities with frontier humor. In what follows, I provide a brief but more
extensive and specific survey of parallels than has been supplied before and
conclude with comments on the function and significance of those parallels.

To begin with, McMurphy is a westerner, a product and an anachronistic
afterimage of the frontier. He has lived all around Oregon and in Texas and
Oklahoma (*CN*, 186). In the frontier spirit of freedom and movement he has
wandered restlessly, "logging, gambling, running carnival wheels, traveling
lightfooted and fast, keeping on the move" (*CN*, 84). His hand is like "a road
map of his travels up and down the West" (*CN*, 27). As already mentioned,
Kesey's family were restless west-walkers, not pioneers or visionaries but just
a simple clan looking for new opportunities.

Drawing upon popular culture, Kesey links McMurphy with the most
familiar hero of the frontier—the cowboy. He smokes Marlboro cigarettes
and is described as "the cowboy out of the TV set walking down the middle of
the street to meet a dare" (*CN*, 172). He has a "drawling cowboy actor's voice"
(*CN*, 232). Before his first meeting with Harding, he says, "this hospital ain't
big enough for the two of us. . . . Tell this Harding that he either meets me
man to man or he's a yaller skunk and better be outta town by sunset"
(*CN*, 24). He has a "cowboy bluster" and a "TV-cowboy stoicism" (*CN*, 62,
73). He sings cowboy songs in the latrine and has Wild Bill Hickok's "dead-
man's hand" tattooed on his shoulder (*CN*, 83, 77). Just before he assaults
Big Nurse he hitches up his shorts "like they were horsehide chaps, and
pushe[s] his cap with one finger like it was a ten-gallon Stetson" (*CN*, 267).
Harding refers to him with an allusion to the Lone Ranger: "I'd like to stand
there at the window with a silver bullet in my hand and ask 'who *wawz* that
'er masked man?' " (*CN*, 258). We all effortlessly absorb such cowboy clichés
from our culture, but Kesey in addition had read Zane Grey (and named a
son Zane) and other writers of Westerns. The widow of Ernest Haycox hired
him while he was at the University of Oregon to write plot summaries of her
husband's novels. Haycox, a major figure in the genre, appeared in *Collier's*
alone an average of thirteen times a year between 1931 and 1949 and did
much to shape the nation's conception of the Western hero.

In similar ways, McMurphy is identified with other frontier types such as
the logger and gambler. As part of a scriptwriting course, Kesey prepared an
outline for a television series to be called "Legends," a treatment of American
folk heroes. He was fascinated by such figures as Paul Bunyan, Davy Crockett,

Mike Fink, and Pecos Bill. McMurphy is a product of that tradition, with its bragging, exaggeration, and humorous treatment of violence. When McMurphy fights the captain of the rental boat and then the two cheerfully sit down to drink beer together, we are witnessing a familiar pattern in frontier humor. When McMurphy and Harding square off to brag about which is the crazier (frequency of voting for Eisenhower being the principal measure), we are witnessing a fresh twist to the ring-tailed roarer confrontations of old-Southwest humor.

Kesey claims that he didn't see the film version of the novel because he was disgusted with the casting of Jack Nicholson as McMurphy. He referred to him as a "wimp." In Kesey's eyes he was too urban, too lacking in the western vernacular strengths that inspired his conception of McMurphy. Nicholson, I suppose, might have been appropriate for Abel Cramer, the main character in "The Kicking Party," but by the time Kesey wrote *Cuckoo's Nest* he had reverted to the wellspring of his western background. His own pencil drawing of McMurphy suggests rugged physical strength.[35]

Americans have always loved the rustic or apparently simple character who appears naive but is actually bright and clever. One version of this type is the television detective Columbo. The type appeared early in American humor in the form of country hicks outsmarting city slickers. It is part of an anti-intellectual current in American humor. Drawing from a rural, oral tradition represented in his family particularly by his maternal grandmother, Kesey composed "Little Tricker the Squirrel Meets Big Double the Bear," which first appeared in his *Demon Box* and then as a separate children's book.[36] This backwoods animal fable in the vein of Joel Chandler Harris's *Uncle Remus* is a story of the clever little guy who defeats the wielder of unjust power. Arthur Maddox, a musician with roots in rural Missouri, composed music to accompany the narration, and Kesey has performed it with symphony orchestras across the country. It is a tribute to his grandmother and the oral tradition she perpetuated, and it suggests one of the sources for McMurphy.

McMurphy is, to a large degree, a hero from that oral tradition, and the bully he combats is not simply Big Nurse, but also the technological Combine she represents. Harding explicitly identifies this aspect of

---

35. Kesey, *Kesey's Garage Sale*, 10.
36. Ken Kesey, *Demon Box* (New York: Viking, 1986).

McMurphy when he acknowledges his intelligence: "an illiterate clod, perhaps, certainly a backwoods braggart with no more sensitivity than a goose,
but basically intelligent nevertheless" (*CN*, 56). Elsewhere, he cautions the
patients to avoid being misled by McMurphy's "back-woodsy ways; he's a
very sharp operator, level-headed as they come" (*CN*, 224). Kesey himself
was a diamond-in-the-rough when he arrived at Stanford from rural Oregon,
but his new friends soon discovered a brilliant mind behind the down-home,
college-jock exterior.

   *Cuckoo's Nest* contains other parallels with frontier humor. For example,
the novel employs homely but vivid similes, such as "shakin' like a dog shittin'
peach pits" (*CN*, 122). McMurphy wrenches language in a way reminiscent of
characters in *Huck Finn* and the Southwestern humor that inspired Twain.
For instance, when Harding mentions "Freud, Jung, and Maxwell Jones,"
McMurphy replies, "I'm not talking about Fred Yoong and Maxwell Jones"
(*CN*, 56). McMurphy often communicates in anecdotes. Their frontier-
humor flavor is illustrated in the one about a rough practical joke that
backfires. A man at a rodeo is tricked into riding a bull blindfolded and
backwards and nevertheless wins (*CN*, 139). This bears a family resemblance
to Twain's anecdote of the genuine Mexican plug in *Roughing It*. Similarly
in the tradition of Twain, McMurphy nearly outdoes Huck Finn with his
creative lying to the service-station attendants in order to protect his friends.
He even receives a discount similar to the way Huck received money with
his lie to the slave hunters that saves Jim (*CN*, 200–201). The novel's
humor is at times scatological and often earthy and exaggerated, as in
the description of Candy reeling in a salmon, "with the crank of the reel
fluttering her breast at such a speed the nipple's just a red blur!" (*CN*,
211). Like a good deal of frontier humor, the novel involves masculine
resistance to feminine order and control. "We are victims of a matriarchy
here," complains Harding (*CN*, 59). Even the novel's narrative method, one
of its most important aspects, can be linked with frontier humor. It is an
original and rather bizarre adaptation of the frame technique often used in
the nineteenth century. Moreover, the use of a hallucinating narrator allows
for the elements of tall tale and exaggeration so characteristic of the native
variety of American humor.

   Another important cultural ingredient in the conception of McMurphy
is the kind of character genially pictured in rascals, subversives, and con
men so endemic to American humor. Walter Blair and Hamlin Hill observe

that "a procession of comic men and women whose life work combined imaginative lying with cynical cheating has been one of the most persistent groups that our humor has portrayed."[37] As new frontiers opened, imaginative scoundrels, in language that raised homely colloquialisms to high art, perpetrated new scams. Everyone is familiar with Twain's king and duke. Several entire books are devoted to the American con man, tracing the type from the Yankee peddler to *The Music Man*. Kesey had a special affinity for this brassy, fast-talking sort of personality. Beginning with his theater activities in college and continuing through the Merry Prankster years up to the present, he has availed himself of every opportunity to play this role.

McMurphy's glib pitchman quality is conveyed by auctioneer and particularly carnival images. On first impression he reminds the narrator of "a car salesman or a stock auctioneer—or one of those pitchmen you see on a sideshow stage, out in front of his flapping banners" (*CN*, 17). He is likened to an "auctioneer spinning jokes to loosen up a crowd before the bidding starts" (*CN*, 22). Three other times we are reminded of his "stock auctioneer" manner, his "rollicking auctioneer voice," and his "auctioneer bellow" (*CN*, 72, 199, 268). Bromden refers to him as "a seasoned con" and "a carnival artist" (*CN*, 220). Harding calls him "a good old red, white, and blue hundred-per-cent American con man" (*CN*, 223). McMurphy himself explains that "the secret of being a top-notch con man is being able to know what the mark *wants*, and how to make him think he's getting it. I learned that when I worked a season on a skillo wheel in a carnival" (*CN*, 74). He talks Dr. Spivey into suggesting in a group meeting that the ward have a carnival (*CN*, 97). He draws eyes to him "like a sideshow barker" (*CN*, 233), and as his example begins to have an effect on his fellow patients, they are infected with the same quality: when Bromden returns from a stint in the "Disturbed" ward for resisting the aides, the faces of the other patients light up "as if they were looking into the glare of a sideshow platform," and Harding does an imitation of a sideshow barker (*CN*, 243).

But as one reflects on the carnival motif, it becomes increasingly interesting and complex. In this world of con or be conned, McMurphy is not always in control. Big Nurse is also a sort of technological-age con artist, and when

37. Walter Blair and Hamlin Hill, *America's Humor: From Poor Richard to Doonesbury* (New York: Oxford, 1978), 43.

her schemes are in ascendancy, she is described as "a tarot-card reader in a glass arcade case" (*CN*, 171) or "one of those arcade gypsies that scratch out fortunes for a penny" (*CN*, 268). And the patients, including McMurphy, are described as "arcade puppets" or "shooting-gallery target[s]" (*CN*, 33, 49). The carnival motif ranges from the vitally human barker toward the mechanized—toward humanoid machines that manipulate people and forecast the future. Harding, describing shock treatment to McMurphy, compares it to a carnival: "it's as if the jolt sets off a wild carnival wheel of images, emotions, memories. These wheels, you've seen them; the barker takes your bet and pushes a button. *Chang!*" (*CN*, 164). McMurphy, of course, has not only seen those wheels, he has operated them, and therefore Harding's words stun and bewilder him. When he realizes he has been committed and is liable to shock treatment, he is transformed from con man to mark: "Why, those slippery bastards have *conned* me, snowed me into holding their bag. If that don't beat all, conned ol' R. P. McMurphy" (*CN*, 166). Later, when he is wheeled back from a lobotomy, Scanlon refers to him as "that crummy sideshow fake lying there on the Gurney" (*CN*, 270). So during the course of the story, McMurphy (and to some extent the other principal patients) function as con men, marks, and sideshow freaks. The novel's poignancy, of course, results from McMurphy's ultimate breaking of the con-or-be-conned cycle by sacrificing himself for others.

Cartoons are another variety of humor that plays a role in the novel. Like the cowboy motif, they are part of popular culture. One of Kesey's characteristic achievements is his use of popular culture (Westerns, horror films, comic books, popular music, etc.) for artistic purposes. And like the cowboy motif, cartoons are related to certain patterns of frontier humor. Bugs Bunny is the quintessential American con man, and Tom and Jerry, Popeye, and others are lively, unsophisticated versions of the little guy versus the bully. America's native forms of humor, with their demotic appeal, naturally provided many themes, characters, and situations for comic strips and animated cartoons.

*Cuckoo's Nest* makes strategic allusions to the cartoon genre. Harding speaks of their "Walt Disney world" (*CN*, 61). When McMurphy reads, it is "a book of cartoons" (*CN*, 151). As in cartoons, characters swell up large when they are angry or feeling strong and shrink when they are embarrassed or frightened. A hallucinating narrator permits such description; that is part of the brilliance of Kesey's narrative strategy. For example, Pete's hand, as Popeye's might, swells into an iron ball when he resists the orderlies, and when he socks one of them against the wall, the wall cracks in the man's shape (*CN*, 52). This is a cartoon cliché, and much of the novel's violence is of this cartoon variety.

But as with the carnival motif, the cartoon imagery has its dark side. The patients are "like cartoon men" in a negative sense. "Their voices are forced and too quick on the comeback to be real talk—more like cartoon comedy speech." Theirs is "a cartoon world where the figures are flat and outlined in black, jerking through some kind of goofy story that might be real funny if it weren't for the cartoon figures being real guys" (*CN*, 37, 36, 34).

What conclusions can be drawn from Kesey's use of these varieties of humor and particularly the parallels with frontier humor? First of all, he was drawing upon an imagination nurtured in distinctive ways by his family and region. He had to step back from the powerful influences of his California experiences in order to allow that imagination to follow its most natural and vigorous inclinations. Second, he used the patterns of frontier humor not simply for comic effect but also because he wished to assert the values embedded within them against a constricting and depersonalizing urban mass society. There is a nostalgic and celebratory quality in their use, combined with a conviction that such values are not merely relics of a vanished frontier. His second novel, less comic and more ambitious, glorifies these values even more forcefully, a fact that disturbed his radical counterculture friends, whose attitude toward frontier values was ambivalent. Though Kesey went on to immerse himself in the attitudes and behavior of urban radical culture, Norman Mailer was correct in observing in the late eighties that "Kesey has stayed close to his roots and was probably absolutely right to do it."[38] Third, Kesey skillfully used native varieties of American humor in order to accomplish serious purposes. The con man–carnival motif is a principal example. Beneath the humor is a subtle and moving examination of institutionalized victimization and the hardy human strength and unpretentious self-sacrifice that can alleviate it. The cartoon motif is likewise implicated in Kesey's sympathetic treatment of what the novel calls the culls of the

38. Quoted in Whitmer and VanWyngarden, *Aquarius Revisited*, 63.

Combine. On the whole, the novel demonstrates the enduring vitality and remarkable adaptability of frontier humor.

Kesey was interested in the question "Why me?" The process of literary creation is too complex to allow a complete answer, but the case of *Cuckoo's Nest* is instructive even in its partial demonstration of how an author transmutes life into art. It contributes to our understanding of the effects of chemical stimulants on the creative imagination; and it informs us about the determining influences of family, place, popular reading and viewing, and national literary-cultural traditions.

# Notes on the Contributors

HOWARD G. BAETZHOLD, Rebecca Clifton Reade Professor of English Emeritus, Butler University, is the author of *Mark Twain and John Bull: The British Connection* and numerous articles in American and British periodicals. He served on the Advisory Board of the *Mark Twain Encyclopedia* and contributed some twenty-six of its entries. With Joseph B. McCullough, University of Nevada, Las Vegas, he has edited a collection of Mark Twain's works, *The Bible According to Mark Twain: Writings on Heaven, Eden, and the Flood.* He is currently an editor of *Tales and Sketches of the Middle Years* (2 vols.) and *Tales and Sketches of the Later Years* (2 or 3 vols.), forthcoming from the Mark Twain Project, and is also John S. Tuckey Memorial Research Fellow at the Elmira College Center for Mark Twain Studies at Quarry Farm.

JOHN W. CROWLEY is a Professor and former Chair of English at Syracuse University. His books include two studies of Howells—*The Black Heart's Truth* and *The Mask of Fiction*—as well as *The White Logic: Alcoholism and Gender in American Modernist Fiction.* Among his edited books are *The Haunted Dusk: American Supernatural Fiction, 1820–1920, New Essays on "Winesburg, Ohio,"* Roger Austen's *Genteel Pagan: The Double Life of Charles Warren Stoddard,* and Charles Jackson's *Arcadian Tales.* His edition of *The Rise of Silas Lapham* is forthcoming from the Oxford University Press.

ROBERT DEMOTT is Professor of English at Ohio University, Athens, Ohio, where he has taught since 1969, and where he has received both the undergraduate and graduate teaching awards. He is a member of the editorial board of the *Steinbeck Newsletter* and coeditor with Elaine Steinbeck of the Library of America's *Steinbeck: Novels and Stories, 1932–1937.* His recent books are *News of Loss* (poems) and *Steinbeck's Typewriter* (essays).

ALBERT J. DEVLIN is the author of *Eudora Welty's Chronicle, Conversations with Tennessee Williams,* and many essays on southern literature. He is a member of the editorial boards of the *Mississippi Quarterly* and the *Tennessee Williams Literary Journal* and served as academic advisor for the Public Broadcasting Service documentary "Tennessee Williams: Orpheus of the American Stage." He is coeditor of *The Selected Letters of Tennessee Williams.*

RICHARD W. DOWELL retired in 1993 after thirty years at Indiana State University, where he was a Professor of English. He was cofounder of the *Dreiser Newsletter (Dreiser Studies)* and served as its coeditor, then editor, for twenty years. He compiled, with Donald Pizer and Frederic Rusch, *Theodore Dreiser; A Bibliography of Primary and Secondary Sources* and *Theodore Dreiser: A Primary Bibliography and Reference Guide,* and he edited *An Amateur Laborer.* He has published many articles and reviews, the majority involving Dreiser.

RICHARD A. HOCKS is Middlebush Professor of English at the University of Missouri. He is the author of *Henry James and Pragmatistic Thought* and *Henry James: A Study of the Short Fiction.* He is also the author of the Henry James chapters in *American Literary Scholarship,* is former president of the James Society, and has coedited the Norton Critical Edition of *The Wings of the Dove.*

JAMES NAGEL, J. O. Eidson Distinguished Professor of American Literature at the University of Georgia, founded the scholarly journal *Studies in American Fiction* and edited it for twenty years. He is the general editor of the *Critical Essays on American Literature* series, published by Macmillan in New York. He also serves as the Executive Coordinator of the American Literature Association. Among his fifteen books are *Stephen Crane and Literary Impressionism, Critical Essays on "Catch-22,"* and *Hemingway in Love and War,* which was selected by the *New York Times* as one of the outstanding books of 1989. His current project is a study of the contemporary short-story cycle.

STEPHEN L. TANNER is Humanities Professor of English at Brigham Young University. He is the author of *Ken Kesey, Paul Elmer More: Literary*

*Criticism as the History of Ideas, Lionel Trilling,* and the forthcoming *Ernest Haycox.* He has published widely in periodicals and is the recipient of four Fulbright Lectureships in Brazil and Portugal.

ALBERT VON FRANK, Professor of English at Washington State University, is the author of *The Sacred Game: Provincialism and Frontier Consciousness in American Literature, 1630–1860* and *An Emerson Chronology.* He is coeditor of *The Poetry Notebooks of Ralph Waldo Emerson* and general editor of *The Complete Sermons of Ralph Waldo Emerson.* He also is the editor of *ESQ: A Journal of the American Renaissance.*

CANDACE WAID is the author of *Edith Wharton's Letters from the Underworld: Fictions of Women and Writing,* as well as numerous essays on Wharton, including introductions for her editions of *The Custom of the Country, Summer, A Backward Glance,* and *The Buccaneers,* and for her selection of Wharton's short fiction, *The Muse's Tragedy and Other Stories.* She is currently editing the Norton Critical Edition of *The Age of Innocence.* An Associate Professor of English and American Studies at Yale University, Waid also writes on Faulkner, Welty, and other writers of the American South.

# Index